POCKET A–Z
WORLD
ATLAS

Previously published as *Atlas A-Z*

D0968167

FOR THE SEVENTH EDITION
Senior Cartographic Editor Simon Mumford
Designer Nimbus Design
Factfile Editors Cambridge International Reference on Current Affairs (CIRCA)
Senior Producer Angela Graef   **Producer (Pre-Production)** Dave Almond

Publisher Andrew Macintyre   **Publishing Director** Jonathan Metcalf
Associate Publishing Director Liz Wheeler   **Art Director** Karen Self

FOR PREVIOUS EDITIONS
Cartographic Director Andrew Heritage
Cartography Roger Bullen, Rob Stokes, Iorwerth Watkins
Project Editor Sam Atkinson   **Art Editor** Karen Gregory

This revised American Edition, 2018. First American Edition, 2001
Published in the United States by DK Publishing,
345 Hudson Street, New York, New York 10014

Previously published as *Atlas A–Z*
Copyright © 1996, 1998, 2001, 2003, 2004, 2005, 2007, 2010, 2012, 2015, 2018
Dorling Kindersley Limited.
DK, a Division of Penguin Random House LLC
18 19 20 21 22   10 9 8 7 6 5 4 3 2 1
001–308257—Oct/2018

Published in Great Britain by Dorling Kindersley Limited.

A catalog record for this book is available from the Library of Congress.
ISBN 978-1-4654-6888-8

DK books are available at special discounts when purchased in bulk for sales promotions,
premiums, fund-raising, or educational use. For details, contact: DK Publishing Special Markets,
345 Hudson Street, New York, New York 10014; SpecialSales@dk.com

Printed and bound in Malaysia

A WORLD OF IDEAS:
SEE ALL THERE IS TO KNOW
www.dk.com

Key to map symbols

ELEVATION

6000m / 19,686ft
4000m / 13,124ft
2000m / 6562ft
1000m / 3281ft
500m / 1640ft
250m / 820ft
100m / 328ft
0
Below sea level

▲ Mountain

• Depression

BORDERS

Full international

Disputed *de facto*

Territorial claim

Cease-fire line

Undefined

State/Province

DRAINAGE FEATURES

River

Seasonal river

Canal

Lake

Seasonal lake

SETTLEMENTS

● Capital city

◎ Major town

○ Minor town

• Major port

COMMUNICATIONS

Major road

Rail

✈ International airport

◈ Insight; facts, figures, and amazing information from around the world

4

Atlas contents

North & Central America 16–17

South America 38–39

Africa 50–51

Europe 62–63

Atlas contents

North & West Asia 94–95

South & East Asia 106–107

Australasia & Oceania 124–125

Country Factfiles 138–359

See overleaf for contents

Factfile contents

Factfile contents

The Political World

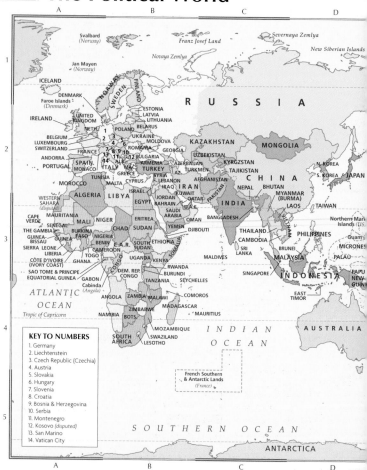

KEY TO NUMBERS

1. Germany
2. Liechtenstein
3. Czech Republic (Czechia)
4. Austria
5. Slovakia
6. Hungary
7. Slovenia
8. Croatia
9. Bosnia & Herzegovina
10. Serbia
11. Montenegro
12. Kosovo (disputed)
13. San Marino
14. Vatican City

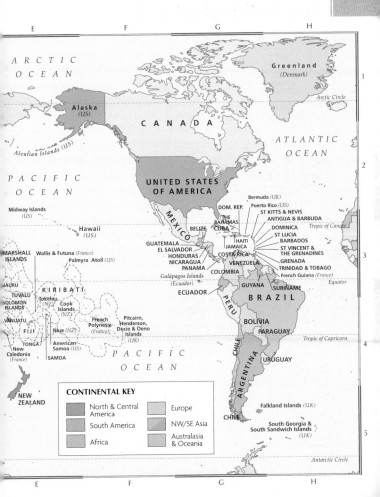

ARCTIC OCEAN

Greenland
(Denmark)

Arctic Circle

Alaska
(US)

CANADA

ATLANTIC
OCEAN

Aleutian Islands (US)

PACIFIC
OCEAN

UNITED STATES
OF AMERICA

Midway Islands
(US)

Bermuda (UK)

DOM. REP.   Puerto Rico (US)
ST KITTS & NEVIS
ANTIGUA & BARBUDA

MEXICO

Hawaii
(US)

BELIZE
CUBA
THE
BAHAMAS

DOMINICA
ST LUCIA
BARBADOS

Tropic of Cancer

MARSHALL
ISLANDS

Wallis & Futuna (France)
Palmyra Atoll (US)

GUATEMALA
EL SALVADOR
HONDURAS
NICARAGUA
PANAMA

HAITI
JAMAICA

COSTA RICA

ST VINCENT &
THE GRENADINES
GRENADA
TRINIDAD & TOBAGO

NAURU

KIRIBATI

COLOMBIA

VENEZUELA

French Guiana (France)

TUVALU

Tokelau
(NZ)

Galápagos Islands
(Ecuador)

GUYANA
SURINAME

Equator

SOLOMON
ISLANDS

Cook
Islands
(NZ)

ECUADOR

BRAZIL

VANUATU

Niue (NZ)

French
Polynesia
(France)

Pitcairn,
Henderson,
Ducie & Oeno
Islands
(UK)

PERU

BOLIVIA

FIJI

TONGA

American
Samoa (US)

PARAGUAY

Tropic of Capricorn

New
Caledonia
(France)

SAMOA

PACIFIC
OCEAN

CHILE

URUGUAY

NEW
ZEALAND

ARGENTINA

CONTINENTAL KEY

North & Central
America

Europe

South America

NW/SE Asia

Africa

Australasia
& Oceania

Falkland Islands (UK)

South Georgia &
South Sandwich Islands
(UK)

CHILE

Antarctic Circle

The Physical World

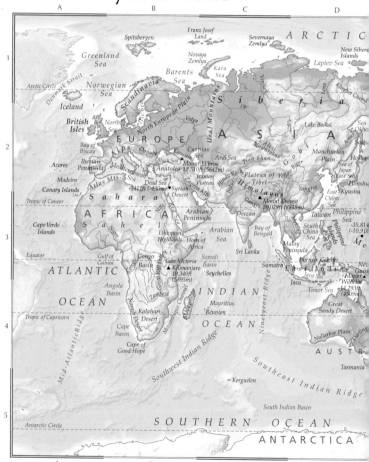

- Spitsbergen
- Greenland Sea
- Franz Josef Land
- Severnaya Zemlya
- ARCTIC
- New Siberian Islands
- Laptev Sea
- Novaya Zemlya
- Kara Sea
- Norwegian Sea
- Iceland
- Denmark Strait
- Arctic Circle
- Barents Sea
- Scandinavia
- Lena
- Khrebet Chersk
- British Isles
- North European Plain
- Ural Mountains
- Siberia
- A S I A
- Ob
- North Sea
- Volga
- Lake Baikal
- Sea of Okho
- Sakh.
- EUROPE
- ALPS
- Danube
- Caspian Sea
- Aral Sea
- Tien Shan
- Altai Mountains
- Gobi
- Manchurian Plain
- Amur
- Bay of Biscay
- Black Sea
- Caucasus
- Mount El'brus 18,510ft (5642m)
- Sea of Japan
- Hokka
- Azores
- Iberian Peninsula
- Mediterranean Sea
- Anatolia
- Hindu Kush
- Plateau of Tibet
- Yellow River
- Yangtze
- Honshu
- Kyushu
- Madeira
- Atlas Mts.
- Dead Sea 1411ft (-430m)
- Syrian Desert
- Zagros Mts
- Iranian Plateau
- Himalayas
- Mount Everest 29,029ft (8848m)
- East China Sea
- Canary Islands
- Sahara
- Tropic of Cancer
- Nile
- Arabian Peninsula
- Deccan
- Taiwan
- Philippine Sea
- -35,81 (-10,91
- AFRICA
- Sahel
- Ethiopian Highlands
- Arabian Sea
- Ganges
- Bay of Bengal
- South China Sea
- Philippine Islands
- Me
- Cape Verde Islands
- Niger
- Horn of Africa
- Somali Basin
- Sri Lanka
- Malay Peninsula
- Equator
- Gulf of Guinea
- Congo Basin
- Lake Victoria
- Seychelles
- Sumatra
- Borneo
- Celebes
- East Indies
- Ne
- Gui
- ATLANTIC
- Congo
- Kilimanjaro 19,340ft (5895m)
- INDIAN
- Java
- Java Sea
- Mount Wilhelm 14,793ft (4509m)
- Angola Basin
- Great Rift Valley
- Zambezi
- Timor Sea
- Gre G
- OCEAN
- Namib Desert
- Kalahari Desert
- Madagascar
- Mauritius
- Réunion
- OCEAN
- Great Sandy Desert
- Tropic of Capricorn
- Cape Basin
- Mozambique Channel
- Nullarbor Plain
- AUSTR
- Cape of Good Hope
- Mid-Atlantic Ridge
- Southwest Indian Ridge
- Ninetyeast Ridge
- Southeast Indian Ridge
- Darling
- Tasmania
- Kerguelen
- South Indian Basin
- Antarctic Circle
- SOUTHERN OCEAN
- ANTARCTICA

E   F   G   H

OCEAN

Siberian Sea

Chukchi Sea

Bering Sea

Aleutian Islands

*Northwest
Pacific
Basin*

Mid-Pacific Mountains

Micronesia

*Solomon
Islands*

Coral
Sea

Fiji

New Caledonia

ASIA

North
Island

Tasman
Sea

New
Zealand

South
Island

Beaufort Sea

Brooks Range

Mackenzie

Denali
(Mount McKinley)
20,305ft (6190m)

Gulf of
Alaska

Coast Mountains

Coast Ranges

Rocky Mountains

Great Plains

Mississippi

Gulf of
Mexico

Hawaiian
Islands

Polynesia

PACIFIC

OCEAN

Galápagos
Islands

Easter Island

East Pacific Rise

Southwest

Pacific

Basin

Ellesmere Island

Queen Elizabeth
Islands

Baffin Island

Baffin
Bay

Greenland

Great Bear
Lake

Great Slave
Lake

Hudson
Bay

Labrador
Sea

NORTH
AMERICA

Great Lakes

Appalachian Mts.

West Indies

Caribbean
Sea

Amazon

Amazon Basin

Peru
Basin

Andes

SOUTH
AMERICA

Gran
Chaco

Paraná

Cerro
Aconcagua
22,838ft
(6961m)

Pampas

Patagonia

Tierra del Fuego

Cape Horn

Drake Passage

Antarctic
Peninsula

Grand Banks
of Newfoundland

North American
Basin

Mid-Atlantic Ridge

ATLANTIC

OCEAN

Brazil
Basin

Argentine
Basin

Falkland Islands

South Georgia

South Sandwich
Islands

Arctic Circle

Tropic of Cancer

Equator

Tropic of Capricorn

Antarctic Circle

1

2

3

4

5

E   F   G   H

Standard Time Zones

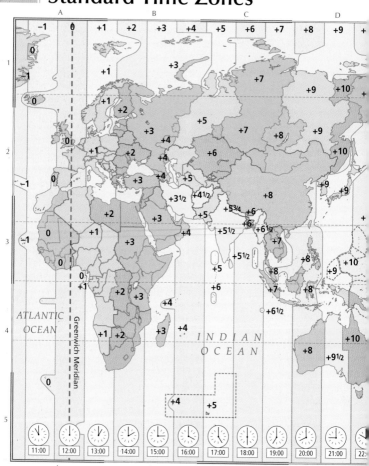

ATLANTIC OCEAN

Greenwich Meridian

INDIAN OCEAN

The world's regions

North & Central America

EUROPE

Franz Josef Land
(Russia)

Svalbard
(Norway)

Jan Mayen
(Norway)

ICELAND

Greenland
(Denmark)

Arctic Circle

Baffin
Bay

Labrador
Sea

Labrador

Laurentian
Mountains

ASIA

Arctic Circle

ARCTIC

OCEAN

North
Pole

Queen Elizabeth
Islands

Baffin Island

Hudson
Bay

C A N A D A

Gr

Reindeer
Lake

Lake Athabasca

Lake Winnipeg

Great Slave Lake

Great Bear
Lake

Beaufort
Sea

Mackenzie

R o c k y   M o u

Bering Strait

ALASKA (US)

Yukon

▲
Mount McKinley (6190m)
Denali
20,306ft

Gulf of
Alaska

PACIFIC

OCEAN

Bering Sea

Aleutian Islands

Snake

St Pierre &
Miquelon
(France)

ATLANTIC

OCEAN

Sargasso Sea

Bermuda
(UK)

Virgin Islands (US)
British Virgin
Islands (UK)
Anguilla (UK)
ANTIGUA &
BARBUDA
Guadeloupe
(France)
ST KITTS
& NEVIS
ST LUCIA
BARBADOS

Turks & Caicos
Islands (UK)

Puerto
Rico
(US)

DOMINICAN
REPUBLIC

MONTSERRAT (UK)
DOMINICA

Martinique (France)
ST VINCENT & THE GRENADINES
GRENADA

TRINIDAD
& TOBAGO

THE
BAHAMAS

HAITI

Bonaire
(Neth.)

Curaçao
(Neth.)
Aruba (Neth.)

CUBA

SOUTH

AMERICA

Cayman Islands
(UK)

JAMAICA

BELIZE

HONDURAS

Gulf of Mexico

NICARAGUA

PANAMA

Andes

Great
Lakes

Lake
Superior

Lake
Huron

Lake Ontario

Lake Erie

Lake
Michigan

Appalachian Mountains

Ohio

Mississippi

Missouri

Arkansas

UNITED STATES

OF AMERICA

Rio Grande

GUATEMALA
EL SALVADOR

COSTA RICA

Sierra Madre Oriental

MEXICO

Sierra Madre Occidental

Colorado

Galápagos Islands
(Ecuador)

PACIFIC

OCEAN

Mount Whitney
14,505ft (4421m)

Death Valley
-282ft (-86m)

Clipperton Island
(French Polynesia)

Equator

Tropic of Cancer

0 km
0 miles

1000

1000

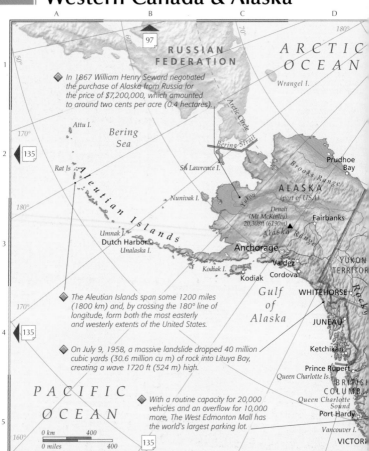

RUSSIAN
FEDERATION

ARCTIC
OCEAN

◆ In 1867 William Henry Seward negotiated
the purchase of Alaska from Russia for
the price of $7,200,000, which amounted
to around two cents per acre (0.4 hectares).

Wrangel I.

Attu I.

*Bering
Sea*

Aleutian Islands

Rat Is

St Lawrence I.

Bering Strait

Arctic Circle

Brooks Range

Prudhoe
Bay

ALASKA
(part of USA)

Nunivak I.

Yukon

Denali
(Mt McKinley)
20,308ft (6190m)

Fairbanks

Umnak I.
Dutch Harbor
Unalaska I.

Anchorage

Alaska Range

Kodiak I.

Valdez

Cordova

YUKON
TERRITORY

Kodiak

Gulf
of
Alaska

WHITEHORSE

◆ The Aleutian Islands span some 1200 miles
(1800 km) and, by crossing the 180° line of
longitude, form both the most easterly
and westerly extents of the United States.

JUNEAU

Rocky

◆ On July 9, 1958, a massive landslide dropped 40 million
cubic yards (30.6 million cu m) of rock into Lituya Bay,
creating a wave 1720 ft (524 m) high.

Ketchikan

Prince Rupert

Queen Charlotte Is.

BRITISH
COLUMBIA

PACIFIC
OCEAN

◆ With a routine capacity for 20,000
vehicles and an overflow for 10,000
more, The West Edmonton Mall has
the world's largest parking lot.

Queen Charlotte
Sound

Port Hardy

Vancouver I.

VICTOR

0 km   400

0 miles   400

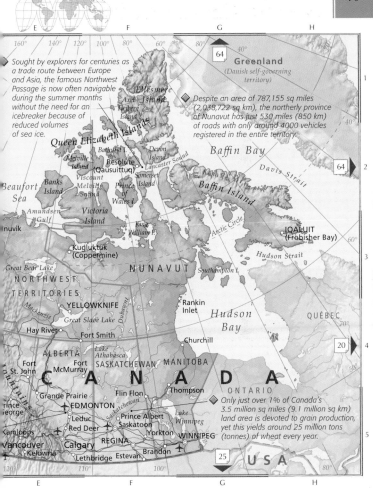

◈ Sought by explorers for centuries as a trade route between Europe and Asia, the famous Northwest Passage is now often navigable during the summer months without the need for an icebreaker because of reduced volumes of sea ice.

◈ Despite an area of 787,155 sq miles (2,038,722 sq km), the northerly province of Nunavut has just 530 miles (850 km) of roads with only around 4000 vehicles registered in the entire territory.

◈ Only just over 1% of Canada's 3.5 million sq miles (9.1 million sq km) land area is devoted to grain production, yet this yields around 25 million tons (tonnes) of wheat every year.

Greenland
(Danish self-governing territory)

Baffin Bay

Davis Strait

Baffin Island

IQALUIT
(Frobisher Bay)

Arctic Circle

Hudson Strait

Ellesmere Island

Axel Heiberg Island

Queen Elizabeth Islands

Bathurst I.

Devon Island

Melville Island

Resolute (Qausuittuq)

Lancaster Sound

Somerset Island

Viscount Melville Sound

Prince of Wales I.

Banks Island

Victoria Island

Amundsen Gulf

King William I.

Beaufort Sea

Inuvik

Great Bear Lake

NORTHWEST TERRITORIES

Mackenzie

YELLOWKNIFE

Great Slave Lake

Hay River

Fort Smith

Dubawnt

NUNAVUT

Southampton I.

Rankin Inlet

Hudson Bay

QUÉBEC

Churchill

Lake Athabasca

ALBERTA

SASKATCHEWAN

MANITOBA

Fort St. John

Fort McMurray

Grande Prairie

Flin Flon

Thompson

ONTARIO

rince eorge

EDMONTON

Leduc

Red Deer

Prince Albert

Saskatoon

Saskatchewan

Yorkton

Lake Winnipeg

amloops

Vancouver

Kelowna

Calgary

REGINA

WINNIPEG

Lethbridge

Estevan

Brandon

C A N A D A

U S A

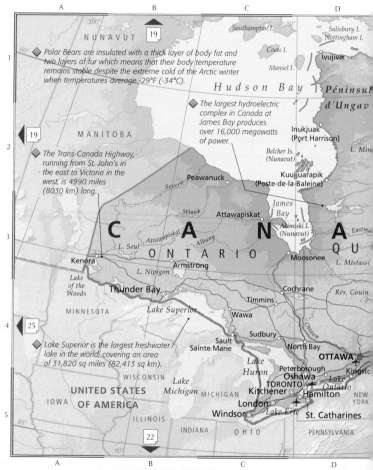

NUNAVUT

◆ Polar Bears are insulated with a thick layer of body fat and two layers of fur which means that their body temperature remains stable despite the extreme cold of the Arctic winter when temperatures average -29°F (-34°C).

MANITOBA

◆ The Trans-Canada Highway, running from St. John's in the east to Victoria in the west, is 4990 miles (8030 km) long.

Southampton I.

Coats I.

Mansel I.

Salisbury I.
Nottingham I.

Ivujivik

H u d s o n   B a y

Péninsul
d'Ungav

◆ The largest hydroelectric complex in Canada at James Bay produces over 16,000 megawatts of power.

Inukjuak
(Port Harrison)

L. Min

Belcher Is.
(Nunavut)

Peawanuck

Kuujjuarapik
(Poste-de-la-Baleine)

Severn

Winisk

Attawapiskat

James
Bay

C   A   N   A

D   A

Attawapiskat

Albany

Akimiski I.
(Nunavut)

Eastma

L. Seul

Kenora

Armstrong

O N T A R I O

QU

L. Nipigon

Moosonee

L. Mistassi

Lake
of the
Woods

Thunder Bay

Cochrane

Rés. Gouin

MINNESOTA

Lake Superior

Timmins

Wawa

Ottawa

◆ Lake Superior is the largest freshwater lake in the world, covering an area of 31,820 sq miles (82,413 sq km).

Sudbury

North Bay

OTTAWA

WISCONSIN

Lake
Huron

Peterborough

Kingsto

UNITED STATES

Lake
Michigan

MICHIGAN

Oshawa
TORONTO

Lake
Ontario

IOWA

OF AMERICA

Kitchener

Hamilton

NEW
YORK

London

ILLINOIS

INDIANA

Windsor

Lake Erie

St. Catharines

OHIO

PENNSYLVANIA

Sault
Sainte Marie

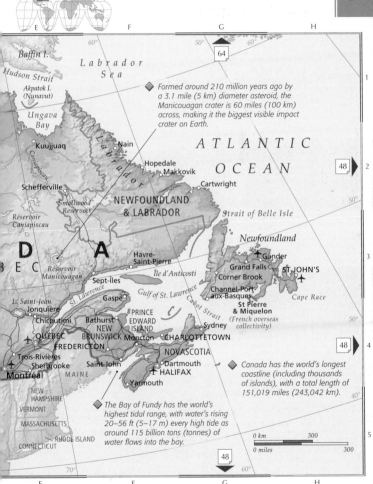

Baffin I.

Hudson Strait

Akpatok I.
(Nunavut)

Ungava
Bay

*Labrador
Sea*

64

Formed around 210 million years ago by
a 3.1 mile (5 km) diameter asteroid, the
Manicouagan crater is 60 miles (100 km)
across, making it the biggest visible impact
crater on Earth.

A T L A N T I C

Nain

O C E A N

Kuujjuaq

Hopedale
Makkovik

Scheffervilie

Cartwright

Labrador

NEWFOUNDLAND
& LABRADOR

Strait of Belle Isle

48

50°

Réservoir
Caniapiscau

Smallwood
Reservoir

Newfoundland

D

A

Havre-
Saint-Pierre

Île d'Anticosti

Gander

Grand Falls

ST. JOHN'S

B E C

Réservoir
Manicouagan

Corner Brook

Sept-Îles

Channel-Port-
aux-Basques

Cape Race

L. Saint-Jean

Gulf of St. Lawrence

St. Lawrence

Gaspé

St Pierre
& Miquelon
(French overseas
collectivity)

50°

Jonquière

Chicoutimi

PRINCE
EDWARD
ISLAND

Cabot Strait

QUÉBEC

Bathurst

NEW
BRUNSWICK

Sydney

48

Trois-Rivières

FREDERICTON

Moncton

CHARLOTTETOWN

40°

Sherbrooke

Saint John

NOVA SCOTIA

Dartmouth

Montréal

MAINE

HALIFAX

Canada has the world's longest
coastline (including thousands
of islands), with a total length of
151,019 miles (243,042 km).

NEW
HAMPSHIRE

Yarmouth

VERMONT

MASSACHUSETTS

The Bay of Fundy has the world's
highest tidal range, with water's rising
20–56 ft (5–17 m) every high tide as
around 115 billion tons (tonnes) of
water flows into the bay.

RHODE ISLAND

CONNECTICUT

0 km   300

0 miles   300

48

70°

60°

◆ The Chicago River originally flowed into Lake Michigan, but was reversed in 1900 by the completion of a canal.

◆ Many US freight trains are over 2 miles (3.2 km) long, made up of almost 200 cars, and can take around 5 minutes to pass a level-crossing.

MINNESOTA

CANADA

ONTARIO

Lake Superior

Superior
Ironwood
Marquette
Sault Ste Marie
Iron Mountain
Ladysmith
Cheboygan
Lake Huron
WISCONSIN
MICHIGAN
Eau Claire
Green Bay
Traverse City
Mississippi
La Crosse
Oshkosh
Lake Michigan
Bay City
IOWA
MADISON
Grand Rapids
Saginaw
Flint
Milwaukee
LANSING
Waukegan
Rockford
Chicago
Ann Arbor
Detroit
Erie
Aurora
South Bend
Lake Erie
Toledo
Cleveland
Joliet
Gary
Youngstown
Rock Island
Fort Wayne
Akron
Galesburg
INDIANA
Mansfield
Canton
Wheeling
Peoria
ILLINOIS
Champaign
Muncie
OHIO
SPRINGFIELD
INDIANAPOLIS
COLUMBUS
Decatur
Dayton
MISSOURI
Effingham
Terre Haute
Cincinnati
Ohio
Bloomington
East St Louis
Huntington
Mt. Vernon
Louisville
CHARLESTON
Evansville
FRANKFORT
Lexington
WEST VIRGINIA
Carbondale
Owensboro
Richmond
Ohio
KENTUCKY
Paducah
Hopkinsville
Bowling Green
London

ARKANSAS

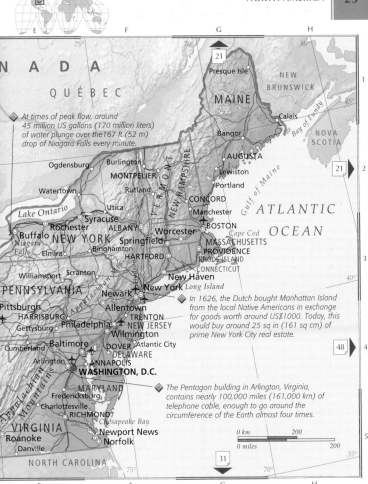

CANADA

QUÉBEC

◆ At times of peak flow, around
45 million US gallons (170 million liters)
of water plunge over the 167 ft (52 m)
drop of Niagara Falls every minute.

Presque Isle

NEW
BRUNSWICK

MAINE

Calais

Bay of Fundy

NOVA
SCOTIA

Bangor

AUGUSTA

Ogdensburg   Burlington

MONTPELIER

Watertown   VERMONT

Lewiston

Portland

Rutland   NEW HAMPSHIRE

CONCORD

Gulf of Maine

ATLANTIC

Lake Ontario   Utica

Manchester

Syracuse   ALBANY   Worcester   BOSTON

OCEAN

Rochester

Buffalo   NEW YORK   Springfield   Cape Cod

Niagara
Falls   Binghamton   HARTFORD   MASSACHUSETTS

Elmira   PROVIDENCE

RHODE ISLAND

CONNECTICUT

Williamsport   Scranton   New Haven

PENNSYLVANIA   Newark   New York   Long Island

◆ In 1626, the Dutch bought Manhattan Island
from the local Native Americans in exchange
for goods worth around US$1000. Today, this
would buy around 25 sq in (161 sq cm) of
prime New York City real estate.

Pittsburgh   Allentown

HARRISBURG   TRENTON

Gettysburg   Philadelphia   NEW JERSEY

Wilmington

Cumberland   Baltimore   DOVER   Atlantic City

DELAWARE

Arlington   ANNAPOLIS

WASHINGTON, D.C.

◆ The Pentagon building in Arlington, Virginia,
contains nearly 100,000 miles (161,000 km) of
telephone cable, enough to go around the
circumference of the Earth almost four times.

MARYLAND

Fredericksburg

Charlottesville

RICHMOND

Chesapeake Bay

VIRGINIA   Newport News

Roanoke   Norfolk

Danville

0 km   200

0 miles   200

NORTH CAROLINA

USA: Central States

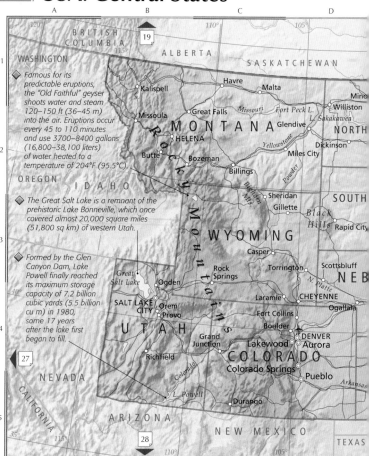

◆ Famous for its predictable eruptions, the "Old Faithful" geyser shoots water and steam 120–150 ft (36–45 m) into the air. Eruptions occur every 45 to 110 minutes and use 3700–8400 gallons (16,800–38,100 liters) of water heated to a temperature of 204°F (95.5°C).

◆ The Great Salt Lake is a remnant of the prehistoric Lake Bonneville, which once covered almost 20,000 square miles (51,800 sq km) of western Utah.

◆ Formed by the Glen Canyon Dam, Lake Powell finally reached its maximum storage capacity of 7.2 billion cubic yards (5.5 billion cu m) in 1980, some 17 years after the lake first began to fill.

BRITISH COLUMBIA

ALBERTA

SASKATCHEWAN

WASHINGTON

Kalispell
Havre
Malta
Mino
Williston

Missoula
Great Falls
Missouri
Fort Peck L.
L. Sakakawea
NORTH

MONTANA
Glendive

HELENA
Yellowstone
Dickinson

Butte
Bozeman
Miles City

Billings
Powder

OREGON
IDAHO

Bighorn Mts.
Sheridan
SOUTH

Gillette
Black Hills
Rapid City

WYOMING

Casper

Great Salt Lake
Rock Springs
Torrington
Scottsbluff
NEB

Ogden
Laramie
CHEYENNE
N. Platte
Ogallala

SALT LAKE CITY
Orem
Provo
Fort Collins

UTAH
Boulder
Lakewood
DENVER
Aurora

Grand Junction
COLORADO

Richfield
Colorado Springs

Colorado
Pueblo
Arkansas

NEVADA
L. Powell
Durango

CALIFORNIA
ARIZONA
NEW MEXICO
TEXAS

E   F   G   H

CANADA

20

MANITOBA   Lake of the Woods   ONTARIO

1

MINNESOTA   Lake Superior

22

Grand Forks   Virginia

DAKOTA   Moorhead   Duluth

BISMARCK   Fargo   Brainerd   ◆ Access to the St. Lawrence Seaway
via the Great Lakes makes Duluth
the most westerly Atlantic port in
the US, some 1100 miles (1770 km)
from the Atlantic Ocean.

45°   2

Aberdeen   St Cloud   SAINT
Minneapolis   PAUL

DAKOTA   Watertown   WISCONSIN   Lake
Michigan

PIERRE   Rochester
Mitchell   Sioux Falls   MICHIGAN

Missouri   Mason City

Sioux City   Dubuque

RASKA   IOWA   Cedar Rapids   ILLINOIS   INDIANA   OHIO

Columbus   DES MOINES   Davenport   40°

North
Platte   Omaha   Council Bluffs   ◆ The deadliest tornado in US
history struck Missouri on
March 18, 1925. Leaving a
continuous 219 mile (352 km)
track, the tornado crossed three
states and killed 695 people.

Platte   LINCOLN   Burlington

Hastings   Kirksville

22

Oakley   Hays   St Joseph   Mississippi
Kansas City   Independence

KANSAS   Kansas City   Missouri   Saint
Louis

TOPEKA   JEFFERSON CITY

Dodge   Pratt   MISSOURI   KENTUCKY
City   Wichita   Springfield

Arkansas   Ozark Plateau   TENNESSEE   85°
35°   5

OKLAHOMA   ARKANSAS   0 km   200
30
0 miles   200

100°   95°   90°

E   F   G   H

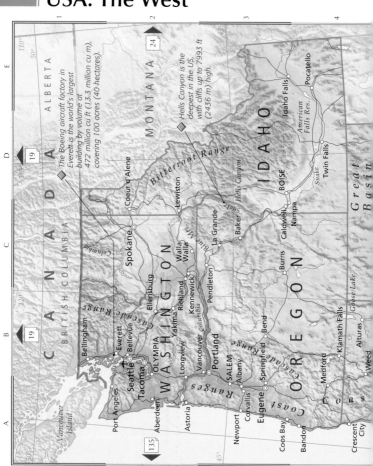

The Boeing aircraft factory in Everett is the world's largest building by volume at 472 million cu ft (13.3 million cu m), covering 100 acres (40 hectares)

Hells Canyon is the deepest in the US, with cliffs up to 7993 ft (2436 m) high.

At Black Rock Desert on October 15, 1997, ThrustSSC, driven by Andy Green, became the first land vehicle to break the sound barrier by achieving a speed of 763 mph (1228 km/h).

Death Valley is not only the lowest point in North America, at -282 ft (-86 m) below sea level, it is also the hottest, with a maximum air temperature of 134°F (57°C) recorded in 1913.

The Golden Gate Bridge, completed in 1937, has 80,000 miles (129,000 km) of wire in its two main cables, weighing a total of 22,200 tons (tonnes).

UTAH

NEVADA

Elko

Susanville

Redding

Ukiah

Santa Rosa

Chico

Yuba City

SACRAMENTO

Oakland

Berkeley

San Francisco

San Jose

Santa Cruz

Monterey

Salinas

Pyramid Lake

Reno

Sparks

CARSON CITY

Fallon

Hawthorne

Tonopah

Ely

Lake Mead

Las Vegas

ARIZONA

Lake Tahoe

Stockton

Modesto

Merced

Bishop

Fresno

Visalia

Mt. Whitney
14,505 ft
4421m

282 ft
(86m)

Death Valley

Mojave Desert

Bakersfield

Lancaster

Mojave

Barstow

San Bernardino

Riverside

Palm Springs

Salton Sea

Colorado

MEXICO

San Diego

Chula Vista

Oceanside

Santa Ana

Huntington Beach

Long Beach

Los Angeles

Pasadena

Oxnard

Santa Barbara

Santa Rosa I.

Santa Catalina I.

San Nicolas I.

San Clemente I.

San Joaquin Valley

CALIFORNIA

Coast Ranges

Sierra Nevada

Ranges

Humboldt

PACIFIC

OCEAN

Channel

Islands

0 km   200

0 miles   200

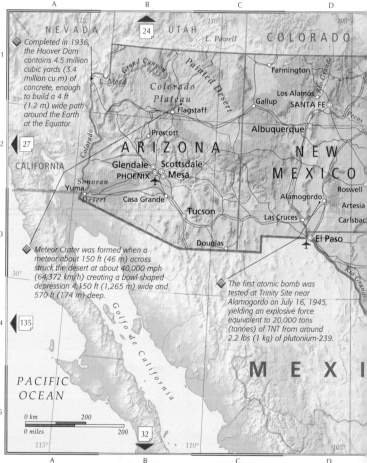

◆ Completed in 1936, the Hoover Dam contains 4.5 million cubic yards (3.4 million cu m) of concrete, enough to build a 4 ft (1.2 m) wide path around the Earth at the Equator.

◆ Meteor Crater was formed when a meteor about 150 ft (46 m) across struck the desert at about 40,000 mph (64,372 km/h) creating a bowl-shaped depression 4,150 ft (1,265 m) wide and 570 ft (174 m) deep.

◆ The first atomic bomb was tested at Trinity Site near Alamogordo on July 16, 1945, yielding an explosive force equivalent to 20,000 tons (tonnes) of TNT from around 2.2 lbs (1 kg) of plutonium-239.

NEVADA · UTAH · COLORADO
L. Powell
Grand Canyon · Painted Desert
L. Mead
Colorado Plateau
Farmington
Los Alamos · SANTA FE
Gallup
Flagstaff
Albuquerque
Prescott
Pecos
Rio Grande
Colorado
A R I Z O N A
N E W
Glendale · Scottsdale
PHOENIX · Mesa
M E X I C O
CALIFORNIA
Sonoran
Desert
Yuma
Casa Grande
Roswell
Alamogordo
Artesia
Las Cruces
Carlsbad
Tucson
Douglas
El Paso
Golfo de California
Rio Grande
PACIFIC
OCEAN
M E X I C

0 km · 200
0 miles · 200

115° · 110° · 105°

E   F   G   H

100°   95°   25

KANSAS

Ponca City

Enid   Tulsa   Broken
Arrow

OKLAHOMA

OKLAHOMA CITY   Shawnee   35°

Borger   Norman

Canadian   Pampa   Lawton

Amarillo   Red River   **ARKANSAS**   30

Clovis   Vernon   Red River   2

Wichita Falls   Paris

Lubbock   Denton

Brownfield   Fort Worth   Arlington   Longview

Hobbs   Abilene   Dallas   Tyler

Sweetwater   Jacksonville

Big Spring   Brazos

Odessa   Midland   Waco   Toledo Bend Res.   Neches   3

Pecos   San Angelo   Colorado   **LOUISIANA**

T E X A S   Bryan   30°

L. Travis   Beaumont

Edwards   AUSTIN   Houston   Port Arthur

Plateau   Pasadena

San Antonio   Texas City

Del Rio   San Antonio   Victoria   Galveston   30   4

Freeport

Eagle Pass

C O   Corpus Christi

Laredo   Kingsville

Padre Island   Gulf

Rio Grande   of

Mexico   5

Brownsville

100°   33   95°   25°

◇ The world's first parking
meter was installed in
Oklahoma City on
July 16, 1935.

◇ On January 10, 1901,
the Lucas Gusher blew
oil 150 ft (46 m) into the
air, flowing at 100,000
barrels a day until it was
eventually capped nine
days later.

With winds estimated at over
145 mph (233 km/h), the 1900
Galveston Hurricane claimed over
8000 lives, making it the deadliest
natural disaster in US history.

USA: The Southeast

A 95° B 90° C D 85°

MISSOURI
[25]

ILLINOIS KENTUCKY

OKLAHOMA

Fayetteville Walnut Ridge Clarksville NASHVILLE
35° Murfreesb
Fort Smith ARKANSAS TENNESSEE
Memphis Chattanooga

North Little Rock Florence Huntsville
LITTLE ROCK Gadsden R
Hot Springs Pine ATLAN
Bluff Columbus Birmingham
[29] Ouachita

Texarkana Monroe MISSISSIPPI Demopolis MONTGOMERY
Shreveport LOUISIANA Meridian Colum
JACKSON ALABAMA
T E X A S Red R. Pearl
Alexandria Hattiesburg Dothan
30° BATON ROUGE Mobile TALLAHASS
[29] Lake Charles Gulfport Pensacola
Lafayette Biloxi Panama City
Metairie New Orleans

Mississippi
Delta

In August 2005 Hurricane Katrina
cut a swath through New Orleans
with winds of up to 175 mph (278 km/h).
At least 1836 people lost their lives
and the area sustained over US$100
billion of damage.

The Mississippi/Missouri river system
drains around one-third of the US,
covering 1,245,000 sq miles
(3,225,000 sq km) including 31
states and two Canadian provinces.

0 km   200
0 miles   200

25° G u l f o f
M e x i c o

5
[33]

95° B 90° C D 85°
A

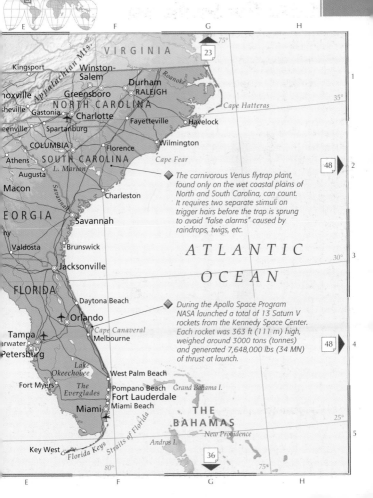

VIRGINIA

Kingsport

Winston-Salem

Durham

RALEIGH

Roanoke

Greensboro

NORTH CAROLINA

Cape Hatteras

noxville

sheville

Gastonia

Charlotte

Fayetteville

Havelock

eenville

Spartanburg

COLUMBIA

Florence

Wilmington

SOUTH CAROLINA

Athens

L. Marion

Cape Fear

Augusta

Charleston

◆ The carnivorous Venus flytrap plant,
found only on the wet coastal plains of
North and South Carolina, can count.
It requires two separate stimuli on
trigger hairs before the trap is sprung
to avoid "false alarms" caused by
raindrops, twigs, etc.

Macon

EORGIA

Savannah

ny

Valdosta

Brunswick

ATLANTIC

Jacksonville

OCEAN

FLORIDA

Daytona Beach

◆ During the Apollo Space Program
NASA launched a total of 13 Saturn V
rockets from the Kennedy Space Center.
Each rocket was 363 ft (111 m) high,
weighed around 3000 tons (tonnes)
and generated 7,648,000 lbs (34 MN)
of thrust at launch.

Orlando

Tampa

Cape Canaveral

Melbourne

arwater

Petersburg

Lake
Okeechobee

West Palm Beach

Fort Myers

The
Everglades

Pompano Beach

Grand Bahama I.

Fort Lauderdale

Miami

Miami Beach

THE
BAHAMAS

New Providence

Key West

Florida Keys

Straits of Florida

Andros I.

23

48

48

36

75°

35°

30°

25°

80°

75°

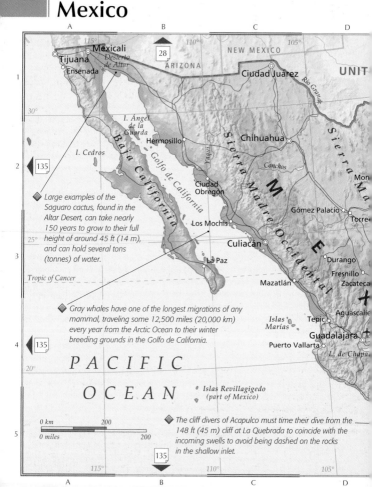

NEW MEXICO

ARIZONA

Tijuana
Mexicali
Ensenada
Desierto de Altar

28

Ciudad Juárez

Rio Grande

UNIT

30°

I. Ángel de la Guarda

I. Cedros

Hermosillo

Chihuahua

Sierra Ma

135

Baja California

Golfo de California

Conchos

Yaqui

M

Mon

Ciudad Obregón

Gómez Palacio

Torre

◆ Large examples of the Saguaro cactus, found in the Altar Desert, can take nearly 150 years to grow to their full height of around 45 ft (14 m), and can hold several tons (tonnes) of water.

Los Mochis

Culiacán

25°

La Paz

Durango

Fresnillo

Zacateca

Tropic of Cancer

Mazatlán

◆ Gray whales have one of the longest migrations of any mammal, traveling some 12,500 miles (20,000 km) every year from the Arctic Ocean to their winter breeding grounds in the Golfo de California.

Islas Marías

Tepic

Aguascalie

Guadalajara

135

Puerto Vallarta

L. de Chapa

PACIFIC

20°

OCEAN

Islas Revillagigedo (part of Mexico)

0 km   200

0 miles   200

◆ The cliff divers of Acapulco must time their dive from the 148 ft (45 m) cliff at La Quebrada to coincide with the incoming swells to avoid being dashed on the rocks in the shallow inlet.

135

Sierra Madre Occidental

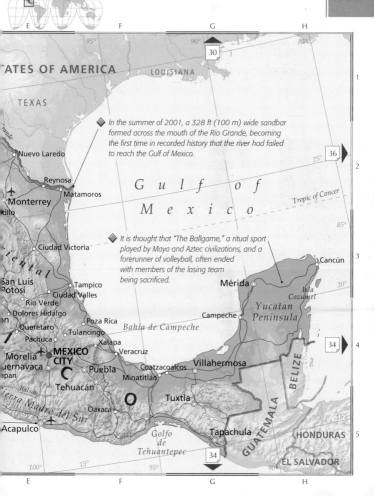

E F G H

STATES OF AMERICA   LOUISIANA

TEXAS

Grande
Nuevo Laredo

Reynosa
Monterrey   Matamoros
tillo

In the summer of 2001, a 328 ft (100 m) wide sandbar formed across the mouth of the Rio Grande, becoming the first time in recorded history that the river had failed to reach the Gulf of Mexico.

G u l f   o f

M e x i c o

Tropic of Cancer

Ciudad Victoria

It is thought that "The Ballgame," a ritual sport played by Maya and Aztec civilizations, and a forerunner of volleyball, often ended with members of the losing team being sacrificed.

Cancún

San Luis
Potosí   Tampico
Río Verde   Ciudad Valles
Dolores Hidalgo
on   Querétaro   Poza Rica
Pachuca   Tulancingo
MEXICO   Xalapa
Morelia   **CITY**   Veracruz
uernavaca   Puebla   Coatzacoalcos
apan   Minatitlán
Tehuacán

Oaxaca

Acapulco

Golfo
de
Tehuantepec

Mérida

Campeche

Bahía de Campeche

Isla
Cozumel

Yucatán
Peninsula

Villahermosa

BELIZE

Tuxtla

GUATEMALA

Tapachula   HONDURAS

EL SALVADOR

Sierra Madre del Sur
Balsas

36

85°

20°

34

15°

5

100°   15°   95°   90°

34

E F G H

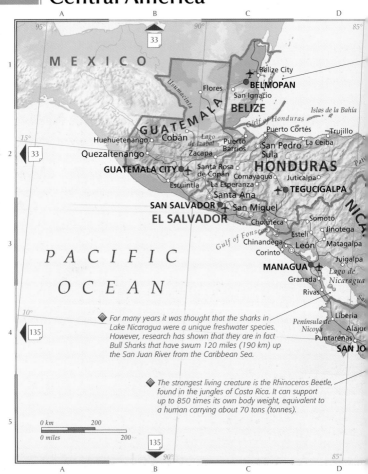

95°   90°   85°

MEXICO

33

GUATEMALA

Belize City
BELMOPAN
Flores
San Ignacio
BELIZE

Islas de la Bahía

Usumacinta

Gulf of Honduras
Puerto Cortés
Trujillo
Huehuetenango
Cobán
Lago de Izabal
Puerto Barrios
San Pedro Sula
La Ceiba
Quezaltenango
Zacapa

HONDURAS

GUATEMALA CITY
Santa Rosa de Copán
Comayagua
Juticalpa

Escuintla
La Esperanza
TEGUCIGALPA

Santa Ana
SAN SALVADOR
San Miguel

EL SALVADOR
Choluteca
Somoto
Estelí
Jinotega

NICA

Chinandega
León
Matagalpa

Corinto

Juigalpa

MANAGUA
Lago de Nicaragua

Granada

Rivas

PACIFIC

OCEAN

Liberia

Península de Nicoya
Alajue

Puntarenas

SAN JO

15°

33

10°

135

For many years it was thought that the sharks in
Lake Nicaragua were a unique freshwater species.
However, research has shown that they are in fact
Bull Sharks that have swum 120 miles (190 km) up
the San Juan River from the Caribbean Sea.

The strongest living creature is the Rhinoceros Beetle,
found in the jungles of Costa Rica. It can support
up to 850 times its own body weight, equivalent to
a human carrying about 70 tons (tonnes).

0 km   200
0 miles   200

135

90°   85°

A   B   C   D

◆ The Great Blue Hole in Lighthouse Reef, a submerged cave some 1000 ft (303 m) in diameter and 400 ft (120 m) deep, was originally explored by Jacques Cousteau, co-inventor of the aqualung.

as Santilla
art of Honduras)

Greater Antilles

HAITI

JAMAICA

◆ In August 1980, Hurricane Allen developed into one of the strongest Atlantic hurricanes in recorded history, reaching Category 5 status with sustained wind speeds of 190 mph (305 km/h).

Bajo Nuevo (part of Colombia)

Cayos Miskitos

Caribbean

Sea

I. de Providencia (part of Colombia)

I. de San Andrés (part of Colombia)

Islas del Maíz

uefields

◆ Each chamber at Gatun Locks on the Panama Canal is 110 ft (33.5 m) wide and 1000 ft (305 m) long. Opened to shipping in 1914, the locks took four years to build and required 2 million cubic yards (1.5 million cu m) of concrete.

OSTA
CA
○ Limón
tago

Colón

Cordillera
lamanca

PANAMA

○ David   Penonomé

PANAMA CITY

Panama Canal   *Isla del Rey*

Gulf of Darien

COLOMBIA

Golfo de Chiriquí   ○ Santiago   ○ Chitré

Golfo de Panamá

Las Tablas

The Caribbean

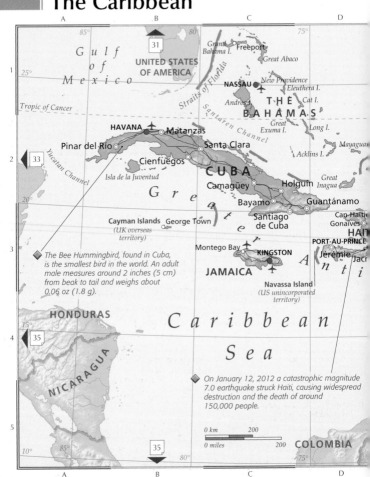

The Bee Hummingbird, found in Cuba, is the smallest bird in the world. An adult male measures around 2 inches (5 cm) from beak to tail and weighs about 0.06 oz (1.8 g).

On January 12, 2012 a catastrophic magnitude 7.0 earthquake struck Haiti, causing widespread destruction and the death of around 150,000 people.

Gulf of Mexico

UNITED STATES OF AMERICA

31

Tropic of Cancer

Straits of Florida

Grand Bahama I. Freeport

Great Abaco

NASSAU New Providence
Eleuthera I.
Andros I. Cat I.

THE BAHAMAS

Great Exuma I. Long I.

Santaren Channel

Mayagua

Acklins I.

HAVANA Matanzas

Pinar del Río

Yucatan Channel

33

Santa Clara

Cienfuegos

Isla de la Juventud

CUBA

Camagüey

Holguín Great Inagua

Bayamo

Guantánamo

Santiago de Cuba

Cap-Haïti
Gonaïves

Cayman Islands George Town
(UK overseas territory)

Montego Bay KINGSTON

JAMAICA

Navassa Island
(US unincorporated territory)

HAITI

PORT-AU-PRINCE

Jérémie Jacm

Anti

HONDURAS

35

NICARAGUA

Caribbean

Sea

35

0 km   200

0 miles   200

COLOMBIA

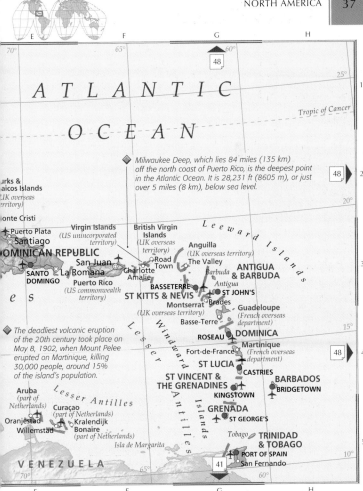

ATLANTIC

OCEAN

Tropic of Cancer

Milwaukee Deep, which lies 84 miles (135 km) off the north coast of Puerto Rico, is the deepest point in the Atlantic Ocean. It is 28,231 ft (8605 m), or just over 5 miles (8 km), below sea level.

Turks & Caicos Islands (UK overseas territory)

Monte Cristi
Puerto Plata
Santiago
DOMINICAN REPUBLIC
SANTO DOMINGO
San Juan
La Romana
Puerto Rico (US commonwealth territory)

Virgin Islands (US unincorporated territory)
British Virgin Islands (UK overseas territory)
Road Town
Charlotte Amalie
BASSETERRE
ST KITTS & NEVIS
Montserrat (UK overseas territory)
Basse-Terre

Anguilla (UK overseas territory)
The Valley
Barbuda
ANTIGUA & BARBUDA
Antigua
ST JOHN'S
Brades
Guadeloupe (French overseas department)

Leeward Islands

ROSEAU DOMINICA
Martinique (French overseas department)
Fort-de-France
ST LUCIA
CASTRIES
ST VINCENT & THE GRENADINES
KINGSTOWN
GRENADA
ST GEORGE'S
BARBADOS
BRIDGETOWN

The deadliest volcanic eruption of the 20th century took place on May 8, 1902, when Mount Pelee erupted on Martinique, killing 30,000 people, around 15% of the island's population.

Aruba (part of Netherlands)
Oranjestad
Curaçao (part of Netherlands)
Willemstad
Kralendijk
Bonaire (part of Netherlands)
Isla de Margarita

Lesser Antilles
Windward Islands

Tobago
TRINIDAD & TOBAGO
PORT OF SPAIN
San Fernando

VENEZUELA

ATLANTIC OCEAN

Equator

49

48

17

17

Caribbean Sea

Greater Antilles

Hispaniola

Jamaica

Puerto Rico

Lesser Antilles

Trinidad

French Guiana (France)

SURINAME (claimed by Suriname)

GUYANA (claimed by Venezuela)

VENEZUELA

Orinoco

Guiana Highlands

Llanos

COLOMBIA

Magdalena

Cauca

Meta

Putumayo

Napo

Marañón

ECUADOR

Chimborazo 20,564ft (6,268m)

Equator

Içá

Río Negro

Represa Balbina

Amazon

Japurá

Negro

Amazon

Juruá

Purus

Madeira

Ucayali

PERU

Andes

BOLIVIA

Beni

Altiplano

Lake Titicaca

BRAZIL

Brasília

Tapajós

Xingu

Tocantins

Araguaia

Planalto da Borborema

São Francisco

Represa de Sobradinho

Brazilian Highlands

Planalto de Mato Grosso

Chapada dos Parecis

Pantan

Mamoré

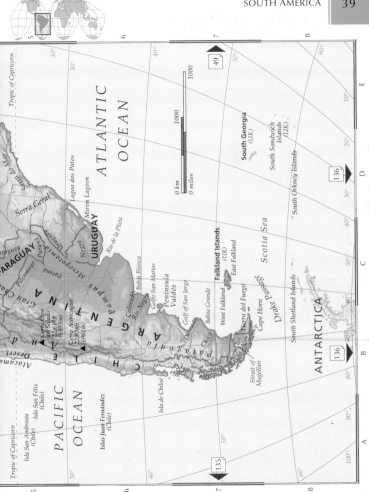

Northern South America

Caribbean Sea

80°

36

75°

Gulf of Venezuela

70°

Less

PANAMA

PACIFIC

OCEAN

35

10°

5°

0° Equator

5°

Santa Marta

Ríohacha

Coro

Barranquilla

Maicao

Maracaibo

CARACA

Cartagena

Valledupar

Cabimas

Maracay

Ciudad Ojeda

Barquisimeto

Valencia

Sincelejo

Lago de Maracaibo

Valera

Acarigua

Montería

Mérida

Guanare

San Juan de los Morros

Cúcuta

Barinas

San Cristóbal

San Fernando

Bucaramanga

Arauca

Bello

Barrancabermeja

Arauca

VEN

Medellín

Quibdó

Itagüí

Tunja

Puerto Carreño

Manizales

Yopal

Pereira

Meta

Armenia

Ibagué

BOGOTÁ

Buenaventura

Villavicencio

COLOMBIA

Cali

Guaviare

Popayán

Neiva

San José del Guaviare

Ne

Pasto

Florencia

Mocoa

Mitú

Esmeraldas

Tulcán

Ibarra

QUITO

Santo Domingo de los Colorados

Ambato

Manta

Caquetá

Portoviejo

Riobamba

Guayaquil

Milagro

ECUADOR

Golfo de Guayaquil

Cuenca

Putumayo

Machala

Loja

PERU

◆ The first coffee seedlings were brought to Colombia in 1804 by Jesuit missionaries; today, Colomb produces over 700,000 tons (tonnes) of coffee beans every year.

◆ Colombia has the highest number of species by area in the world. There are over 1700 endemic bird species; more than all of Europe and North America combined.

42

135

A   B   C   D

Antilles   **GRENADA**

ATLANTIC

Isla de Margarita

Carúpano

TRINIDAD & TOBAGO

Cumaná

1

Barcelona

Maturín

Tucupita

OCEAN

10°

El Tigre

The Serpent's Mouth

Orinoco

Ciudad Guayana

The Guiana Shield is one of the Earth's oldest surfaces, formed around 2 billion years ago.

Ciudad Bolívar

Embalse de Guri

(claimed by Venezuela)

ZUELA

GEORGETOWN

Nieuw Amsterdam

49

2

Caroní

Cuyuni

Bartica

New Amsterdam

St.-Laurent-du-Maroni

Salto Ángel

Rockstone

PARAMARIBO

Casiquiare

GUYANA

Linden

Sinnamary

Kourou

5°

Caroní

G u i a n a

W.J. van Blommesteinmeer

SURINAME

CAYENNE

Parima

H i g h l a n d s

Angel Falls (Salto Ángel) plunge a total of 3212 ft (979 m) to form the world's highest waterfall.

Orinoco

French Guiana

(French overseas department)

3

Essequibo

Courantyne

Maroni

Acarai Mts.

(claimed by Suriname)

(claimed by Suriname)

The European Space Agency launch facility at Kourou takes advantage of the Earth's spin near the equator to gain 10 percent more payload than an equivalent launch at Cape Canaveral in the US.

Equator

4

A m a z o n

B R A Z I L

43

B a s i n

2.47 acres (1 hectare) of Amazon rain forest can contain more than 750 types of trees and 1500 plant species, amounting to around 900 tons (tonnes) of living plant material.

5

0 km   200

0 miles   200

37

49

43

43

Lake Titicaca is the largest lake in South America at 3220 sq miles (8340 sq km). With an altitude of 12,500 ft (3810 m) it is also the world's highest navigable lake.

BOLIVIA'S TWO CAPITALS

La Paz - seat of government

Sucre - legal capital

E · F · G · H

50° · 40°

48

SURINAME

French Guiana
(French overseas department)

The Amazon River is 4049 miles (6516 km) long, with an average flow of 7.7 million cubic feet (219,000 cu m) of water entering the Atlantic Ocean every second.

Macapá

Ilha Caviana de Fora

Ilha de Marajó

Belém

Amazon

Santarém

A T L A N T I C

Equator

São Luís

Paranaíba

O C E A N

Fortaleza

San Fernando de Noronha (part of Brazil)

49

Represa de Tucuruí

Imperatriz

Teresina

Mossoró

Xingu

Z   I   L

Carolina

Natal

Campina Grande

João Pessoa

Tocantins

Juàzeiro do Norte

Recife

les Pires

São Francisco

Araguaia

Represa de Sobradinho

Juàzeiro

Maceió

10°

M a t o   G r o s s o

Taguatinga

Feira de Santana

Aracaju

Cuiabá

B r a z i l i a n

Salvador

Anápolis

BRASÍLIA

H i g h l a n d s

Itabuna

49

Goiânia

Vitória da Conquista

Montes Claros

Governador Valadares

Uberlândia

Uberaba

Divinópolis

Belo Horizonte

Campo Grande

Ribeirão Preto

Paraná

Vitória

Marília

Campinas

Nova Iguaçu

Campos

20°

Londrina

Sorocaba

Taubaté

Juiz de Fora

São Paulo

Rio de Janeiro

44

Tropic of Capricorn

30°

50° · 40°

E · F · G · H

Paraguay, Uruguay & South Brazil

◆ Formed by river deposits washed down from the Andes and Brazilian Shield, the Gran Chaco is virtually free of stones. It is composed of sand and silt sediments that are up to 10,000 ft (3050 m) thick.

◆ With a maximum height of 269 ft (82 m) and a total width of 1.7 miles (2.7 km) Iguaçu Falls has a peak flow rate of 452,000 cu ft/s (12,799 cu m/s) which would fill five Olympic size swimming pools every second.

Map labels:

BOLIVIA
BRA
Gran Chaco
General Eugenio A. Garay
Fuerte Olimpo
Mariscal Estigarribia
PARAGUAY
São José do Rio Preto
Campo Grande
Presidente Prudente
Maril
Bauru
Dourados
Paraná
Ourinhos
Tropic of Capricorn
Pozo Colorado
Concepción
Maringá
Londrina
Pilcomayo
Coronel Oviedo
Ciudad del Este
Ponta Grossa
ASUNCIÓN
Lambare
Villarrica
Guarapuava
Curitiba
Caazapá
San Juan Bautista
Iguaçu
Joinville
Pilar
Encarnación
Pelotas
Paraná
Blumenau
Florianópoli
Lajes
Carazinho
São Borja
Passo Fundo
Erechim
Uruguay
Caxias do Sul
Santa Maria
Serra
Uruguaiana
Canoas
Artigas
Porto Alegre
Rivera
Bagé
Lagoa dos Patos
ARGENTINA
Salto
Tacuarembó
Pelotas
Paysandú
Negro
Melo
Rio Grande
Fray Bentos
URUGUAY
Mirim Lagoon
Mercedes
Durazno
Chuy
Trinidad
Las Piedras
MONTEVIDEO
San Carlos
Rio de la Plata

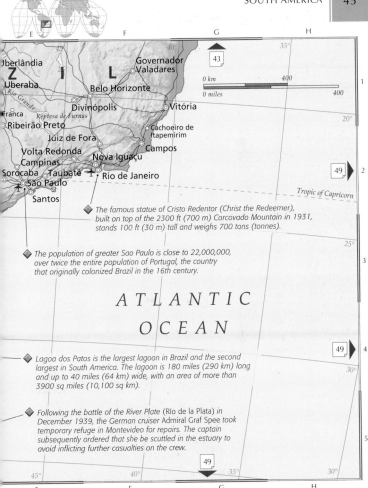

E F G H

Uberlândia

Z I L

Uberaba

Governador
Valadares

Rio Grande

Belo Horizonte

Divinópolis

França

Ribeirão Preto

Represa de Furnas

Vitória

Juiz de Fora

Cachoeiro de
Itapemirim

Volta Redonda

Campos

Campinas

Nova Iguaçu

Sorocaba

Taubaté

Rio de Janeiro

Sao Paulo

Santos

Tropic of Capricorn

0 km 400

0 miles 400

◆ The famous statue of Cristo Redentor (Christ the Redeemer),
built on top of the 2300 ft (700 m) Corcovado Mountain in 1931,
stands 100 ft (30 m) tall and weighs 700 tons (tonnes).

◆ The population of greater Sao Paulo is close to 22,000,000,
over twice the entire population of Portugal, the country
that originally colonized Brazil in the 16th century.

ATLANTIC

OCEAN

◆ Lagoa dos Patos is the largest lagoon in Brazil and the second
largest in South America. The lagoon is 180 miles (290 km) long
and up to 40 miles (64 km) wide, with an area of more than
3900 sq miles (10,100 sq km).

◆ Following the battle of the River Plate (Río de la Plata) in
December 1939, the German cruiser Admiral Graf Spee took
temporary refuge in Montevideo for repairs. The captain
subsequently ordered that she be scuttled in the estuary to
avoid inflicting further casualties on the crew.

E F G H

Southern South America

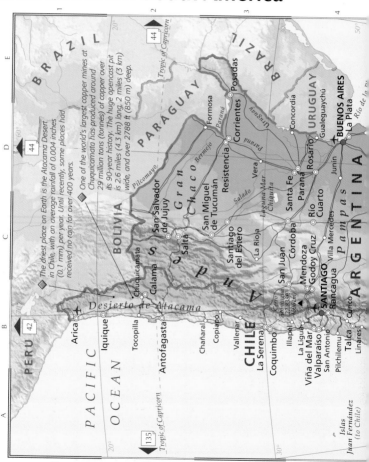

The driest place on Earth is the Atacama Desert in Chile, with an average rainfall of 0.004 inches (0.1 mm) per year. Until recently, some places had received no rain for over 400 years.

One of the world's largest copper mines at Chuquicamata has produced around 29 million tons (tonnes) of copper over its 90-year history. The huge opencast pit is 2.6 miles (4.3 km) long, 2 miles (3 km) wide, and over 2788 ft (850 m) deep.

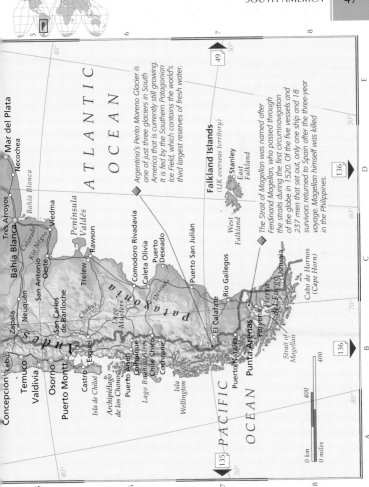

ATLANTIC OCEAN

PACIFIC OCEAN

Mar del Plata
Necochea
Tres Arroyos
Bahía Blanca
Bahía Blanca
Viedma
Colorado
Río Negro
Península
Valdés
San Antonio
Oeste
Neuquén
Zapala
San Carlos
de Bariloche
Rawson
Trelew
Chubut
Comodoro Rivadavia
Caleta Olivia
Puerto
Deseado
Deseado
Puerto San Julián

Argentina's Perito Moreno Glacier is one of just three glaciers in South America that is currently still growing. It is fed by the Southern Patagonian Ice Field, which contains the world's third largest reserves of fresh water.

Falkland Islands
(UK overseas territory)
Stanley
East
Falkland
West
Falkland

The Strait of Magellan was named after Ferdinand Magellan, who passed through the straits during the first circumnavigation of the globe in 1520. Of the five vessels and 237 men that set out, only one ship and 18 survivors returned to Spain after the three-year voyage. Magellan himself was killed in the Philippines.

Concepción
Temuco
Valdivia
Osorno
Puerto Montt
Castro
Isla de Chiloé
Archipiélago
de los Chonos
Puerto Aisén
Coihaique
Chile Chico
Cochrane
Lago Buenos Aires
Isla
Wellington
El Calafate
Río Gallegos
Puerto Natales
Punta Arenas
Porvenir
Tierra del Fuego
Ushuaia
Cabo de Hornos
(Cape Horn)
Strait of
Magellan

Lago
Musters

Patagonia

Andes

Esquel

Lebu

Lago
Buenos Aires

0 km   400
0 miles   400

The Atlantic Ocean

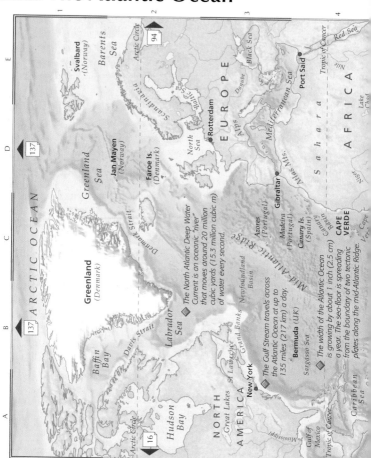

ARCTIC OCEAN

EUROPE

AFRICA

NORTH AMERICA

Greenland (Denmark)

Svalbard (Norway)

Barents Sea

Arctic Circle

Greenland Sea

Jan Mayen (Norway)

Faroe Is. (Denmark)

Scandinavia

Baltic Sea

Black Sea

Danube

Nile

Red Sea

Tropic of Cancer

Port Said

Mediterranean Sea

Sahara

Lake Chad

Niger

Cape

CAPE VERDE

Canary Basin

Canary Is. (Spain)

Madeira (Portugal)

Azores (Portugal)

Gibraltar

Atlas Mts.

Alps

North Sea

Rotterdam

Denmark Strait

Baffin Bay

Davis Strait

Hudson Bay

Arctic Circle

Labrador Sea

Newfoundland Basin

Grand Banks

St. Lawrence

Great Lakes

Mississippi

Gulf of Mexico

Tropic of Cancer

Caribbean Sea

New York

Sargasso Sea

Bermuda (UK)

Mid-Atlantic Ridge

The North Atlantic Deep Water Current is an oceanic "river" that moves around 20 million cubic yards (15.3 million cubic m) of water every second.

The Gulf Stream travels across the Atlantic Ocean at up to 135 miles (217 km) a day.

The width of the Atlantic Ocean is growing by about 1 inch (2.5 cm) a year. The sea-floor is spreading from the boundary of two tectonic plates along the mid-Atlantic Ridge.

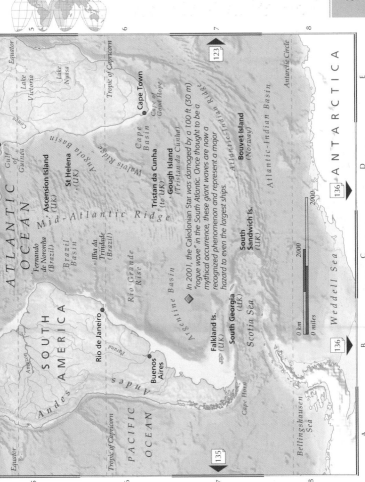

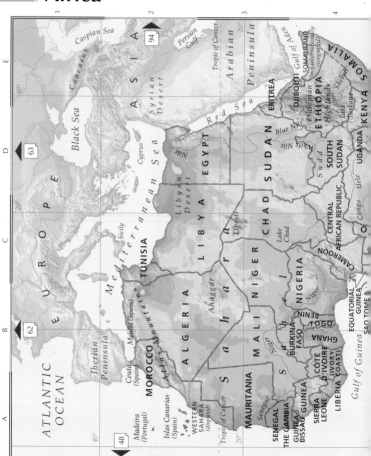

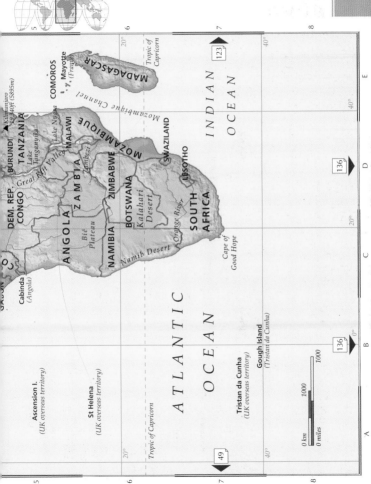

ATLANTIC OCEAN

INDIAN OCEAN

Ascension I.
(UK overseas territory)

St Helena
(UK overseas territory)

Tristan da Cunha
(UK overseas territory)

Gough Island
(Tristan da Cunha)

Tropic of Capricorn

Tropic of Capricorn

MADAGASCAR

Mayotte
(France)

COMOROS

Kilimanjaro
19,340ft (5895m)

BURUNDI

TANZANIA

DEM. REP.
CONGO

Lake
Tanganyika

Lake Nyasa

Great Rift Valley

MALAWI

MOZAMBIQUE

Mozambique Channel

ANGOLA

Cabinda
(Angola)

ZAMBIA

Zambezi

ZIMBABWE

Biê
Plateau

NAMIBIA

BOTSWANA

Kalahari
Desert

SWAZILAND

LESOTHO

Namib Desert

Orange River

SOUTH
AFRICA

Cape of
Good Hope

0 km   1000
0 miles   1000

123

136

136

49

Northwest Africa

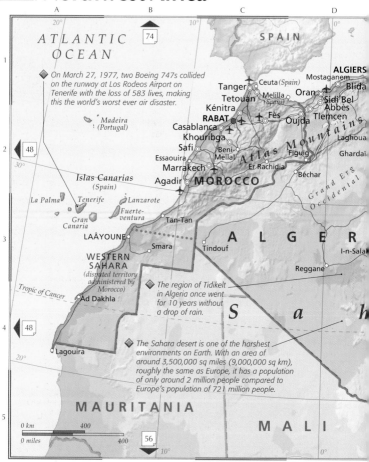

ATLANTIC
OCEAN

SPAIN

◆ On March 27, 1977, two Boeing 747s collided
on the runway at Los Rodeos Airport on
Tenerife with the loss of 583 lives, making
this this world's worst ever air disaster.

ALGIERS

Tanger   Ceuta (Spain)   Mostaganem   Blida
Tetouán   Melilla   Oran   Sidi Bel
        (Spain)   Abbès
Kénitra   Fès   Oujda   Tlemcen
RABAT
Casablanca   Laghoua
Khouribga   Figuig   Ghardaï
        Beni-
Safi   Mellal   Er Rachidia   Béchar
Essaouira
Marrakech   MOROCCO
Agadir

Madeira
(Portugal)

Islas Canarias
(Spain)

La Palma   Tenerife   Lanzarote
    Gran   Fuerte-
    Canaria   ventura

Tan-Tan

LAÂYOUNE   A L G E R

Smara   Tindouf   I-n-Sala

WESTERN
SAHARA
(disputed territory
administered by
Morocco)   Reggane

Tropic of Cancer

◆ The region of Tidikelt
in Algeria once went
for 10 years without
a drop of rain.

Ad Dakhla   S a h

◆ The Sahara desert is one of the harshest
environments on Earth. With an area of
around 3,500,000 sq miles (9,000,000 sq km),
roughly has the same as Europe, it has a population
of only around 2 million people compared to
Europe's population of 721 million people.

Lagouira

MAURITANIA

M A L I

0 km   400
0 miles   400

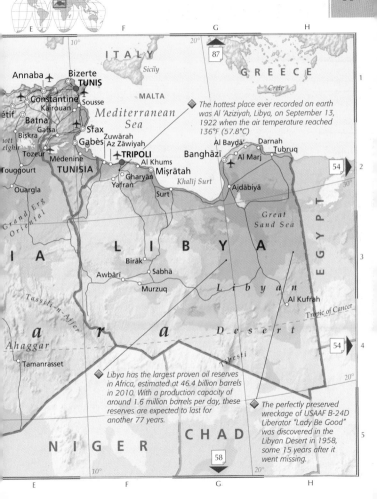

E   F   G   H

I T A L Y

Sicily

MALTA

Mediterranean Sea

Annaba

Bizerte
TUNIS

Constantine

Kairouan

Sousse

tif

Batna

Gafsa

Sfax

Biskra

Zuwārah

Az Zāwiyah

Touggourt

Gabès

TRIPOLI

Al Khums

Tozeur

Médenine

Gharyān

TUNISIA

Yafran

Surt

Ouargla

Misrātah

Khalīj Surt

Al Bayda'

Darnah

Tubruq

Banghāzī

Al Marj

Ajdābiyā

Great Sand Sea

I A

L I B Y A

E G Y P T

Birāk

Awbārī

Sabhā

Murzuq

Libyan

Al Kufrah

Tropic of Cancer

Tassili-n-Ajjer

a

r   *a*

Desert

Ahaggar

Tamanrasset

Tbesti

N I G E R

C H A D

Grand Erg Oriental

ott
elghir

The hottest place ever recorded on earth was Al 'Azīzīyah, Libya, on September 13, 1922 when the air temperature reached 136°F (57.8°C)

Libya has the largest proven oil reserves in Africa, estimated at 46.4 billion barrels in 2010. With a production capacity of around 1.6 million barrels per day, these reserves are expected to last for another 77 years.

The perfectly preserved wreckage of USAAF B-24D Liberator "Lady Be Good" was discovered in the Libyan Desert in 1958, some 15 years after it went missing.

GREECE

Crete

87

54

54

58

10°   20°   30°   20°

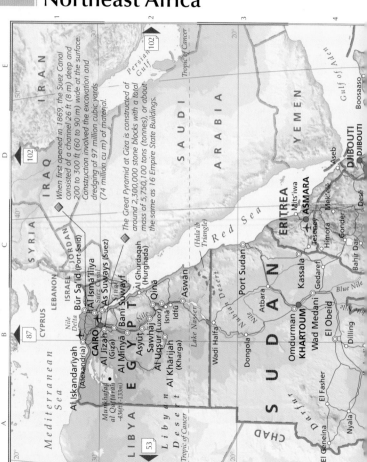

When first opened in 1869, the Suez Canal consisted of a channel 26 ft (8 m) deep and 200 to 300 ft (60 to 90 m) wide at the surface. Construction involved the excavation and dredging of 97 million cubic yards (74 million cu m) of material.

The Great Pyramid at Giza is constructed of around 2,300,000 stone blocks with a total mass of 5,750,100 tons (tonnes), or about the same as 16 Empire State Buildings.

Mediterranean Sea

IRAN

IRAQ

SYRIA

LEBANON

ISRAEL

JORDAN

CYPRUS

Persian Gulf

Gulf of Aden

SAUDI ARABIA

YEMEN

Boosaaso

DJIBOUTI
DJIBOUTI

Aseb

ERITREA

ASMARA

Mits'iwa

Mekele

Desē

Red Sea

Gonder

Himora

Bahir Dar

Jesenēy

Kassala

Gedaref

Port Sudan

Atbara

Dongola

Wadi Halfa

Lake Nasser

Nubian Desert

Blue Nile

Nile

White Nile

Omdurman
KHARTOUM

Wad Medani

El Obeid

Dilling

El Fasher

Nyala

El Geneina

Darfur

SUDAN

CHAD

Bür Sa'īd (Port Said)

Al Ismā'īlīya

As Suways (Suez)

Suez Canal

Sinai

Al Iskandarīyah
(Alexandria)

Nile Delta

CAIRO

Al Jīzah
(Giza)

Al Minyā

Asyūţ

Sawhāj

Banī Suwayf

Al Ghurdaqah
(Hurghada)

Qinā

Al Uqşur (Luxor)

Isnā

Idfū

Aswān

At Khārijah
(Kharga)

EGYPT

Munkhafad
al Qattārah
-436ft (-133m)

Libyan Desert

LIBYA

Tropic of Cancer

(Hala'ib
Triangle)

102

102

87

53

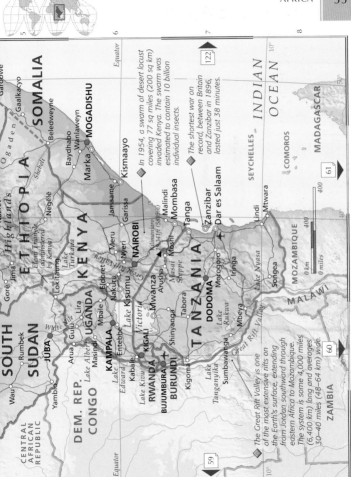

In 1954, a swarm of desert locust covering 77 sq miles (200 sq km) invaded Kenya. The swarm was estimated to contain 10 billion individual insects.

The shortest war on record, between Britain and Zanzibar in 1896, lasted just 38 minutes.

The Great Rift Valley is one of the most extensive rifts on the Earth's surface, extending from Jordan southward through eastern Africa to Mozambique. The system is some 4,000 miles (6,400 km) long and averages 30–40 miles (48–64 km) wide.

Map labels:
Garoowe
Gaalkacyo
SOMALIA
Beledweyne
Wanlaweyn
MOGADISHU
Baydhabo
Marka
Kismaayo
Ogaden
Shebeli
Nazrēt
Highlands
ETHIOPIA
Gorē
Jima
Negēlē
Elliot Triangle (administered by Kenya)
Lake Turkana
Jamaame
Garissa
Malindi
Mombasa
Meru
Nyeri
NAIROBI
Kilimanjaro 19,341ft (5895m)
Moshi
Arusha
Masai Steppe
Tanga
Zanzibar
Dar es Salaam
INDIAN OCEAN
SEYCHELLES
COMOROS
MADAGASCAR
MOZAMBIQUE
Mtwara
Lindi
Songea
Iringa
Morogoro
DODOMA
Mbeya
Lake Nyasa
MALAWI
Lake Rukwa
Tabora
Shinyanga
Lake Victoria
Mwanza
KENYA
TANZANIA
Eldoret
Nakuru
Lake Kisumu
Kampala
Entebbe
Mbale
Kabale
Lira
Gulu
Arua
Masindi
UGANDA
White Nile
Rumbek
Wau
Yambio
JUBA
SOUTH SUDAN
CENTRAL AFRICAN REPUBLIC
DEM. REP. CONGO
Lake Albert
Lake Edward
Lake Kivu
KIGALI
RWANDA
BUJUMBURA
BURUNDI
Kigoma
Lake Tanganyika
Sumbawanga
Great Rift Valley
ZAMBIA
Equator
Gallabat
Addis Ababa

0 km 400
0 miles 400

59
60
61
122

West Africa

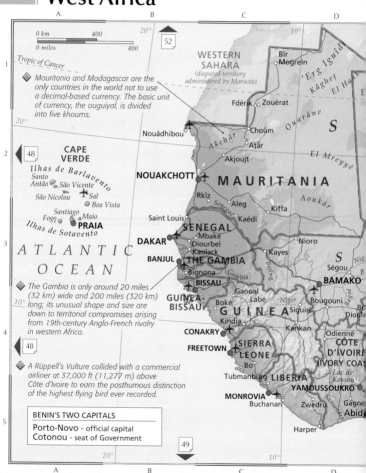

0 km 400
0 miles 400

Tropic of Cancer

20°

◆ Mauritania and Madagascar are the
only countries in the world not to use
a decimal-based currency. The basic unit
of currency, the ouguiyal, is divided
into five khoums.

20°

WESTERN
SAHARA
(disputed territory
administered by Morocco)

Bîr
Mogreïn

'Erg Iguîdi

Kâghet   El Hank

Fdérik   Zouérat

Ouarâne

Choûm

Nouâdhibou

Akchâr

Atâr

El Mreyyé

Akjoujt

CAPE
VERDE

48

Ilhas de Barlavento
Santo
Antão   São Vicente
São Nicolau   Sal
Boa Vista

Santiago
Fogo   Maio
PRAIA
Ilhas de Sotavento

ATLANTIC

OCEAN

NOUAKCHOTT

MAURITANIA

Aoukâr

Rkîz   Aleg   Kiffa

Saint Louis   Kaédi   Nioro

SENEGAL   Mbaké
DAKAR   Diourbel
Kaolack   Kayes
BANJUL
THE GAMBIA
BISSAU
Bignona

Ségou

BAMAKO

◆ The Gambia is only around 20 miles
(32 km) wide and 200 miles (320 km)
long; its unusual shape and size are
down to territorial compromises arising
from 19th-century Anglo-French rivalry
in western Africa.

10°

GUINEA-
BISSAU

Gaoual   Niger
Boké   Labé   Bougouni
GUINEA   Siguiri   Dioula
Kindia   Kankan

48

CONAKRY

FREETOWN

SIERRA
LEONE

Bo

Odienné
CÔTE
D'IVOIRE
(IVORY COA

◆ A Rüppell's Vulture collided with a commercial
airliner at 37,000 ft (11,277 m) above
Côte d'Ivoire to earn the posthumous distinction
of the highest flying bird ever recorded.

Tubmanburg   LIBERIA

MONROVIA

Lac de
Kossou

YAMOUSSOUKRO

Gagn

Abid

Buchanan

Zwedru

BENIN'S TWO CAPITALS

Porto-Novo - official capital
Cotonou - seat of Government

Harper

49

20°   10°

Nouâdhibou

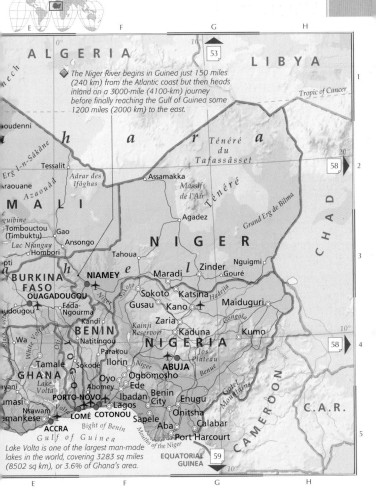

E · 0° · F · 10° G · H

ALGERIA   LIBYA

◆ The Niger River begins in Guinea just 150 miles
(240 km) from the Atlantic coast but then heads
inland on a 3000-mile (4100-km) journey
before finally reaching the Gulf of Guinea some
1200 miles (2000 km) to the east.

Tropic of Cancer

oudenni

S   a   h   a   r   a   Ténéré
du
Tafassâsset

Tessalit

araouane   Adrar des   Assamakka
Ifóghas   Massif
Azaouâd   de l'Aïr   Ténéré
MALI   Gao   Agadez   Grand Erg de Bilma
guibine   Ansongo
Tombouctou
(Timbuktu)   NIGER   CHAD
Lac Niangay   Tahoua
Hombori

pti
a   h   e   Maradi   l   Zinder   Nguigmi
BURKINA   NIAMEY   Gouré
FASO   Sokoto
OUAGADOUGOU   Sokoto Katsina
Fada-   Gusau   Kano   Maiduguri
udougou   Ngourma   Zaria   Hadejia
Kandi   Kaduna   Kumo
BENIN   Gongola
Wa   Natitingou   Kainji
Parakou   Reservoir   NIGERIA
Jos
GHANA Tamale   Sokode   Ilorin   Niger ABUJA Plateau
Lake   Benue
Volta   Oyo   Ogbomosho
Abomey Ede
masi   Nsawam PORTO-NOVO   Ibadan Benin
amankese ACCRA LOMÉ COTONOU Lagos City Enugu
Sapele   Onitsha   Cameroun
Bight of Benin Aba Calabar   Mountains
Gulf of Guinea   Port Harcourt   C.A.R.
Mouths
of the Niger
CAMEROON

Lake Volta is one of the largest man-made
lakes in the world, covering 3283 sq miles
(8502 sq km), or 3.6% of Ghana's area.

EQUATORIAL
GUINEA   59

E · F · 10° G · H

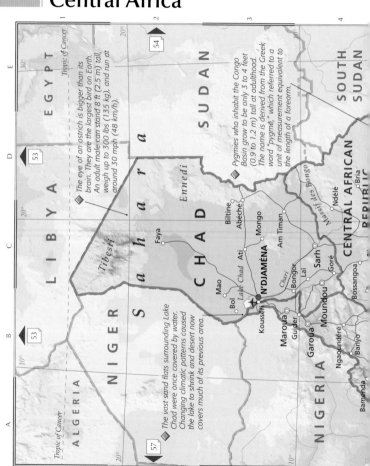

The eye of an ostrich is bigger than its brain. They are the largest bird on Earth. An adult male can stand 8 ft (2.5 m) tall, weigh up to 300 lbs (135 kg), and run at around 30 mph (48 km/h).

Pygmies who inhabit the Congo Basin grow to be only 3 to 4 feet (0.9 to 1.2 m) tall at adulthood. The name is derived from the Greek word "pygmé," which referred to a unit of measurement equivalent to the length of a forearm.

The vast sand flats surrounding Lake Chad were once covered by water. Changing climatic patterns caused the lake to shrink and desert now covers much of its previous area.

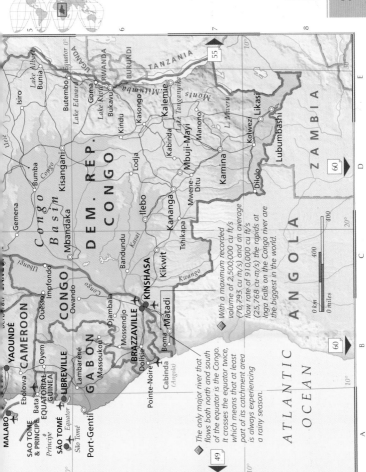

TANZANIA

55

Lake Albert
Bunia
Isiro
Butembo
Lake Edward
Goma
Lake Kivu
Bukavu
RWANDA
BURUNDI
UGANDA
Equator

Lake Tanganyika
Monts Mitumba
Kalemie
L. Mweru
Likasi
Kolwezi
Lubumbashi
Kindu
Kasongo
Manono
Kamina
Dilolo
ZAMBIA

Gemena
Bumba
Kisangani
Lodja
Mbuji-Mayi
Mwene-Ditu
Kabinda

C o n g o
B a s i n
Mbandaka
Ilebo
Kananga
Tshikapa
Kasai
Kwango
Kwilu

D E M . R E P . C O N G O

Ubangi
Uele
Uele
Congo
Impfondo
Ouésso
Owando
Djambala
Bandundu
Kikwit

C O N G O
CAMEROON
YAOUNDÉ
Ebolowa
Oyem
Bata
EQUATORIAL
GUINEA
MALABO
SÃO TOMÉ
& PRÍNCIPE
SÃO TOMÉ
Príncipe
São Tomé
LIBREVILLE
Lambaréné
Massoukou
Mossendjo
Dolisie
Pointe-Noire
Cabinda
(Angola)
BRAZZAVILLE
KINSHASA
Matadi
Boma
Port-Gentil
G A B O N
Equator

A N G O L A

A T L A N T I C

O C E A N

With a maximum recorded
volume of 2,500,000 cu tr/s
(70,793 cu m/s) and an average
flow rate of 910,000 cu tr/s
(25,768 cu m/s) the rapids at
Inga Falls on the Congo river are
the biggest in the world.

The only major river that
flows both north and south
of the equator is the Congo.
It crosses the equator twice,
which means that at least
part of its catchment area
is always experiencing
a rainy season.

60

60

49

0 km   400
0 miles   400

0°   10°   20°   30°

5   6   7   8

Southern Africa

0 km 400
0 miles 400

ATLANTIC
OCEAN

◆ The Okavango River pours
some 14.4 billion cubic yards
(11 billion cu m) of water into
the Okavango Delta each year.
It drains away through a maze of
lagoons, channels, and islands
covering around 5800 sq miles
(15,000 sq km), before eventually
disappearing into the sands of the
Kalahari Desert to the south.

◆ The Kalahari Desert is the largest
continuous sand surface in the world.
Iron oxide gives a distinctive red
color to the sand, which is over
200 ft (60 m) deep in places.

Tropic of Capricorn

SOUTH AFRICA'S THREE CAPITALS

Pretoria - administrative capital
Cape Town - legislative capital
Bloemfontein - judicial capital

DEM. REP.
CONGO

Tangan

Cabinda
(Angola) Cabinda

Ambriz
Uige
N'Dalatando
LUANDA
Lucapa
Saurimo

Malanje

Sumbe
Lobito
Benguela
Cuanza
ANGOLA
Kuito
Huambo
Zambezi
Menongue
Ndola
Mufulira
Chingola
Kitwe
Luanshya
ZAMBIA

Lubango
Namibe
Tombua
N'Giva
Cubango
Cunene
Rundu
Okavango
Choma
Livingstone
Victoria
Falls
LUSAKA
Lak
Kari

Etosha
Pan
Tsumeb
Grootfontein
Okavango Delta
Maun
NAMIBIA
Ghanzi
Bulawayo
Francistown
ZIM

WINDHOEK
Kalahari
Mahalapye
BOTSWANA

Swakopmund
Walvis Bay
Rehoboth
Desert
GABORONE
Lobatse
PRETORI
Limpopo

Keetmanshoop
Mmabatho
Soweto
Johannesburg

Lüderitz
Karasburg
Kroonstad
MASER

Kimberley

Orange
BLOEMFONTEIN
LESOTHO

**SOUTH
AFRICA**
Middelburg

Beaufort West

Bellville
CAPE TOWN
Cape of Good Hope
George
Port
Elizabeth
East
London

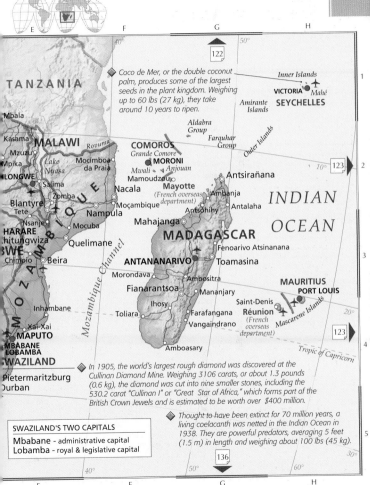

In 1905, the world's largest rough diamond was discovered at the Cullinan Diamond Mine. Weighing 3106 carats, or about 1.3 pounds (0.6 kg), the diamond was cut into nine smaller stones, including the 530.2 carat "Cullinan I" or "Great Star of Africa," which forms part of the British Crown Jewels and is estimated to be worth over $400 million.

Thought to have been extinct for 70 million years, a living coelacanth was netted in the Indian Ocean in 1938. They are powerful predators, averaging 5 feet (1.5 m) in length and weighing about 100 lbs (45 kg).

Coco de Mer, or the double coconut palm, produces some of the largest seeds in the plant kingdom. Weighing up to 60 lbs (27 kg), they take around 10 years to ripen.

SWAZILAND'S TWO CAPITALS

Mbabane - administrative capital
Lobamba - royal & legislative capital

Europe

A   B   C   D

137

Arctic Circle

40°   20°   0°

Limit of winter pack ice

ICELAND

Lofo

*Norwegian
Sea*

40°

Faroe Islands
(Denmark)

48

*Outer
Hebrides*

*British
Isles*

Vaner

Ireland
IRELAND

Britain

**UNITED
KINGDOM**

*North
Sea*

DENMARK

40°

*Celtic
Sea*

A T L A N T I C

NETHERLANDS

Elbe

Nor

English Channel

BELGIUM

LUX.

GERMANY

**CZEC
REPUB
(CZEC**

O C E A N

Seine

Loire

Rhine

Bay of Biscay

FRANCE

*Massif
Central*

SWITZ.

LIECH

AUSTRI

Garonne

Rhône

Po

▲ Mont Blanc
15,771 ft (4807 m)

SLOVENI

48

PORTUGAL

Pyrenees

MONACO

Iberian

SPAIN

ANDORRA

**SAN
MARINO**

CROAT

**BOS
& HE**

Duero

Tagus

Ebro

Peninsula

Corsica

I T A L Y

*Madeira
(to Portugal)*

Strait of Gibraltar

**VATICAN
CITY**

Sardinia

*Tyrrhenian
Sea*

Gibraltar
(UK)

Balearic Islands

M e d i t e r r a n e a n

20°

*Canary Islands
(to Spain)*

Atlas   Mountains

Sicily

AFRICA

MALTA

50

0°

A   B   C   D

0 km   800
0 miles   800

E   F   G   H

Barents Sea

North Cape
Ostrov Kolguyev

Kola
Peninsula
*White
Sea*

FINLAND

Gulf of Bothnia

Northern Dvina

Lake Onega

Åland

Lake
Ladoga

ESTONIA

LATVIA

LITHUANIA

KALININGRAD
(part of Russia)

Baltic Sea

Ural Mountains

R U S S I A

POLAND

BELARUS

Eu ro pean Plain

*Central
Russian
Upland*

Volga Uplands

Volga

Ural

Aral Sea

Vistula

Bug

*Pripet
Marshes*

Dnieper Lowlands

Dnieper

Don

Carpathian Mts.

Dniester

UKRAINE

SLOVAKIA

MOLDOVA

HUNGARY

ROMANIA

*Sea of
Azov*

Crimea

(Since 2014 the Ukrainian
territory of Crimea has been
annexed by Russia)

Caspian Sea

SERBIA

Danube

BULGARIA

KOSOVO

Balkan Mts.

MACED.

TURKEY

ALBANIA

*Aegean
Sea*

GREECE

Peloponnese

*Ionian
Sea*

Crete

Black Sea

Caucasus

El'brus
18,510ft
(5642m)

Anatolia

A S I A

Cyprus

20°   40°   60°   80°   60°

80°

40°

60°

20°   40°

The North Atlantic

At 836,100 sq miles (2,166,600 sq km), Greenland is the largest island in the world. However, 677,700 sq miles (1,756,000 sq km) of this is a massive ice sheet so heavy that the central land area has sunk to form to a basin more than 1000 ft (300 m) below sea level.

The Jakobshavn Glacier is among the world's fastest glaciers, often moving 100 feet (30 m) a day, and calves around 20 billion tons (tonnes) of icebergs every year.

Devon Island

Ellesmere Island

Nares Strait

NUNAVUT

Arctic Circle

Qaanaaq

Innaanganeq

Knud Rasmussen Land

Savissivik

Hudson Bay

Qimusseriarsuaq

Baffin Bay

Kullorsuaq

CANADA

Baffin Island

Limit of summer pack ice

Davis Strait

Qeqertarsuaq

Qeqertarsuaq

Qasigiannguit

QUÉBEC

Hudson Strait

Cumberland Sound

Frobisher Bay

Sisimiut

Kong Frederik IX Land

Ungava Bay

Greenland

(Danish self-governing territory)

Maniitsoq

NUUK

Kong Christian IX Land

Gunnbjørn Field
12,139 ft (3700m)

Paamiut

Kong Frederik VI Kyst

Ammassalik

Ivittuut

Denmark

Qaqortoq

Limit of winter pack ice

Nanortalik

Faxa

Labrador Sea

Nunap Isua
(Kap Farvel)

ATLANTIC OCEAN

NEWFOUNDLAND & LABRADOR

0 km   800
0 miles   800

90° 80° 70° 60° 50° 40° 30°

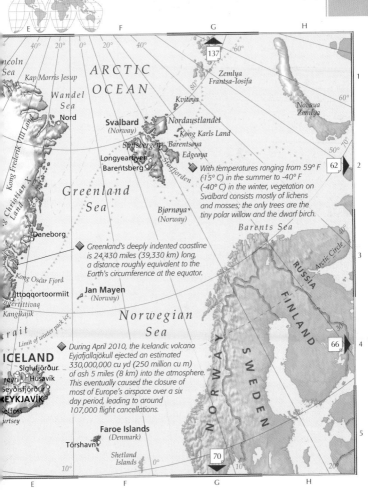

ARCTIC OCEAN

137

Zemlya
Frantsa-Iosifa

Kap Morris Jesup

Wandel
Sea

Nord

Kvitøya

Novaya
Zemlya

ncoln
Sea

Svalbard
(Norway)

Nordaustlandet

Kong Karls Land

Spitsbergen

Barentsøya
Edgeøya

62

Longyearbyen

Barentsberg

With temperatures ranging from 59° F
(15° C) in the summer to -40° F
(-40° C) in the winter, vegetation on
Svalbard consists mostly of lichens
and mosses; the only trees are the
tiny polar willow and the dwarf birch.

Kong Frederik VIII Land

Greenland
Sea

Bjørnøya
(Norway)

Barents Sea

8 Christian
IX Land

Daneborg

Greenland's deeply indented coastline
is 24,430 miles (39,330 km) long,
a distance roughly equivalent to the
Earth's circumference at the equator.

Arctic Circle

RUSSIA

FINLAND

Kong Oscar Fjord

Jan Mayen
(Norway)

66

ttoqqortoormiit

ivertittivaq

Kangikajik

Norwegian
Sea

rait

Limit of winter pack ice

During April 2010, the Icelandic volcano
Eyjafjallajökull ejected an estimated
330,000,000 cu yd (250 million cu m)
of ash 5 miles (8 km) into the atmosphere.
This eventually caused the closure of
most of Europe's airspace over a six
day period, leading to around
107,000 flight cancellations.

ICELAND

Siglufjörður

reyri • Húsavík

eyðisfjörður

REYKJAVÍK

elfoss

urtsey

NORWAY

SWEDEN

Faroe Islands
(Denmark)

Tórshavn

Shetland
Islands

70

E F G H

Scandinavia & Finland

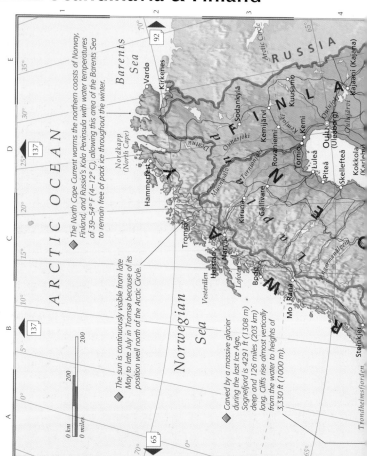

The North Cape Current warms the northern coasts of Norway, Finland, and Russia's Kola Peninsula with water temperatures of 39–54° F (4–12° C), allowing this area of the Barents Sea to remain free of pack ice throughout the winter.

The sun is continuously visible from late May to late July in Tromsø because of its position well north of the Arctic Circle.

Carved by a massive glacier during the last Ice Age, Sognefjord is 4291 ft (1308 m) deep and 126 miles (203 km) long. Cliffs rise almost vertically from the water to heights of 3,330 ft (1000 m).

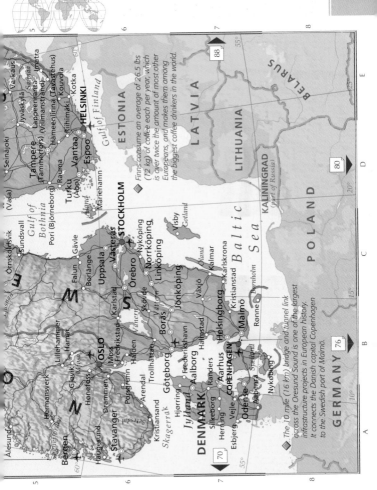

Finns consume an average of 26.5 lbs (12 kg) of coffee each per year, which is over twice the amount of most other Europeans, and makes them among the biggest coffee drinkers in the world.

The 10 mile (16 km) bridge and tunnel link across the Øresund Sound is one of the largest infrastructure projects in European history. It connects the Danish capital Copenhagen to the Swedish port of Malmö.

ESTONIA

LATVIA

LITHUANIA

BELARUS

KALININGRAD (part of Russia)

POLAND

GERMANY

DENMARK

Gulf of Finland

Baltic Sea

Gulf of Bothnia

Skagerrak

Jylland

Åland

Öland

Gotland

Bornholm

HELSINKI
Vantaa
Espoo
Turku (Åbo)
Tampere (Tammerfors)
Rauma
Pori (Björneborg)
Mariehamn
Hämeenlinna (Tavastehus)
Lahti
Riihimäki
Kotka
Kouvola
Lappeenranta (Villmanstrand)
Imatra
Kuopio
Jyväskylä
Seinäjoki
Vaasa (Vasa)
Varkaus

STOCKHOLM
Västerås
Uppsala
Örebro
Norrköping
Nyköping
Linköping
Jönköping
Växjö
Kalmar
Kristianstad
Karlskrona
Visby
Falun
Borlänge
Karlstad
Skövde
Borås
Vänern
Vättern
Halmstad
Helsingborg
Malmö
Ronne

Gävle
Sundsvall
Örnsköldsvik

OSLO
Lillehammer
Hamar
Gjøvik
Moss
Fredrikstad
Halden
Honefoss
Drammen
Porsgrunn
Arendal
Kristiansand
Stavanger
Haugesund
Bergen
Ålesund
Hermansverk
Trollhättan
Göteborg
Frederikshavn
Hjørring
Ålborg
Randers
Århus
Silkeborg
Herning
Vejle
Esbjerg
Odense
Åbenrå
Nyköbing
COPENHAGEN
Sjælland

Sundet

88
80
76
70

The Low Countries

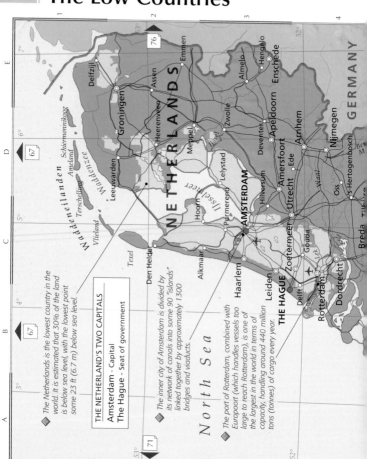

THE NETHERLAND'S TWO CAPITALS

Amsterdam - Capital
The Hague - Seat of government

The Netherlands is the lowest country in the world. It is estimated that 30% of the land is below sea level, with the lowest point some 23 ft (6.7 m) below sea level.

The inner city of Amsterdam is divided by its network of canals into some 90 "islands" linked together by approximately 1300 bridges and viaducts.

The port of Rotterdam, combined with Europoort (which handles vessels too large to reach Rotterdam), is one of the largest in the world in terms of capacity, handling around 440 million tons (tonnes) of cargo every year.

NETHERLANDS

GERMANY

North Sea

Waddeneilanden

Schiermonnikoog
Ameland
Terschelling
Vlieland
Waddenzee

Texel

Den Helder

Alkmaar
Hoorn
Purmerend
Haarlem
AMSTERDAM
Hilversum
Leiden
Delft
THE HAGUE
Zoetermeer
Gouda
Rotterdam
Dordrecht

Leeuwarden
Groningen
Delfzijl
Assen
Emmen
Heerenveen
Meppel
Zwolle
Deventer
Apeldoorn
Almelo
Hengelo
Enschede
Arnhem
Nijmegen
's-Hertogenbosch
Ede
Amersfoort
Utrecht
Oss
Breda
Lek
Lelystad
IJsselmeer
IJssel
Waal

76
67
67
71

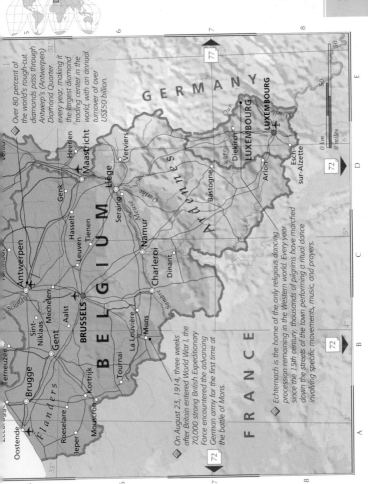

Over 80 percent of the world's rough-cut diamonds pass through Antwerp's (Antwerpen) Diamond Quarter every year, making it the largest diamond trading center in the world, with an annual turnover of over US$50 billion.

Echternach is the home of the only religious dancing procession remaining in the Western world. Every year since the 15th century, thousands of pilgrims have marched down the streets of the town performing a ritual dance involving specific movements, music, and prayers.

On August 23, 1914, three weeks after Britain entered World War I, the 70,000 strong British Expeditionary Force encountered the advancing German army for the first time at the battle of Mons.

GERMANY

BELGIUM

LUXEMBOURG

FRANCE

The British Isles

ATLANTIC

OCEAN

Midges have the fastest wing-beat of any insect, and are able to flap their wings at around 60,000 beats per minute.

The Giant's Causeway comprises approximately 37,000 interlocking dark basalt polygonal columns; they were formed by volcanic activity around 55 million years ago.

After the surrender of the German fleet in 1918 and its internment in Scapa Flow, over 50 ships were scuttled by the German crews on June 21, 1919, to prevent them falling into British hands.

With a depth of 788 ft (240 m) and a length of about 23 miles (36 km), Loch Ness contains the largest volume of fresh water in Great Britain.

North Sea

Faroe Islands

Shetland Islands

Lerwick

Orkney Islands

Kirkwall

Thurso

Ullapool

Moray Firth

Elgin

Inverness

Loch Ness

SCOTLAND

Grampian Mts.

Aberdeen

Dundee

Perth

Firth of Tay

Stirling

Firth of Forth

EDINBURGH

Isle of Lewis

Stornoway

The Minch

The Little Minch

Outer Hebrides

North Uist

South Uist

Barra

Skye

Isle of Skye

Mull

Oban

Iona

Loch Lomond

Greenock

Glasgow

Fort William

Islay

Firth of Clyde

Ayr

Southern Uplands

UNITED KINGDOM

ATLANTIC

OCEAN

FRANCE

IRELAND

ENGLAND

WALES

LONDON

DUBLIN

CARDIFF

Sligo
Galway
Ennis
Limerick
Tralee
Killarney
Cork
Waterford
Wexford
Wicklow
Athlone
Dundalk
Newry
Douglas
Bantry Bay

Lough Corrib
Lough Mask
Lough Ree
Lough Derg
Shannon
Barrow
Blackwater
Wicklow Mts.

Isles of Scilly
Land's End
Penzance
Plymouth
Exeter
Barnstaple
Taunton
Bournemouth
Salisbury
Bath
Bristol
Newport
Swansea
Gloucester
Worcester
Stratford-upon-Avon
Birmingham
Brecon Beacons
Aberystwyth
Cardigan Bay
Fishguard
Milford Haven
Bangor
Anglesey
Holyhead
Shrewsbury
Chester
Stoke-on-Trent
Derby
Leicester
Coventry
Oxford
Reading
Southampton
Portsmouth
Isle of Wight
Brighton
Canterbury
Dover
Southend-on-Sea
Ipswich
Colchester
Cambridge
Peterborough
Norwich
Grimsby
Lincoln
Nottingham
Sheffield
Manchester
Bradford
Leeds
York
Kingston upon Hull
Bolton
Blackpool
Preston
Lancaster
Liverpool
Darwen

The Wash
The Fens
Severn
Dartmoor
Exmoor

English Channel

Irish Sea

Channel Islands
St. Peter Port
Guernsey
(British Crown Dependency)
St. Helier
Jersey
(British Crown Dependency)

Channel Tunnel

◆ Every year over 1.5 billion pints (850 million liters) of Guinness® Irish stout are consumed in over 120 countries around the world.

◆ The River Severn has the second highest tidal range in the world, as much as 50 ft (15 m), often giving rise to a tidal bore. In September 1996, one such wave carried a surfer for 5.7 miles (9 km).

◆ With evidence of teaching beginning as early as 1096, Oxford University is the second oldest university in the world.

0 km   100
0 miles   100

68
72
74
48

France, Andorra & Monaco

Work began on the 31-mile (50-km) Channel Tunnel in 1987. Earth was removed at the rate of 2400 tons (tonnes) a day until completion, seven years later. Around 10.5 million cu yards (8 million cu m) had been excavated.

Champagne bottles are placed neck down into a freezing brine bath (bac à glace), freezing only the bottle's neck to form a plug that keeps the wine—and the bubbles—in the bottle while sediments are removed.

On July 1, 1916, the British suffered 58,000 casualties on the opening day of the Somme Offensive. Five months later, after advancing only a few miles, there had been 420,000 British, 200,000 French and 500,000 German casualties.

North Sea

UNITED KINGDOM

NETHERLANDS

GERMANY

BELGIUM

LUXEMBOURG

FRANCE

Channel Tunnel

Dunkerque
Calais
Boulogne-sur-Mer
Lille
Douai
Arras
Amiens
Somme
Laon
Reims
Châlons-en-Champagne
Marne
Thionville
Metz
Nancy
Strasbourg
Colmar
Mulhouse
Belfort
Vesoul
Épinal
Bar-le-Duc
Troyes
Auxerre
Dijon
PARIS
Beauvais
Rouen
Dieppe
Seine
Mantes-la-Jolie
Versailles
Chartres
Orléans
Bourges
Blois
Tours
Le Mans
Loire
Angers
Laval
Rennes
St-Brieuc
Quimper
Lorient
Vannes
St-Nazaire
Nantes
La Roche-sur-Yon
Brest
Cherbourg
Le Havre
Caen
St-Lô
St-Malo
Alençon

Normandie

Bretagne

English Channel

Channel Islands
Guernsey
(British Crown Dependencies) Jersey
Île d'Ouessant
Belle Île

Bay of Biscay

Moselle
Meuse
Vosges
Bourgogne

76
65
71
71
71

ITALY

Mont Blanc
15,771 ft (4807m)

Geneva

Villeurbanne
Annecy
Lyon
Roanne
St-Étienne Chambéry
St-Chamond Grenoble
Vichy

Limoges
Clermont
Ferrand
Périgueux
Aurillac
Le Puy
Valence

MONACO
Nice
Côte d'Azur
Cannes
Îles
d'Hyères
Toulon
Aix-en-
Provence
Avignon Provence
Arles
Marseille

Ligurian
Sea

Bastia
78

Corse
(Corsica)
Ajaccio

Sardinia

Massif
Central
Cévennes
Mende
Nîmes
Béziers
Montpellier
Narbonne
Perpignan

Rodez
Albi
Tarn
Montauban
Toulouse
Carcassonne

Rhône

Golfe
du Lion

One of history's great leaders,
Napoleon Bonaparte, was born
on August 15, 1769, at Ajaccio
in Corsica.

84

The word denim comes from "de Nîmes,"
this being the town where the fabric was
originally produced.

Mediterranean Sea

Angoulême

Bordeaux
Périgueux
Dordogne
Cahors
Lot
Agen
Garonne
Auch
Mont-de-Marsan
Tarbes
Bayonne
Pau

P y r é n é e s

ANDORRA
ANDORRA
LA VELLA

The lowest point in Andorra is Riu Runer,
at 2756 ft (840m) above sea level.

Balearic
Islands

84

S P A I N

The Tour de France
bicycle race is typically held over
some 21 day-long stages covering
around 2200 miles (3500 km) for
the coveted yellow jersey.

Chateau Lafite was
sold at auction for
US$233,972 (or
US$46,000 per
glass) making it
the most expensive
standard bottle
of wine ever sold.

75

0 km   100

0 miles   100

Spain & Portugal

71

48

ATLANTIC

OCEAN

40°

◈ Port has been produced in the Duoro
Valley under strict regulation since
the 1750s. Brandy is added to the
grape juice to fortify and
strengthen the wine.

◈ Portugal produces around half of the
world's cork and has regulations for
protecting cork trees dating back to
1320. Despite a recent decline, around
12 billion bottles of wine are sealed
with cork stoppers every year.

48

◈ Gibraltar was seized by a combined Anglo-Dutch fleet
under Admiral Rooke in 1704. British sovereignty was
then formalized in 1713 by the Treaty of Utrecht, and
Gibraltar eventually became a British colony in 1830.

35°

52

Ferrol
A Coruña
Avilés
Gijón/Xixón
Oviedo
Galicia
Lugo
Santiago de Compostela
Cordillera Cantábrica
León
Pontevedra
Vigo
Ourense
Miño
Emb. de Ricobayo
Palen
Viana do Castelo
Chaves
Braga
Bragança
Valladolid
Póvoa de Varzim
Guimarães
Zamora
Matosinhos
Vila Real
Duero
Porto
Vila Nova de Gaia
Douro
S
Aveiro
Viseu
Salamanca
Coimbra
Covilhã
Sistema Centra
Figueira da Foz
PORTUGAL
Plasencia
Castelo Branco
Tagus
Caldas da Rainha
Cáceres
Tagus
Sintra
Santarém
Portalegre
Cascais
Mérida
LISBON
Badajoz
Setúbal
Alcácer do Sal
Beja
Sierra Morena
Sines
Córdoba
Algarve
Guadiana
Sevilla
Lagos
Huelva
Andalucía
Cabo de São Vicente
Faro
Olhão
Antequer
Málag
El Puerto de Santa María
Cádiz
Marb
Algeciras
Gibralt
(UK)
Ceuta
(Spain)

MOROCCO

0 km   100
0 miles   100

10°

5°

Work continues on the Sagrada Família, Gaudí's unfinished cathedral. Begun in 1882, construction passed the mid-point in 2010 and is now due to be completed in around 2025.

Seat of many great civilizations throughout history, the name Mediterranean translates as "sea between the lands."

Spain produces just under half of the world's olive oil, which amounted to around 1.2 million tons (tonnes) in 2009. Of this, roughly 30 percent is the highest quality "extra-virgin" olive oil.

Germany & The Alpine States

The Kiel Canal is 61 miles (98 km) long and one of the busiest canals in the world, with around 45,000 ships a year passing between the Baltic and the North Sea.

Early in the morning of Sunday, August 13, 1961, work began on the Berlin Wall, which would eventually run for 66 miles (107 km) between east and west Berlin, cutting through 192 streets.

During what became known as "The Berlin Airlift" a total of 2,326,406 tons (tonnes) of supplies were flown into Berlin over an 18-month period to break a Soviet blockade of the city.

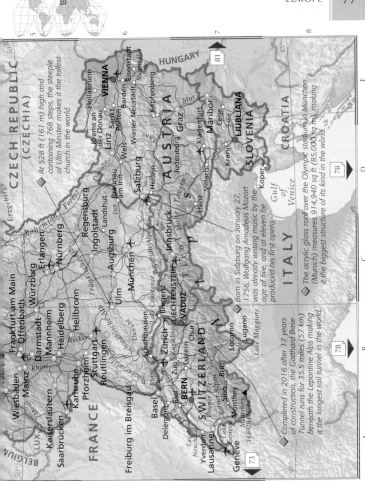

CZECH REPUBLIC
(CZECHIA)

HUNGARY

81

VIENNA

Hollabrunn
Krems an
der Donau
Sankt
Pölten
Baden
Eisenstadt
Wiener Neustadt
Mur
Graz
Kapfenberg
Maribor
LJUBLJANA
SLOVENIA
CROATIA
Kranj
Celje
Klagenfurt
Koper
Gulf
of
Venice

Erzgebirge

Bohemian Forest

Regensburg
Landshut
Ingolstadt
Nürnberg
Erlangen
Würzburg
Offenbach
Frankfurt am Main
Darmstadt
Mainz
Wiesbaden

Franconian Alps

Augsburg
München
Ulm

Donau
Braunau
am Inn
Inn
Linz
Wels
AUSTRIA
Salzburg
Hallein
Judenburg

Danube

Innsbruck
LIECHTENSTEIN
VADUZ
TIROL
Hohe Tauern
Lienz
Villach

ITALY

At 528 ft (161 m) high and
containing 768 steps, the steeple
of Ulm Minster makes it the tallest
church in the world.

Born in Salzburg on January 27,
1756, Wolfgang Amadeus Mozart
was already writing music by the
age of five, and at eleven he
produced his first opera.

The acrylic glass roof over the
Olympic stadium in München
(Munich) measures 914,940 sq ft
(85,000 sq m), making it the
biggest structure of its kind in the
world.

FRANCE

Kaiserslautern
Saarbrücken

Rhine

Mannheim
Heidelberg
Heilbronn
Karlsruhe
Pforzheim
Stuttgart
Reutlingen

Neckar

Black Forest

Freiburg im Breisgau

Schaffhausen
Bregenz

Lake Constance

Zürich
Zug
Chur

SWITZERLAND

Delémont
Basel
Biel
BERN
Sion
Brig
Monthey

Lake Neuchâtel

Yverdon
Lausanne
Genève

Lake Geneva

Matterhorn
14,692 ft (4,478 m)

Lake Maggiore

Locarno
Lugano

Completed in 2016 after 17 years
of construction, the Gotthard Base
Tunnel runs for 35.5 miles (57 km)
beneath the Lepontine Alps making
it the longest rail tunnel in the world.

78

78

73

BELGIUM
LUX.

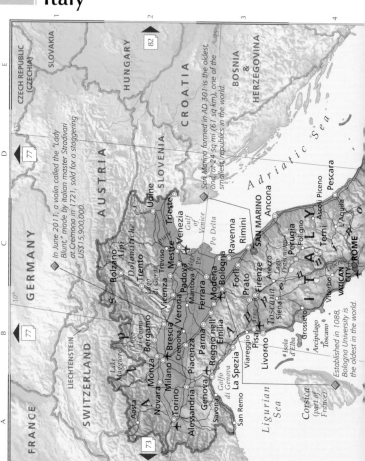

In June 2011, a violin called the "Lady Blunt," made by Italian master Stradivari at Cremona in 1721, sold for a staggering US$15,900,000.

San Marino formed in AD 301 is the oldest, and, at 24 sq mi (61 sq km), one of the smallest, republics in the world.

Established in 1088, Bologna University is the oldest in the world.

Strait of Otranto

Bari
Altamura
Taranto
Brindisi
Lecce
Gallipoli

Golfo di Taranto

Crotone

Catanzaro

Ionian Sea

Mt. Etna began some 300,000 years ago as a submarine volcano and has since grown to a cone with a base 30 miles (48 km) wide and 10,922 ft (3329 m) high.

Salerno

Potenza

Cosenza

Reggio di Calabria

Stretto di Messina

Isola Stromboli

Isola Vulcano

Isola Lipari

Messina

Isole Eolie

Napoli
Torre del Greco

Golfo di Salerno

Golfo di Gaeta

Isola di Capri

VALLETTA
MALTA

Isola d'Ustica

Cefalù

Palermo

Catania

Siracusa

Sicilia (Sicily)

Ragusa

Caltanissetta

Malta Channel

Gozo

The George cross that appears on the Maltese flag was awarded to the islanders by King George VI of Britain for their heroism during World War II.

Tyrrhenian Sea

Trapani

Isole Egadi

Marsala

Agrigento

Isola di Pantelleria

Isole Pelagie

Mediterranean Sea

Sardegna (Sardinia)

Nuoro

Oristano

Cagliari

Alghero

Iglesias

The medical school at Salerno is the oldest in Europe, established during the 11th and 12th centuries.

Strait of Sicily

TUNISIA

0 km   100
0 miles 100

Built between 1747 and 1795, the Zaluski Library in Warsaw was one of the world's first public libraries.

Founded in Gdansk shipyard in 1980, the Solidarity trade union, and its leader Lech Walesa, played a key role in the downfall of communism across much of eastern Europe.

In November 1989, the so-called "Velvet Revolution" saw Czechoslovakia split into the Czech Republic (Czechia) and Slovakia.

LATVIA

LITHUANIA

BELARUS

KALININGRAD
(part of Russia)

Courland
Lagoon

Baltic Sea

SWEDEN

DENMARK

Bornholm
(part of Denmark)

Pomeranian
Bay

Zalew
Szczecinski

GERMANY

Odra

Gulf of
Gdańsk

Elbląg

Gdynia
Gdańsk

Słupsk

Koszalin

Czluchow

Szczecin

Gozow
Wielkopolski

Zielona
Góra

Pila

Noteć

Bydgoszcz

Toruń

Grudziądz

Wisła

Włocławek

Poznań

Warta

Kalisz

Legnica

Wrocław

Oder

Olsztyn

Ostrołęka

Płock

Łódź

Warta

M a z u r y

Białystok

Narew

Bug

WARSAW

Radom

Wisła

Kielce

Lublin

Ostrowiec
Świętokrzyski

P O L A N D

0 km   100
0 miles   100

UKRAINE

Rzeszów • Tarnów • Kraków

CZECH REPUBLIC (CZECHIA)

Karlovy Vary • Kladno • PRAGUE
Pilzeň
Stratonice • Tábor • Jihlava
Prostějov
České Budějovice • Brno

Ostrava
Wodzisław Śląski • Rybnik
Bielsko-Biała

Olomouc

Žilina
Martin

Trenčín
Trnava
BRATISLAVA

SLOVAKIA
Prešov • Košice
Poprad
Banská Bystrica
Lučenec
Ózd
Miskolc

Nyíregyháza
Debrecen

Győr
Tatabánya
Székesfehérvár
Veszprém
Zalaegerszeg
Nagykanizsa
Szombathely
Sopron

BUDAPEST
Szolnok
Kecskemét
Szeged
Békéscsaba

H U N G A R Y
Szekszárd
Kaposvár
Pécs
Baja

Great Hungarian Plain

ROMANIA

SERBIA

AUSTRIA

SLOVENIA

ITALY

CROATIA

BOSNIA & HERZEGOVINA

Adriatic Sea

◆ Built in 1357, Charles Bridge was the only crossing point of the Vltava in Prague until the 19th century.

◆ With a surface area of around 231 sq mi (598 sq km), Lake Balaton has an average depth of only 11 ft (3.25 m).

◇ The Great Hungarian Plain (Alföld) stretches south from Budapest to the borders of Croatia and Serbia and east to Ukraine and Romania. It covers an area of 20,000 sq miles (51,800 sq km) and is almost completely flat.

Southeast Europe

The Danube forms all or part of the border between nine different European nations: Germany, Austria, Slovakia, Hungary, Croatia, Serbia, Romania, Bulgaria, and Ukraine.

At 11:15 am, on June 28, 1914, Archduke Francis Ferdinand and his wife were shot dead by Gavrilo Princip in Sarajevo. This single act precipitated World War I, which eventually leed to the death of almost 10 million troops.

Born in Zagreb in 1892, Marshall Tito was the president of the former Yugoslavia from 1953 until his death in 1980.

The modern necktie has its origins in 17th century Croatia as a knotted "cravat" that was worn by

BULGARIA

ROMANIA

SERBIA

SLOVAKIA

HUNGARY

AUSTRIA

SLOVENIA

CROATIA

BOSNIA & HERZEGOVINA

FED. BOSNE I HERCEGOVINE

REP. SRPSKA

VOJVODINA

Danube

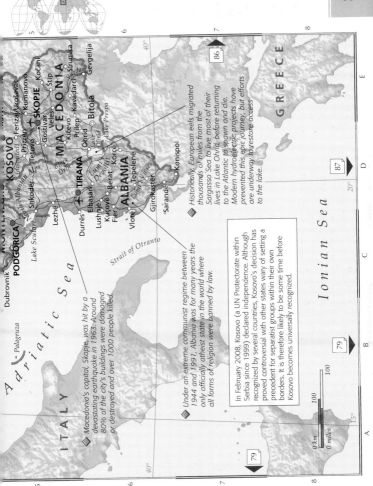

Adriatic Sea

ITALY

Ionian Sea

GREECE

KOSOVO
MONTENEGRO
Dubrovnik
Palagruža
Lake Scutari
PODGORICA
Albanian Alps
Prizren
Ferizaj/Uroševac
Peć
disputed
Gjakovë
Shkodër
Lezhë
Durrës
Drini
TIRANA
Lushnjë
Elbasan
Kuçovë
Berat
Fier
Vlorë
Strait of Otranto
Gjirokastër
Sarandë
Konispol

SKOPJE
Kumanovo
Kočani
Štip
Veles
Gostivar
MACEDONIA
Tetovo
Kičevo
Prilep
Kavadarci
Strumica
Gevgelija
Bitola
Ohrid
Lake Ohrid
Lake Prespa
Drini i Zi
Korçë
Tepelenë
Drino
Vjosa
Devoll
Osum
ALBANIA

♦ Macedonia's capital, Skopje, was hit by a
devastating earthquake in 1963. Around
80% of the city's buildings were damaged
or destroyed and over 1000 people killed.

♦ Under an extreme communist regime between
1944 and 1991, Albania was for many years the
only officially atheist state in the world where
all forms of religion were banned by law.

♦ Historically, European eels migrated
thousands of miles from the
Sargasso Sea to live most of their
lives in Lake Ohrid, before returning
to the Atlantic to spawn and die.
Modern hydroelectric projects have
prevented this epic journey, but efforts
are underway to restore access
to the lake.

In February 2008, Kosovo (a UN Protectorate within
Serbia since 1999) declared independence. Although
recognized by several countries, Kosovo's decision has
proved controversial with other states wary of setting a
precedent for separatist groups within their own
borders. It is therefore likely to be some time before
Kosovo becomes universally recognized.

0 km   100
0 miles   100

The Mediterranean

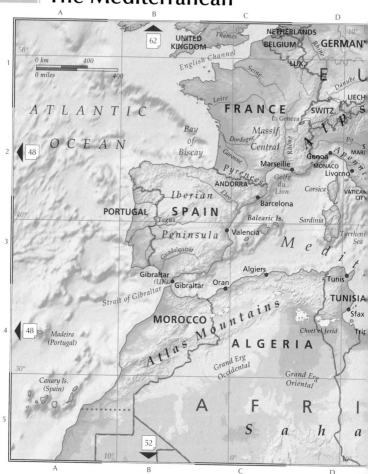

ATLANTIC OCEAN

UNITED KINGDOM

NETHERLANDS
BELGIUM
GERMAN*
LUX.
E U
LIECH.
SWITZ.
FRANCE
A L P S
Thames
English Channel
Seine
Loire
Rhine
Danube
L. Geneva
Massif
Central
Dordogne
Rhône
Po
MARI
Genoa
MONACO
Livorno
Marseille
Apenni
Bay of Biscay
Garonne
Pyrenees
ANDORRA
Golfe du Lion
Corsica
VATICAN CITY
Iberian
SPAIN
PORTUGAL
Ebro
Barcelona
Balearic Is.
Sardinia
Tagus
Peninsula
Valencia
M e d i t
Tyrrheni Sea
Guadalquivir
Algiers
Tunis
Gibraltar (UK)
Gibraltar
Oran
TUNISIA
Strait of Gibraltar
Sfax
MOROCCO
Atlas Mountains
Chott el Jerid
Trip
Madeira (Portugal)
ALGERIA
Grand Erg Occidental
Grand Erg Oriental
Canary Is. (Spain)
A
F R I
S a h a

50°
40°
30°
10°
10°

0 km   400
0 miles   400

62
48
48
52

EUROPE

POLAND
CZECH REP.
(CZECHIA)
AUSTRIA
SLOVAKIA
HUNGARY
SLOVENIA
CROATIA
BOS. &
HERZ.
Dinaric Alps
Hungarian
Plain
Carpathian Mountains
UKRAINE
(Since 2014 the Ukrainian territory of Crimea has been annexed by Russia)
MOLDOVA
Dniester
Danube
Delta
Sea
of Azov
Crimea
RUSSIA
Don
Dnieper

SERBIA
KOSOVO
(disputed)
MON.
ITALY
Adriatic Sea
Naples
ALBANIA
ROMANIA
Danube
BULGARIA
Balkan Mts.
Rhodope Mts.
MACEDONIA
Pindus Mts.

Black Sea

Bosporus
Caucasus
GEORGIA

GREECE
Aegean
Sea
Lesbos
Piraeus
Peloponnese
Ionian
Sea
Sicily
Kos
Rhodes
TURKEY
Anatolia
Izmir
Taurus Mts.
Lake
Van

MALTA
Crete
CYPRUS
SYRIA
Euphrates
Tigris
IRAQ

Mediterranean Sea
LEBANON
Haifa
ISRAEL
Port Said
Nile
Delta
Suez Canal
Mt. Lebanon
Syrian Desert
JORDAN
ASIA

Gulf of Sirte

LIBYA
EGYPT
Libyan
Desert
Nile
Red Sea
SAUDI
ARABIA
Arabian
Peninsula

63

94

94

54

Bulgaria & Greece

Bulgaria is one of the few countries in the world where locals shake their heads from side to side to mean "yes" and nod up and down for "no."

Sofia's skyline is dominated by the gold domes of the Alexander Nevski Memorial Church, which took craftsmen and artists some thirty years to build between 1882 and 1912.

Built between 447 and 438 BCE, the Parthenon survived almost unscathed for over 2000 years until, in 1687, a gunpowder magazine beneath the building exploded, causing considerable damage.

ROMANIA

SERBIA

BULGARIA

Black Sea

Dobrich
Varna
Razgrad
Shumen
Burgas
Ruse
Yambol
Siliven
Stara Zagora
Gabrovo
Lovech
Pleven
Kazanlŭk
Plovdiv
Veliko Tŭrnovo
Vratsa
SOFIA
Pernik
Pazardzhik
Velingrad
Khaskovo
Vidin

Balkan Mountains
Rhodope Mountains

TURKEY

Marmara Denizi

Orestiáda
Komotiní
Xánthi
Drama
Kavala
Thásos
Akrotírio Pínes
Akrotírio Drépano
Akrotírio Palioúri
Thessaloníki
Sérres
Petrích
Kílkis
Kateríni
Véroia
Kozáni
Flórina
Blagoevgrad
Kardítsa
Tríkala
Lárisa
Vólos
Ioánnina
Préveza
Kérkyra
Lake Prespa

MACEDONIA

KOSOVO
(disputed)

ALBANIA

GREECE

Pindos

Thracian Sea

Samothráki
Límnos
Lésvos
Mitilíni

Voreíes Sporádes

Alexandroúpoli

Danube
Marítsa
Tundzha
Iskŭr
Axiós
Strimónas
Thermaïkós Kólpos
Pineiós

TURKEY

Aegean Sea

Lefkáda

Lefkimmi

Agrínio

Ionia

Chalkída

ATHENS

Korinthiakós Kólpos

Korinthos

Peiraiás

Peloponnisos

Trípoli

Pátra

Kefalloniá

Ionian Sea

Iónia Nisiá
(Ionian Islands)

Mirtóo Pelagos

Kalámata

Spárti

Zákynthos

Kýthira

Chíos Chíos

Sámos

Ikaría

Kykládes
(Cyclades)

Ándros

Kéa
(Tziá)

Tínos

Mýkonos

Náxos

Páros

Íos

Amorgós

Mílos

Santoríni

Astypálaia

Dodekánisa
(Dodecanese)

Kos

Kárpathos

Ródos
(Rhodes)

Ródos

Kritikó Pélagos
(Sea of Crete)

Irákleio

Chaniá

Kríti
(Crete)

Mediterranean Sea

The first Olympic athletics
festival was held at Olympia
in around 776 BCE.

The Corinth Canal was completed in 1893 after
11 years of work. The canal is 4 miles (6.3 km)
long, 80 ft (25 m) wide, and 26 ft (8 m) deep.
The central section runs along a 260 ft- (79 m-)
deep cutting through solid rock.

Only about 100 of the 2000
or so Greek Islands are
permanently inhabited.

The Minoans developed the first Hellenic
civilization 4000 years ago, based at the
luxurious palace of Knossos. Unfortunately,
in 1400 BCE, this civilization came to an
abrupt end, destroyed by a catastrophic
event, probably a tidal wave.

0 km   100

0 miles   100

The Baltic States & Belarus

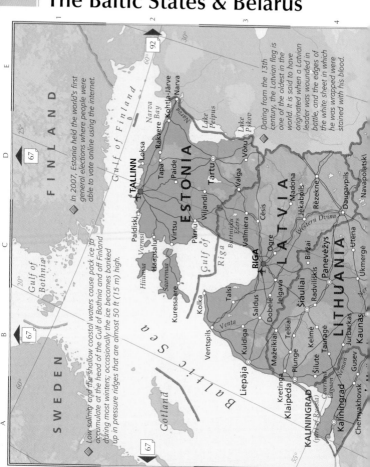

In 2007, Estonia held the world's first general elections where people were able to vote online using the internet.

Dating from the 13th century, the Latvian flag is one of the oldest in the world. It is said to have originated when a Latvian leader was wounded in battle, and the edges of the white sheet in which he was wrapped were stained with his blood.

Low salinity and the shallow coastal waters cause pack ice to accumulate at the head of the Gulf of Bothnia and off Finland during most winters; occasionally the ice becomes banked up in pressure ridges that are almost 50 ft (15 m) high.

RUSSIA

BELARUS

UKRAINE

POLAND

VILNIUS

MINSK

Western Dvina

Hlybokaye/Glubokoye
Lyepyel'/Lepel'
Vitsyebsk/Vitebsk
Orsha
Baryssaw/Borisov
Mahilyow/Mogilëv
Krychaw/Krichev
Horki/Gorki
Zhodzina/Zhodino
Maladzyechna/Molodechno
Babruysk/Bobruysk
Zhlobin
Svietlahorsk/Svetlogorsk
Homyel'/Gomel'
Rechytsa/Rechitsa
Kalinkavichy/Kalinkovichi
Mazyr/Mozyr
Slutsk
Salihorsk/Soligorsk
Baranavichy/Baranovichi
Luninyets/Luninets
Pinsk
Slonim
Vawkavysk/Volkovysk
Hrodna/Grodno
Druskininkai
Alytus
Kobryn/Kobrin
Brest

Bjarezina

Ptsich

Pripet

Neman (Nyoman)

Pripet Marshes

Dnjapro (Dnieper)

Sozh/Sož

Dnjapro (Dnieper)

Kupjels'ke Vdskh

90

91

90

80

The largest dump truck in the world is produced in Belarus. The BelAZ-75710 weighs 350 tons (tonnes) when empty and can carry a load of 450 tons (tonnes). Each of its 8 wheels is 13ft (4 m) high, and it costs about US$7.5 million.

Covering an area of approximately 34,000 sq miles (88,000 sq km), Pripet Marshes are the largest area of marshland in Europe.

Formed in 1945 from the northern half of German East Prussia, and ceded to Russia under the Potsdam agreement, Kaliningrad oblast became a true enclave, completely separated from the rest of Russia, when Lithuania and Belarus achieved their independence in 1991.

0 km 100
0 miles 100

Ukraine, Moldova & Romania

POLAND

BELARUS

◆ On April 25, 1986, engineers accidentally initiated an uncontrolled chain reaction in the number 4 reactor of the Chornobyl' nuclear power plant. The resulting explosion released 8 tons (tonnes) of radioactive material in the world's worst-ever nuclear accident.

Pripet Marshes

Kovel'

Luts'k

Korosten'

Rivne

L'viv

Zhytomyr

SLOVAKIA

Ternopil'

U K R

Ivano-Frankivs'k

Khmel'-nyts'kyy

Vinnytsya

◆ Vlad Dracula or Vlad the Impaler was the real-life prince upon whom Bram Stoker based his famous Count Dracula. Dracula was born in Transylvania in 1431 in the town of Sighisoara.

Uzhhorod

Kam''yanets'-Podil's'kyy

Chernivtsi

Transnistr

Satu Mare

Dniester

Suceava

Botoşani

Ríbniţa

Bălţi

Baia Mare

MOLDOVA

Oradea

Dej

Dubăsari

HUNGARY

Transylvania

Piatra-Neamţ

CHIŞINĂU

Cluj-Napoca

Iaşi

Tiraspol

Arad

Târgu Mureş

Bacău

Bender (Tighina)

Alba Iulia

Sighişoara

Basarabeasca

Timişoara

Deva

R O M A N I A

Sibiu

Focşani

SERBIA

Reşiţa

Carpaţii Meridionali

Braşov

Galaţi

Reni

Râmnicu Vâlcea

Buzău

Brăila

Tulcea

◆ In 1889, Timisoara became the first city in Europe to have electric street lighting.

Piteşti

Târgovişte

Drobeta-Turnu Severin

Ploieşti

Craiova

BUCHAREST

Constan

Corabia

Danube

Eforie Sud

Giurgiu

Mangalia

BULGARIA

RUSSIA

30°　　35°　　40°

◆ A monument in central Kyiv stands as testament to the 7–12 million Ukrainian peasants who died during the Great Famine, or Holodomor, of 1932–33.

Shostka

Chernihiv

Chornobyl'
Kyyivs'ke Vdskh.
✝ KYIV
Kaniv's'ke Vdskh.

Sumy

Bila Tserkva
Lubny

A I N E

Kharkiv

Cherkasy
Kremenchuts'ke Vdskh.
Poltava
Kremenchuk

Donets

Syeverodonets'k

Slov''yans'k
Pavlohrad
Horlivka

Luhans'k
Kostyantynivka
Yenakiyeve
Khrustal'nyy
(Krasnyy Luch)

Oleksandriya

Kropyvnyts'kyy
(Kirovohrad)
Dnipro
(Dnipropetrovs'k)
Makiyivka
Donets'k

Kryvyy Rih
Nikopol'
Zaporizhzhya

Pivdennyy Buh

Mariupol'

Mykolayiv
Kakhovs'ka Vdskh.
Melitopol'
Berdyans'k

Kherson
Kakhovka
Dnieper

Odesa

Sea of Azov
(since 2014 the Ukrainian territory of Crimea has been annexed by Russia)

◆ In 1872, an iron foundry was established at Donets'k by British industrialist John Hughes (from whom the town's pre-Revolutionary name Yuzovka was derived) to produce rails for the growing Russian transportation network.

Karkinits'ka Zatoka

Kryms'kyy Pivostriv

Kerch

RUSSIA

Yevpatoriya
Simferopol'
Sevastopol'
Yalta

Black Sea

◆ Odesa was one of the major flashpoints in the Russian Revolution of 1905, and was the scene of the mutiny on the warship Potemkin, when sailors protesting against the serving of rotten meat eventually killed several of the ship's officers.

0 km　　100
0 miles　　100

European Russia

The port of Murmansk remains ice-free throughout the winter thanks to the Gulf Stream, whereas St. Petersburg, 600 miles (965 km) to the south on the Baltic Sea, is ice-bound between December and May.

96
137
137
66

ARCTIC OCEAN

Karskoye More

Barents Sea

Novaya Zemlya

Ostrov Vaygach

Ostrov Kolguyev

(Ural Mountains)

Arctic Circle

Vorkuta

Pechora

Usa

RUSSIA

Murmansk

Kol'skiy Poluostrov

Beloye More

Belove More

Arkhangel'sk

Mezen'

Pinega

Severnaya Dvina

Ukhta

Syktyvkar

Kotlas

Petrozavodsk

Onezhskoye Ozero

Onega

Vologda

Yaroslavl'

Ladozhskoye Ozero

FINLAND

Velikiy Novgorod

Cherepovets

Rybinskoye Vdkhr.

Tver'

NORWAY

SWEDEN

Gulf of Bothnia

Gulf of Finland

Sankt Peterburg (St Peterburg)

Pskov

ESTONIA

Velikiye Luki

Smolensk

Norwegian Sea

Baltic Sea

LATVIA

LITHUANIA

BELARUS

Arctic Circle

0 km   400
0 miles   400

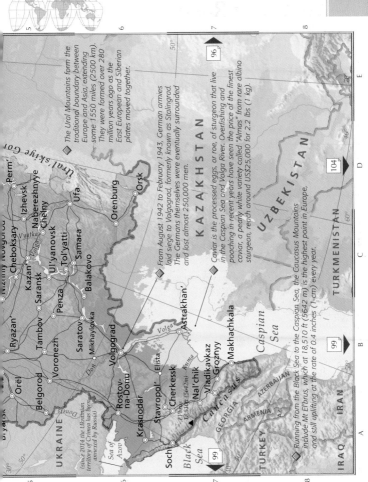

The Ural Mountains form the traditional boundary between Europe and Asia, extending some 1550 miles (2500 km). They were formed over 280 million years ago as the East European and Siberian plates moved together.

From August 1942 to February, 1943, German armies laid siege to Volgograd, formerly known as Stalingrad. The Germans themselves were eventually surrounded and lost almost 250,000 men.

Caviar is the processed eggs, or roe, of sturgeon that live in the Caspian Sea and Volga River. Overfishing and poaching in recent years have seen the price of the finest caviar, a pearly white variety called "Almas" from rare albino sturgeon, reach around US$25,000 for 2.2 lbs (1 kg).

Running from the Black Sea to the Caspian Sea, the Caucasus Mountains include Mt El'brus, which at 18,510 ft (5642 m) is the highest point in Europe, and still uplifting at the rate of 0.4 inches (1-cm) every year.

(since 2014 the Ukrainian territory of Crimea has been annexed by Russia)

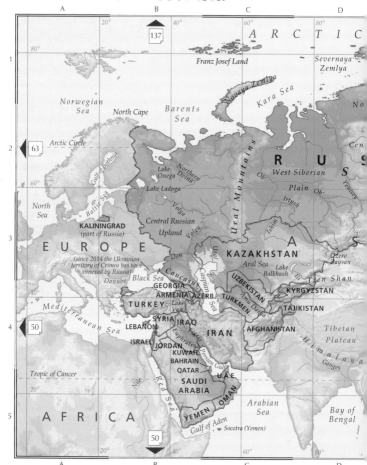

ARCTIC

137

Franz Josef Land

Severnaya
Zemlya

Norwegian
Sea

North Cape

Barents
Sea

Novaya Zemlya

Kara Sea

No

80°

63

Arctic Circle

60°

Gulf of Bothnia

Lake
Onega

Northern
Dvina

Lake Ladoga

Ural Mountains

Ob'

West Siberian
Plain

Ob'

Irtysh

R U S S

A

Cen

Yenisey

North
Sea

Baltic Sea

KALININGRAD
(part of Russia)

Central Russian
Upland

Volga

Volga

Don

Ural

EUROPE

(since 2014 the Ukrainian
territory of Crimea has been
annexed by Russia)

Danube

Black Sea

Caucasus

Caspian Sea

KAZAKHSTAN

Aral Sea

Lake
Balkhash

Ozero
Zaysan

Ili

Tien Shan

GEORGIA

ARMENIA AZERB.

UZBEKISTAN

Amu Darya

TURKMEN.

KYRGYZSTAN

TURKEY

Lake
Van

TAJIKISTAN

40°

Mediterranean Sea

SYRIA

IRAQ

Tigris

IRAN

AFGHANISTAN

Tibetan
Plateau

LEBANON

Euphrates

Himalaya

ISRAEL

JORDAN

KUWAIT

Persian Gulf

Ganges

Tropic of Cancer

50

BAHRAIN

QATAR

U.A.E.

20°

Nile

Red Sea

SAUDI
ARABIA

OMAN

AFRICA

YEMEN

Arabian
Sea

Bay of
Bengal

Gulf of Aden

Socotra (Yemen)

50

20°

40°

60°

80°

E   120°   F   140°   G   160°   H   180°

137

O C E A N

80°

1

New Siberian Islands

Laptev Sea

East Siberian
Sea

Wrangel Island

rian Lowland

Chukchi
Sea

Anabar   Olenëk   Lena   Yana   Indigirka   Kolyma

Long Strait

rian Plateau

Arctic Circle

16

Bering Strait

S   e   r   i   a

Velikaya

60°

2

Lena   Amga

Bering
Sea

Vitim

Lake
Baikal

Sea of
Okhotsk

Kamchatka

Aleutian Islands

Amur   Zeya

Argun

Sakhalin

Kuril Islands

3

o b i

Yellow River

Sea of
Japan
(East Sea)

(administered by
Russian Federation,
claimed by Japan.)

40°

Yangtze

East
China
Sea

P A C I F I C

O C E A N

16

4

Tropic of Cancer

20°

Mekong

South
China
Sea

0 km   800

0 miles   800

5

125

E   120°   F   140°   G   160°   H   180°

Russia & Kazakhstan

ARCTIC

NORWAY
66
SWEDEN
DENMARK
GERMANY
FINLAND
KALININGRAD
(part of Russia)
POLAND
LITH. LAT. EST.
91
Pskov
Sankt-Peterburg (St Petersburg)
Velikiy
Novgorod
UKRAINE
BELARUS
Arkhangel'sk
Murmansk
Barents Sea
Zemlya
Frantsa-
Iosifa

MOSCOW
Cherepovets
Vologda
Bryansk
Yaroslavl'
MOLDOVA
Tula
Ryazan'
Nizhniy
Novgorod
Kirov
Kazan'
Syktyvkar
Perm'
Vorkuta
Nori'
Salekhard
Voronezh
Izhevsk
Serov
Yekaterinburg
Nizhnevartov.

(since 2014
the Ukrainian
territory of
Crimea has
been annexed
by Russia)

Rostov-na-Donu
Volgograd
Samara
Ufa
Chelyabinsk
Sochi
Stavropol'
Nal'chik
Ural'sk
Orenburg
Kostanay
Petropavlovsk
Krasnoyar:
GEORGIA
Astrakhan
Groznyy
Orsk
Rudnyy
Omsk
Tom
ARM.
Makhachkala
Kokshetau
Novosibirsk
Kemero
102
AZ.
Aktau
KAZAKHSTAN
ASTANA
Pavlodar
Barnaul
Kemer
Caspian Sea
Karagandy
Novokuzne:
Zhezkazgan
Semey
Ust'-Kamenogors
Aral
Sea
Kyzylorda
Balkhash
Shymkent
Taraz
Ozero
Balkhash
Taldykorgan
TURKMENISTAN
UZBEKISTAN
IRAN
KYRGYZSTAN
Almaty
CHINA

Zapadno-
Sibirskaya
Ravnina
Ural'skiye Gory
Ob'
R
Karskoye Mor
Novaya Zemlya

104

Arctic Circle

OCEAN

100° 120° 140°   160°   80°   180°   70°   60°

◆ Also known as the "Road of Bones," construction
of the 1262 mile (2031 km) road between Yakutsk
and Magadan took over twenty years and cost
the lives of a huge number of prisoners from
Stalin's notorious Gulag camps.

Ostrov
Vrangelya

18

Pevek

Anadyr'

Vostochno-
Sibirskoye More

Ambarchik

Bering
Sea

180°

Novosibirskiye
Ostrova

*ernaya
*entiya

*ostrov
*aymyr

More
Laptevykh

Ozero
Taymyr

Tiksi

Ossora

134

Ust'-Kamchatsk

Poluostrov
Kamchatka

50°

Olenëk

Lena

Verkhoyanskiy Khrebet

Magadan

Petropavlovsk
-Kamchatskiy

160°

*ednesibirskoye
Ploskogor'ye

Okhotsk

Sea of
Okhotsk

A S I A

Yakutsk

ibir

Suntar

Sakhalin

Kuril Islands

Siberia)

Lena

Komsomol'sk-
na-Amure

*nsk

Bratsk

Skovorodno

134

Ozero
Baykal

Blagoveshchensk

Yuzhno-
Sakhalinsk

Irkutsk

Chita

Khabarovsk

40°

Ulan-Ude

Amur

JAPAN

C H I N A

Vladivostok

◆ The Trans-Siberian Railroad, completed in 1916, runs
5578 miles (9297 km) between Moscow and Vladivostok.
Crossing eight time zones, the journey takes six days.

0 km   500

0 miles   500

MONGOLIA

100°   140°   120°   130°

110

E   F   G   H

Turkey & the Caucasus

An average of 50,000 commercial ships pass through the Bosporus a year, along with thousands of ferries and smaller passenger boats. The strait is three times busier than the Suez Canal and four times as busy as the Panama Canal.

ROMANIA

BULGARIA

Black Sea

86

GREECE

Edirne ● ● Kırklareli

Tekirdağ ●

Çanakkale Boğazı (Dardanelles)

Marmara Denizi

İstanbul ●

Bosporus

Zonguldak ●

Küre Dağları

Sinop ●

Kastamonu ●

Samsu

Karabük ●

Çapik Daği

Çanakkale ●

İzmit ●

Bursa ●

Adapazarı ●

Eskişehir ●

Çankırı ●

ANKARA ★

Çorum ●

Toka

Balıkesir ●

Kütahya ●

A n a t o l i a

Kırıkkale ●

T U R K

Sivas ●

Ayvalık ●

Lésvos

Manisa ●

İzmir ●

Afyon ●

Uşak ●

Nevşehir ●

Kızıl Irmak

i a

Kayseri ●

Chíos

Sámos

Aydın ●

Tuz Gölü

Niğde ●

Kahraman maraş

Bodrum ●

Muğla ●

Denizli ●

Isparta ●

Konya ●

Osmaniye ●

Ereğli ●

Adana ●

Gazian

87

Antalya ●

Toros Dağları

Mersin ●

Tarsus ●

İskenderun ●

Antak

Dalaman ●

Antalya Körfezi

Kríti

Kárpathos

Megísti

Ródos

TURKISH REPUBLIC OF NORTHERN CYPRUS *(recognized only by Turkey)*

Girne (Kerýneia) ●

Gazimağusa (Ammóchostos, Famagust

NICOSIA ★

M e d i t e r r a n e a n S e a

Páfos ●

Lárnaka ●

Lemesós (Limassol) ●

CYPRUS

LEBANON

RUSSIA

◆ The Spitak earthquake struck Armenia
in 1988, killing at least 25,000 people
and devastating the country's infrastructure.

Caspian
Sea

Gagra
Sokhumi
Ochamchire

Caucasus

Kutaisi

GEORGIA

TBILISI · Rustavi

Poti

Batumi

Hopa

Rize

rabzon

Enguri

Vanadzor · Gäncä
Gyumri

Kars

ARMENIA

YEREVAN

Quba

Mingäçevir

Sumqayıt
BAKU

AZERBAIJAN

Sevana Lich
Nagornyy-
Karabakh

Xankändi

Büyükağrı Dağı
(Mount Ararat)
16,853ft (5137m)

Naxçıvan

AZERBAIJAN

Länkäran

Erzurum

Erzincan

Elazig

Malatya

Diyarbakır

Adiyaman

Şanlıurfa

Muş

Güney Doğu Toroslar

Van
Gölü

Siirt

Batman

Mardin

Van

◆ Azerbaijan has substantial oil reserves
located in and around the Caspian Sea.
They were some of the earliest oilfields
in the world to be exploited.

IRAN

◆ The salty water of Lake Van inhibits all animal
life except the Pearl Mullet, a small fish that
has adapted to the harsh conditions.

◆ Atatürk Dam, one of the largest dams in the world, was completed in 1990.
The reservoir behind the dam covers an area of 315 sq miles (816 sq km)
and often requires interruptions in the flow of the Euphrates River
to maintain water levels.

SYRIA

IRAQ

0 km   200

0 miles   200

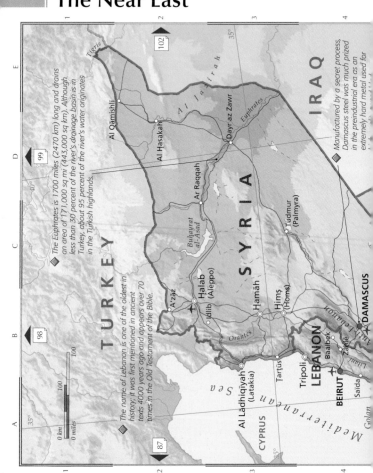

The Euphrates is 1700 miles (2470 km) long and drains an area of 171,000 sq mi (443,000 sq km). Although less than 30 percent of the river's drainage basin is in Turkey, about 95 percent of the river's water originates in the Turkish highlands.

The name of Lebanon is one of the oldest in history; it was first mentioned in ancient texts 4000 years ago and appears over 70 times in the Old Testament of the Bible.

Manufactured by a secret process, Damascus steel was much prized in the preindustrial era as an extremely hard metal used for

TURKEY

IRAQ

SYRIA

LEBANON

CYPRUS

Al Qāmishlī

Al Ḩasakah

Ar Raqqah

Dayr az Zawr

Euphrates

Al Jazīrah

Tigris

A'zāz

Halab (Aleppo)

Idlib

Buḩayrat al-Asad

Hamāh

Tudmur (Palmyra)

Ḩimş (Homs)

Baalbek

Zaḩlé

Al Lādhiqīyah (Latakia)

Tarţūs

Tripoli

Saïda

BEIRUT

DAMASCUS

Golan

Orontes

Litani

Lebanon

Anti Lebanon

Mediterranean Sea

0 km   100
0 miles   100

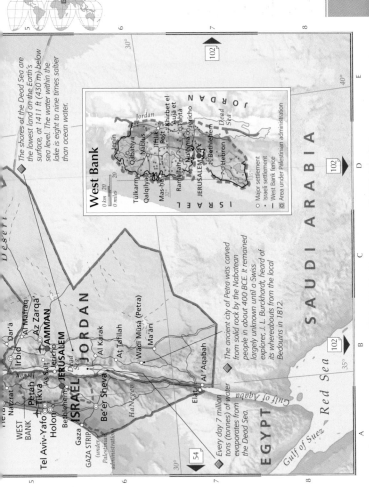

The shores of the Dead Sea are the lowest land on the Earth's surface, at 1411 ft (430 m) below sea level. The water within the lake is eight to nine times saltier than ocean water.

West Bank

0 km 20
0 miles 20

○ Major settlement
• Israeli settlement
— West Bank fence
▨ Area under Palestinian administration

JORDAN

Jordan
Jenin
Túlkarm
Qabátiya
Nåbus
Qalqilya
Jiftlik
Mas-ha
Khirbet el
'Auja et
Tahta
Jericho
Ram Allah
Nu'eima
Ma'ale Adummim
JERUSALEM
Bethlehem
Hebron
ISRAEL
Dead Sea

The ancient city of Petra was carved from solid rock by the Nabatean people in about 400 BCE. It remained largely unknown until a Swiss explorer, J. L. Burckhardt, heard of its whereabouts from the local Bedouins in 1812.

Every day 7 million tons (tonnes) of water evaporates from the Dead Sea.

SAUDI ARABIA

JORDAN

Desert

Dará
Al Mafraq
Irbid
Az Zarqá
AMMAN
Naphali
Nazerat
Petah Tikva
Tel Aviv-Yafo
Holon
JERUSALEM
Bethlehem
Jericho
As Salt
Al Karak
At Tafilah
Wádi Músa (Petra)
Ma'án
Be'er Sheva
Ha Negeve
Elat
Al 'Aqabah

ISRAEL

WEST BANK (under Palestinian administration)

GAZA STRIP (under Palestinian administration)

Gaza

Jordan

EGYPT

Gulf of Suez
Red Sea
Gulf of Aqaba

The Middle East

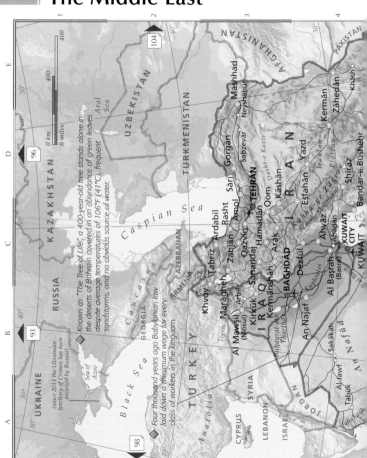

Known as "The Tree of Life", a 400-year-old tree stands alone in the deserts of Bahrain covered in an abundance of green leaves despite average temperatures of 106°F (41°C), frequent sandstorms, and no obvious source of water.

(since 2014 the Ukrainian territory of Crimea has been annexed by Russia)

Four thousand years ago Babylonian law laid down a minimum wage for every class of workers in the kingdom.

RUSSIA

UKRAINE

KAZAKHSTAN

UZBEKISTAN

TURKMENISTAN

AFGHANISTAN

PAKISTAN

GEORGIA

AZERBAIJAN

ARMENIA

TURKEY

SYRIA

LEBANON

ISRAEL

CYPRUS

JORDAN

IRAQ

IRAN

KUWAIT

Black Sea

Sea of Azov

Caspian Sea

Aral Sea

Anatolia

Caucasus

Dasht-e Kavir

Dasht-e Lut

Plateau of Iran

Kūh-e Zagros

Zagros Mountains

An Nafūd

Bīḩayrat al Tharthār

Tigris

Euphrates

Mashhad

Neyshābūr

Sabzevār

Gorgān

Sārī

Āmol

Rasht

Ardabīl

Tabrīz

Khvoy

Marāgheh

Arbīl

Kirkūk

Al Mawşil
(Mosul)

Zanjān

Qazvīn

Hamadān

Sanandaj

Kermānshāh

Arāk

Qom

TEHRAN

Kāshān

Eşfahān

Yazd

Shīrāz

Kermān

Zāhedān

Khāsh

Bandar-e Būshehr

Ahvāz

Dezfūl

Ābādān

Al Başrah
(Basra)

BAGHDĀD

An Najaf

Sakākah

Al Jawf

Thāmūd(?)

KUWAIT
CITY

0 km   400

0 miles   400

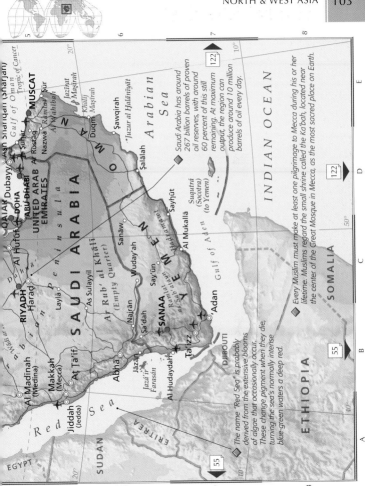

Saudi Arabia has around 267 billion barrels of proven oil reserves, with around 60 percent of this still remaining. At maximum output, the region can produce around 10 million barrels of oil every day.

Every Muslim must make at least one pilgrimage to Mecca during his or her lifetime. Muslims regard the small shrine called the Ka'bah, located near the center of the Great Mosque in Mecca, as the most sacred place on Earth.

The name "Red Sea" is probably derived from the extensive blooms of algae that occasionally occur. These change pigment when they die, turning the sea's normally intense blue-green waters a deep red.

Central Asia

◆ Since 1960, the Aral Sea has shrunk by 90 percent, becoming extremely saline and consequently losing all but one of its once-abundant fish species.

◆ The desert of Kara Kum (Garagum) occupies over 70 percent of Turkmenistan, severely limiting human settlement across much of the country.

◆ The Kara Kum (Garagum) Canal, the world's longest irrigation canal, stretches some 850 miles (1375 km) and is known as the "River of Life," since it irrigates large areas of arid land.

KAZAKHSTA

Aral Sea

Ustyurt Plateau

Nukus
Koneürgenç
Daşoguz   Urganch   Uchquduq
UZBEKISTAN   To'rtko'l   Zarafshc
                                         Aydarko'
                                         Ko'li
Türkmenbaşy   Navoi
Hazar   Balkanabat
          Bereket   Buxoro
TURKMENISTAN   Garagum   Samarqa
Caspian   Serdar   Seÿdi   Qarshi
Sea   Baharly   Türkmenabat
          Gökdepe
Abadan   Mary   Bayramaly   Atamyrat
AŞGABAT   Garagum Kanaly   Saýat
          Kaka   Tejen   Murgap   Āqcha
                                         Shibirghan   Mazar-e Sha
IRAN   Bala Murghab   Maimanah
                         Serhetabat   Darya-ye Murghāb
          Herāt   Harīrūd
          AFGHANISTAN
          Farāh
                         Gereshk   Qalā
          Zaranj   Kandahār
          Dasht-e-Mārgow

0 km   200
0 miles   200

Turan Lowland

Amu Darya

Darya-ye Helmand

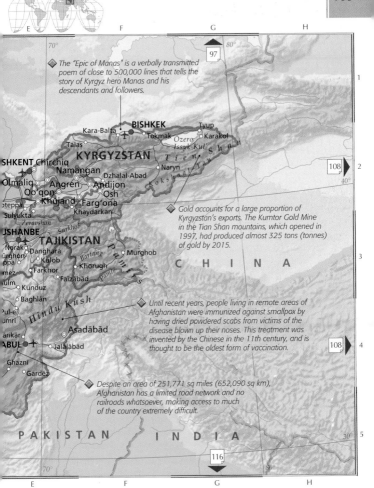

E · F · G · H

70° · 80°

97

◆ The "Epic of Manas" is a verbally transmitted poem of close to 500,000 lines that tells the story of Kyrgyz hero Manas and his descendants and followers.

Kara-Balta · **BISHKEK** · Tyup
Talas · Tokmak · Karakol
Ozero Issyk-Kul'
KYRGYZSTAN · *Tien Shan*

SHKENT · Chirchiq · Naryn · 108

Namangan
Olmaliq · Angren · Dzhalal-Abad · 40°
Qo'qon · Andijon · *Kokshaal*
Khujand · Farg'ona · Osh
oteppa · Khaydarkan
Sulyukta · *Zeravshan* · *Surkhob*

◆ Gold accounts for a large proportion of Kyrgyzstan's exports. The Kumtor Gold Mine in the Tian Shan mountains, which opened in 1997, had produced almost 325 tons (tonnes) of gold by 2015.

USHANBE · **TAJIKISTAN** · *Pamirs*
Norak · Danghara · Murghob
urghon- · Kulob · *Bartang*
mez · Farkhor · Khorugh · *Pamir* · **C H I N A**
ulm · Faizābād
· Kŭnduz
· Baghlān · *Hindu Kush*

◆ Until recent years, people living in remote areas of Afghanistan were immunized against smallpox by having dried powdered scabs from victims of the disease blown up their noses. This treatment was invented by the Chinese in the 11th century, and is thought to be the oldest form of vaccination.

Pul-e · Asadābād · 108
arikar
ABUL · Jalālābād

Ghazni
· Gardēz

◆ Despite an area of 251,771 sq miles (652,090 sq km), Afghanistan has a limited road network and no railroads whatsoever, making access to much of the country extremely difficult.

P A K I S T A N · **I N D I A** · 30°

70° · 116 · 30°

E · F · G · H

South & East Asia

Black Sea

Caspian Sea

Aral Sea

Syr Darya

Lake Balkhash

Irtysh

Yenisey

Lake Baikal

Uvs Nuur

Hovsgol Nuur

MONGOLIA

Tien Shan

Altai Mountains

Gobi

Yellow River

Iranian Plateau

A S I A

Hindu Kush

Takla Makan Desert

Altun Shan

Kunlun Mountains

Plateau of Tibet

CHIN

PAKISTAN

Indus

Sutlej

Himalayas

Yamuna

Ganges

NEPAL

Brahmaputra

Saluveen

Mekong

Yan

Thar Desert

Rann of Kachchh

Mount Everest 29,029ft (8848m)

BHUTAN

BANGLADESH

Gulf of Khambhat

INDIA

Deccan

Western Ghats

Eastern Ghats

MYANMAR (BURMA)

Irrawaddy

Red River

Xi Jia

VIETNA

LAOS

Arabian Sea

THAILAND

Mekong

CAMBO

Tônle Sa

Laccadive Islands (to India)

Bay of Bengal

Andaman Islands (to India)

Andaman Sea

Gulf of Thailand

SRI LANKA

Gulf of Mannar

Nicobar Islands (to India)

MAL

MALDIVES

SINGAPORE

Sumatra

INDIAN

OCEAN

Equator

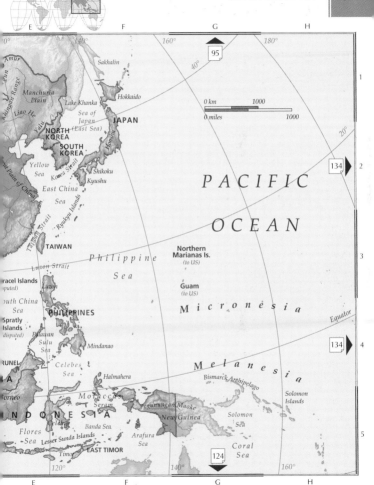

E   F   G   H

95

0 km   1000
0 miles   1000

Amur

Sakhalin

Manchuria
Plain

Stanovoy Range

Amur

Sun

Liao He

Hokkaido

Lake Khanka

Sea of
Japan
(East Sea)

JAPAN

**NORTH
KOREA**

Yalu

**SOUTH
KOREA**

Honshu

Yellow
Sea

Great Plain of China

Korea Strait

Shikoku

Kyushu

134

East China
Sea

Ryukyu Islands

P A C I F I C

O C E A N

Taiwan Strait

TAIWAN

Philippine

Sea

Luzon Strait

Northern
Marianas Is.
(to US)

Paracel Islands
(disputed)

Luzon

South China
Sea

Guam
(to US)

Spratly
Islands
(disputed)

PHILIPPINES

M i c r o n e s i a

134

BRUNEI

Palawan

Sulu
Sea

Mindanao

Equator

MALAYSIA

Celebes
Sea

Halmahera

M e l a n e s i a

Borneo

Bismarck Archipelago

Solomon
Islands

INDONESIA

Moluccas

Seram

Pegunungan Maoke

New Guinea

Solomon
Sea

Flores
Sea

Banda Sea

Arafura
Sea

Coral
Sea

Timor

Lesser Sunda Islands

EAST TIMOR

124

E   F   G   H

Western China & Mongolia

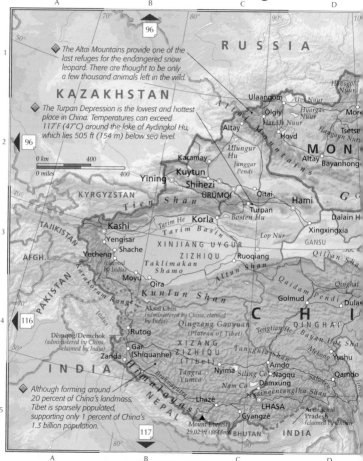

◆ The Altai Mountains provide one of the last refuges for the endangered snow leopard. There are thought to be only a few thousand animals left in the wild.

◆ The Turpan Depression is the lowest and hottest place in China. Temperatures can exceed 117°F (47°C) around the lake of Aydingkol Hu, which lies 505 ft (154 m) below sea level.

◆ Although forming around 20 percent of China's landmass, Tibet is sparsely populated, supporting only 1 percent of China's 1.3 billion population.

RUSSIA

KAZAKHSTAN

KYRGYZSTAN

TAJIKISTAN

AFGH.

PAKISTAN

INDIA

NEPAL

BHUTAN

MONGOLIA

Altai Mountains

Hangayn Nuruu

GOBI

GANSU

Qilian Shan

Qinghai

QINGHAI

Qaidam Pendi

Bayan Har Shan

Arunachal Pradesh (claimed by China)

Himalayas

Tien Shan

Karakoram Range

Kunlun Shan

Altun Shan

Tangla Shan

Nyainqentanglha Shan

CHINA

XINJIANG UYGUR ZIZHIQU

XIZANG ZIZHIQU (Tibet)

Qingzang Gaoyuan (Plateau of Tibet)

Taklimakan Shamo

Tarim Basin

Junggar Pendi

Ulaangom
Olgiy
Altay
Hovd
Altay
Bayanhongor
Mörön
Tsetserleg
Uvs Nuur
Har Us Nuur
Hyargas Nuur
Hövsgöl Nuur

Karamay
Yining
Kuytun
Shihezi
ÜRÜMQI
Qitai
Turpan
Hami
Dalain Hob
Xingxingxia
Bosten Hu
Lop Nur
Korla
Kashi
Yengisar
Shache
Yecheng
(claimed by India)
Moyu
Qira
Ruoqiang
Golmud
Dulan
Qinghai
Yushu
Qamdo
Amdo
Naqqu
Damxung
LHASA
Gyangzê
Lhazê
Nyima
Siling Co
Nam Co
Tangra Yumco
Rutog
Gar (Shiquanhe)
Zanda
Dêmqog/Demchok (administered by China, claimed by India)
Aksai Chin (administered by China, claimed by India)
Ulungur Hu

Tarim He
Tongtian He
Mekong He
Salween He
Brahmaputra
Indus

Mount Everest 29,029ft (8848m)

0 km 400
0 miles 400

96
96
116
117

50°
40°
30°
70°
80°
90°

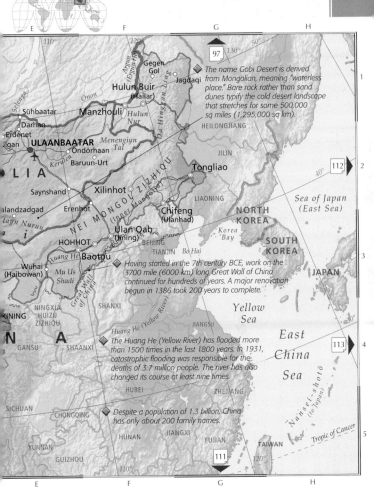

97

The name Gobi Desert is derived from Mongolian, meaning "waterless place." Bare rock rather than sand dunes typify the cold desert landscape that stretches for some 500,000 sq miles (1,295,000 sq km).

Having started in the 7th century BCE, work on the 3700 mile (6000 km) long Great Wall of China continued for hundreds of years. A major renovation begun in 1386 took 200 years to complete.

The Huang He (Yellow River) has flooded more than 1500 times in the last 1800 years. In 1931, catastrophic flooding was responsible for the deaths of 3.7 million people. The river has also changed its course at least nine times.

Despite a population of 1.3 billion, China has only about 200 family names.

112
113
111

E   110°   F   120°   G   130°   H

Sühbaatar
Darhan
Erdenet
Ilgan
ULAANBAATAR
Öndörhaan
Baruun-Urt
Saynshand
alandzadgad
tayn Nuruu
i
Wuhai
(Haibowan)
XINING

Onon
Selenga
Kerulen
Menengiyn
Tal
Erdenet

Arxan
(Ergun He)
Gegen
Gol
Hulun Buir
(Hailar)
Manzhouli
Hulun
Nur
Jagdaqi

Da Hinggan Ling

Tongliao

NEI MONGGOL ZIZHIQU
(Inner Mongolia)

Xilinhot
Erenhot
Chifeng
(Ulanhad)
Ulan Qab
(Jining)
HOHHOT
Baotou
Huang He

Mu Us
Shadi

Great Wall
of China

NINGXIA
HUIZU
ZIZHIQU

GANSU   SHAANXI   SHANXI

SICHUAN   CHONGQING

YUNNAN   GUIZHOU

HUBEI

HUNAN   JIANGXI

HEILONGJIANG

JILIN

LIAONING

NORTH
KOREA

SOUTH
KOREA

Korea
Bay

BEIJING
TIANJIN   Bo Hai

JIANGSU

Huang He (Yellow River)

Yellow
Sea

ZHEJIANG

FUJIAN   TAIWAN

Sea of Japan
(East Sea)

JAPAN

East
China
Sea

Nansei-shotō
(to Japan)

Tropic of Cancer

CHINA

LIA

40°

30°

50°

120°

110°

130°

Eastern China & Korea

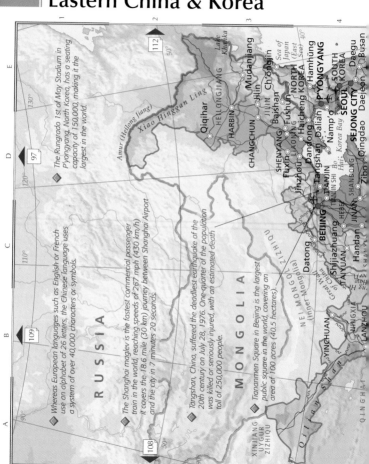

The Rungrado 1st of May Stadium in Pyongyang, North Korea, has a seating capacity of 150,000, making it the largest in the world.

Whereas European languages such as English or French use an alphabet of 26 letters, the Chinese language uses a system of over 40,000 characters or symbols.

The Shanghai maglev is the fastest commercial passenger train in the world, reaching speeds of 267 mph (430 km/h). It covers the 18.6 mile (30 km) journey between Shanghai Airport and the city in 7 minutes 20 seconds.

Tangshan, China, suffered the deadliest earthquake of the 20th century on July 28, 1976. One-quarter of the population was killed or seriously injured, with an estimated death toll of 250,000 people.

Tiananmen Square in Beijing is the largest public square in the world, covering an area of 100 acres (40.5 hectares).

JAPAN

Jeju-do

Nansei-shotō (part of Japan)

Yellow Sea

East China Sea

Okinawa

Tropic of Cancer

JIANGSU

SHANGHAI

Nanjing

Bengbu

Kaifeng

ZHENGZHOU

HENAN

Hefei

Huainan

ANHUI

Wuxi

Jiaxing

HANGZHOU

Ningbo

Jingdezhen

ZHEJIANG

Wenzhou

C H I N A

HUBEI

WUHAN

JIANGXI

Shangrao

FUZHOU

Lichuan

Yueyang

NANCHANG

Jinhua

CHANGSHA

HUNAN

Hengyang

FUJIAN

Xiamen

Xi'an

SHAANXI

Hanzhong

SICHUAN

Mianyang

CHENGDU

Nanchong

Leshan Zigong CHONGQING

GUIZHOU

GUANGXI

Guiyang

ZHUANG ZIZHIQU

Liuzhou

GUANGZHOU

GUANGDONG

Dongguan

Shantou

Macao (Special Admin. Region)

Hong Kong (Special Administrative Region)

YUNNAN

KUNMING

NANNING

Red River

Gulf of Tonkin

HAINAN

Hainan Dao

Paracel Islands (disputed by China, Taiwan, and Vietnam)

South China Sea

Spratly Islands (disputed by China, Malaysia, Philippines, Taiwan, and Vietnam)

Jinsha Jiang

Jialing Jiang

Yalong Jiang

XIZANG ZIZHIQU (Tibet)

Hengduan Shan

Wuliang Shan

Mekong

Salween

MYANMAR (BURMA)

LAOS

THAILAND

V I E T N A M

CAMBODIA

TAICHUNG

TAIPEI

TAIWAN

Taichung

Taichung Strait

Tainan

Kaohsiung

Luzon Strait

PACIFIC OCEAN

PHILIPPINES

(China and Taiwan claim all of each other's territory)

SOUTH KOREA'S TWO CAPITALS

Seoul - capital

Sejong City - administrative capital

Li is the family name for over 87 million people in China.

In 2016, the Duge bridge became the highest in the world with the road deck sitting over 1854 ft (565 m) above the Beipan River.

134

121

118

118

400

400

50 km

50 miles

Japan

Kuril Islands
(administered by
Russia, claimed
by Japan)

Ostrov Iturup

Ostrov Shikotan

Sea of
Okhotsk

Ostrov Kunashir

Nemuro

Kushiro

Kitami

Hokkaidō

Abashiri

Ostrov
Sakhalin

Asahikawa

Obihiro

Tomakomai

Hakodate

Hachinohe

Morioka

Honshū

Sendai

Fukushima

Kōriyama

Iwaki

Hitachi

On Friday March 11, 2011
a 9.0 magnitude earthquake
struck off the east coast of
Japan triggering massive
tsunami waves up to 133 ft
(40 m) high that devastated
coastal regions and left a
death toll in excess of
15,000 people

Pérouse Strait

Wakkanai

Rebun-tō

Rishiri-tō

Sapporo

Otaru

Aomori

Akita

Niigata

Sado

Shinano-gawa

Toyama

Nagano

Okushiri-tō

At 33.4 miles (53.8 km), 14.3 miles (23.3 km)
of which lie under the Tsugaru Strait, the Seikan
Tunnel is the second longest tunnel in the
world. Construction began in 1964 and took
24 years to complete.

Sea of Japan

(East Sea)

J A P A N

The Toyota Motor Corporation was first established in
1937 as a spin-off from Toyoda Automatic Loom
Works. In 2012, the company became the first in
the world to produce 10 million vehicles a year,
equivalent to one every 3.1 seconds.

R U S S I A

C H I N A

NORTH KOREA

Liancourt Rocks

134

97

97

110

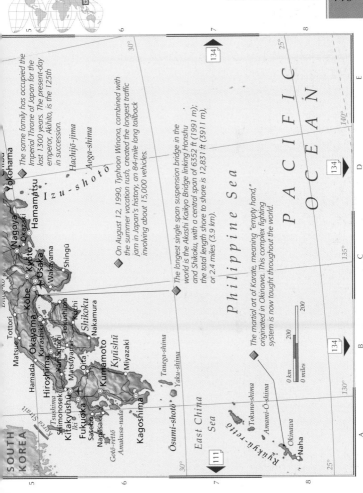

The same family has occupied the Imperial Throne of Japan for the last 1300 years. The present-day emperor, Akihito, is the 125th in succession.

On August 12, 1990, Typhoon Winona, combined with the summer vacation rush, created the longest traffic jam in Japan's history, an 84-mile long tailback involving about 15,000 vehicles.

The longest single span suspension bridge in the world is the Akashi Kaikyo Bridge linking Honshu and Shikoku, with a central span of 6352 ft (1991 m); the total length shore to shore is 12,831 ft (3911 m), or 2.4 miles (3.9 km).

The martial art of Karate, meaning "empty hand," originated in Okinawa. This complex fighting system is now taught throughout the world.

Map labels

SOUTH KOREA

Tsushima Strait

PACIFIC OCEAN

Philippine Sea

East China Sea

Izu-shotō

Hachijō-jima

Aoga-shima

Yokohama
Nagoya
Kyōto
Kōbe
Ōsaka
Hamamatsu
Okazaki
Wakayama
Shingū
Tottori
Matsue
Okayama
Kurashiki
Hamada
Hiroshima
Shimonoseki
Iwakuni
Matsuyama
Tokushima
Takamatsu
Kōchi
Nakamura
Shikoku
Kitakyūshū
Fukuoka
Iki
Ōita
Kumamoto
Kyūshū
Sasebo
Nagasaki
Miyazaki
Gotō-rettō
Amakusa-nada
Kagoshima
Tanega-shima
Yaku-shima
Osumi-shotō
Tokuno-shima
Amami-Ō-shima
Ryūkyū-rettō
Okinawa
Naha

0 km   200
0 miles   200

Southern India & Sri Lanka

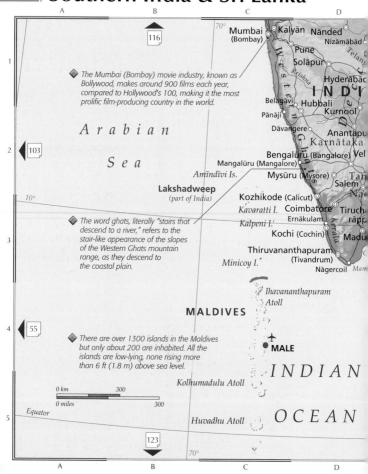

A   B   C   D

116

70°   Mumbai   Kalyān   Nānded
(Bombay)   Nizāmābād

Pune   Telang
Solāpur

Hyderābāc

INDI

Belagāvi   Hubbali   Kurnool

Pānāji

Dāvangere   Anantapu

Karnātaka

Bengalūru (Bangalore)   Vel

Mangalūru (Mangalore)

Amīndīvi Is.   Mysūru (Mysore)   Tan
Salem

Lakshadweep   Kozhikode (Calicut)   Coimbatore   Tiruch
(part of India)   Kavaratti I.   Ernākulam   rāpp

Kalpeni I.   Kochi (Cochin)   Madu

Thiruvananthapuram
(Tivandrum)

Minicoy I.   Nāgercoil   Man

A r a b i a n

S e a

*The Mumbai (Bombay) movie industry, known as
Bollywood, makes around 900 films each year,
compared to Hollywood's 100, making it the most
prolific film-producing country in the world.*

103

*The word ghats, literally "stairs that
descend to a river," refers to the
stair-like appearance of the slopes
of the Western Ghats mountain
range, as they descend to
the coastal plain.*

Ihavananthapuram
Atoll

MALDIVES

55

*There are over 1300 islands in the Maldives
but only about 200 are inhabited. All the
islands are low-lying, none rising more
than 6 ft (1.8 m) above sea level.*

●MALE

INDIAN

Kolhumadulu Atoll

0 km   300
0 miles   300

Equator

OCEAN

Huvadhu Atoll

123

70°

A   B   C   D

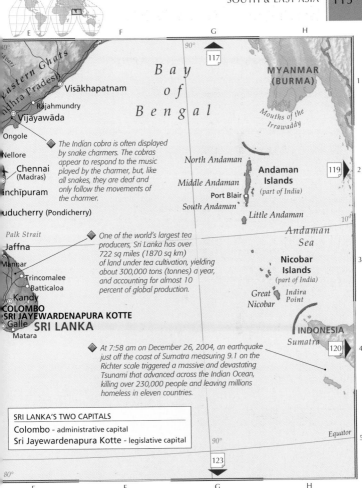

E   F   G   H

90°

117

MYANMAR (BURMA)

Eastern Ghats

Andhra Pradesh

Visākhapatnam

Rājahmundry

Vijayawāda

Ongole

Nellore

Chennai (Madras)

anchīpuram

uducherry (Pondicherry)

B a y
o f
B e n g a l

Mouths of the Irrawaddy

1

The Indian cobra is often displayed by snake charmers. The cobras appear to respond to the music played by the charmer, but, like all snakes, they are deaf and only follow the movements of the charmer.

North Andaman

Middle Andaman

Port Blair

South Andaman

Little Andaman

Andaman Islands
(part of India)

119

2

10°

Palk Strait

Jaffna

Mannar

Trincomalee

Batticaloa

Kandy

COLOMBO

SRI JAYEWARDENAPURA KOTTE

Galle

SRI LANKA

Matara

One of the world's largest tea producers, Sri Lanka has over 722 sq miles (1870 sq km) of land under tea cultivation, yielding about 300,000 tons (tonnes) a year, and accounting for almost 10 percent of global production.

Andaman Sea

Nicobar Islands
(part of India)

Great Nicobar

Indira Point

3

INDONESIA

Sumatra

120

At 7:58 am on December 26, 2004, an earthquake just off the coast of Sumatra measuring 9.1 on the Richter scale triggered a massive and devastating Tsunami that advanced across the Indian Ocean, killing over 230,000 people and leaving millions homeless in eleven countries.

4

SRI LANKA'S TWO CAPITALS

Colombo - administrative capital

Sri Jayewardenapura Kotte - legislative capital

Equator

90°

5

123

80°

E   F   G   H

North India & Pakistan

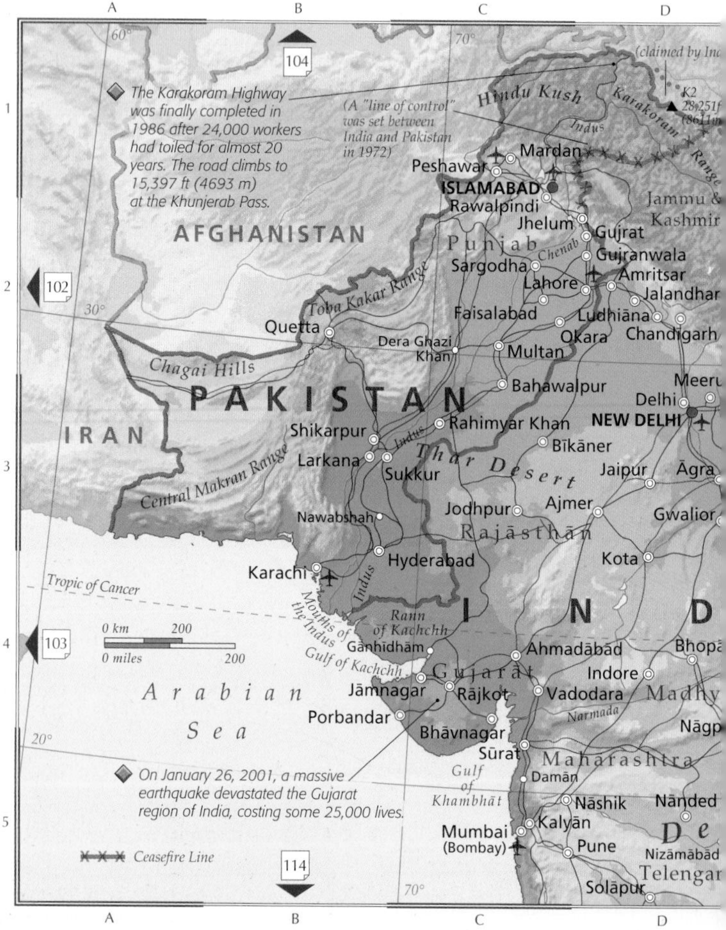

A
B
C
D
1
2
3
4
5
60°
70°
30°
20°
104
102
103
114
The Karakoram Highway was finally completed in 1986 after 24,000 workers had toiled for almost 20 years. The road climbs to 15,397 ft (4693 m) at the Khunjerab Pass.
(A "line of control" was set between India and Pakistan in 1972)
(claimed by Ind
K2 28,251f (8611m
Hindu Kush
Karakoram Range
Indus
Mardan
Peshawar
ISLAMABAD
Rawalpindi
Jammu & Kashmir
Jhelum
Gujrat
AFGHANISTAN
Punjab
Chenab
Gujranwala
Sargodha
Amritsar
Lahore
Jalandhar
Toba Kakar Range
Faisalabad
Ludhiāna
Quetta
Okara
Chandigarh
Dera Ghazi Khan
Multan
Chagai Hills
Bahawalpur
Meeru
PAKISTAN
Delhi
NEW DELHI
IRAN
Shikarpur
Rahimyar Khan
Bīkāner
Larkana
Thar Desert
Jaipur
Āgra
Sukkur
Central Makran Range
Jodhpur
Ajmer
Gwalior
Nawabshah
Rajāsthān
Hyderabad
Kota
Karachi
Tropic of Cancer
Indus
Mouths of the Indus
Rann of Kachchh
INDIA
0 km 200
0 miles 200
Gānhīdhām
Ahmadābād
Bhopā
Gulf of Kachchh
Gujarāt
Indore
Jāmnagar
Rājkot
Vadodara
Madhy
Arabian Sea
Narmada
Porbandar
Nāgp
Bhāvnagar
Sūrat
Mahārāshtra
On January 26, 2001, a massive earthquake devastated the Gujarat region of India, costing some 25,000 lives.
Gulf of Khambhāt
Damān
Nāshik
Nānded
Kalyān
Mumbai (Bombay)
Pune
Nizāmābād
Ceasefire Line
Telengar
Solāpur

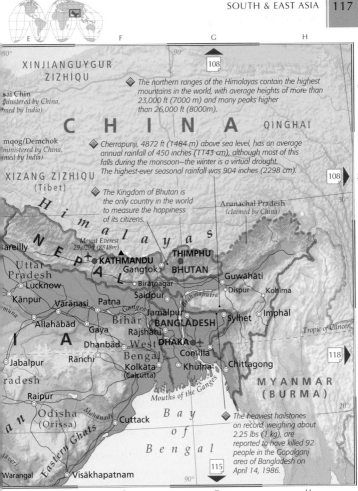

108

XINJIANGUYGUR
ZIZHIQU

sai Chin
*inistered by China,
med by India*

◆ The northern ranges of the Himalayas contain the highest
mountains in the world, with average heights of more than
23,000 ft (7000 m) and many peaks higher
than 26,000 ft (8000m).

C H I N A   QINGHAI

mqog/Demchok
ministered by China,
med by India

◆ Cherrapunji, 4872 ft (1484 m) above sea level, has an average
annual rainfall of 450 inches (1143 cm), although most of this
falls during the monsoon—the winter is a virtual drought.
The highest-ever seasonal rainfall was 904 inches (2298 cm).

108

XIZANG ZIZHIQU
(Tibet)

◆ The Kingdom of Bhutan is
the only country in the world
to measure the happiness
of its citizens.

Arunachal Pradesh
(claimed by China)

H
i
m
a
l
a
y
a
s

areilly

Mount Everest
29,029ft (8848m)▲

N
E
P
A
L

KATHMANDU
Gangtok

THIMPHU
BHUTAN

Guwāhāti

Uttar
Pradesh

Birātnagar

Dispur

Kohima

Lucknow

Saidpur

Jamalpur

Sylhet

Imphāl

Kānpur

Vārānasi

Patna

Ganges

BANGLADESH

Brahmaputra

Tropic of Cancer

Allahābād

muna

Bihār

DHAKA

118

I
A

Gaya

Rājshāhi

West

Comilla

Dhanbād

Bengal

Khulna

Chittagong

Jabalpur

Rānchi

Kolkāta
(Calcutta)

M Y A N M A R
(B U R M A)

radesh

Raipur

Mouths of the Ganges

Odisha
(Orissa)

an

Mahanadi

Cuttack

B a y
o f
B e n g a l

◆ The heaviest hailstones
on record, weighing about
2.25 lbs (1 kg), are
reported to have killed 92
people in the Gopalganj
area of Bangladesh on
April 14, 1986.

averi

Eastern Ghats

Warangal

Visākhapatnam

115

Mainland Southeast Asia

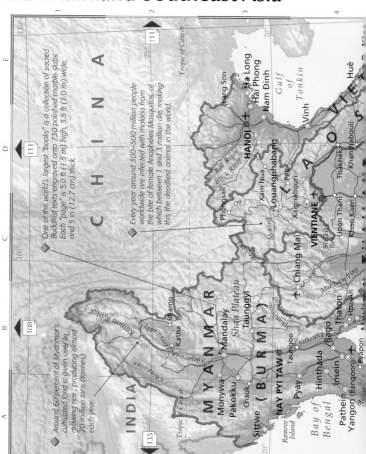

One of the world's largest 'books' is a collection of sacred Buddhist texts engraved onto 730 polished marble slabs. Each 'page' is 5.0 ft (1.5 m) high, 3.5 ft (1.0 m) wide, and 5 in (12.7 cm) thick.

Every year around 300–500 million people worldwide are infected with malaria from the bite of female Anopheles Mosquitos, of which between 1 and 3 million die, making this the deadliest animal in the world.

Around 60 percent of Myanmar's cultivated land is given over to growing rice, producing almost 20 million tons (tonnes) each year.

CHINA

INDIA

MYANMAR (BURMA)

LAOS

VIETNAM

Kumon Range

Shan Plateau

Bay of Bengal

Gulf of Tonkin

Tropic of Cancer

HANOI · Ha Long · Hai Phong · Nam Dinh

Lang Son

Vinh

Huê

Phongsali

Xam Nua

Louangphabang

Xaignabouli

VIENTIANE

Thakhek

Khanthabouli

Udon Thani

Khon Kaen

Chiang Mai

Bhamo

Katha

Mandalay

Monywa

Taunggyi

Taungoo

Pakokku

Chauk

NAY PYI TAW

Pyay

Hinthada

Thaton

Hpa-An

Bago

Insein

Yangon (Rangoon)

Pathein

Sittwe

Ramree Island

Prapon

Mekong

Red River

Black River

Ou

Salween

Chindwin

Irrawaddy

Ayeyarwady

Sittoung

Mae Nam Ping

Nan

Quy Nhon

Nha Trang
Da Lat
Stung Treng
Kampong Cham
Ho Chi Minh

CAMBODIA
Suy Rieng
Can Tho

Muang Khong
Samraong
Kampong Chhnang
PHNOM PENH
Rach Gia

Mouths of the Mekong

Ratchasima
Kampong
Kampot
Stœng Sên
Tonle Sap
Battambang
Sihanoukville

South

China Sea

Ayutthaya
Chon Buri
BANGKOK
Samraong
Ko Chang

Pattaya
Gulf of Thailand
Pattani
Yala

Ratchaburi
Ko Phangan
Ko Samui
Chumphon
Isthmus of Kra
Nakhon Si
Thammarat
Songkhla

Malay Peninsula
MALAYSIA
Strait of Malacca

Dawei

Myeik
Mergui Archipelago
Surat Thani
Trang
Hat Yai
Phuket
Ko Phuket

INDONESIA
Sumatra

Mottama

Nicobar Islands
(part of India)

Andaman Sea

INDIAN OCEAN

Following years of conflict, it is estimated that as many as 6 million landmines remain buried in the soils of Cambodia.

Bangkok's full ceremonial name is:
Krungthepmahanakhon
Amonrattanakosin
Mahintharayutthaya
Mahadilokphop
Noppharatratchathaniburirom
Udomratchaniwetmahasathan
Amonphimanawatansathit
Sakkathattiyawitsanukamprasit,
which is the longest place name in the world.

The world's smallest mammal is the Kitti's hog-nosed bat, also known as the bumblebee bat, of Thailand, weighing less than 0.09 oz (2.5 g).

0 km   200
0 miles   200

Maritime Southeast Asia

MYANMAR (BURMA)

THAILAND

LAOS

VIETNAM

CAMBODIA

Gulf of Tonkin

Paracel Islands
(disputed by China, Taiwan, and Vietnam)

South China Sea

Spratly Islands
(disputed by China, Malaysia, Philippines, Taiwan, and Vietnam)

0 km 400
0 miles 400

MALAYSIA'S TWO CAPITALS
Kuala Lumpur - Capital
Putrajaya - Administrative capital

Andaman Sea

Nicobar Islands
(to India)

Isthmus of Kra

Gulf of Thailand

◆ The Rafflesia plant has the largest single flow
in the world. The bloom, 3 ft (90 cm) in
diameter, attracts insects by imitating
the foul smell of rotting flesh.

Bandaaceh

Strait of Malacca

George Town

Kota Bharu

Kuala Terengganu

Kota Kinabalu

Taiping

Ipoh

Kuantan

BANDAR SERI BEGAWAN

Medan

Klang

KUALA LUMPUR

BRUNEI

Pematangsiantar

PUTRAJAYA

MALAYSIA

Kuching

Sibu

Sarawak

Pegunungan Müller

Pulau Simeulue

Danau Toba

Johor Bahru

Borneo

Sibolga

SINGAPORE

Equator

Pulau Nias

Pekanbaru

Pontianak

Kapuas

Kalimantan

Samarir

Sumatera (Sumatra)

Padang

Pegunungan Barisan

Bukit Barisan

Selat Karimata

Balikpapa

Pulau Siberut

Batang Hari

Jambi

Bangka

Banjarmasin

Kepulauan Mentawai

Palembang

Pulau Belitung

Java Sea

Bengkulu

Makas

INDIAN OCEAN

Bandar Lampung

Selat Sunda

JAKARTA

Tegal

Pekalongan

Semarang

Kudus

Suraba

◆ In August 1883, a devastating volcanic
eruption destroyed most of the island of
Krakatau and triggered a tsunami that
claimed around 35,000 lives.

Bogor

Sukabumi

Bandung

Cilacap

Jawa (Java)

Magelang

Yogyakarta

Surakarta

Madiun

Kediri

Malang

Denpasar

Matara

Jember

Bali

Bali

Philippine

Sea

◆ The Philippines take their name from Philip II
of Spain, who was king when the islands were
colonized during the 16th century.

PHILIPPINES

P   A   C   I   F   I   C

O   C   E   A   N

MICRONESIA

PALAU

◆ Indonesia is the world's largest archipelago,
with over 17,500 islands stretching
3100 miles (5000 km) between the Indian
and Pacific oceans.

Northern
Mariana
Islands
(to US)

Guam (to US)

Yap

Babeldaob

Equator

Luzon Strait
Babuyan Channel

Tuguergarao
Ilagan
Luzon
Dagupan
eles   Cabanatuan
NILA   Lucena
angas
Minoon   Naga
Sibuyan   Legazpi City
Sea   Calbayog
Roxas City   Tacloban
Iloilo   Cadiz
Bacolod   Cebu
City   Butuan
Bohol Sea   Cagayan de Oro
Iligan   Mindanao
nboanga   Davao

General
Santos   Kepulauan
Talaud

Kepulauan
Sangir

Manado

Gorontalo

Gulf of
Tomini   Molucca Sea   Kepulauan
Banggai   Pulau Morotai

Sulawesi
(Celebes)   Kepulauan
Banggai

Kendari

Parepare   Pulau
Buton
Makassar

N   E   S   I   A

Banda Sea

Pulau
Buru

Pulau
Seram

Kepulauan
Kai

Pulau
Yamdena

Halmahera   Pulau
Biak

Sorong   Jazirah
Doberai

Ceram Sea   Wahai
Ambon

Maluku (Moluccas)

Kepulauan
Aru

Sungai Mamberamo

Pegunungan Maoke

Papua
(Irian Jaya)

New   Guinea

Digul

Jayapura

PAPUA
NEW
GUINEA

ores Sea   Wetar
Strait   Kepulauan
Tanimbar

usa - Tenggara   Kepulauan Alor
Flores   Kepulauan Leti   DILI

Sumba   Savu Sea   EAST TIMOR   Arafura   Sea

mba   Kupang   Timor

Timor Sea

Tores Strait

AUSTRALIA

Puerto
Princesa

Sulu Sea

Sulu Archipelago

Celebes Sea

Java Gulf

The Indian Ocean

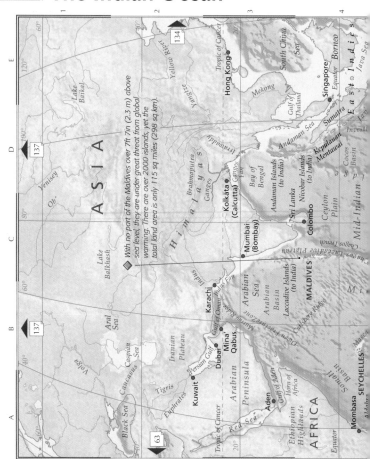

With no part of the Maldives over 7ft 7in (2.3 m) above sea level, they are under great threat from global warming. There are over 2000 islands, yet the total land area is only 115 sq miles (298 sq km).

Australasia & Oceania

Philippine Sea

Northern Mariana Islands *(to US)*

Wake Island *(to US)*

MARSHALL ISLANDS

Ratak Chain

Saipan

Guam *(to US)*

M i c r o n e s i a

Philippines

Yap

MICRONESIA

C a r o l i n e   I s l a n d s

Ralik Chain

Sulu Sea

Babeldaob

Chuuk Islands

Pohnpei

Kosrae

Tunga *(Gilbert Islan...*

Celebes Sea

PALAU

M e l a n e

Nauru

NAURU

Banaba

KIRIBATI

Borneo

TUV

Bismarck Archipelago

s i a

Celebes

Equator

Bismarck Sea

New Britain

Solomon Sea

Solomon Islands

SOLOMON ISLANDS

Banda Sea

Mount Wilhelm 14,793ft (4509m)

New Guinea

Solomon Islands

Guadalcanal

Santa Cruz Islands

VANUATU

Arafura Sea

PAPUA NEW GUINEA

Timor

Flores

Torres Strait

Coral Sea

Espíritu Santo

Malekula

Efate

Vanua

Vit. Levu

Timor Sea

Arnhem Land

Gulf of Carpentaria

Cape York Peninsula

Coral Sea Islands *(to Australia)*

New Caledonia *(to France)*

Ashmore & Cartier Islands *(to Australia)*

New Caledonia

INDIAN OCEAN

AUSTRALIA

Great Sandy Desert

Macdonnell Ranges

Simpson Desert

Great Barrier Reef

Norfolk Island *(to Australia)*

Gibson Desert

Uluru (Ayers Rock)

L. Eyre North

Grey Range

Darling

Lord Howe Island *(to Australia)*

North

Tropic of Capricorn

Great Victoria Desert

L. Torrens

Great Dividing Range

North Island

NEW ZEALAND

Nullarbor Plain

Murray

Mount Kosciuszko 7310ft (2228m)

Cape Leeuwin

Great Australian Bight

Kangaroo Island

Bass Strait

Tasman Sea

South Island

Aoraki (Mt Cook) 12,218ft (3724m)

Tasmania

Antipo Isla

Auckland Islands *(to New Zealand)*

E   F   G   H

160°   140°   120°

107

Hawaiian Islands
(to US)   20°   1

Johnston Atoll
(to US)

P A C I F I C   O C E A N

Kingman Reef
(to US)

Palmyra Atoll
(to US)   Teraina
                        Tabuaeran
Baker & Howland   • Kiritimati
Islands
(to US)   **134**   2

Jarvis Island
(to US)

KIRIBATI   Equator

hoenix Islands   Malden Island
                        Starbuck Island   KIRIBATI

Tokelau   Northern Cook Islands   Penrhyn   Millennium
(to NZ)   Island
is &   Manihiki   Flint Island
ance)   • Marquesas Islands
SAMOA
            American   Cook Islands
ONGA   Samoa   *(to NZ)*
va'u   *(to US)*
oup.   Tuamotu Islands
            Niue
            (to NZ)   Society Islands
Tongatapu   • Tahiti
Group   Southern Cook Islands   Rarotonga

                        Îles Australes   French Polynesia   Pitcairn,
nadec Islands   *(to France)*   Henderson,
New Zealand)   Ducie &
                              Maroliri   Oeno Islands
                                                      (to UK)   20°   **134**   4
                                          Pitcairn Island
                                                      Tropic of Capricorn

P

                        0 km   1000

                        0 miles   1000

Chatham Islands
(to New Zealand)   5

160°   140°   40°

136

E   F   G   H

The Southwest Pacific

130°   140°   150°   160°   170°

Guam
(US unincorporated
territory)
HAGÁTÑA

134

**MARSHALL
ISLANDS**

Ratak Chain

1

10°

Yap

Caroline Islands

Mi cr o n e s i a

Ralik Chain

*Majuro
Atoll*

NGERULMUD

Chuuk Is.

Pohnpei
PALIKIR

PALAU

MICRONESIA

Kosrae

121

2

0° *Equator*

◆ The Pitohui bird has a poison on its feathers and skin
similar to the poison arrow tree frog, making it the
only known example of a poisonous bird.

NAURU

Tar

Ban

PAPUA NEW GUINEA

INDONESIA

Bismarck Archipelago *New Ireland*

3

*Mt Wilhelm
14,793ft (4509m)* ▲ **Madang**

New Guinea

Lae

Bougainville I.

New Britain

*New
Georgia
Islands*

M e l a n e s i a

PORT MORESBY

*Solomon
Sea*

HONIARA *Santa Cruz
Islands*

10° *Arafura*

Sea

**SOLOMON
ISLANDS**

4

128

*Gulf
of
Carpentaria*

Coral Sea

Banks Is

VANUATU

◆ Found only in the rainforest of New Guinea,
Queen Alexandra's Birdwing, with a wingspan
of 11 inches (280 mm), is the
largest butterfly in the world.

Coral Sea Islands
(Australian external
territory)

PORT VILA

20°

New Caledonia
(French self-governing
territory of
special status)

5

AUSTRALIA

*Îles
Loyauté*

NOUMÉA

Tropic of Capricorn

130°   140°   150°   160°   170°

131

A   B   C   D

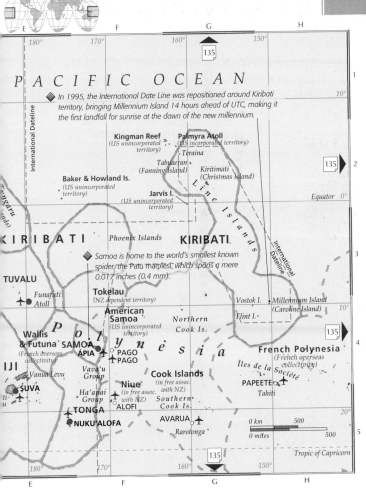

PACIFIC OCEAN

◆ In 1995, the International Date Line was repositioned around Kiribati territory, bringing Millennium Island 14 hours ahead of UTC, making it the first landfall for sunrise at the dawn of the new millennium.

International Dateline

Kingman Reef
(US unincorporated territory)

Palmyra Atoll
(US incorporated territory)

Teraina

Tabuaeran
(Fanning Island)

Kiritimati
(Christmas Island)

Baker & Howland Is.
(US unincorporated territory)

Jarvis I.
(US unincorporated territory)

Line Islands

Equator 0°

KIRIBATI

Phoenix Islands

KIRIBATI

International Dateline

◆ Samoa is home to the world's smallest known spider, the Patu marplesi, which spans a mere 0.017 inches (0.4 mm).

TUVALU

Funafuti Atoll

Tokelau
(NZ dependent territory)

American Samoa
(US unincorporated territory)

Northern Cook Is.

Vostok I.

Millennium Island
(Caroline Island)

Flint I.

Wallis & Futuna
(French overseas collectivity)

SAMOA
APIA

PAGO PAGO

French Polynesia
(French overseas collectivity)

Îles de la Société

PAPEETE

Tahiti

Polynesia

IJI

Vanua Levu

SUVA

ti u

Vava'u Group

Ha'apai Group

Niue
(in free assoc. with NZ)

ALOFI

Cook Islands
(in free assoc. with NZ)

Southern Cook Is.

TONGA

NUKU'ALOFA

AVARUA

Rarotonga

0 km   500

0 miles   500

Tropic of Capricorn

Western Australia

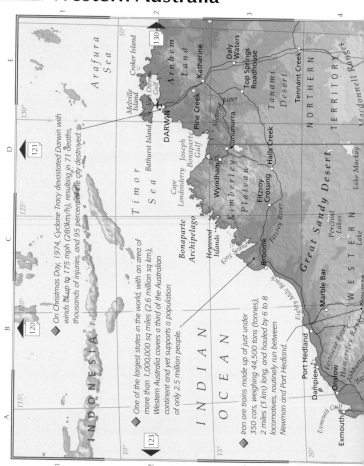

On Christmas Day, 1974, Cyclone Tracy devastated Darwin with winds of up to 175 mph (280km/h), resulting in 71 deaths, thousands of injuries, and 95 percent of the city destroyed.

One of the largest states in the world, with an area of more than 1,000,000 sq miles (2.6 million sq km), Western Australia covers a third of the Australian continent and yet supports a population of only 2.5 million people.

Iron ore trains made up of just under 350 cars, weighing 44,500 tons (tonnes), 2 miles (3 km) long, and hauled by 6 to 8 locomotives, routinely run between Newman and Port Hedland.

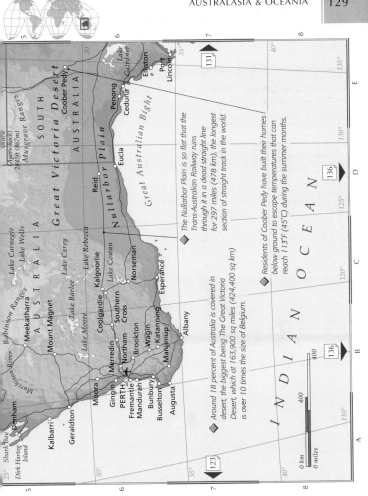

The Nullarbor Plain is so flat that the Trans-Australian Railway runs through it in a dead straight line for 297 miles (478 km), the longest section of straight track in the world.

Residents of Coober Pedy have built their homes below ground to escape temperatures that can reach 113°F (45°C) during the summer months.

Around 18 percent of Australia is covered in desert, the biggest being The Great Victoria Desert, which at 163,900 sq miles (424,400 sq km) is over 10 times the size of Belgium.

Eastern Australia

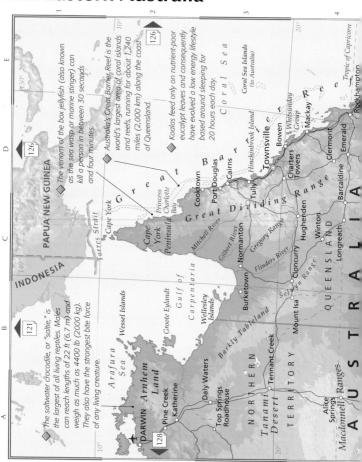

The venom of the box jellyfish (also known as the sea wasp or marine stinger) can kill a person in between 30 seconds and four minutes.

Australia's Great Barrier Reef is the world's largest area of coral islands and reefs, running for about 1,240 miles (2,000 km) along the coast of Queensland.

Koalas feed only on nutrient-poor eucalypt leaves and consequently have evolved a low energy lifestyle based around sleeping for 20 hours each day.

The saltwater crocodile, or "saltie," is the largest of all living reptiles. Males can reach lengths of 22 ft (6.7 m) and weigh as much as 4400 lb (2000 kg). They also have the strongest bite force of any living creature.

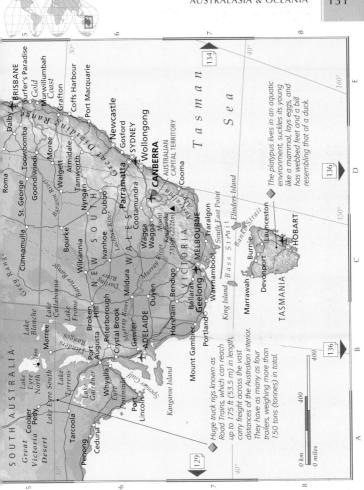

The platypus lives in an aquatic environment, suckles its young like a mammal, lays eggs, and has webbed feet and a bill resembling that of a duck.

Huge road rigs known as Road Trains, which can reach up to 175 ft (53.5 m) in length, carry freight across the vast distances of the Australian interior. They have as many as four trailers, weighing more than 150 tons (tonnes) in total.

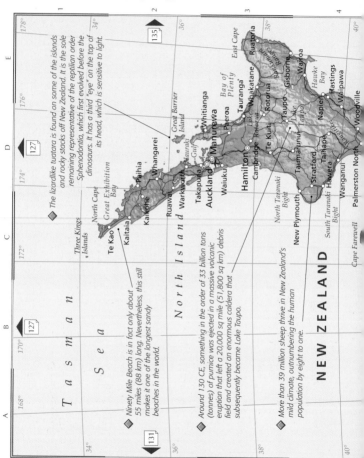

The lizardlike tuatara is found on some of the islands and rocky stacks off New Zealand. It is the sole remaining representative of the reptilian order Sphenodontia, which first evolved before the dinosaurs. It has a third "eye" on the top of its head, which is sensitive to light.

Ninety Mile Beach is in fact only about 55 miles (88 km) long. Nevertheless, this still makes it one of the longest sandy beaches in the world.

Around 130 CE, something in the order of 33 billion tons (tonnes) of pumice was ejected in a massive volcanic eruption that left a 20,000 sq mile (51,800 sq km) debris field and created an enormous caldera that subsequently became Lake Taupo.

More than 39 million sheep thrive in New Zealand's mild climate, outnumbering the human population by eight to one.

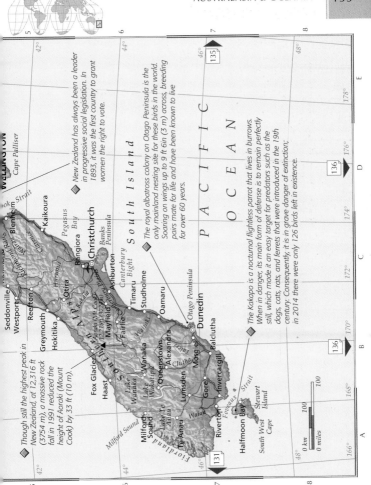

New Zealand has always been a leader in progressive social legislation. In 1893, it was the first country to grant women the right to vote.

The royal albatross colony on Otago Peninsula is the only mainland nesting site for these birds in the world. Soaring on wings up to 9 ft 6 in (3 m) across, breeding pairs mate for life and have been known to live for over 60 years.

The kakapo is a nocturnal flightless parrot that lives in burrows. When in danger, its main form of defense is to remain perfectly still, which made it an easy target for predators such as the dogs, cats, rats, and ferrets that were introduced in the 19th century. Consequently it is in grave danger of extinction; in 2014 there were only 126 birds left in existence.

Though still the highest peak in New Zealand, at 12,316 ft (3754 m), a massive rock fall in 1991 reduced the height of Aoraki (Mount Cook) by 33 ft (10 m).

PACIFIC

OCEAN

South Island

WELLINGTON

Cape Palliser

Blenheim

Cook Strait

Kaikoura

Pegasus Bay

Christchurch

Rangiora

Banks Peninsula

Ashburton

Canterbury Bight

Timaru

Mayfield

Studholme

Fairlie

Oamaru

Otago Peninsula

Dunedin

Balclutha

Mosgiel

Alexandra

Queenstown

Gore

Invercargill

Lumsden

Riverton

Te Anau

Stewart Island

Halfmoon Bay

Foveaux Strait

South West Cape

Fiordland

Milford Sound

Lake Te Anau

Lake Wakatipu

Lake Wanaka

Wanaka

Haast

Fox Glacier

Aoraki/Mt Cook 12,316 ft (3754 m)

Otira

Hokitika

Greymouth

Reefton

Westport

Seddonville

SOUTHERN ALPS

0 km 100

0 miles 100

The Pacific Ocean

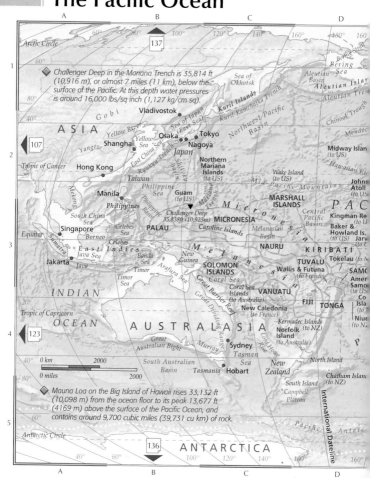

◆ Challenger Deep in the Mariana Trench is 35,814 ft (10,916 m), or almost 7 miles (11 km), below the surface of the Pacific. At this depth water pressures is around 16,000 lbs/sq inch (1,127 kg/cm sq).

◆ Mauna Loa on the Big Island of Hawaii rises 33,132 ft (10,098 m) from the ocean floor to its peak 13,677 ft (4169 m) above the surface of the Pacific, and contains around 9,700 cubic miles (39,731 cu km) of rock.

Arctic Circle

Bering Sea

Sea of Okhotsk

Aleutian Basin

Aleutian Islands

Aleutian Trench

Chinook Trough

Gobi

ASIA

Vladivostok

Sea of Japan (East Sea)

Kuril Islands

Kuril-Kamchatka Trench

Northwest Pacific Basin

Mendo

Yellow River

Yellow Sea

Osaka

Tokyo

Shanghai

Nagoya

Yangtze

East China Sea

Japan

Midway Islan (to US)

Hawaiian Ri

Tropic of Cancer

Hong Kong

Taiwan

Ryukyu Islands

Shikoku Basin

Northern Mariana Islands (to US)

Wake Island (to US)

Johns Atoll (to

Manila

Philippine Sea

Guam (to US)

Challenger Deep 35,838ft (10,923m)

Mariana Trench

Mid Pacific Mountains

Central Pacific Basin

MARSHALL ISLANDS

PAC

Philippines

Kingman R

South China Sea

Singapore

Celebes Sea

Borneo

PALAU

MICRONESIA

Caroline Islands

Micronesia

Melanesian Basin

NAURU

Baker & Howland Is. (to US)

Equator

Sumatra

Java Sea

Celebes

East Indies

Banda Sea

New Guinea

KIRIBATI

Jakarta

Java

Timor Sea

Arafura Sea

SOLOMON ISLANDS

Melanesia

Coral Sea

Tokelau (to N

Wallis & Futuna (to France)

Sam Samo (to U

INDIAN

Great Barrier Reef

Coral Sea Islands (to Australia)

VANUATU

New Caledonia (to France)

FIJI

TONGA

Co Isla (to

Tropic of Capricorn

OCEAN

AUSTRALASIA

Great Dividing Range

Kermadec Islands (to NZ)

Norfolk Island (to Australia)

Niue (to N

Great Australian Bight

Murray

Sydney

Lord Howe Rise

North Island

0 km 2000

South Australian Basin

Tasmania

Tasman Sea

Hobart

New Zealand

South Island

Chatham Islan (to NZ)

0 miles 2000

Campbell Plateau

International Dateline

Pacific

Antar

Antarctic Circle

ANTARCTICA

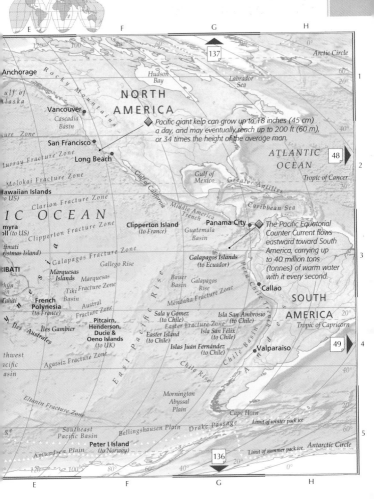

E   F   G   H

137

Arctic Circle

Anchorage

Hudson
Bay

Labrador
Sea

ulf of
Alaska

Rocky Mountains

Vancouver

NORTH
AMERICA

Cascadia
Basin

Pacific giant kelp can grow up to 18 inches (45 cm)
a day, and may eventually reach up to 200 ft (60 m),
or 34 times the height of the average man.

ATLANTIC
OCEAN

48

San Francisco

Long Beach

ure Zone

Murray Fracture Zone

Molokai Fracture Zone

Gulf of
California

Gulf of
Mexico

Greater Antilles

Tropic of Cancer

awaiian Islands
(to US)

IC OCEAN

Middle America Trench

Caribbean Sea

myra
oll (to US)

Clarion Fracture Zone

Clipperton Fracture Zone

Clipperton Island
(to France)

Panama City

Guatemala
Basin

The Pacific Equatorial
Counter Current flows
eastward toward South
America, carrying up
to 40 million tons
(tonnes) of warm water
with it every second.

tīmati
ristmas Island)

Galapagos Fracture Zone

Gallego Rise

Galapagos Islands
(to Ecuador)

RIBATI

Marquesas
Islands

Marquesas

Tiki Fracture Zone

Bauer
Basin

Galapagos
Rise

Callao

Mendaña Fracture Zone

SOUTH

hyn
o US)

French
Polynesia
(to France)

Tahiti

Austral
Fracture Zone

Sala y Gómez

Isla San Ambrosio
(to Chile)

AMERICA

Tropic of Capricorn

Iles Gambier

Pitcairn,
Henderson,
Ducie &
Oeno Islands
(to UK)

Easter Fracture Zone

Easter Island
(to Chile)

Isla San Félix
(to Chile)

Islas Juan Fernández
(to Chile)

Valparaiso

49

Iles Australes

East Pacific Rise

Agassiz Fracture Zone

thwest
cific
asin

Chile Rise

Chile Basin

Eltanin Fracture Zone

Mornington
Abyssal
Plain

8°

Southeast
Pacific Basin

Peter I Island
(to Norway)

Bellingshausen Plain

Cape Horn

Drake Passage

Limit of winter pack ice

Antarctic Circle

Amundsen Plain

Limit of summer pack ice

136

E   F   G   H

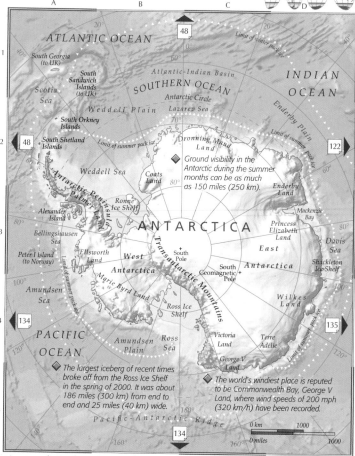

ATLANTIC OCEAN

Atlantic-Indian Basin

SOUTHERN OCEAN

INDIAN OCEAN

South Georgia (to UK)

South Sandwich Islands (to UK)

Scotia Sea

Antarctic Circle

Lazarev Sea

Weddell Plain

Enderby Plain

South Orkney Islands

48

South Shetland Islands

Dronning Maud Land

Limit of summer pack ice

122

Weddell Sea

Coats Land

Enderby Land

◆ Ground visibility in the Antarctic during the summer months can be as much as 150 miles (250 km).

Ronne Ice Shelf

Mackenzie Bay

Antarctic Peninsula

Palmer Land

Princess Elizabeth Land

Alexander Island

ANTARCTICA

East

80°

Bellingshausen Sea

South Pole

Davis Sea

Peter I Island (to Norway)

Ellsworth Land

West Antarctica

South Geomagnetic Pole

Antarctica

Shackleton Ice Shelf

Amundsen Sea

Marie Byrd Land

Transantarctic Mountains

Wilkes Land

134

Ross Ice Shelf

135

PACIFIC OCEAN

Amundsen Plain

Ross Sea

Victoria Land

Terre Adélie

George V Land

◆ The largest iceberg of recent times broke off from the Ross Ice Shelf in the spring of 2000. It was about 186 miles (300 km) from end to end and 25 miles (40 km) wide.

◆ The world's windiest place is reputed to be Commonwealth Bay, George V Land, where wind speeds of 200 mph (320 km/h) have been recorded.

Pacific-Antarctic Ridge

134

0 km   1000

0 miles   1000

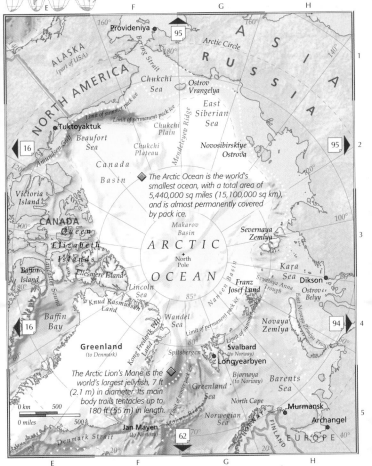

ALASKA
(part of USA)

NORTH AMERICA

RUSSIA

ASIA

Arctic Circle

Providentiya

Bering Strait

Chukchi
Sea

Ostrov
Vrangelya

East
Siberian
Sea

Limit of summer pack ice

Limit of permanent pack ice

Chukchi
Plain

Mendeleyev Ridge

Chukchi
Plateau

Novosibirskiye
Ostrova

Tuktoyaktuk

Beaufort
Sea

Amundsen Gulf

Canada
Basin

◆ The Arctic Ocean is the world's
smallest ocean, with a total area of
5,440,000 sq miles (15,100,000 sq km),
and is almost permanently covered
by pack ice.

Victoria
Island

CANADA

Queen
Elizabeth
Islands

Makarov
Basin

Severnaya
Zemlya

ARCTIC

+ North
Pole

Kara
Sea

Dikson

Baffin
Island

Ellesmere Island

OCEAN

Nansen Basin

Severnaya Anna
Trough

Franz
Josef Land

Ostrov
Belyy

Lancaster Sound

Lincoln
Sea

Knud Rasmussen
Land

Baffin
Bay

Wandel
Sea

Limit of permanent pack ice

Limit of summer pack ice

Novaya
Zemlya

East Novaya Zemlya Trough

Greenland
(to Denmark)

Kong Frederik VIII Land

Spitsbergen

Svalbard
(to Norway)

Longyearbyen

◆ The Arctic Lion's Mane is the
world's largest jellyfish, 7 ft
(2.1 m) in diameter. Its main
body trails tentacles up to
180 ft (55 m) in length.

Bjørnøya
(to Norway)

Greenland
Sea

Barents
Sea

North Cape

Murmansk

0 km   500
0 miles   500

Jan Mayen
(to Norway)

Denmark Strait

Norwegian
Sea

Limit of winter pack ice

FINLAND

EUROPE

Archangel

95

16

95

16

94

62

The world factfiles

North & Central America

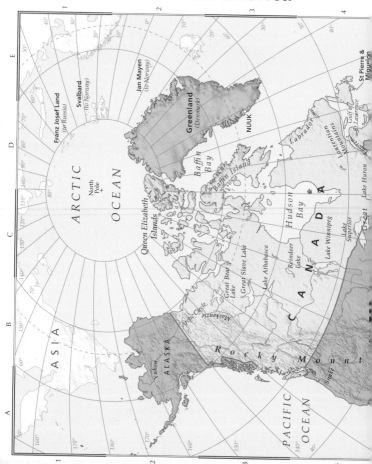

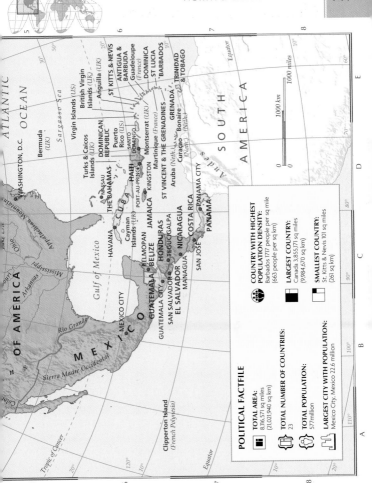

ATLANTIC OCEAN

Sargasso Sea

Bermuda (UK)

Virgin Islands (US)

British Virgin Islands (UK)

Anguilla (UK)

ST KITTS & NEVIS

ANTIGUA & BARBUDA

Guadeloupe (France)

DOMINICA

Martinique (France)

ST LUCIA

BARBADOS

ST VINCENT & THE GRENADINES

GRENADA

Montserrat (UK)

Aruba (Neth.)

Curaçao (Neth.)

Bonaire (Neth.)

TRINIDAD & TOBAGO

SOUTH AMERICA

Andes

Equator

1000 miles

1000 km

WASHINGTON, D.C.

Appalachian Mountains

Ohio

Mississippi

Arkansas

Turks & Caicos Islands (UK)

NASSAU

THE BAHAMAS

Puerto Rico (US)

SANTO DOMINGO

DOMINICAN REPUBLIC

HAITI

PORT-AU-PRINCE

CUBA

HAVANA

Cayman Islands (UK)

JAMAICA

KINGSTON

BELMOPAN

BELIZE

GUATEMALA CITY

GUATEMALA

TEGUCIGALPA

HONDURAS

SAN SALVADOR

EL SALVADOR

MANAGUA

NICARAGUA

SAN JOSÉ

COSTA RICA

PANAMA CITY

PANAMA

Gulf of Mexico

MEXICO CITY

UNITED STATES OF AMERICA

Rio Grande

M E X I C O

Sierra Madre Occidental

Tropic of Cancer

Colo

Clipperton Island (French Polynesia)

Equator

POLITICAL FACTFILE

TOTAL AREA:
8,116,571 sq miles
(21,021,940 sq km)

TOTAL NUMBER OF COUNTRIES:
23

TOTAL POPULATION:
577 million

LARGEST CITY WITH POPULATION:
Mexico City, Mexico 22.6 million

COUNTRY WITH HIGHEST POPULATION DENSITY:
Barbados 1717 people per sq mile
(663 people per sq km)

LARGEST COUNTRY:
Canada 3,855,171 sq miles
(9,984,670 sq km)

SMALLEST COUNTRY:
St Kitts & Nevis 101 sq miles
(261 sq km)

South America

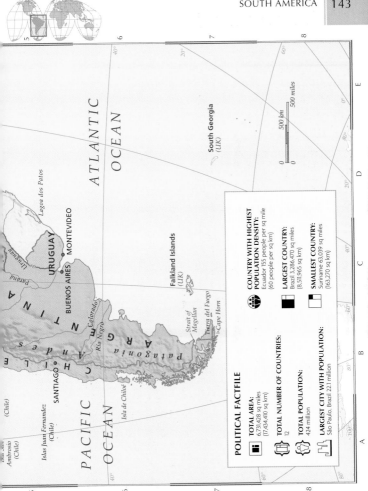

ATLANTIC

OCEAN

South Georgia
(UK)

PACIFIC

OCEAN

Lagoa dos Patos

URUGUAY

MONTEVIDEO

BUENOS AIRES

Paraná

Uruguay

Falkland Islands
(UK)

ARGENTINA

CHILE

Andes

Patagonia

Rio Negro

Colorado

Strait of
Magellan

Tierra del Fuego

Cape Horn

SANTIAGO

Isla de Chiloé

Islas Juan Fernández
(Chile)

Isla San
Ambrosio
(Chile)

500 km

500 miles

0

0

POLITICAL FACTFILE

TOTAL AREA:
6,731,428 sq miles
(17,434,410 sq km)

TOTAL NUMBER OF COUNTRIES:
12

TOTAL POPULATION:
424 million

LARGEST CITY WITH POPULATION:
São Paulo, Brazil 22.1 million

COUNTRY WITH HIGHEST POPULATION DENSITY:
Ecuador 155 people per sq mile
(60 people per sq km)

LARGEST COUNTRY:
Brazil 3,286,470 sq miles
(8,511,965 sq km)

SMALLEST COUNTRY:
Suriname 63,039 sq miles
(163,270 sq km)

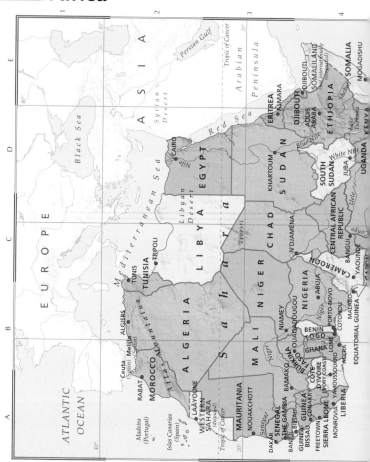

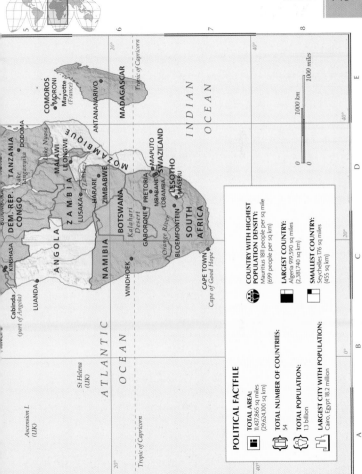

COMOROS
MORONI
Mayotte
(France)
MADAGASCAR
ANTANANARIVO

Tropic of Capricorn

INDIAN
OCEAN

TANZANIA
DODOMA
Lake Nyasa
Lake Tanganyika
DEM. REP.
CONGO
KINSHASA
MALAWI
LILONGWE
Zambezi
MOZAMBIQUE
MAPUTO
SWAZILAND
MBABANE
LOBAMBA
LESOTHO
MASERU

ANGOLA
LUANDA
Cabinda
(part of Angola)

ZAMBIA
LUSAKA
ZIMBABWE
HARARE
BOTSWANA
GABORONE
Kalahari
Desert
PRETORIA
SOUTH
AFRICA
BLOEMFONTEIN

NAMIBIA
WINDHOEK
Orange River

CAPE TOWN
Cape of Good Hope

ATLANTIC
OCEAN

St Helena
(UK)

Ascension I.
(UK)

Tropic of Capricorn

0   1000 km
0   1000 miles

POLITICAL FACTFILE

TOTAL AREA:
11,437,865 sq miles
(29,624,000 sq km)

TOTAL NUMBER OF COUNTRIES:
54

TOTAL POPULATION:
1.3 billion

LARGEST CITY WITH POPULATION:
Cairo, Egypt: 18.2 million

COUNTRY WITH HIGHEST POPULATION DENSITY:
Mauritius 1811 people per sq mile
(699 people per sq km)

LARGEST COUNTRY:
Algeria 919,590 sq miles
(2,381,740 sq km)

SMALLEST COUNTRY:
Seychelles 176 sq miles
(455 sq km)

Europe

POLITICAL FACTFILE

TOTAL AREA:
3,739,678 sq miles
(9,685,756 sq km)

TOTAL NUMBER OF COUNTRIES:
46

TOTAL POPULATION:
720 million

LARGEST CITY WITH POPULATION:
Moscow, European Russia 17 million

**COUNTRY WITH HIGHEST
POPULATION DENSITY:**
Monaco 50,667 people per sq mile
(19,487 people per sq km)

LARGEST COUNTRY:
European Russia 1,527,341 miles
(3,955,818 sq km)

SMALLEST COUNTRY:
Vatican City, Italy 0.17 sq miles
(0.44 sq km)

REYKJAVÍK

ICELAND

Arctic Circle

Norwegian Sea

Faroe Islands
(Denmark)

Shetland Islands

Outer
Hebrides

Orkney Islands

British
Isles

North
Sea

OSLO

IRELAND

UNITED
KINGDOM

DENMARK

DUBLIN

COPENHAGEN

LONDON

AMSTERDAM

NETH.

BELGIUM

THE HAGUE

BERLIN

BRUSSELS

GERMANY

PARIS

LUXEMBOURG

LUXEMBOURG

PRAC

CZECH REPU
(CZECHIA)

Loire

Rhine

LIECH.

BRATISLA

Bay of Biscay

FRANCE

BERN

VIENN

SWITZERLAND

AUSTRIA

SLOVEN

Garonne

LJUBLJANA

ZAGRE

ATLANTIC

OCEAN

PORTUGAL

Ebro

MONACO

CROATIA

SARA

SAN MARINO

BOS
H&

ANDORRA

Corsica

LISBON

MADRID

VATICAN CITY

Tagus

SPAIN

ROME

Madeira
(Portugal)

Guadalquivir

Balearic Islands

Sardinia

Gibraltar
(UK)

Ceuta
(Spain)

Mediterra

Melilla
(Spain)

Canary Islands
(Spain)

Sicily

AFRICA

VALLETTA

MALTA

E F G H

20° 40° 70° 60° 80° 60°

1

Ob'

Irtysh 80°

Ural Mountains

Northern Dvina

Lake Onega

Lake Ladoga R U S S I A 2 50°

HELSINKI

OCKHOLM
TALLINN
ESTONIA
LATVIA RIGA MOSCOW
LITHUANIA *Volga*
Ural 3
ALININGRAD VILNIUS
(Russia) MINSK
BELARUS *Aral Sea*
WARSAW *Don*
OLAND
KYIV *Caspian Sea*
UKRAINE 40°
LOVAKIA since 2014 the Ukrainian
UDAPEST MOLDOVA territory of Crimea has been 4
UNGARY CHIŞINĂU annexed by Russia)
ROMANIA *Dnieper*
RBIA *Caucasus* 60°
BELGRADE BUCHAREST
MONTENEGRO *Danube*
PODGORICA *Black Sea*
PRISHTINE/PRIŠTINA A
S SKOPJE SOFIA BULGARIA S
MACED. TURKEY I
TIRANA A
ALBANIA

GREECE 0 1000 km 5
0 1000 miles

ATHENS

e a *Cyprus* 30°

Crete

E F G H

Asia

E F G H

POLITICAL FACTFILE

TOTAL AREA:
17,006,354 sq miles
(44,046,472 sq km)

TOTAL NUMBER OF COUNTRIES:
49

TOTAL POPULATION:
4.5 billion

LARGEST CITY WITH POPULATION:
Guangzhou, China 45.6 million

**COUNTRY WITH HIGHEST
POPULATION DENSITY:**
Singapore 24,153 people per sq mile
(9344 people per sq km)

LARGEST COUNTRY:
Asiatic Russia 5,065,394 sq miles
(13,119,382 sq km)

SMALLEST COUNTRY:
Maldives 116 sq miles
(300 sq km)

Sea of Okhotsk

Kuril Islands

NORTH KOREA

ONGYANG

ING

SEOUL

SEJONG CITY

SOUTH KOREA

JAPAN

TOKYO

Tropic of Cancer

Ryukyu Islands

TAIPEI

TAIWAN

PACIFIC OCEAN

MANILA

PHILIPPINES

Equator

0   1000 km
0   1000 miles

NEI

BANDAR SERI BEGAWAN

LA

ONESIA

DILI

EAST TIMOR

AUSTRALASIA
& OCEANIA

1

2

3

4

5

Australasia & Oceania

Philippine Sea

Wake Island
(to US)

Northern Mariana Islands
(US)

○ HAGÅTÑA
Guam
(US)

MARSHALL ISLANDS

Maju Atoll

Micronesia

● PALIKIR

Caroline Islands

NGERULMUD
Babeldaob

MICRONESIA

Tarau Atoll

PALAU

Melanesia

NAURU
● NAURU

KIRIBAT

ASIA

Equator

PAPUA NEW GUINEA

PORT MORESBY

SOLOMON ISLANDS
HONIARA

TUVA

Fun

VANUATU

Ashmore & Cartier Islands
(Australia)

Coral Sea Islands
(Australia)

PORT VILA

S

New Caledonia
(France)

F

INDIAN OCEAN

NOUMÉA

AUSTRALIA

Great Dividing Range

Norfolk Island
(Australia)

Lake Eyre North

Lord Howe Island
(Australia)

Lake Torrens

Darling

NEW ZEALAND

Tropic of Capricorn

Murray ● CANBERRA

WELLINGTO

Tasman Sea

Tasmania

E   F   G   H

160°   140°   120°

POLITICAL FACTFILE

TOTAL AREA:
3,244,632 sq miles (8,403,608 sq km)

TOTAL NUMBER OF COUNTRIES:
14

TOTAL POPULATION:
40 million

LARGEST CITY WITH POPULATION:
Sydney, Australia 5.0 million

COUNTRY WITH HIGHEST POPULATION DENSITY:
Nauru 1605 people per sq mile (619 people per sq km)

LARGEST COUNTRY:
Australia 2,967,893 sq miles (7,686,850 sq km)

SMALLEST COUNTRY:
Nauru 8.1 sq miles (21 sq km)

Johnston Atoll
(US)

20° — 1

ker & Howland
Islands
(US)

Jarvis Island
(US)

— 2

P A C I F I C

P   *o*   *l*   *y*   *n*   *e*   *s*   *i*   *a*

KIRIBATI

Phoenix Islands

KIRIBATI

O C E A N

Equator

Tokelau
(NZ)

Marquesas Islands

llis &
una

Cook Islands
(NZ)

American
Samoa
(US)

SAMOA
A'UTU   ÁPIA   PAGO PAGO

PAPEETE

— 3

TONGA

Niue
(NZ)

Society Islands

P   *o*   *l*   *y*   *n*   *e*   *s*   *i*   *a*

NUKU'
ALOFA

AVARUA

French Polynesia
(France)

Pitcairn,
Henderson,
Ducie &
Oeno Islands
(UK)

ermadec Islands
(New Zealand)

Îles Australes

20° — 4

Tropic of Capricorn

International Dateline

P

1000 km

0   1000 miles

— 5

Chatham Islands
(New Zealand)

160°   140°   120°   100°

E   F   G   H

Key to factfile maps

FOREWORD

This factfile is intended as a guide to a world that is continually changing as political fashions and personalities come and go. Nevertheless, all the material in these factfiles has been researched from the most up-to-date and authoritative sources to give an incisive portrait of the geographical, social, and economic characteristics that make each country unique.

KEY TO MAP SYMBOLS

ELEVATION

- 4000m/13,124ft
- 3000m/9843ft
- 2000m/6562ft
- 1000m/3281ft
- 500m/1640ft
- 200m/656ft
- 0
- Below sea level

BORDERS

——— Full international

------ Disputed de facto

·········· Territorial claim

✳✳✳✳✳✳ Cease-fire line

——— State/Province

DRAINAGE FEATURES

——— River

·········· Seasonal river

˖˖˖˖˖˖˖ Canal

⬭ Lake

⬭ Seasonal lake

SYMBOLS

● Capital city

○ Major town

✈ International airport

▲ Mountain

The asterisk in the Factfile denotes the country's official language(s)

Date of formation denotes the date of political origin or independence of a state, i.e. its emergence as a recognizable entity in the modern political world

The area figure denotes total land area

Afghanistan

About 75% of this landlocked Asian country is inaccessible. Governments struggle to assert control in the face of Islamist *Taliban* insurgency and clan-based politics.

GEOGRAPHY

Predominantly mountainous. Highest range is the Hindu Kush. Mountains are bordered by fertile plains. Desert plateau in the south.

CLIMATE

Harsh continental. Hot, dry summers. Cold winters with heavy snow, especially in the Hindu Kush.

PEOPLE & SOCIETY

Mujahideen factions fought first against Soviet invaders (from 1979), and then against each other (after 1989). *Taliban* insurgents won control in 1996 and imposed a strict Islamist regime: women were denied all rights and ethnic tensions were exacerbated. In 2001, a US-led intervention justified as a "war on terrorism" ousted the *Taliban*. NATO assistance against the subsequent insurgency ended in 2014, since when there has been an upsurge in violence.

THE ECONOMY

Mainly agricultural, severely disrupted by war. Illicit opium trade is big cash earner. Natural gas pipeline planned from the Caspian Sea to Pakistan.

INSIGHT: *In the national sport, Buzkashi ('goat-grabbing'), horseriders must snatch a carcass from their opponents and get it to the goal.*

	3000m/9843ft
	2000m/6562ft
	1000m/3281ft
	500m/1640ft
	200m/656ft

0   100 km
0   100 miles

FACTFILE

OFFICIAL NAME: Islamic Republic of Afghanistan

DATE OF FORMATION: 1919

CAPITAL: Kabul

POPULATION: 35.5 million

TOTAL AREA: 250,000 sq. miles (647,500 sq. km)

DENSITY: 141 people per sq. mile

LANGUAGES: Pashtu*, Tajik, Dari*, Farsi, other

RELIGIONS: Sunni Muslim 80%, Shi'a Muslim 19%, other 1%

ETHNIC MIX: Pashtun 38%, Tajik 25%, Hazara 19%, Uzbek and Turkmen 15%, other 3%

GOVERNMENT: Nonparty system

CURRENCY: Afghani = 100 puls

Albania

Lying at the southeastern end of the Adriatic Sea, Albania was the last east European country to liberalize its economy. The regional strife of the 1990s has left a difficult legacy.

GEOGRAPHY

Narrow coastal plain. Interior is mostly hills and mountains. Forest and scrub cover over 40% of the land.

CLIMATE

Mediterranean coastal climate, with warm summers and cool winters. Mountains receive heavy rains or snows in winter.

PEOPLE & SOCIETY

The pace of economic, political, and judicial reforms remain a major issue. Albania's application for EU membership reached candidate status in 2014. Mosques and churches have reopened in what was once the world's only officially atheist state. The Greek minority in the south suffers much discrimination.

◆ **INSIGHT:** *The Albanians' name for their country, Shqipërisë, means "Land of the Eagles"*

THE ECONOMY

Oil and natural gas reserves have potential to offset rudimentary infrastructure and lack of foreign investment. Organized crime problem.

FACTFILE

OFFICIAL NAME: Republic of Albania

DATE OF FORMATION: 1912

CAPITAL: Tirana

POPULATION: 2.9 million

TOTAL AREA: 11,100 sq. miles (28,748 sq. km)

DENSITY: 274 people per sq. mile

LANGUAGES: Albanian*, Greek

RELIGIONS: Muslim (mainly Sunni) 68%, Roman Catholic 12%, Albanian Orthodox 8%, nonreligious 6%, other 6%

ETHNIC MIX: Albanian 98%, Greek 1%, other 1%

GOVERNMENT: Parliamentary system

CURRENCY: Lek = 100 qindarka (qintars)

Algeria

On the Mediterranean coast, and independent from France since 1962, Algeria is now Africa's largest country. Its regime used the army to keep Islamists from power in 1992.

GEOGRAPHY
85% of the country lies within the Sahara Desert. Fertile coastal region with plains and hills rises to meet the Atlas Mountains.

CLIMATE
Coastal areas are warm and temperate, with most rainfall during the mild winters. The south is very hot, with negligible rainfall.

PEOPLE & SOCIETY
Algerians are predominantly Arab, under 35 years of age, and urban. Berbers consider the mountainous Kabylia region in the northeast to be their homeland. They have been granted greater ethnic rights in recent years. The Sahara sustains just 500,000 people, mainly oil workers or Tuareg nomads herding goats and camels. The suppression of the Islamists led to civil war; national reconciliation was achieved, though remains fragile.

THE ECONOMY
Oil and natural gas exports. Political turmoil has led to exodus of skilled foreign labor. Limited agriculture.

◆ **INSIGHT:** *Some of the world's highest dunes are located in the deserts of east central Algeria*

FACTFILE

OFFICIAL NAME: People's Democratic Republic of Algeria

DATE OF FORMATION: 1962

CAPITAL: Algiers

POPULATION: 41.3 million

TOTAL AREA: 919,590 sq. miles (2,381,740 sq. km)

DENSITY: 45 people per sq. mile

LANGUAGES: Arabic*, Tamazight*, French

RELIGIONS: Sunni Muslim 99%, Christian and Jewish 1%

ETHNIC MIX: Arab 75%, Berber 24%, European and Jewish 1%

GOVERNMENT: Presidential system

CURRENCY: Algerian dinar = 100 centimes

Andorra

A tiny landlocked principality, Andorra lies high in the eastern Pyrenees between France and Spain. It held its first full elections in 1993. Tourism is the main source of income.

GEOGRAPHY
High mountains, with six deep, glaciated valleys that drain into the Valira River as it flows into Spain.

CLIMATE
Cool, wet springs followed by dry, warm summers. Mountain snows linger until March.

PEOPLE & SOCIETY
Low taxes attract wealthy expatriates: significant levels of income and investment are prerequisites for residency. A referendum in 1993 ended 715 years of semifeudal status, but Andorran society remains conservative. Over ten million visitors arrive each year, mainly for skiing and duty-free shopping.

◆ INSIGHT: *Andorra's coprincipality status dates from the 13th century. The "princes" are the president of France and the bishop of Urgel in Spain.*

THE ECONOMY
Tourism and duty-free sales dominate the economy. Banking secrecy laws and low consumer taxes promote investment and commerce. France and Spain effectively decide economic policy. The country is dependent on imported food and raw materials.

FACTFILE

OFFICIAL NAME: Principality of Andorra

DATE OF FORMATION: 1278

CAPITAL: Andorra la Vella

POPULATION: 77,000

TOTAL AREA: 181 sq. miles (468 sq. km)

DENSITY: 428 people per sq. mile

LANGUAGES: Spanish, Catalan*, French, Portuguese

RELIGIONS: Roman Catholic 94%, other 6%

ETHNIC MIX: Spanish 46%, Andorran 28%, other 18%, French 8%

GOVERNMENT: Parliamentary system

CURRENCY: Euro = 100 cents

Angola

Located in southwest Africa, Angola suffered a civil war following independence from Portugal in 1975, until a 2002 peace deal. Hundreds of thousands of people died.

GEOGRAPHY
Most of the land is hilly and grass-covered. Desert in the south. Mountains in the center and north.

CLIMATE
Varies from temperate to tropical. Rainfall decreases north to south. Coast is cooler and dry.

PEOPLE & SOCIETY
Civil war pitched the ruling Ambundu-dominated, then-Marxist MPLA against UNITA, representing the Ovimbundu. Peace has held since 2002, except for ongoing separatist conflict in the oil-rich Cabinda exclave. Only a small elite has benefited from Angola's oil wealth; unemployment, corruption, and widespread poverty are key issues.

◆ **INSIGHT:** *Angola has the greatest number of amputees (caused by landmines) in the world*

THE ECONOMY
Abundant natural resources, but long civil war damaged economy. Since the war ended, oil production has driven growth. Diamonds also exported.

2000m/6562ft
1000m/3281ft
500m/1640ft
200m/656ft
Sea Level

0   200 km
0   200 miles

FACTFILE

OFFICIAL NAME: Republic of Angola
DATE OF FORMATION: 1975
CAPITAL: Luanda
POPULATION: 29.8 million
TOTAL AREA: 481,351 sq. miles (1,246,700 sq. km)
DENSITY: 62 people per sq. mile

LANGUAGES: Portuguese*, Umbundu, Kimbundu, Kikongo
RELIGIONS: Roman Catholic 40%, Protestant 38%, nonreligious 12%, other 10%
ETHNIC MIX: Ovimbundu 37%, other 25%, Ambundu 25%, Bakongo 13%
GOVERNMENT: Presidential system
CURRENCY: Readjusted kwanza = 100 lwei

Antarctica

The circumpolar continent of Antarctica is almost entirely covered by ice, some up to 3 miles (4.8 km) thick. It contains 90% of the Earth's freshwater reserves and is designated as a nature reserve, devoted to peace and science.

GEOGRAPHY
The bulk of Antarctica's ice is contained in the Greater Antarctic Ice Sheet – a huge dome that rises steeply from the coast and flattens to a plateau in the interior.

CLIMATE
Antarctica is a cold desert. Strong winds create a storm belt around the continent, which brings clouds, fog, and blizzards. The lowest temperature ever recorded was –128.6°F (–89.2°C).

PEOPLE & SOCIETY
No indigenous population. In the summer as many as 10,000 scientists and logistical staff work at the 44 permanent, and 33 seasonal, research stations; only around 1000 remain for the winter. A few Chilean settler families live on King George Island. Around 40,000 tourists visit each year, mostly by cruise ship to the Antarctic Peninsula.

Territorial Claims:

Chilean claim
Argentinian claim
Brazilian zone of interest
British claim
Norwegian undefined limit
Australian claim
French claim
New Zealand claim

The Antarctic Treaty of 1959 holds all territorial claims in abeyance in the interest of international cooperation

FACTFILE

DATE OF FORMATION: 1961
TOTAL AREA: 5,405,000 sq. miles (14,000,000 sq. km)

◆ **INSIGHT:** *If the ice sheets of Antarctica were to melt, the world's oceans would rise by as much as 200–210 ft (60–65 m)*

Antigua & Barbuda

A former colony of Spain, France, and the UK, Antigua and Barbuda lies at the outer edge of the Leeward Islands group in the Caribbean, and includes the uninhabited islet of Redonda.

GEOGRAPHY
Mainly low-lying limestone and coral islands with some higher volcanic areas. Antigua's coast is indented with bays and harbors.

CLIMATE
Tropical, moderated by trade winds and sea breezes. Humidity and rainfall are low for the region.

PEOPLE & SOCIETY
Most are of African origin; small communities of Europeans, South Asians. Women's status has risen with improved access to education. The Bird family dominated politics from 1960 to 2004; their Antigua Labor Party returned to power in 2014. Hurricane Irma destroyed 90% of buildings on Barbuda in 2017.

◆ **INSIGHT:** In 1865, Redonda was "claimed" by an eccentric Englishman as a kingdom for his son

THE ECONOMY
Tourism is key. Rebuilding Barbuda will take years. Reputation of financial services hurt by international fraud case. Internet gambling industry mired in trade dispute with US.

FACTFILE

OFFICIAL NAME: Antigua and Barbuda

DATE OF FORMATION: 1981

CAPITAL: St. John's

POPULATION: 101,000

TOTAL AREA: 170 sq. miles (442 sq. km)

DENSITY: 594 people per sq. mile

LANGUAGES: English*, English patois

RELIGIONS: Other Christian 49%, other 19%, Anglican 19%, Seventh-day Adventist 13%

ETHNIC MIX: Black African 87%, mixed race 5%, Hispanic 3%, other 3%, White 2%

GOVERNMENT: Parliamentary system

CURRENCY: E. Caribbean $ = 100 cents

Argentina

Argentina occupies most of southern South America.
After 30 years of intermittent military rule, democracy returned
in 1983. Economic crash in 2001 led to largest-ever debt default.

GEOGRAPHY
The Andes form a natural border
with Chile in the west. East are the
heavily wooded plains (Gran Chaco) and
treeless but fertile Pampas plains. Bleak
and arid Patagonia lies in the south.

CLIMATE
The Andes are semiarid in the north
and snowy in the south. Pampas have a
mild climate with summer rains.

PEOPLE & SOCIETY
People are largely of European
descent; over one-third are of Italian
origin. Indigenous peoples are now a tiny
minority, living mainly in Andean regions
or in the Gran Chaco. The middle classes
were worst hit by the banking collapse
and economic meltdown of 2001–2002.

◆ **INSIGHT:** *The Tango originated
in the poorer quarters of Buenos
Aires at the end of the 19th century*

THE ECONOMY
Agricultural exports led recovery.
Recession again in 2014, another default.
Pro-market reforms. Inflation now falling.

FACTFILE

OFFICIAL NAME: Argentine Republic

DATE OF FORMATION: 1816

CAPITAL: Buenos Aires

POPULATION: 44.3 million

TOTAL AREA: 1,068,296 sq. miles
(2,766,890 sq. km)

DENSITY: 42 people per sq. mile

LANGUAGES: Spanish*, Italian, Amerindian
languages

RELIGIONS: Roman Catholic 71%, Protestant
15%, nonreligious 11%, other 3%

ETHNIC MIX: Indo-European 97%, Mestizo
(European–Amerindian) 2%, Amerindian 1%

GOVERNMENT: Presidential system

CURRENCY: Argentine peso = 100 centavos

Armenia

The smallest of the former USSR's republics, Armenia lies landlocked in the Lesser Caucasus Mountains. After 1988, a confrontation with Azerbaijan dominated national life.

GEOGRAPHY
Rugged and mountainous, with expanses of semidesert and a large lake in the east: Sevana Lich.

CLIMATE
Continental climate, with little rainfall in the lowlands. The winters are often bitterly cold.

PEOPLE & SOCIETY
Christianity is the dominant religion, but minority groups are well integrated. War with Azerbaijan over the exclave of Nagorno Karabakh forced 350,000 Armenians living in Azerbaijan to return home, many to live in poverty. There are close and important ties to the 11-million-strong Armenian diaspora.

◆ **INSIGHT:** *In the 4th century, Armenia became the first country to adopt Christianity as its state religion*

THE ECONOMY
Agriculture accounts for a sixth of GDP; overseas remittances are almost as significant. Main products are wine, tobacco, potatoes, and fruit. Well-developed machine-building and manufacturing – includes textiles and bottling of mineral water.

FACTFILE
OFFICIAL NAME: Republic of Armenia

DATE OF FORMATION: 1991

CAPITAL: Yerevan

POPULATION: 2.9 million

TOTAL AREA: 11,506 sq. miles (29,800 sq. km)

DENSITY: 252 people per sq. mile

LANGUAGES: Armenian*, Azeri, Russian

RELIGIONS: Orthodox Christian 89%, other 8%, nonreligious 2%, Armenian Catholic Church 1%

ETHNIC MIX: Armenian 98%, Yezidi 1%, other 1%

GOVERNMENT: Parliamentary system

CURRENCY: Dram = 100 luma

Australia

An island continent in its own right, Australia is the world's sixth-largest country. Europeans first settled in New South Wales, from 1788. Most people now live in coastal cities.

GEOGRAPHY
Located between the Indian and Pacific oceans, Australia has a variety of landscapes, including tropical rainforests, the arid plateaus, ridges, and vast deserts of the "red center," the lowlands and river systems draining into Lake Eyre, rolling tracts of pastoral land, and magnificent beaches around much of the coastline. In the far east are the mountains of the Great Dividing Range. Famous natural features include Uluru (Ayers Rock) and the Great Barrier Reef.

CLIMATE

The west and south are semi-arid with hot summers. The arid interior can reach 120°F (50°C) in the central desert areas. The north is hot throughout the year, and humid during the summer monsoon. East, southeast, and southwest coastal areas are temperate.

PEOPLE & SOCIETY
The first settlers arrived in Australia at least 100,000 years ago. Today, the Aborigines make up around 2% of the population. European colonization began in 1788, and was dominated by British and Irish immigrants, some of whom were convicts. White-only immigration drives brought many Europeans to Australia, but since the 1960s multiculturalism has been encouraged and most new settlers are Asian; Cantonese has overtaken Italian as the second most widely spoken language. Wealth disparities are small, but Aborigines, the exception in an otherwise integrated society, are marginalized: their average life expectancy is around ten years less than other Australians. Illegal immigration is a key political divide; Liberal–National government policies aim to turn back asylum seekers or process and resettle them offshore.

FACTFILE

OFFICIAL NAME: Commonwealth of Australia

DATE OF FORMATION: 1901

CAPITAL: Canberra

POPULATION: 24.5 million

TOTAL AREA: 2,967,893 sq. miles (7,686,850 sq. km)

DENSITY: 8 people per sq. mile

LANGUAGES: English*, Cantonese, other

RELIGIONS: Roman Catholic 28%, nonreligious 24%, Anglican 19%, other Christian 15%, other 9%, United Church 5%

ETHNIC MIX: British 34%, Australian 27%, other 24%, Irish 8%, Italian 4%, Chinese 3%

GOVERNMENT: Parliamentary system

CURRENCY: Australian dollar = 100 cents

THE ECONOMY

Efficient agriculture: beef, wheat, wool, wine. Large resource base, including coal, gas, iron, and bauxite. Protectionism abandoned to open up Australian markets. Concentration on trade with Asia: China's huge demand for coal and minerals make it Australia's dominant trading partner, and rising Asian visitor arrivals have strengthened tourism. Overreliance on mining has left manufacturing neglected. Unemployment is a persistent problem. Droughts, floods, and cyclones have dented economic growth in recent years.

◆ **INSIGHT:** *Australia has the most endemic mammals and reptiles in the world. Species include marsupials such as the kangaroo and wombat, the egg-laying platypus, and the freshwater crocodile*

INDIAN OCEAN

Arafura Sea

Timor Sea

Bamaga ○ Cape York

PACIFIC OCEAN

Darwin ○

Arnhem Land

Gulf of Carpentaria

Kimberley Plateau

Great Barrier Reef

Coral Sea

NORTHERN TERRITORY

Cairns ○

Port Hedland ○

Townsville ○

Great Sandy Desert

Lake Disappointment ○ Lake Mackay

Macdonnell Ranges ○ Alice Springs

Mount Isa ○

Mackay ○

Hamersley Range

Gibson Desert

QUEENSLAND

Rockhampton ○

Uluru (Ayers Rock) ▲ 2831 ft (863m)

Simpson Desert

Bundaberg ○

Fraser I.

Carnarvon ○

WESTERN

Lake Carnegie

Great Victoria Desert

Lake Eyre

SOUTH

Gympie ○

Toowoomba ○ ○ Brisbane
Ipswich ○ Gold Coast
Surfers Paradise
Grafton ○

Meekatharra ○

AUSTRALIA

AUSTRALIA

Flinders Ranges

Darling

Coffs Harbour ○

Geraldton ○

Kalgoorlie ○

Nullarbor Plain

Port Augusta ○

Broken Hill ○

NEW SOUTH WALES

Newcastle ○

Whyalla ○ ○ Port Pirie

Wagga Wagga ○ ○ Sydney

Perth ○
Fremantle ○
Rockingham ○
Bunbury ○

Darling Range

Esperance ○

Port Lincoln ○

Elizabeth ○
Adelaide ○

Albury ○ Wollongong ○

Murray

✦ CANBERRA
Australian Capital Territory

Cape Leeuwin

Albany ○

Kangaroo I.

Bendigo ○

VICTORIA

Australian Alps

Great Australian Bight

Geelong ○ ○ Melbourne

Tasman Sea

Burnie ○

Bass Strait

TASMANIA ○ Launceston

1000m/3281ft
500m/1640ft
200m/656ft
Sea Level
Below Sea Level

Hobart ○

South East Cape

0   400 km
0   400 miles

Austria

Bordering eight countries in the heart of Europe, Austria was created in 1918 after the collapse of the Habsburg Empire. Neutral after World War II, it joined the EU in 1995.

GEOGRAPHY
Mainly mountainous. Alps and foothills cover the west and south. Lowlands in the east are part of the Danube River basin.

CLIMATE
Temperate continental climate. The western Alpine regions have colder winters and more rainfall.

PEOPLE & SOCIETY
Though Austrians speak German, they like to stress their distinctive identity in relation to Germany. Vienna is a major cultural center. Minorities are few; there are some ethnic Croats, Slovenes, and Hungarians, plus refugees from conflict in former Yugoslavia. Though strongly Roman Catholic, Austrian society is less conservative than some southern German *Länder*. Class divisions remain strong.

THE ECONOMY
Large manufacturing base, despite lack of energy resources. The skilled labor force is key to high-tech exports. Eurozone member. Limited GDP growth has returned since 2009 recession.

INSIGHT: *Many of the world's great composers were Austrian, including Mozart, Haydn, Schubert, and Strauss*

3000m/9843ft
2000m/6562ft
1000m/3281ft
500m/1640ft
200m/656ft
Sea Level

FACTFILE
OFFICIAL NAME: Republic of Austria
DATE OF FORMATION: 1918
CAPITAL: Vienna
POPULATION: 8.7 million
TOTAL AREA: 32,378 sq. miles (83,858 sq. km)
DENSITY: 272 people per sq. mile
LANGUAGES: German*, Croatian, Slovenian, Hungarian (Magyar)
RELIGIONS: Roman Catholic 75%, nonreligious 12%, other Christian 8%, Muslim 4% other 1%
ETHNIC MIX: Austrian 93%, Croat, Slovene, and Hungarian 6%, other 1%
GOVERNMENT: Parliamentary system
CURRENCY: Euro = 100 cents

Azerbaijan

Situated on the western coast of the Caspian Sea, it was the first Soviet republic to declare independence in 1991. Territorial disputes with Armenia have dominated politics since.

GEOGRAPHY

Caucasus Mountains in west, including Naxçivan exclave south of Armenia. Flat, low-lying terrain on the coast of the Caspian Sea.

CLIMATE

Low rainfall. Continental, with bitter winters, inland. Subtropical in coastal regions.

PEOPLE & SOCIETY

Azeris, a Muslim people with ethnic links to Turks, form a large majority. Since independence, thousands of Armenians, Russians, and Jews have left, but half a million Azeri refugees have arrived, fleeing war with Armenia over the disputed enclave of Nagorno Karabakh. Armenians there operate with de facto independence. The status of women deteriorated after the fall of communism but they are slowly regaining their former social position.

THE ECONOMY

Oil and natural gas exports drive economic growth. Pipeline to Ceyhan, Turkey, has opened up European market. Severe pollution in Baku.

INSIGHT: *The fire-worshipping Zoroastrian faith originated in Azerbaijan in the 6th century BCE*

FACTFILE

OFFICIAL NAME: Republic of Azerbaijan

DATE OF FORMATION: 1991

CAPITAL: Baku

POPULATION: 9.8 million

TOTAL AREA: 33,436 sq. miles (86,600 sq. km)

DENSITY: 293 people per sq. mile

LANGUAGES: Azerbaijani*, Russian

RELIGIONS: Shi'a Muslim 68%, Sunni Muslim 26%, Russian Orthodox 3%, Armenian Apostolic Church (Orthodox) 2%, other 1%

ETHNIC MIX: Azeri 91%, other 3%, Lazs 2%, Russian 2%, Armenian 2%

GOVERNMENT: Presidential system

CURRENCY: New manat = 100 gopik

The Bahamas

Located off the Florida coast in the western Atlantic, the Bahamas comprises an archipelago of some 700 islands and 2400 cays, only around 30 of which are inhabited.

GEOGRAPHY
Long, mainly flat coral formations with a few low hills. Some islands have pine forests, lagoons, and mangrove swamps.

CLIMATE
Subtropical. Hot summers and mild winters. Heavy rainfall, especially in summer. Hurricanes can strike in July–December.

PEOPLE & SOCIETY
Around 70% of the population live on New Providence. Tourism employs over half of the labor force. There are marked wealth disparities, from urban professionals in the banking sector to traditional fishermen on outlying islands and illegal Haitian and Cuban immigrants. More women are now entering the professions. Government priorities are tackling narcotics trafficking and combating money laundering.

THE ECONOMY
Major tourist destination, especially for US visitors. Financial services: banking and insurance.

INSIGHT: *The country's extensive merchant fleet consists mainly of "flag-of-convenience" vessels registered by foreign owners*

FACTFILE

OFFICIAL NAME: Commonwealth of the Bahamas

DATE OF FORMATION: 1973

CAPITAL: Nassau

POPULATION: 391,000

TOTAL AREA: 5382 sq. miles (13,940 sq. km)

DENSITY: 101 people per sq. mile

LANGUAGES: English*, English Creole, French Creole

RELIGIONS: Baptist 36%, other 29%, Anglican 14%, Roman Catholic 12%, Pentecostal 9%

ETHNIC MIX: Black African 85%, European 12%, Asian and Hispanic 3%

GOVERNMENT: Parliamentary system

CURRENCY: Bahamian dollar = 100 cents

Bahrain

Bahrain is an archipelago of 49 islands between the Qatar peninsula and the Saudi Arabian mainland. Only three of the islands are inhabited. It was the first Gulf emirate to export oil.

GEOGRAPHY

All islands are low-lying. The largest, Bahrain Island, is mainly sandy plains and salt marshes.

CLIMATE

Summers are hot and humid. Winters are mild. Low rainfall.

PEOPLE & SOCIETY

Key social division is between the Shi'a majority and Sunni minority. Sunnis hold the best jobs in bureaucracy and business; Shi'as tend to do menial work. Bahrain is socially liberal. The al-Khalifa family has ruled since 1783, but changed Bahrain to a constitutional monarchy in 2002. Protests calling for greater democracy rocked the country after the 2011 "Arab Spring" but achieved little.

◆ INSIGHT: The 16 Hawar Islands were awarded to Bahrain in 2001 after a lengthy dispute with Qatar

THE ECONOMY

Main exports are refined petroleum and aluminum products.
Oil reserves expected to last 10-15 years; natural gas is of increasing importance. Major Middle East offshore banking center.

FACTFILE

OFFICIAL NAME: Kingdom of Bahrain
DATE OF FORMATION: 1971
CAPITAL: Manama
POPULATION: 1.5 million
TOTAL AREA: 239 sq. miles (620 sq. km)
DENSITY: 5495 people per sq. mile

LANGUAGES: Arabic*
RELIGIONS: Muslim (mainly Shi'a) 70%, other 30%
ETHNIC MIX: Bahraini 46%, Asian 46%, other Arab 5%, other 3%
GOVERNMENT: Mixed monarchical-parliamentary system
CURRENCY: Bahraini dinar = 1000 fils

Bangladesh

Bangladesh lies at the north end of the Bay of Bengal and frequently suffers devastating floods, cyclones, and famine. It seceded from Pakistan in 1971.

GEOGRAPHY

Mostly flat alluvial plains and deltas of the Brahmaputra and Ganges rivers. Southeast coasts are fringed with mangrove forests.

CLIMATE

Hot and humid. During the monsoon, water levels can rise 20 ft (6 m) above sea level.

PEOPLE & SOCIETY

After a period of military rule, Bangladesh returned to democracy in 1991; political instability has continued, however, and corruption is a problem. Just over a quarter of the population live in poverty, but living standards are improving. Women are prominent in politics, but their rights are neglected.

◆ **INSIGHT:** *Torrential monsoon rains flood two-thirds of the country every year*

THE ECONOMY

Agriculture is vulnerable to unpredictable climate. Bangladesh accounts for 80% of world jute fiber exports. Poor infrastructure deters investment. Growing textile industry.

FACTFILE

OFFICIAL NAME: People's Republic of Bangladesh

DATE OF FORMATION: 1971

CAPITAL: Dhaka

POPULATION: 165 million

TOTAL AREA: 55,598 sq. miles (144,000 sq. km)

DENSITY: 3186 people per sq. mile

LANGUAGES: Bengali*, Urdu, Chakma, Marma, Garo, Khasi, Santhali, Tripuri, Mro

RELIGIONS: Muslim (mainly Sunni) 90%, Hindu 9%, other 1%

ETHNIC MIX: Bengali 98%, other 2%

GOVERNMENT: Parliamentary system

CURRENCY: Taka = 100 poisha

Barbados

Barbados is the most easterly of the Caribbean islands.
Once solely inhabited by the native Arawak, Barbados
was first colonized by British settlers in the 1620s.

GEOGRAPHY
Encircled by coral reefs. Fertile and
predominantly flat, with a few gentle hills
to the north.

CLIMATE
Moderate tropical climate. Sunnier
and drier than its more mountainous
neighbors.

PEOPLE & SOCIETY
Independent from the UK since
1966. Some latent tension between the
economically dominant white community
and the majority black population, but
violence is rare. Increasing social mobility
has enabled black Barbadians to enter
the professions. Despite political stability,
and good welfare and education services,
pockets of abject poverty remain.

◆ INSIGHT: *Barbados retains a strong
British influence and is referred to by its
neighbors as "Little England"*

THE ECONOMY
Well-developed tourism sector
based on climate and accessibility.
Financial services, offshore banking,
and information processing are key
industries. Sugar production has
dwindled. High cost of living.

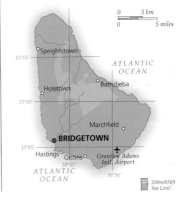

FACTFILE

OFFICIAL NAME: Barbados
DATE OF FORMATION: 1966
CAPITAL: Bridgetown
POPULATION: 285,000
TOTAL AREA: 166 sq. miles (430 sq. km)
DENSITY: 1717 people per sq. mile
LANGUAGES: Bajan (Barbadian English), English*

RELIGIONS: Anglican 24%, nonreligious 21%,
other 21%, Pentecostal 20%,
Seventh-day Adventist 6%, Methodist 4%,
Roman Catholic 4%
ETHNIC MIX: Black African 93%, mixed race 3%,
White 3%, other 1%
GOVERNMENT: Parliamentary system
CURRENCY: Barbados dollar = 100 cents

Belarus

Literally "White Russia," Belarus lies landlocked in eastern Europe. It reluctantly became independent when the USSR broke up in 1991. It has few resources other than agriculture.

GEOGRAPHY

Mainly plains and low hills. The Dnieper and Dvina rivers drain the eastern lowlands. Vast Pripet Marshes in the southwest.

CLIMATE

Extreme continental climate. Winters are long, sub-freezing, but mainly dry; summers are hot.

PEOPLE & SOCIETY

Only 2% of people are non-Slav, so ethnic tension is minimal. Russian culture dominates. Belarus was the slowest ex-Soviet state to implement political reform; President Lukashenka has been labeled as Europe's last dictator. Enthusiasm for a merger with Russia has waned. Wealth is held by a small ex-Communist elite. Fallout from the 1986 Chernobyl nuclear disaster in Ukraine still seriously affects health and the environment.

THE ECONOMY

Industry outmoded and mainly state-owned. Depends on Russia for energy and raw materials: tensions over natural gas prices and oil transit.

INSIGHT: *The number of cancer and leukemia cases soared after the 1986 Chernobyl disaster*

FACTFILE

OFFICIAL NAME: Republic of Belarus

DATE OF FORMATION: 1991

CAPITAL: Minsk

POPULATION: 9.5 million

TOTAL AREA: 80,154 sq. miles (207,600 sq. km)

DENSITY: 119 people per sq. mile

LANGUAGES: Belarussian*, Russian*

RELIGIONS: Orthodox Christian 73%, Roman Catholic 12%, other 12%, nonreligious 3%

ETHNIC MIX: Belarussian 86%, Russian 8%, Polish 3%, other 2%, Ukrainian 1%

GOVERNMENT: Presidential system

CURRENCY: Belarussian rouble = 100 kopeks

Belgium

Belgium lies in northwestern Europe. Its history has been marked by tensions between the majority Dutch-speaking (Flemish) and minority French-speaking (Walloon) communities.

GEOGRAPHY

Low-lying coastal plain covers two-thirds of the country. Land becomes hilly and forested in the southeast (Ardennes).

CLIMATE

Maritime climate with Gulf Stream influences. Mild temperatures, with heavy cloud cover and rain. More rainfall and weather fluctuations at the coast.

PEOPLE & SOCIETY

Since 1970, Flemish regions have become more prosperous than those of the minority Walloons, overturning traditional roles and increasing friction. Belgium moved to a federal system from 1980 in order to contain tensions, but recent fractious politics have raised doubts over the union's survival. The Flemish separatist N-VA heads the Flanders government and since 2010 has been the largest party at federal level. Brussels hosts key EU institutions.

THE ECONOMY

Variety of industrial exports, including steel, glassware, cut diamonds, and textiles. High levels of public debt. Bureaucracy larger than European average.

INSIGHT: *Belgium holds the world record for the country with the longest period without a government*

FACTFILE

OFFICIAL NAME: Kingdom of Belgium
DATE OF FORMATION: 1830
CAPITAL: Brussels
POPULATION: 11.4 million
TOTAL AREA: 11,780 sq. miles (30,510 sq. km)
DENSITY: 900 people per sq. mile

LANGUAGES: Dutch*, French*, German*
RELIGIONS: Roman Catholic 88%, other 10%, Muslim 2%
ETHNIC MIX: Fleming 58%, Walloon 33%, other 6%, Italian 2%, Moroccan 1%
GOVERNMENT: Parliamentary system
CURRENCY: Euro = 100 cents

Belize

Belize lies on the eastern shore of the Yucatan Peninsula. Formerly called British Honduras, Belize was the last Central American country to gain its independence, in 1981.

GEOGRAPHY

Almost half the land area is forested. Low mountains in southeast. Flat swampy coastal plains.

CLIMATE

Tropical. Very hot and humid, with May–December rainy season.

PEOPLE & SOCIETY

English-speaking black Creoles are outnumbered by Spanish speakers, including native *mestizos* (European–Amerindian) and immigrants from neighboring states. The Creoles have traditionally dominated society, but high levels of emigration to the US have weakened their influence. The Afro-Carib *garifuna* have their own language. Corruption, and trafficking of people and narcotics, are major problems.

 INSIGHT: *Belize's barrier reef is the second-largest in the world*

THE ECONOMY

Tourism, agriculture, and offshore banking. Oil extraction began in 2005. Sugar, oil, textiles, citrus, bananas, lobsters, and shrimp are exported. Hurricane damage is a recurring problem.

FACTFILE

OFFICIAL NAME: Belize
DATE OF FORMATION: 1981
CAPITAL: Belmopan
POPULATION: 367,000
TOTAL AREA: 8867 sq. miles
(22,966 sq. km)
DENSITY: 42 people per sq. mile

LANGUAGES: English Creole, Spanish, English*, Mayan, Garifuna (Carib)
RELIGIONS: Roman Catholic 40%, other Christian 34%, nonreligious 16%, other 10%
ETHNIC MIX: *Mestizo* 49%, Creole 24%, Maya 10%, Other 11%, Garifuna 6%
GOVERNMENT: Parliamentary system
CURRENCY: Belizean dollar = 100 cents

Benin

Benin stretches north from the west African coast. In 1990, Benin became one of the pioneers of African democratization, ending 17 years of one-party Marxist-Leninist rule.

GEOGRAPHY

Sandy coastal region. Numerous lagoons lie just behind the shoreline. Forested plateaus inland. Mountains in the northwest.

CLIMATE

Hot and humid in the south. Two rainy seasons. Hot, dusty *harmattan* winds blow during the December–February dry season.

PEOPLE & SOCIETY

There are 42 different ethnic groups. The southern Fon have tended to dominate politics. Other major groups are the Adja and Yoruba. The northern Fulani follow a nomadic lifestyle. North–south tension is mainly due to the south being more developed. French culture, centered on Cotonou, is highly prized. Substantial differences in wealth reflect a strongly hierarchical society.

THE ECONOMY

Agriculture employs almost three-quarters of the workforce: cash crops include cotton, oil palm, and cashew nuts. Smuggling is a serious problem. France is the main aid donor.

INSIGHT:

Voodoo is thought to have originated in Benin, and was taken to Haiti by slaves

500m/1640ft
200m/656ft
Sea Level

0   100 km
0   100 miles

FACTFILE

OFFICIAL NAME: Republic of Benin

DATE OF FORMATION: 1960

CAPITALS: Porto-Novo; Cotonou

POPULATION: 11.2 million

TOTAL AREA: 43,483 sq. miles (112,620 sq. km)

DENSITY: 262 people per sq. mile

LANGUAGES: Fon, Bariba, Yoruba, Adja, Houeda, Somba, French*

RELIGIONS: Indigenous beliefs and Voodoo 50%, Christian 30%, Muslim 20%

ETHNIC MIX: Fon 41%, other 21%, Adja 16%, Yoruba 12%, Bariba 10%

GOVERNMENT: Presidential system

CURRENCY: CFA franc = 100 centimes

Bhutan

Perched in the eastern Himalayas between India and China lies the landlocked Kingdom of Bhutan. It is largely closed to the outside world to protect its culture; TV was banned until 1999.

GEOGRAPHY
Low, tropical southern strip rising through fertile central valleys to high Himalayas in the north. Around 70% of the land is forested.

CLIMATE
South is tropical; north is alpine, cold, and harsh. Central valleys warmer in east than west.

PEOPLE & SOCIETY
The king was absolute monarch until 1998, and the first democratic elections were held a decade later. Most people are devoutly Buddhist and originate from Tibet. The Hindu Nepalese settled in the south. Bhutan has 20 languages. In 1988, Dzongkha (a Tibetan dialect native to just 16% of the people) was made the official language. The Nepalese community regard this as "cultural imperialism," causing considerable ethnic tensions.

THE ECONOMY
Reliant on India for trade. Most people farm their own plots of land and herd cattle and yaks. Steep land unsuited for cultivation. Developing hydropower. Grows cash crops for Asian markets.

 INSIGHT: *In 2004 Bhutan became the first country in the world to ban smoking and the sale of tobacco*

4000m/13124ft
3000m/9843ft
2000m/6562ft
1000m/3281ft
500m/1640ft
200m/656ft
Sea Level

0   50 km
0   50 miles

FACTFILE

OFFICIAL NAME: Kingdom of Bhutan
DATE OF FORMATION: 1656
CAPITAL: Thimphu
POPULATION: 798,000
TOTAL AREA: 18,147 sq. miles (47,000 sq. km)
DENSITY: 44 people per sq. mile

LANGUAGES: Dzongkha*, Nepali, Assamese
RELIGIONS: Mahayana Buddhist 75%, Hindu 25%
ETHNIC MIX: Drukpa 50%, Nepalese 35%, other 15%
GOVERNMENT: Mixed monarchical–parliamentary system
CURRENCY: Ngultrum = 100 chetrum

Bolivia

Landlocked high in central South America, Bolivia is one of the region's poorest countries. La Paz is the world's highest capital city: 13,385 feet (3631 m) above sea level.

GEOGRAPHY

A high windswept plateau, the *altiplano*, lies between two Andean mountain ranges. Semiarid grasslands to the east; dense tropical forests to the north.

CLIMATE

Altiplano has extreme tropical climate, with night-frost in winter. North and east are hot and humid.

PEOPLE & SOCIETY

Wealthy Spanish-descended families have traditionally controlled the economy. The indigenous majority faces widespread discrimination. Amerindian Evo Morales, president from 2005, is cutting poverty, redistributing land, and pushing for inter-national recognition of legal coca use.

◆ INSIGHT: *Between 1825 and 1982 Bolivia averaged more than one armed coup a year*

THE ECONOMY

Gold, silver, zinc, tin, oil, natural gas: all vulnerable to world price fluctuations. Social issues and nationalization of natural gas sector deter investors. Major coca producer. Lack of manufacturing. Resources centered in eastern provinces.

FACTFILE

OFFICIAL NAME: Plurinational State of Bolivia
DATE OF FORMATION: 1825
CAPITALS: Sucre; La Paz (administrative)
POPULATION: 11.1 million
TOTAL AREA: 424,162 sq. miles (1,098,580 sq. km)
DENSITY: 27 people per sq. mile

LANGUAGES: Aymara*, Quechua*, Spanish*
RELIGIONS: Roman Catholic 77%, Protestant 16%, nonreligious 4%, other 3%
ETHNIC MIX: Quechua 37%, Aymara 32%, mixed race 13%, European 10%, other 8%
GOVERNMENT: Presidential system
CURRENCY: Boliviano = 100 centavos

Bosnia & Herzegovina

Perched in the highlands of southeast Europe, Bosnia and Herzegovina was the focus of the bitter ethnic conflict that accompanied the early 1990s dissolution of the Yugoslav state.

GEOGRAPHY

Hills and mountains, with narrow river valleys. Lowlands in the north. Mainly deciduous forest covers about half of the total area.

CLIMATE

Continental. Hot summers and cold, often snowy winters.

PEOPLE & SOCIETY

Despite sharing the same origin and spoken language, Bosnians have been divided by history between Orthodox Serbs, Roman Catholic Croats, and Muslim Bosniaks. Ethnic cleansing was practiced by all sides in the civil war, displacing about 60% of the population. Now the country is politically divided into two entities (Serb and Bosniak).

INSIGHT: *The murder of Archduke Ferdinand of Austria in Sarajevo in 1914 triggered the First World War*

THE ECONOMY

Potential to recover status as a thriving economy centered on tourism, energy, and manufacturing. More foreign investment is needed. The country applied for EU membership in 2016.

FACTFILE

OFFICIAL NAME: Bosnia and Herzegovina

DATE OF FORMATION: 1992

CAPITAL: Sarajevo

POPULATION: 3.5 million

TOTAL AREA: 19,741 sq. miles (51,129 sq. km)

DENSITY: 177 people per sq. mile

LANGUAGES: Bosnian*, Serbian*, Croatian*

RELIGIONS: Muslim (mainly Sunni) 53%, Orthodox Christian 35%, Roman Catholic 8%, nonreligious 3%, other 1%

ETHNIC MIX: Bosniak 48%, Serb 34%, Croat 16%, other 2%

GOVERNMENT: Parliamentary system

CURRENCY: Marka = 100 pfeninga

Botswana

Landlocked in the heart of southern Africa, Botswana boasts the world's largest inland river delta. The country is a major diamond producer, but is badly affected by HIV/AIDS.

GEOGRAPHY

Lies on vast plateau, high above sea level. Hills in the east. Kalahari Desert in center and southwest. Swamps and salt pans elsewhere and in Okavango Basin.

CLIMATE

Dry and prone to drought. Summer wet season, April–October. Winters are warm, with cold nights.

PEOPLE & SOCIETY

The nomadic San bushmen, the first inhabitants, are marginalized. One in five adults is living with HIV (only Swaziland and Lesotho are worse affected) but the government provides free anti-retroviral drugs. Diamond revenue has widened wealth inequalities.

◆ **INSIGHT:** *Water, Botswana's most precious resource, is honored in the name of the currency – pula*

THE ECONOMY

Overreliance on diamonds: vulnerable to world price fluctuations. Copper, nickel, and beef also exported. Tourism aimed at wealthy wildlife enthusiasts. Significant coal reserves.

FACTFILE

OFFICIAL NAME: Republic of Botswana

DATE OF FORMATION: 1966

CAPITAL: Gaborone

POPULATION: 2.3 million

TOTAL AREA: 231,803 sq. miles (600,370 sq. km)

DENSITY: 11 people per sq. mile

LANGUAGES: Setswana, English*, Shona, San, Khoikhoi, isiNdebele

RELIGIONS: Christian 80%, nonreligious 15%, traditional beliefs 4%, other 1%

ETHNIC MIX: Tswana 79%, Kalanga 11%, other 10%

GOVERNMENT: Presidential system

CURRENCY: Pula = 100 thebe

Brazil

Covering almost half of South America, Brazil is the site of the world's largest and ecologically most important rainforest. The country has immense natural and economic resources.

GEOGRAPHY

Rainforest grows around the massive Amazon River and its delta, covering almost half of Brazil's total land area. Apart from the basin of the River Plate to the south, the rest of the country consists of highlands. The mountainous east is part-forested and part-desert. The coastal plain in the southeast has swampy areas. The Atlantic coastline is 1240 miles (2000 km) long.

CLIMATE

Brazil's share of the Amazon Basin has a model tropical equatorial climate, with high temperatures and rainfall all year round. The Brazilian plateau has far greater seasonal variation. The dry northeast suffers frequent droughts, though coastal regions are occasionally flooded by bouts of torrential rain. The south has hot summers and cool winters.

PEOPLE & SOCIETY

Diverse population includes Amerindians, black people of African descent, European immigrants, and those of mixed race. Amerindians suffer prejudice from most other groups. Shanty towns in the cities attract poor migrants from the northeast. Urban crime, violent land disputes, and unchecked development in Amazonia tarnish Brazil's image as a modern nation. Catholicism and the family unit remain strong.

THE ECONOMY

Rich resources, agriculture (coffee, sugar, soybeans); in recession after commodity export boom. Prestige of soccer world cup and 2016 Olympics contrast with underinvestment in basic infrastructure; high youth unemployment and social tensions.

Equato

COLOMB

PERL

FACTFILE

OFFICIAL NAME: Federative Rep. of Brazil
DATE OF FORMATION: 1822
CAPITAL: Brasília
POPULATION: 209 million
TOTAL AREA: 3,286,470 sq. miles (8,511,965 sq. km)
DENSITY: 64 people per sq. mile

LANGUAGES: Portuguese*, German, Japanese, Italian, Spanish, Polish, Amerindian languages
RELIGIONS: Roman Catholic 61%, Protestant 26%, nonreligious 8%, other 5%
ETHNIC MIX: White 48%, mixed race 43%, Black 8%, other 1%
GOVERNMENT: Presidential system
CURRENCY: Real = 100 centavos

INSIGHT: Since 1900, a third of Brazil's indigenous Amerindian groups have become extinct due to disease, starvation, or the forceful taking of land by miners, loggers, and settlers

ENEZUELA

Boa Vista

French Guiana (France)

SURINAME

GUYANA

Guiana Highlands

Macapá

ATLANTIC

Rio Negro

Branco

OCEAN

Amazon

Ilha de Marajó

Belém

Equator

á

A m a z o n

B a s i n

Manaus

Madeira

Santarém

Amazon

Tapajós

São Luís

Parnaíba

Teresina

Fortaleza

San Fernando de Noronha

Purus

Xingu

Iriri

Tocantins

Imperatriz

to Velho

Branco

São Manuel

Aripuanã

Juruena

Juazeiro do Norte

Represa de Sobradinho

Campina Grande

Natal

João Pessoa

Olinda

Recife

Chapada dos Parecis

Guaporé

Planalto de Mato Grosso

Taguatinga

São Francisco

Maceió

10°

BOLIVIA

Paraguay

Cuiabá

Pantanal

Araguaia

BRASÍLIA

Goiânia

B r a z i l i a n

H i g h l a n d s

Montes Claros

Aracaju

Feira de Santana

Salvador

Itabuna

Vitória da Conquista

60°

Uberlândia

Uberaba

Governador Valadares

Campo Grande

Bauru

Belo Horizonte

PARAGUAY

Paraná

Londrina

Ribeirão Preto

Campinas

Nova Iguaçu

São Paulo

Santos

Duque de Caxias

Rio de Janeiro

Vitória

Campos

20°

Curitiba

Joinville

Florianópolis

ATLANTIC

ARGENTINA

Caxias do Sul

Porto Alegre

OCEAN

30°

Pelotas

Lagoa dos Patos

50°

Rio Grande

Mirim Lagoon

URUGUAY

	2000m/6562ft
	1000m/3281ft
	500m/1640ft
	200m/656ft
	Sea Level

0   500 km

0   500 miles

40°

Brunei

Lying on the northern coast of the island of Borneo, Brunei is surrounded and divided in two by the Malaysian state of Sarawak. It has been independent since 1984.

GEOGRAPHY
Mostly dense lowland rainforest and mangrove swamps, with some mountains in the southeast.

CLIMATE
Tropical. Six-month rainy season with very high humidity.

PEOPLE & SOCIETY
Malays benefit from positive discrimination. Many in the Chinese community are stateless. Since a failed rebellion in 1962, Brunei has been ruled by decree of the sultan. In 1990, "Malay Muslim Monarchy" was introduced, promoting Islamic values as state ideology. Women, less restricted than in some Muslim states, usually wear headscarves but not the veil.

◆ **INSIGHT:** *The sultan spent US$350 million building the world's largest palace at Bandar Seri Begawan*

THE ECONOMY
Oil and natural gas production has brought one of the world's highest standards of living. Massive overseas investments. Major consumer of high-tech gadgets, electronic devices, and Western designer clothes.

FACTFILE

OFFICIAL NAME: Brunei Darussalam
DATE OF FORMATION: 1984
CAPITAL: Bandar Seri Begawan
POPULATION: 423,000
TOTAL AREA: 2228 sq. miles (5770 sq. km)
DENSITY: 208 people per sq. mile

LANGUAGES: Malay*, English, Chinese
RELIGIONS: Muslim (mainly Sunni) 79%, Christian 9%, Buddhist 8%, other 4%
ETHNIC MIX: Malay 66%, other 21%, Chinese 10%, indigenous 3%
GOVERNMENT: Monarchy
CURRENCY: Brunei dollar = 100 cents

Bulgaria

Located in southeastern Europe, Bulgaria was under communist rule from 1947 to 1989. Significant political and economic reform since then enabled it to join the EU in 2007.

GEOGRAPHY

Mountains run east–west across center and along southern border. Danube plain in north, Thracian plain in southeast. Black Sea to the east.

CLIMATE

Hot summers, cooler at the coast. Snowy winters, especially in mountains. East winds bring seasonal extremes.

PEOPLE & SOCIETY

The communists tried forcibly to suppress cultural identities; once free movement was allowed in 1989, there was a large exodus of Bulgarian Turks. Privatizations in the 1990s left many Turks landless, prompting further emigration. Roma suffer discrimination at all levels of society. Women have equal rights in theory, but society remains patriarchal. EU accession included caveats demanding further action against organized crime, human trafficking, and corruption.

THE ECONOMY

Good agricultural production, including grapes, for well-developed wine industry, and tobacco. Expertise in software development. Industry and infrastructure are outdated.

INSIGHT: *Archaeologists have found evidence of wine-making in Bulgaria dating back over 5000 years*

FACTFILE

OFFICIAL NAME: Republic of Bulgaria
DATE OF FORMATION: 1908
CAPITAL: Sofia
POPULATION: 7.1 million
TOTAL AREA: 42,822 sq. miles (110,910 sq. km)
DENSITY: 166 people per sq. mile

LANGUAGES: Bulgarian*, Turkish, Romani
RELIGIONS: Orthodox Christian 75%, Muslim 15%, nonreligious 5%, other 3%, Protestant 1%, Roman Catholic 1%
ETHNIC MIX: Bulgarian 85%, Turkish 9%, Roma 5%, other 1%
GOVERNMENT: Parliamentary system
CURRENCY: Lev = 100 stotinki

Burkina Faso

The west African state of Burkina Faso was known as Upper Volta until 1984. It became a multiparty state in 1991, though military ruler Blaise Compaoré held power until 2014.

GEOGRAPHY
The Sahara covers the north of the country. The south is largely savanna. The three main rivers are the Black, White, and Red Voltas.

CLIMATE
Tropical. Dry, cool weather November–February. Erratic rain March–April, mostly in southeast.

PEOPLE & SOCIETY
No single ethnic group is dominant, but the Mossi, from around Ouagadougou, have always played an important part in government. The people from the west are much more ethnically mixed. Extreme poverty has led to a strong sense of egalitarianism. Most women are still denied access to education, though their absence from public life belies their real power and social influence.

THE ECONOMY
Cotton is the major cash crop, but the encroaching Sahara Desert is restricting agriculture. Beneficiary of foreign debt cancellation plans.

INSIGHT: *Droughts and poor soils mean that many Burkinabés seek work southward in Ghana and Côte d'Ivoire*

FACTFILE

OFFICIAL NAME: Burkina Faso
DATE OF FORMATION: 1960
CAPITAL: Ouagadougou
POPULATION: 19.2 million
TOTAL AREA: 105,869 sq. miles (274,200 sq. km)
DENSITY: 182 people per sq. mile

LANGUAGES: Mossi, Fulani, French*, Tuareg, Dyula, Songhai
RELIGIONS: Muslim 61%, Christian 23%, traditional beliefs 15%, other 1%
ETHNIC MIX: Mossi 48%, other 21%, Peul 10%, Lobi 7%, Bobo 7%, Mandé 7%
GOVERNMENT: Presidential system
CURRENCY: CFA franc = 100 centimes

Burundi

Small, densely populated, and landlocked, Burundi lies just south of the equator, on the Nile–Congo watershed in central Africa. It is one of the poorest countries in the world.

GEOGRAPHY
Hilly with high plateaus in center and savanna in the east. Great Rift Valley on western side.

CLIMATE
Temperate, with high humidity. Heavy and frequent rainfall, mostly October–May. Highlands have frost.

PEOPLE & SOCIETY
Burundi has been riven by ethnic conflict between majority Hutu and the Tutsi, who controlled the army – with repeated large-scale massacres: hundreds of thousands of people died between 1993 and 2004. The constitution now guarantees an ethnic balance in the government and army. Twa pygmies were not involved in the conflict.

◆ **INSIGHT:** *Burundi's fertility rate is one of the highest in Africa. On average, women have six children*

THE ECONOMY
Overwhelmingly agricultural economy, mostly subsistence. Small quantities of gold and tungsten. Potential of oil in Lake Tanganyika. Ongoing political fragility.

FACTFILE

OFFICIAL NAME: Republic of Burundi

DATE OF FORMATION: 1962

CAPITAL: Bujumbura

POPULATION: 10.9 million

TOTAL AREA: 10,745 sq. miles (27,830 sq. km)

DENSITY: 1101 people per sq. mile

LANGUAGES: Kirundi*, French*, Kiswahili

RELIGIONS: Roman Catholic 65%, Protestant 23%, other 7%, Muslim 3%, Seventh-day Adventist 2%

ETHNIC MIX: Hutu 85%, Tutsi 14%, Twa 1%

GOVERNMENT: Presidential system

CURRENCY: Burundi franc = 100 centimes

Cambodia

Located on the Indochinese peninsula in southeast Asia, Cambodia has emerged from genocide, civil war, and invasion from Vietnam. Tourism has rebounded, and is a key income earner

GEOGRAPHY
Mostly low-lying basin. Tônlé Sap (Great Lake) drains into the Mekong River. Forested mountains and plateau east of the Mekong.

CLIMATE
Tropical. High temperatures throughout the year. Heavy rainfall during May–October monsoon.

PEOPLE & SOCIETY
Devastated by US bombing, then by the Khmer Rouge regime, whose extreme Marxist program killed over a million between 1975 and 1979, Cambodia then endured further civil conflict and Vietnamese occupation. The effects are still felt, reflected in the high rates of orphans, widows, and land-mine victims. A fragile stability has lasted since elections in 1993. Hun Sen, in office since 1985, is the world's longest-serving prime minister. Poverty is widespread.

THE ECONOMY
Economy is heavily aid-reliant. Garment industry is growing, and accounts for 80% of exports. Rubber, rice, and timber are also exported. Land disputes and corruption issues.

INSIGHT: *Cambodia has many impressive temples (including Angkor Wat), which date from when the country was the center of the Khmer Empire*

FACTFILE

OFFICIAL NAME: Kingdom of Cambodia
DATE OF FORMATION: 1953
CAPITAL: Phnom Penh
POPULATION: 16 million
TOTAL AREA: 69,900 sq. miles (181,040 sq. km)
DENSITY: 235 people per sq. mile

LANGUAGES: Khmer*, French, Chinese, Vietnamese, Cham
RELIGIONS: Buddhist 97%, Muslim 2%, other (mostly Christian) 1%
ETHNIC MIX: Khmer 90%, Vietnamese 5%, other 4%, Chinese 1%
GOVERNMENT: Parliamentary system
CURRENCY: Riel = 100 sen

Cameroon

Situated in the corner of the Gulf of Guinea, Cameroon was effectively a one-party state for 30 years. Multiparty elections, since 1992, regularly return that same party to power.

GEOGRAPHY

Over half the land is forested: equatorial rainforest in north, evergreen forest and wooded savanna in south. Mountains in the west.

CLIMATE

South is equatorial, with plentiful rainfall, declining inland. Far north is beset by drought.

PEOPLE & SOCIETY

Around 230 ethnic groups; no single group is dominant. The Bamileke is the largest, though it has never held political power. North is poorer than the south. Tensions are greater between majority French- and minority English-speakers than between ethnic groups.

◆ **INSIGHT:** *Cameroon's name derives from the Portuguese word* camarões, *after the shrimp fished by the early European explorers*

THE ECONOMY

Oil and gas reserves. Diversified agricultural economy – timber, cocoa, cotton, bananas, coffee. High youth unemployment. Corruption. Port for Chad and CAR. Poor infrastructure.

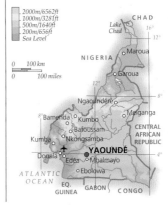

2000m/6562ft
1000m/3281ft
500m/1640ft
200m/656ft
Sea Level

0   100 km
0   100 miles

CHAD
Lake Chad
16°
12°
Maroua
NIGERIA
Garoua
12°
8°
Ngaoundéré
Bamenda   Kumbo   Meiganga
8°
Bafoussam   CENTRAL AFRICAN REPUBLIC
Kumba   Nkongsamba
Douala   YAOUNDÉ
Edéa   Mbalmayo   4°
ATLANTIC OCEAN   Ebolowa
EQ.   GABON   CONGO
GUINEA

FACTFILE

OFFICIAL NAME: Republic of Cameroon
DATE OF FORMATION: 1960
CAPITAL: Yaoundé
POPULATION: 24.1 million
TOTAL AREA: 183,567 sq. miles (475,400 sq. km)
DENSITY: 134 people per sq. mile

LANGUAGES: Bamileke, Fang, Fulani, French*, English*
RELIGIONS: Roman Catholic 35%, traditional beliefs 25%, Muslim 22%, Protestant 18%
ETHNIC MIX: Cameroon highlanders 31%, Bantu 27%, other 21%, Kirdi 11%, Fulani 10%
GOVERNMENT: Presidential system
CURRENCY: CFA franc = 100 centimes

Canada

Canada extends from the Arctic to its US border along the 49th parallel. Unified under British rule from 1763, its development and expansion attracted large-scale immigration.

GEOGRAPHY

The world's second-largest country, stretching north to Cape Colombia on Ellesmere Island, south to Lake Erie, and across five time zones from the Pacific seaboard to Newfoundland. Arctic tundra and islands in the far north give way southward to forests, interspersed with lakes and rivers, and then the vast Canadian Shield, which covers over half the area of Canada. Rocky Mountains in west, beyond which are the Coast Mountains, islands, and fjords. Fertile lowlands in the east.

CLIMATE

Ranges from polar and subpolar in the north, to continental in the south. Winters in the interior are colder and longer than on the coast, with temperatures well below freezing and deep snow; summers are hotter. Pacific coast has the mildest winters.

PEOPLE & SOCIETY

Two-thirds of the population live in the Great Lakes–St. Lawrence lowlands fostering some shared cultural values with the neighboring US. Key differences however, include wider welfare provision French-speaking Québécois, outnumbere by Canadians of English, Scottish, or Irish descent, have pressed for constitutional recognition as a "distinct society" to preserve their culture. Immigration policie have promoted ethnic diversity, with mo recent arrivals from Asian countries addin to sizable communities notably of Italian, German, Dutch, Polish, or Ukrainian origin Indigenous peoples, historically victims o discrimination, now seek redress and recognition of land claims. The Inuit-governed territory of Nunavut, covering nearly a quarter of Canada's land area, wa created from a portion of the Northwest Territories in 1999. Women are well represented in government but less in to business roles.

FACTFILE

OFFICIAL NAME: Canada
DATE OF FORMATION: 1867
CAPITAL: Ottawa
POPULATION: 36.6 million
TOTAL AREA: 3,855,171 sq. miles (9,984,670 sq. km)
DENSITY: 10 people per sq. mile

LANGUAGES: English*, French*, Chinese, other
RELIGIONS: Roman Catholic 39%, other Christian 28%, nonreligious 24%, other 6%, Muslim 3%
ETHNIC ORIGIN: European descent 80%, Asian 15%, First Nations and Métis 5%
GOVERNMENT: Parliamentary system
CURRENCY: Canadian dollar = 100 cents

THE ECONOMY

Canadians enjoy high living standards, with smaller wealth disparities than in the US. Plentiful resources provide exports, cheap energy, and raw materials for manufacturing. Primary exports drive growth when global demand is strong, but Alberta's oil industry in particular depends heavily on world prices. Manufactured exports flourished with the creation in 1994 of the NAFTA free trade area, and the country weathered the recession caused by the 2008–2009 global downturn relatively well. A housing boom helped create additional jobs, but the economy remains vulnerable to changing conditions and policies in the US.

INSIGHT: *The Magnetic North Pole, where the dipping needle of a compass stands still, migrates across northern Canada*

	3000m/9843ft
	2000m/6562ft
	1000m/3281ft
	500m/1640ft
	200m/656ft
	Sea Level

0   400 km
0   400 miles

Cape Verde

Off the west coast of Africa, in the Atlantic Ocean, lies the group of islands that make up Cape Verde, a Portuguese colony until it gained independence in 1975.

GEOGRAPHY

Ten main islands and eight smaller islets, all of volcanic origin. Mostly mountainous, with steep cliffs and rocky headlands.

CLIMATE

Warm and very dry. Subject to droughts that can last for years at a time. Frequent winds carry Saharan dust.

PEOPLE & SOCIETY

Most people are of mixed Portuguese–African origin (*Mestiço*); the rest are descendants of African slaves or more recent immigrants. Creolization of the culture negates ethnic tensions. Over half of the population live on Santiago. More Cape Verdeans live abroad (mostly in the US) than on the islands.

◆ **INSIGHT:** *Poor soils and lack of surface water mean that Cape Verde is dependent on food aid*

THE ECONOMY

Despite lack of rain and arable land, most people are subsistence farmers. No natural resources. Clothing and shoes are exported. Tourism. Mid-Atlantic location ensures work maintaining ships and planes.

FACTFILE

OFFICIAL NAME: Republic of Cabo Verde

DATE OF FORMATION: 1975

CAPITAL: Praia

POPULATION: 540,000

TOTAL AREA: 1557 sq. miles (4033 sq. km)

DENSITY: 347 people per sq. mile

LANGUAGES: Portuguese Creole, Portuguese*

RELIGIONS: Roman Catholic 97%, other 2%, Protestant (Church of the Nazarene) 1%

ETHNIC MIX: *Mestiço* 71%, African 28%, European 1%

GOVERNMENT: Mixed presidential-parliamentary system

CURRENCY: Escudo = 100 centavos

Central African Republic

The Central African Republic (CAR) is a landlocked
country lying between the basins of the Chad and Congo Rivers.
Politics suffers frequent interruption by coups and rebellions.

GEOGRAPHY
Comprises a low plateau,
covered by scrub or savanna. North
is arid. Equatorial rainforests in the
south. The Ubangi River forms the
border with the Democratic Republic
of the Congo.

CLIMATE
The south is equatorial; the
north is hot and dry. Rain occurs all
year round, with heaviest falls
between July and October.

PEOPLE & SOCIETY
The Baya and Banda are the
largest ethnic groups, but the lingua
franca is Sango, a trading creole spoken
by the minorities in the south who have
traditionally provided most political
leaders. Recent rebellions by northern
militias have displaced thousands of
people. The UN ranks the CAR as the
world's least developed country.

THE ECONOMY
Dominated by subsistence farming.
Exports include diamonds, cotton,
timber, and coffee. Aid needed to
support refugees. Instability and
poor infrastructure hinder progress.

◆ INSIGHT: *"Emperor" Bokassa's
eccentric rule from 1965 to 1979 was
followed by military dictatorship until
democracy was restored in 1993*

FACTFILE

OFFICIAL NAME: Central African Republic
DATE OF FORMATION: 1960
CAPITAL: Bangui
POPULATION: 4.7 million
TOTAL AREA: 240,534 sq. miles
(622,984 sq. km)
DENSITY: 20 people per sq. mile

LANGUAGES: Sango*, Banda, Gbaya,
French*
RELIGIONS: Traditional beliefs 35%, Roman
Catholic 25%, Protestant 25%, Muslim 15%
ETHNIC MIX: Baya 33%, Banda 27%,
other 17%, Mandjia 13%, Sara 10%
GOVERNMENT: Presidential system
CURRENCY: CFA franc = 100 centimes

Chad

Landlocked in north-central Africa, Chad has had a turbulent history since independence from France in 1960. Intermittent periods of civil war followed a military coup in 1975.

GEOGRAPHY

Mostly plateaus sloping westward to Lake Chad. Northern third is Sahara. Tibesti Mountains in north rise to 10,826 ft (3300 m).

CLIMATE

Three distinct zones: desert in north, semiarid region in center, and tropics in south.

PEOPLE & SOCIETY

Most people live in the southwest. The northern third has only 100,000 people, mainly Muslim Toubou nomads. Democracy was restored in 1996 by ex-coup leader Idriss Déby, who has won all elections since. Instability has continued, first with tension between Muslims and southern Christians and, more recently, with rebellions in the east.

◆ INSIGHT: Lake Chad is drying up: it is now estimated to be less than 10% of the size it was in 1963.

THE ECONOMY

The discovery of oil, and the opening of a pipeline to the coast via Cameroon, are transforming Chad's economy, though the new wealth is unlikely to reach most people.

3000m/9843ft
2000m/6562ft
1000m/3281ft
500m/1640ft
200m/656ft
Sea Level

FACTFILE

OFFICIAL NAME: Republic of Chad
DATE OF FORMATION: 1960
CAPITAL: N'Djaména
POPULATION: 14.9 million
TOTAL AREA: 495,752 sq. miles (1,284,000 sq. km)
DENSITY: 31 people per sq. mile

LANGUAGES: French*, Sara, Arabic*, Maba
RELIGIONS: Muslim 51%, Christian 35%, traditional beliefs 7%, animist 7%
ETHNIC MIX: Other 30%, Sara 28%, Mayo-Kebbi 12%, Arab 12%, Ouaddai 9%, Kanem-Bornou 9%
GOVERNMENT: Presidential system
CURRENCY: CFA franc = 100 centimes

Chile extends in a ribbon down the west coast of South America. It returned to elected civilian rule in 1989 after a referendum forced out military dictator General Pinochet.

GEOGRAPHY
Fertile valleys in the center between the coast and the Andes. Atacama Desert in north. Deep-sea channels, lakes, and fjords in south.

CLIMATE
Arid in the north. Hot, dry summers and mild winters in the center. Higher Andean peaks have glaciers and year-round snow. Very wet and stormy in the south.

PEOPLE & SOCIETY
Most people are *mestizo* (mixed Spanish–Amerindian descent), and are highly urbanized. General Pinochet's dictatorship was brutally repressive, but the business and middle classes prospered. Around a third of the population live in Santiago, many in large slums. There are three main indigenous groups, including the Rapa Nui of Easter Island.

THE ECONOMY
World's biggest copper producer, but price vulnerable to global fluctuations. Also exports other minerals, paper, fishmeal, fruits, wine, and salmon. Strong foreign investment.

INSIGHT:
Chile's Atacama Desert is the driest place on Earth, making it the perfect location for hi-tech space observatories

	4000m/13124ft
	3000m/9843ft
	2000m/6562ft
	1000m/3281ft
	Sea Level

0   300 km
0   300 miles

FACTFILE
OFFICIAL NAME: Republic of Chile
DATE OF FORMATION: 1818
CAPITAL: Santiago
POPULATION: 18.1 million
TOTAL AREA: 292,258 sq. miles (756,950 sq. km)
DENSITY: 63 people per sq. mile

LANGUAGES: Spanish*, Amerindian languages
RELIGIONS: Roman Catholic 64%, Protestant 17%, nonreligious 16%, other 3%
ETHNIC MIX: *Mestizo* and European 95%, Mapuche 4%, other Amerindian 1%
GOVERNMENT: Presidential system
CURRENCY: Chilean peso = 100 centavos

China

Adjoining 14 countries, China covers much of east Asia, and has the world's largest population. A one-party Communist state since 1949, it is a dominant force in global manufacturing.

GEOGRAPHY

A land of huge physical diversity, China has a long Pacific coastline to the east. Two-thirds of the country is uplands. The southwestern mountains include Tibet, the world's highest plateau. In the northwest, the Tien Shan Mountains separate the arid Tarim and Dzungarian basins. The rolling hills and plains of the low-lying east are home to two-thirds of the population.

CLIMATE

China is divided into two main climatic regions. The north and west are semiarid or arid, with extreme temperature variations. The south and east are warmer and more humid, with year-round rainfall. Winter temperatures vary with latitude, but are warmest on the subtropical southeast coast. Summer temperatures are more uniform, rising above 70°F (21°C).

PEOPLE & SOCIETY

Most are Han Chinese; fewer than one in ten belong to other ethnic groups. Among the 55 recognized minorities, some have disproportionate political significance as they live in strategic border areas. A deeply resented policy of resettling Han Chinese in remote regions led to uprisings in Xinjiang and Tibet. The former one-child family policy, designed to curb population growth, brought some small groups close to extinction before exceptions were allowed. In 2016, policy changed to allow second children, due to concerns about the aging workforce. Society is traditionally patriarchal, with several generations living together. However, economic change is breaking down social controls; unemployment and divorce are rising, the puritanism of the past has given way to materialism, and social media use, on China's own networks, has exploded. By 2017 most Chinese people owned smartphones.

FACTFILE

OFFICIAL NAME: People's Republic of China

DATE OF FORMATION: 960

CAPITAL: Beijing

POPULATION: 1.41 billion

TOTAL AREA: 3,705,386 sq. miles (9,596,960 sq. km)

DENSITY: 391 people per sq. mile

LANGUAGES: Mandarin*, Cantonese, other

RELIGIONS: Nonreligious or traditional beliefs 73%, Buddhist 16%, other 7%, Christian 3%, Muslim 1%

ETHNIC MIX: Han 92%, other 4%, Zhuang 1%, Hui 1%, Manchu 1%, Uighur 1%

GOVERNMENT: One-party state

CURRENCY: Yuan = 10 jiao = 100 fen

THE ECONOMY

Since its first steps away from rigid central planning in 1978, China has seen rapid and sustained growth, becoming the world's second-largest economy and leading exporter. Liberalization came fastest in the south where the emerging business class was strongest. Faced with a global downturn from 2008, China used stimulus packages to boost domestic spending; its huge demand for consumer goods and raw materials helped drive global recovery. Recent five-year plans have emphasized social infrastructure and education, continuing growth at a more moderate pace, and making industry more efficient and sustainable.

◆ **INSIGHT:** *China has the world's oldest continuous civilization. Its recorded history began 4000 years ago, with the Shang dynasty*

4000m/13124ft
3000m/9843ft
2000m/6562ft
1000m/3281ft
500m/1640ft
200m/656ft
Sea Level

0   400 km
0   400 miles

Colombia

Lying in northwest South America, Colombia has coastlines on both the Caribbean and the Pacific. It is primarily noted for its coffee, emeralds, gold, and cocaine trafficking.

GEOGRAPHY

The densely forested and almost uninhabited east is separated from the western coastal plains by the Andes, which divide into three ranges (cordilleras) with intervening valleys.

CLIMATE

Coastal plains are hot and wet. The highlands are much cooler. The equatorial east has two wet seasons.

PEOPLE & SOCIETY

Most people are of mixed blood. Blacks and Amerindians have the least political representation. Civil conflict since the 1960s has killed over 250,000 people and displaced six million; a peace deal was signed in 2016. The fighting was deeply entwined with the narcotics trade. Violent crime is common.

 INSIGHT: *Colombia is the world's main source of emeralds*

THE ECONOMY

Healthy and diversified export sector – includes coffee, oil, and coal. Growth potential, but narcotics-related violence and corruption deter foreign investors. World's largest cocaine producer.

3000m/9843ft
2000m/6562ft
1000m/3281ft
500m/1640ft
Sea Level

0   200 km
0   200 miles

FACTFILE

OFFICIAL NAME: Republic of Colombia

DATE OF FORMATION: 1819

CAPITAL: Bogotá

POPULATION: 49.1 million

TOTAL AREA: 439,733 sq. miles (1,138,910 sq. km)

DENSITY: 122 people per sq. mile

LANGUAGES: Spanish*, Wayuu, Páez, other Amerindian languages

RELIGIONS: Roman Catholic 79%, Protestant 13%, nonreligious 6%, other 2%

ETHNIC MIX: *Mestizo* 58%, White 20%, European–African 14%, African 4%, African–Amerindian 3%, Amerindian 1%

GOVERNMENT: Presidential system

CURRENCY: Colombian peso = 100 centavos

Comoros

Off the east African coast, between Mozambique and Madagascar, lies the archipelago republic of the Comoros, comprising three main islands and a number of smaller islets.

GEOGRAPHY
Main islands are of volcanic origin and are heavily forested. The remainder are coral atolls.

CLIMATE
Hot and humid all year round, especially on the coasts. November to May is the hottest and wettest period.

PEOPLE & SOCIETY
The Comoros has absorbed a diversity of people over the years, including Africans, Arabs, Polynesians, and Persians. There have also been Portuguese, Dutch, French, and Indian immigrants. Ethnic discord is rare, but regional tensions between islands are marked. The country is politically unstable and there have been frequent coups. The islands have their own legislative assemblies and governors. A political and business elite controls most of the wealth.

THE ECONOMY
One of the world's poorest countries. Subsistence-level farming. Vanilla and cloves are main cash crops. Lack of basic infrastructure.

INSIGHT: *The Comoros is the world's largest producer of ylang-ylang – an extract from tree blossom used in manufacturing perfumes*

FACTFILE

OFFICIAL NAME: Union of the Comoros
DATE OF FORMATION: 1975
CAPITAL: Moroni
POPULATION: 796,000
TOTAL AREA: 838 sq. miles
(2170 sq. km)
DENSITY: 925 people per sq. mile

LANGUAGES: Arabic*, Comoran*, French*
RELIGIONS: Muslim (mainly Sunni) 98%, Roman Catholic 1%, other 1%
ETHNIC MIX: Comoran 97%, other 3%
GOVERNMENT: Presidential system
CURRENCY: Comoros franc = 100 centimes

Congo

Astride the equator in west-central Africa, this former
French colony emerged from 20 years of Marxist-Leninist rule in
1990. Democracy was soon overshadowed by years of violence.

GEOGRAPHY

Mostly forest- or savanna-covered plateaus, drained by the Ubangi and Congo river systems. Narrow coastal plain is lined with sand dunes and lagoons.

CLIMATE

Hot, tropical. Temperatures rarely fall below 86°F (30°C). Two wet and two dry seasons. Rainfall is heaviest south of the equator.

PEOPLE & SOCIETY

One of the most tribally conscious and heavily urbanized countries in Africa, with most people living in the Brazzaville–Pointe-Noire region. The main tensions are between the majority Bakongo and the Mbochi, to which long-term president Denis Sassou-Nguesso belongs. Conflict with "ninja" rebels in the Pool region, around Brazzaville, flared up again from 2016.

THE ECONOMY

Oil accounts for 90% of exports. Timber. Foreign debt high, despite two-thirds' reduction in 2010. Industrial base around Brazzaville and Pointe-Noire.

INSIGHT: *In 1970, Congo became the first African country to declare itself a communist state*

FACTFILE

OFFICIAL NAME: Republic of the Congo

DATE OF FORMATION: 1960

CAPITAL: Brazzaville

POPULATION: 5.3 million

TOTAL AREA: 132,046 sq. miles
(342,000 sq. km)

DENSITY: 40 people per sq. mile

LANGUAGES: Kongo, Teke, Lingala, French*

RELIGIONS: Traditional beliefs 50%, Roman Catholic 35%, Protestant 13%, Muslim 2%

ETHNIC MIX: Bakongo 51%, Teke 17%, other 16%, Mbochi 11%, Mbédé 5%

GOVERNMENT: Presidential system

CURRENCY: CFA franc = 100 centimes

Congo, Dem. Rep. (DRC)

A former Belgian colony in east-central Africa, the Democratic Republic of the Congo (DRC) is Africa's second-largest country and the scene of one of its worst regional wars.

GEOGRAPHY
Rainforested basin of Congo River occupies 60% of the land area. High mountain ranges and lakes stretch down the eastern border.

CLIMATE
Tropical and humid. Distinct wet and dry seasons south of the equator. The north is mainly wet.

PEOPLE & SOCIETY
There are 12 main ethnic groups and around 190 smaller ones. Civil war from 1996 drew neighboring countries into a bloody conflict. The indigenous forest pygmies, victimized in the war, are now a marginalized group. Various peace deals have been undermined by splinter rebel groups or intercommunal violence.

THE ECONOMY
Rich resource base: minerals (copper, coltan, cobalt, diamonds) dominate export earnings. War and decades of corruption have caused economic collapse. Food aid is needed to ease humanitarian crisis.

◆ INSIGHT: *The DRC's rainforests comprise 6% of the world's, and 50% of Africa's, remaining woodlands*

FACTFILE

OFFICIAL NAME: Democratic Republic of the Congo
DATE OF FORMATION: 1960
CAPITAL: Kinshasa
POPULATION: 81.3 million
TOTAL AREA: 905,563 sq. miles (2,345,410 sq. km)

DENSITY: 93 people per sq. mile
LANGUAGES: Kiswahili, Tshiluba, French*
RELIGIONS: Christian 70%, Kimbanguist 10%, Muslim 10%, traditional beliefs and other 10%
ETHNIC MIX: Other 55%, Mongo, Luba, Kongo, and Mangbetu-Azande 45%
GOVERNMENT: Presidential system
CURRENCY: Congolese franc = 100 centimes

Costa Rica

Costa Rica, Central America's most stable country, is rich in pristine scenery and exotic wildlife. Its neutrality in foreign affairs is long-standing, but it has strong ties with the US

GEOGRAPHY
Coastal plains of swamp and savanna rise to a fertile central plateau, which leads to a mountain range with active volcanic peaks.

CLIMATE
Hot and humid in coastal regions. Temperate central uplands. High annual rainfall.

PEOPLE & SOCIETY
Most people are *mestizo*, of partly Spanish–partly Amerindian origin. There is a black, English-speaking minority and around 35,000 indigenous Amerindians. Plantation owners are the wealthiest group, while one in five people live in poverty. Nonetheless, living standards are high for the region, and education and healthcare provision is good.

INSIGHT: *Costa Rica's 1949 constitution bans a national army*

THE ECONOMY
Main cash crops: bananas, coffee, and pineapples; vulnerable to fluctuating world prices. Growing industrial base. Stability has attracted multinationals. History of high inflation. Pioneer of eco-tourism. Plans to be the world's first carbon neutral country (by 2021).

FACTFILE

OFFICIAL NAME: Republic of Costa Rica

DATE OF FORMATION: 1838

CAPITAL: San José

POPULATION: 4.9 million

TOTAL AREA: 19,730 sq. miles (51,100 sq. km)

DENSITY: 249 people per sq. mile

LANGUAGES: Spanish*, English Creole, Bribri, Cabecar

RELIGIONS: Roman Catholic 62%, Protestant 25%, nonreligious 9%, other 4%

ETHNIC MIX: *Mestizo* and European 96%, Amerindian 3%, Black 1%

GOVERNMENT: Presidential system

CURRENCY: C.R. colón = 100 céntimos

Côte d'Ivoire (Ivory Coast)

One of the larger nations along the coast of west Africa, Côte d'Ivoire is the world's biggest cocoa producer. Since 2002 its image of stability has been rocked by civil war and electoral chaos.

 GEOGRAPHY
Sandy coastal strip and rainforested interior, with savanna plateau in north.

CLIMATE
Hot all year. Two wet seasons in south; north has one, with lower rainfall.

PEOPLE & SOCIETY
Over 60 tribes; largest is the Baoulé (an Akan group). Southern Christians harbor resentment against non-Ivorian Muslims in the north. Plantations employ millions of migrant workers (including children), though thousands fled back to Burkina during the 2002–2007 civil war. In 2010 President Laurent Gbagbo was ousted when he refused to accept defeat in elections. Rebel fighters were merged into the army: mutinies are a problem.

INSIGHT: *The Basilica of Our Lady of Peace in Yamoussoukro is the largest church in the world*

THE ECONOMY
Main cash crops are cocoa and coffee. Oil is now a major export. Good infrastructure. Lack of professional training. Instability deters investment.

■ 1000m/3281ft	
■ 500m/1640ft	
■ 200m/656ft	
□ Sea Level	

0   100 km
0   100 miles

FACTFILE

OFFICIAL NAME: Republic of Côte d'Ivoire
DATE OF FORMATION: 1960
CAPITAL: Yamoussoukro
POPULATION: 24.3 million
TOTAL AREA: 124,502 sq. miles (322,460 sq. km)
DENSITY: 198 people per sq. mile
LANGUAGES: Akan, French*, Krou, Voltaique

RELIGIONS: Muslim 43%, Nonreligious or traditional beliefs 23%, Roman Catholic 17%, Evangelical 12%, Other 5%
ETHNIC MIX: Akan 42%, Voltaique 18%, Mandé du Nord 17%, Krou 11%, Mandé du Sud 10%, other 2%
GOVERNMENT: Presidential system
CURRENCY: CFA franc = 100 centimes

Croatia

Though it was controlled by Hungary from medieval times and was a part of the Yugoslav state for much of the 20th century, Croatia has a very strong national identity.

GEOGRAPHY
Rocky, mountainous Adriatic coastline is dotted with islands. Interior is a mixture of wooded mountains and broad valleys.

CLIMATE
The interior has a temperate continental climate. Mediterranean climate along the Adriatic coast.

PEOPLE & SOCIETY
Croats are distinguished from Bosniaks and Serbs by their Roman Catholic faith and use of the Latin alphabet. Many Serbs fled Croatia during the early 1990s conflict that accompanied Yugoslavia's breakup. Croatia's entry into the EU, delayed by border disputes with Slovenia, finally occurred in 2013.

◆ **INSIGHT:** *Croatia only regained control of Serb-occupied Eastern Slavonia, around Vukovar, in 1998*

THE ECONOMY
The war cost the economy an estimated $50 billion. Unemployment has been persistently high. Corruption deters foreign investment. Tourism is mainly on the Dalmatian coast. EU membership.

FACTFILE

OFFICIAL NAME: Republic of Croatia
DATE OF FORMATION: 1991
CAPITAL: Zagreb
POPULATION: 4.2 million
TOTAL AREA: 21,831 sq. miles
(56,542 sq. km)
DENSITY: 192 people per sq. mile

LANGUAGES: Croatian*
RELIGIONS: Roman Catholic 84%, nonreligious 7%, Orthodox Christian 4%, other 3%, Muslim 2%
ETHNIC MIX: Croat 92%, Serb 4%, other 3%, Bosniak 1%
GOVERNMENT: Parliamentary system
CURRENCY: Kuna = 100 lipa

Cuba

A former Spanish colony, Cuba is the largest island in the Caribbean. It became the only communist country in the Americas after Fidel Castro seized power in 1959.

GEOGRAPHY
Mostly fertile plains and basins. Three mountainous areas. Forests of pine and mahogany cover one-quarter of the country.

CLIMATE
Subtropical. Hot all year round, and very hot in summer. Heaviest rainfall in the mountains. Hurricanes can strike in the fall; north coast damaged in 2017.

PEOPLE & SOCIETY
The communist regime has reduced formerly extreme wealth disparities, given education a high priority, and established an efficient health service. Political dissent, however, is not tolerated. A dramatic fall in living standards since the late 1980s has led thousands of Cubans to flee to the US, to seek asylum. About 70% of Cubans are of Spanish descent. There is little ethnic tension.

THE ECONOMY
Sugar industry now superseded by tourism and nickel. US trade embargo, since 1961. Shortages drive black market. Parallel use of US dollar (1993–2004), and then convertible peso, boosted investment but created a "dollarized" elite: dual peso system to be scrapped.

INSIGHT: *Fidel Castro was the world's longest-serving non-hereditary ruler, in power from 1959 to 2006. His brother Raúl was then president for a further 12 years.*

FACTFILE

OFFICIAL NAME: Republic of Cuba

DATE OF FORMATION: 1902

CAPITAL: Havana

POPULATION: 11.5 million

TOTAL AREA: 42,803 sq. miles (110,860 sq. km)

DENSITY: 269 people per sq. mile

LANGUAGES: Spanish*

RELIGIONS: Nonreligious 49%, Roman Catholic 40%, atheist 6%, other 4%, Protestant 1%

ETHNIC MIX: White 65%, *Mulatto* (mixed race) 25%, Black 10%

GOVERNMENT: One-party state

CURRENCY: Cuban peso = 100 centavos

Cyprus

Cyprus lies south of Turkey in the eastern Mediterranean. Since 1974, it has been partitioned between the Turkish-occupied north and the Greek-Cypriot south.

GEOGRAPHY
Mountains in the center-west give way to a fertile plain in the east, flanked by hills to the northeast.

CLIMATE
Mediterranean. Summers are hot and dry. Winters are mild, with snow in the mountains.

PEOPLE & SOCIETY
The Greek majority practice Orthodox Christianity. Since the 16th century, a minority community of Turkish Muslims has lived in the north of the island. In 1974 Turkish troops occupied the north and proclaimed the Turkish Republic of Northern Cyprus (TRNC), but it is recognized only by Turkey. Over 100,000 mainland Turks have settled there since. UN-led mediation failed to reunite the island ahead of EU accession in 2004, so the north was left out of membership; peace talks continue.

THE ECONOMY
Tourism. Eurozone member. Weathered 2009 downturn, but banks crashed in 2013: Cypriots lost savings under IMF/EU bailout terms. North lacks investment and wages are lower.

◆ **INSIGHT:** *The Green Line, which separates north from south, was opened for the first time in 2003*

FACTFILE

OFFICIAL NAME: Republic of Cyprus
DATE OF FORMATION: 1960
CAPITAL: Nicosia
POPULATION: 1.2 million
TOTAL AREA: 3571 sq. miles (9250 sq. km)
DENSITY: 336 people per sq. mile

LANGUAGES: Greek*, Turkish*
RELIGIONS: Orthodox Christian 78%, Muslim 18%, other 4%
ETHNIC MIX: Greek 81%, Turkish 11%, other 8%
GOVERNMENT: Presidential systems
CURRENCY: Euro = 100 cents (Turkish lira in TRNC = 100 kurus)

Czech Republic (Czechia)

Once part of Czechoslovakia, a central European communist state in 1948–1989, the Czech Republic peacefully dissolved its union with Slovakia in 1993. It joined the EU in 2004.

GEOGRAPHY
Landlocked in central Europe. Bohemia, the western territory, is a plateau surrounded by mountains. Moravia, in the east, is characterized by hills and lowlands.

CLIMATE
Cool, sometimes cold winters and warm summer months, which bring most of the annual rainfall.

PEOPLE & SOCIETY
Secular and urban society, with high divorce rates (around 50%). Czechs make up the vast majority of the population, while the next largest group are Moravians. The Slovaks left in the Czech Republic after partition are now permitted dual citizenship. Ethnic tensions are few, but there is widespread hostility toward the Roma minority. A new commercial elite is emerging alongside postcommunist entrepreneurs.

THE ECONOMY
Traditional heavy industries (car-making, machinery, iron) have been successfully privatized. Skilled workforce, low unemployment. Prague attracts tourists. Plans to join euro are on hold.

INSIGHT: *Charles University in Prague was founded in the 13th century*

1000m/3281ft
500m/1640ft
200m/656ft
Sea Level

0   50 km
0   50 miles

FACTFILE

OFFICIAL NAME: Czech Republic
DATE OF FORMATION: 1993
CAPITAL: Prague
POPULATION: 10.6 million
TOTAL AREA: 30,450 sq. miles (78,866 sq. km)
DENSITY: 348 people per sq. mile

LANGUAGES: Czech*, Slovak, Hungarian (Magyar)
RELIGIONS: Nonreligious 72%, Roman Catholic 21%, other 6%, Orthodox Christian 1%
ETHNIC MIX: Czech 86%, Moravian 7%, other 5%, Slovak 2%
GOVERNMENT: Parliamentary system
CURRENCY: Czech koruna = 100 haleru

Denmark

Denmark occupies the Jutland peninsula and over 400 islands in southern Scandinavia. Greenland and the Faroe Islands are self-governing associated territories.

GEOGRAPHY

Fertile farmland covers two-thirds of the terrain, which is among the flattest in the world. About 100 islands are inhabited.

CLIMATE

Damp, temperate climate with mild summers and cold, wet winters. Rainfall is moderate.

PEOPLE & SOCIETY

Income distribution is the most even in the West. Danish liberalism is challenged over immigration: cultural clashes have arisen with immigrant minorities. Almost all women now work; Denmark is a world leader in childcare provision. Marriage is becoming less common, even for couples with children.

◆ **INSIGHT:** *Denmark is Europe's oldest kingdom – the monarchy dates back to the 10th century*

THE ECONOMY

Natural gas and oil reserves. Skilled workforce key to high-tech industrial success. Pork, bacon, and dairy products are exported. Opted not to join the euro, though its currency is pegged.

200m/656ft
Sea Level

Skagerrak

Aalborg

Kattegat

Jutland

Viborg   Randers

Silkeborg

Herning   Århus

Horsens

Esbjerg   Vejle   Roskilde   COPENHAGEN

Kolding   Odense

Svendborg   Fyn   Sjælland   Næstved

Sønderborg

North Sea

GERMANY   Lolland   Nykøbing   Falster

Helsingør

Baltic Sea

Bornholm
Rønne

0   50 km
0   50 miles

FACTFILE

OFFICIAL NAME: Kingdom of Denmark
DATE OF FORMATION: 950
CAPITAL: Copenhagen
POPULATION: 5.7 million
TOTAL AREA: 16,639 sq. miles
(43,094 sq. km)
DENSITY: 348 people per sq. mile

LANGUAGES: Danish*
RELIGIONS: Evangelical Lutheran 95%, Roman Catholic 3%, Muslim 2%
ETHNIC MIX: Danish 96%, other (including Scandinavian and Turkish) 3%, Faroese and Inuit 1%
GOVERNMENT: Parliamentary system
CURRENCY: Danish krone = 100 øre

Djibouti

A city-state with a desert hinterland, Djibouti lies in northeast Africa on the Red Sea. Once known as the French Territory of the Afars and Issas, independence came in 1977.

GEOGRAPHY
Mainly low-lying desert and semidesert, with a volcanic mountain range in the north.

CLIMATE
Almost no rain, though the monsoon is very humid. The 109°F (45°C) heat of summer is unbearable.

PEOPLE & SOCIETY
The main ethnic groups are the Issas in the south, and the nomadic Afars in the north: tensions led to conflict in 1991–1994. Smaller tribal groups make up the rest of the population, and the rural peoples are mostly nomadic. Wealth is concentrated in Djibouti city. France exerts considerable influence in Djibouti, supporting it financially and maintaining a naval base and garrison. The US, China, Italy, and Japan also have bases there. Djibouti hosts over 25,000 refugees from Yemen, Somalia, and elsewhere.

THE ECONOMY
Djibouti's major assets are its ports in a key Red Sea location.

INSIGHT: *Chewing the leaves of the mildly narcotic qat shrub is an age-old social ritual in Djibouti*

1000m/3281ft
500m/1640ft
200m/656ft
Sea Level
Below Sea Level

FACTFILE

OFFICIAL NAME: Republic of Djibouti
DATE OF FORMATION: 1977
CAPITAL: Djibouti
POPULATION: 942,000
TOTAL AREA: 8494 sq. miles (22,000 sq. km)
DENSITY: 105 people per sq. mile

LANGUAGES: Somali, Afar, French*, Arabic*
RELIGIONS: Muslim (mainly Sunni) 94%, Christian 6%
ETHNIC MIX: Issa 60%, Afar 35%, other 5%
GOVERNMENT: Presidential system
CURRENCY: Djibouti franc = 100 centimes

Dominica

Dominica is renowned as the Caribbean island that resisted European colonization until the 18th century. It achieved independence from the UK in 1978.

GEOGRAPHY
Mountainous and densely forested. Volcanic activity has given the land very fertile soils, hot springs, geysers, and black sand beaches.

CLIMATE
Tropical, cooled by constant trade winds. Heavy annual rainfall. Tropical depressions and hurricanes are likely June–November.

PEOPLE & SOCIETY
Most Dominicans are descendants of African slaves brought over to work on banana plantations. The Carib Territory in the northeast is home to the only surviving indigenous community in the Caribbean. Wealth disparities are not as marked as elsewhere in the region, but in 2017 all Dominicans were affected by Hurricane Maria, which caused US$1.3 billion of destruction (more than double the GDP), and damaged most buildings.

THE ECONOMY
Based on bananas, but has lost preferential access to EU market. Some diversification: flowers, coffee, and fruit. Agriculture vulnerable to hurricanes. Eco-tourism. Some offshore banking.

◆ INSIGHT: *Dominica is known as "Nature Island," due to its spectacular flora and fauna*

FACTFILE

OFFICIAL NAME: Commonwealth of Dominica

DATE OF FORMATION: 1978

CAPITAL: Roseau

POPULATION: 73,000

TOTAL AREA: 291 sq. miles (754 sq. km)

DENSITY: 252 people per sq. mile

LANGUAGES: French Creole, English*

RELIGIONS: Roman Catholic 62%, Protestant 30%, nonreligious 6%, other 2%

ETHNIC MIX: Black 87%, mixed race 9%, Carib 3%, other 1%

GOVERNMENT: Parliamentary system

CURRENCY: East Caribbean dollar = 100 cents

Dominican Republic

The Dominican Republic occupies the eastern two-thirds of the island of Hispaniola in the Caribbean. Spanish-speaking, it seeks closer ties to the anglophone West Indies.

GEOGRAPHY

Highlands and rainforested mountains – including the highest peak in the Caribbean, Pico Duarte – interspersed with fertile valleys. Extensive coastal plain in the east.

CLIMATE

Hot and humid close to sea level, cooler at altitude. Heavy rainfall, especially in the northeast.

PEOPLE & SOCIETY
White landowners – especially those descended from the original Spanish settlers – form the wealthy elite. The mixed-race majority controls commerce and forms the bulk of the professional middle classes. White and mixed-race women are entering the professions. Great disparities of wealth exist; the black and Haitian-immigrant populations occupy the bottom of the social ladder.

THE ECONOMY
Mining (nickel and gold), sugar, bananas, tobacco, and textiles. Tourism, remittances, and exports all rely heavily on US market. Hidden economy based on trans-shipment of narcotics to US.

INSIGHT: *Santo Domingo is the oldest city in the Americas. It was founded in 1496 by the brother of Christopher Columbus*

FACTFILE

OFFICIAL NAME: Dominican Republic
DATE OF FORMATION: 1865
CAPITAL: Santo Domingo
POPULATION: 10.8 million
TOTAL AREA: 18,679 sq. miles (48,380 sq. km)
DENSITY: 578 people per sq. mile

LANGUAGES: Spanish*, French Creole
RELIGIONS: Roman Catholic 57%, Protestant 23%, nonreligious 18%, other 2%
ETHNIC MIX: Mixed race 73%, European 16%, Black African 11%
GOVERNMENT: Presidential system
CURRENCY: Dominican Republic peso = 100 centavos

East Timor

East Timor occupies the once Portuguese-owned eastern half of the island of Timor. Invaded by Indonesia in 1975, it became independent in 2002 following a long struggle.

GEOGRAPHY

A narrow coastal plain gives way to forested highlands. The mountain backbone rises to 9715 ft (2963 m).

CLIMATE

Tropical. Heavy rain in wet season (December–March), then dry and hot, particularly in the north.

PEOPLE & SOCIETY

The population is almost entirely Roman Catholic. The Timorese are a mix of Malay and Papuan peoples, and many indigenous Papuan tribes survive. There is an urban Chinese minority, and ethnic Indonesian settlers became numerous after 1975 annexation. Preindependence violence in 1999 was politically rather than ethnically motivated. Over half of people are under 25. Women do not have access to the professions, and levels of domestic violence are notably high. Living standards are low.

THE ECONOMY

Widespread poverty. Dependent on Timor Sea oil reserves, but these: could run out soon. Government wants to renegotiate maritime border with Australia. Oil revenue is funding jobs, utilities, and infrastructure.

◆ **INSIGHT:** *Once dependent on sandalwood, the economy now relies almost entirely on oil under the Timor Sea*

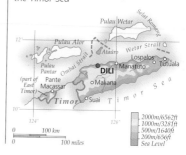

FACTFILE

OFFICIAL NAME: Democratic Republic of Timor-Leste

DATE OF FORMATION: 2002

CAPITAL: Dili

POPULATION: 1.3 million

TOTAL AREA: 5756 sq. miles (14,874 sq. km)

DENSITY: 230 people per sq. mile

LANGUAGES: Tetum* (Portuguese/Austronesian), Bahasa Indonesia, Portuguese*

RELIGIONS: Roman Catholic 96%, Protestant 2%, other 2%

ETHNIC MIX: Papuan groups c. 85%, Indonesian c. 13%, Chinese 2%

GOVERNMENT: Parliamentary system

CURRENCY: US dollar = 100 cents

Ecuador

Once part of the Inca heartland, Ecuador lies on the western coast of South America. Its territory includes the fascinating Galápagos Islands, 610 miles (970 km) to the west.

GEOGRAPHY
Broad coastal plain, inter-Andean central highlands, and dense jungle in upper Amazon basin.

CLIMATE
The climate is hot and moist on the coast, cool in the Andes, and hot equatorial in the Amazon basin.

PEOPLE & SOCIETY
Most people are of Amerindian–Spanish extraction (*mestizo*). Black communities exist on the coast. The strong and largely unified Amerindian movement leads the pressure for social reform. Recent left-wing policies have given greater rights to women, the poor, and Amerindians. Extreme poverty has halved from 17% in 2006 to 8.7% in 2016.

◆ **INSIGHT:** *Darwin's studies on the Galápagos Islands in 1856 played a major part in his theory of evolution*

THE ECONOMY
Oil accounts for around a third of exports: vulnerable to price fluctuations. World's biggest banana exporter. Use of US dollar offers stability, but less control. Earthquake damage in 2016.

FACTFILE

OFFICIAL NAME: Republic of Ecuador
DATE OF FORMATION: 1830
CAPITAL: Quito
POPULATION: 16.6 million
TOTAL AREA: 109,483 sq. miles (283,560 sq. km)
DENSITY: 155 people per sq. mile

LANGUAGES: Spanish*, Quechua, other Amerindian languages
RELIGIONS: Roman Catholic 79%, Protestant 13%, nonreligious 5%, other 3%
ETHNIC MIX: *Mestizo* 79%, Black African 7%, Amerindian 7%, White 6%, other 1%
GOVERNMENT: Presidential system
CURRENCY: US dollar = 100 cents

Egypt

Occupying the northeast corner of Africa, Egypt is divided by the highly fertile Nile Valley. A long tradition of ethnic and religious tolerance has been shaken by the rise in Islamism.

GEOGRAPHY

Fertile Nile Valley separates arid Libyan Desert from smaller semiarid eastern desert. Sinai peninsula has mountains in the south.

CLIMATE

Summers are very hot, but winters are cooler. Rainfall is negligible, except on the coast.

PEOPLE & SOCIETY

Mubarak's military-backed regime was ousted in a popular uprising in the "Arab Spring" of 2011, but the subsequent elected Muslim Brotherhood government was in turn ousted. Clashes between Muslims and Copts are rising. Women's access to education and economic status are threatened by Islamism. Rapidly growing population. Poverty in the south.

◆ INSIGHT: *In 450 BCE Herodotus visited the already-ancient pyramids*

THE ECONOMY

Oil, gas, gold, cotton, and textiles. Tolls from the Suez Canal. Tourism and foreign investment affected by terrorist attacks and ongoing political instability.

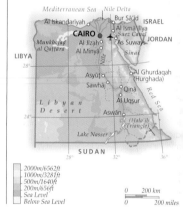

Map labels: Mediterranean Sea, Nile Delta, Al Iskandariyah, Bûr Sa'îd, ISRAEL, Al Isma'îlîya, Suez Canal, JORDAN, CAIRO, Al Jîzah, As Suways, LIBYA, Munkhafad al Qattâra, Al Minyâ, Sinai, 28°, Asyût, Al Ghurdaqah (Hurghada), Sawhâj, Qinâ, Red Sea, Libyan Desert, Al Uqsur, 24°, Aswân, (Hala'ib Triangle), Lake Nasser, SUDAN, 28°, 32°, 36°

2000m/6562ft
1000m/3281ft
500m/1640ft
200m/656ft
Sea Level
Below Sea Level

0   200 km
0   200 miles

FACTFILE

OFFICIAL NAME: Arab Republic of Egypt
DATE OF FORMATION: 1936
CAPITAL: Cairo
POPULATION: 97.6 million
TOTAL AREA: 386,660 sq. miles (1,001,450 sq. km)
DENSITY: 254 people per sq. mile

LANGUAGES: Arabic*, French, English, Berber
RELIGIONS: Muslim (mainly Sunni) 90%, Coptic Christian and other 9%, other Christian 1%
ETHNIC MIX: Egyptian 99%, other (Nubian, Armenian, Greek, Berber) 1%
GOVERNMENT: Presidential system
CURRENCY: Egyptian pound = 100 piastres

El Salvador

El Salvador is Central America's smallest and most densely populated country. Recovery from the 1980s civil war has been set back by earthquakes and other natural disasters.

GEOGRAPHY

El Salvador is a narrow coastal belt backed by two mountain ranges. There is a central plateau. The country is located within a seismic zone, and there are more than 20 volcanic peaks.

CLIMATE

Tropical coastal belt is very hot, with seasonal rains. Cooler, temperate climate in highlands.

PEOPLE & SOCIETY

Ethnic tensions are few. Economic disparities sparked the 1981–1991 civil war between the US-backed government and left-wing FMLN guerrillas; 75,000 people died, many of them unarmed civilians, and human rights abuses were widespread. In 2009 the FMLN won the presidency, but wealth disparities still exist despite some reform. Gangs now control much of daily life; the murder rate has risen again since a short truce.

THE ECONOMY

Coffee, sugar. Garment industry. Overseas remittances. Frequent natural disasters damage infrastructure and deepen country's reliance on aid. Most businesses suffer extortion by gangs. Violence deters investors and tourism.

INSIGHT: *Independent since 1841, El Salvador is named after Jesus Christ, "the savior" of Christians*

FACTFILE

OFFICIAL NAME: Republic of El Salvador

DATE OF FORMATION: 1841

CAPITAL: San Salvador

POPULATION: 6.4 million

TOTAL AREA: 8124 sq. miles (21,040 sq. km)

DENSITY: 800 people per sq. mile

LANGUAGES: Spanish*

RELIGIONS: Roman Catholic 50%, Protestant 36%, nonreligious 12%, other 2%

ETHNIC MIX: Mestizo 86%, White 13%, other and Amerindian 1%

GOVERNMENT: Presidential system

CURRENCY: Salvadorean colón = 100 centavos; US dollar = 100 cents

Equatorial Guinea

Comprising the mainland territory of Río Muni and five islands on the west coast of central Africa, Equatorial Guinea, despite its name, lies just north of the equator.

 GEOGRAPHY

The islands are mountainous and volcanic. The mainland is lower, with mangrove swamps along the coast.

 CLIMATE

The island of Bioco is extremely wet and humid. The mainland is only marginally drier and cooler.

PEOPLE & SOCIETY

The only Spanish-speaking country in Africa. Río Muni is sparsely populated: most people there are Fang, an ethnic group also found in Cameroon and northern Gabon. Bioco is populated by Bubi and a minority of Creoles known as Fernandinos. Tensions between the two territories have been reignited by the discovery of oil off Bioco. President Obiang Nguema has held power since 1979. Wealth is concentrated in the ruling clan; most people are farmers, living at the subsistence level.

 THE ECONOMY

Oil and gas now account for almost all of exports; the government has promised to reinvest oil funds in development. Timber also exported.

 INSIGHT: *In 2003, state radio declared President Obiang Nguema to be "like God in Heaven"*

2000m/6562ft	
1000m/3281ft	
500m/1640ft	
200m/656ft	
Sea Level	

MALABO

Isla da Bioco

Bight of Biafra

ATLANTIC OCEAN

CAMEROON

Micomeseng

Gulf of Guinea

Bata   Niefang

Mbini   Mongomo

Río Muni   Uolo

Cabo San Juan   Etembue

Cogo   Nsoc

Isla de Corisco

GABON

0   40 km
0   40 miles

FACTFILE

OFFICIAL NAME: Republic of Equatorial Guinea

DATE OF FORMATION: 1968

CAPITAL: Malabo

POPULATION: 1.3 million

TOTAL AREA: 10,830 sq. miles (28,051 sq. km)

DENSITY: 120 people per sq. mile

LANGUAGES: Spanish*, Fang, Bubi, French*

RELIGIONS: Roman Catholic 90%, other 10%

ETHNIC MIX: Fang 85%, other 11%, Bubi 4%

GOVERNMENT: Presidential system

CURRENCY: CFA franc = 100 centimes

Eritrea

Lying along the southwest shore of the Red Sea, Eritrea won a long war for independence from Ethiopia in 1993. The two neighbors fought a bitter border war in 1998–2000.

GEOGRAPHY
Mostly consists of rugged mountains, bush, and the Danakil Desert, which falls below sea level.

CLIMATE
Warm in the mountains; desert areas are hot. Droughts from July onward are common.

PEOPLE & SOCIETY
Tigrinya-speakers, mainly Orthodox Christians, are the most numerous of nine main ethnic groups. A strong sense of nationhood has been forged by war. Women played a vital role in combat. Over three-quarters of people are subsistence farmers. Multiparty elections, due under the 1997 constitution, are yet to be held.

INSIGHT: *Eritrea was modern Italy's first African colony. It's named for the ancient Greek for Red Sea: Erythra Thalassa*

THE ECONOMY
Legacy of disruption and destruction from wars; resettlement of refugees. Susceptible to drought and famine: dependent on food aid. Most of the population live at subsistence level. Potential for extraction of gold, copper, and oil. Red Sea location: port at Massawa.

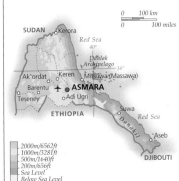

	2000m/6562ft
	1000m/328ft
	500m/1640ft
	200m/656ft
	Sea Level
	Below Sea Level

FACTFILE

OFFICIAL NAME: State of Eritrea

DATE OF FORMATION: 1993

CAPITAL: Asmara

POPULATION: 5.1 million

TOTAL AREA: 46,842 sq. miles (121,320 sq. km)

DENSITY: 112 people per sq. mile

LANGUAGES: Tigrinya*, English*, Tigre, Afar, Arabic*, Saho, Bilen, Kunama, Nara, Hadareb

RELIGIONS: Christian 50%, Muslim 48%, other 2%

ETHNIC MIX: Tigray 50%, Tigre 31%, other 9%, Saho 5%, Afar 5%

GOVERNMENT: Mixed presidential–parliamentary system

CURRENCY: Nakfa = 100 cents

Estonia

The smallest and most Western-oriented of the former Soviet-ruled Baltic states, Estonia is also the most developed, but its standard of living is well below the EU average.

GEOGRAPHY

Estonia's terrain is flat, boggy, and partly forested, with over 1500 islands. Lake Peipus forms much of the eastern border with Russia.

CLIMATE

Maritime, with some continental extremes. Harsh winters, with cool summers and damp springs.

PEOPLE & SOCIETY

Estonians are related ethnically and linguistically to the Finns. Friction between ethnic Estonians and the large Russian minority led to a reassertion of Estonian culture and language. Outright discrimination against the Russian language was only ended in 2000. Estonians are predominantly Lutheran. Families are small. The divorce rate has reduced since the 1980s peak. Market reforms have increased prosperity; a few people have become very rich.

THE ECONOMY

Timber, oil shale. Service-based economy. Low debt burden. Good productivity and competitiveness. Joined EU in 2004, but first EU country to enter recession in 2008. Drastic spending cuts aided quick revival. Adopted euro in 2011.

INSIGHT: *Estonia pioneered online voting in 2007, and voting by cell phone in 2011*

FACTFILE

OFFICIAL NAME: Republic of Estonia
DATE OF FORMATION: 1991
CAPITAL: Tallinn
POPULATION: 1.3 million
TOTAL AREA: 17,462 sq. miles (45,226 sq. km)
DENSITY: 75 people per sq. mile

LANGUAGES: Estonian*, Russian
RELIGIONS: Nonreligious 45%, Orthodox Christian 25%, Lutheran 20%, other 10%
ETHNIC MIX: Estonian 70%, Russian 25%, other 2%, Ukrainian 2%, Belarussian 1%
GOVERNMENT: Parliamentary system
CURRENCY: Euro = 100 cents

Ethiopia

The former empire of Ethiopia once dominated northeast Africa. A Marxist regime in 1974–1991, now a free-market democracy, it has suffered economic, civil, and natural crises.

GEOGRAPHY

Great Rift Valley divides desert lowlands in northeast and southeast from mountainous northwest. Ethiopian Plateau drained mainly by the Blue Nile.

CLIMATE

Moderate, with summer rains. Highlands are warm, with night frost and snowfalls on the mountains.

PEOPLE & SOCIETY

Around 80 nationalities speak over 200 languages. Oromo (or Gallas) are largest group. Ethnic representation is a major political issue. Sporadic conflict with Eritrea since its secession. Orthodox Christianity has a very ancient history in Ethiopia. Former emperor Haile Selassie inspired Rastafarianism.

◆ **INSIGHT:** *King Solomon and the Queen of Sheba are said to have founded the Kingdom of Abyssinia (Ethiopia) c. 1000 BCE*

THE ECONOMY

Overwhelmingly dependent on agriculture; coffee is main export crop. War-damaged infrastructure and periodic serious droughts and famines undermine growth. There is a heavy reliance on food aid. Landlocked since secession of Eritrea.

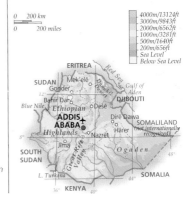

0 200 km	4000m/13124ft
0 200 miles	3000m/9843ft
	2000m/6562ft
	1000m/3281ft
	500m/1640ft
	200m/656ft
	Sea Level
	Below Sea Level

FACTFILE

OFFICIAL NAME: Federal Democratic Republic of Ethiopia

DATE OF FORMATION: 1896

CAPITAL: Addis Ababa

POPULATION: 105 million

TOTAL AREA: 435,184 sq. miles (1,127,127 sq. km)

DENSITY: 245 people per sq. mile

LANGUAGES: Amharic*, Tigrinya, other

RELIGIONS: Orthodox Christian 44%, Muslim 34%, Protestant 18%, traditional beliefs 3%, other 1%

ETHNIC MIX: Oromo 34%, Amhara 27%, other 23%, Somali 6%, Tigray 6%, Sidama 4%

GOVERNMENT: Parliamentary system

CURRENCY: Birr = 100 cents

Fiji

A volcanic archipelago in the South Pacific, with two large islands and 880 islets. Tensions between native Fijians and the Indian minority have sparked a succession of coups.

GEOGRAPHY
Main islands are mountainous, fringed by coral reefs. Remainder are limestone and coral formations.

CLIMATE
Tropical. High temperatures all year round. Cyclones are a hazard.

PEOPLE & SOCIETY
The British introduced workers from India in the late 19th century, and by 1946 their descendants outnumbered the ethnic Fijians. Ethnic-Fijian nationalism is strong. Many Indo-Fijians left after the 1987 coup, restoring ethnic Fijians to a majority. The first Indo-Fijian-dominated government was ousted in 2000. The army led another coup in 2006: elections were held in 2014. Women are lobbying for more rights.

 INSIGHT: *Both Fijians and Indians practice fire-walking; Indians walk on hot embers, Fijians on heated stones*

THE ECONOMY
Tourism recovering from instability. Coups have also caused international isolation. Sugar industry declining. Also exports mineral water, gold, textiles, timber, and fish. Cyclone damage in 2016.

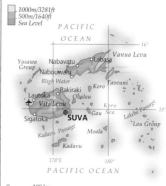

FACTFILE
OFFICIAL NAME: Republic of Fiji
DATE OF FORMATION: 1970
CAPITAL: Suva
POPULATION: 899,000
TOTAL AREA: 7054 sq. miles (18,270 sq. km)
DENSITY: 127 people per sq. mile
LANGUAGES: Fijian*, English*, Hindi*, Urdu, Tamil, Telugu
RELIGIONS: Methodist 35%, Hindu 28%, other Christian 21%, Roman Catholic 9%, Muslim 6%, other and nonreligious 1%
ETHNIC MIX: Melanesian 57%, Indian 38%, other 5%
GOVERNMENT: Parliamentary system
CURRENCY: Fiji dollar = 100 cents

Finland

Finland's language and national identity have been influenced by both its Scandinavian and Russian neighbors. Once aligned with the USSR, Finland is now a member of the EU.

GEOGRAPHY

South and center are flat, with low hills and many lakes. Uplands and low mountains in the north. 60% of the land area is forested.

CLIMATE

Long, harsh winters with frequent snowfalls. Short, warmer summers. Rainfall is low, and decreases northward.

PEOPLE & SOCIETY

One in four of the population lives in the Greater Helsinki region. Swedish-speakers live mainly in the Åland Islands in the southwest. The Sámi (Lapps) lead a seminomadic existence inside the Arctic Circle. Women make up 48% of the labor force, continuing a long tradition of equality between the sexes. Finnish women were the first in Europe to get the vote, in 1906, and the first in the world able to stand for parliament. Families tend to be close-knit.

THE ECONOMY

Strong engineering and electronics sectors: home of Nokia. Wood, pulp, and paper production.

INSIGHT: *Finland has Europe's largest inland waterway system*

FACTFILE

OFFICIAL NAME: Republic of Finland

DATE OF FORMATION: 1917

CAPITAL: Helsinki

POPULATION: 5.5 million

TOTAL AREA: 130,127 sq. miles (337,030 sq. km)

DENSITY: 47 people per sq. mile

LANGUAGES: Finnish*, Swedish*, Sámi

RELIGIONS: Evangelical Lutheran 78%, nonreligious 19%, other 2%, Orthodox Christian 1%

ETHNIC MIX: Finnish 93%, other (including Sámi) 7%

GOVERNMENT: Parliamentary system

CURRENCY: Euro = 100 cents

France

Stretching across western Europe, from the English Channel (la Manche) to the Mediterranean Sea, France was Europe's first modern republic, and is still a leading industrial power.

GEOGRAPHY

Broad plain covers northern half of the country. High mountain ranges in the east and southwest, with a mountainous plateau in the center.

CLIMATE

Three main climates: temperate and damp northwest; continental east; and Mediterranean south.

PEOPLE & SOCIETY

Strong national identity coexists with pronounced regional differences, including local languages. Immigration laws have been tightened since the 1970s, but ethnic minorities growing up in city suburbs feel increasingly alienated. Wearing the veil is banned in public. New equality laws were passed in 2014.

INSIGHT: *France is the most popular tourist destination in the world, with over 80 million visitors a year*

THE ECONOMY

Chemicals, electronics, heavy engineering, cars, and aircraft typify a strong and diversified export sector. World leader in cosmetics, perfumes, and quality wines. Modernized agriculture.

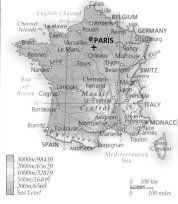

3000m/9843ft
2000m/6562ft
1000m/3281ft
500m/1640ft
200m/656ft
Sea Level

0   100 km
0   100 miles

FACTFILE

OFFICIAL NAME: French Republic

DATE OF FORMATION: 987

CAPITAL: Paris

POPULATION: 65 million

TOTAL AREA: 211,208 sq. miles (547,030 sq. km)

DENSITY: 306 people per sq. mile

LANGUAGES: French*, Provençal, German, Breton, Catalan, Basque

RELIGIONS: Christian 51%, nonreligious 40%, Muslim 6%, other 2%, Jewish 1%

ETHNIC MIX: French 86%, North African 5%, Black 5%, German 2%, Breton 1%, other 1%

GOVERNMENT: Mixed presidential–parliamentary system

CURRENCY: Euro = 100 cents

Gabon

Gabon is a former French colony straddling the equator on Africa's west coast. Independent since 1960, it returned to multiparty politics in 1990, after 22 years of one-party rule.

GEOGRAPHY
Low plateaus and mountains lie beyond the coastal strip. Two-thirds of the land is covered by rainforest.

CLIMATE
Hot and tropical, with little distinction between seasons. Cold Benguela current cools the coast.

PEOPLE & SOCIETY
Some 40 different languages are spoken. The Fang, who live mainly in the north, are the largest ethnic group, but have yet to gain control of the government. Oil wealth has led to the growth of an affluent middle class, but one in three people still live in poverty. Menial jobs are done by immigrant workers. Education follows the French system. With 87% of people living in towns, Gabon is one of Africa's most urbanized countries. The government is encouraging population growth.

THE ECONOMY
Oil accounts for 75% of exports, but reserves are dwindling: struggling to diversify economy. High debt problem. Tropical hardwoods and manganese.

◆ **INSIGHT:** *Libreville was founded as a settlement for freed French slaves in 1849*

```
           CAMEROON
EQUATORIAL        CONGO
 GUINEA     Oyem
        Makokou
+ LIBREVILLE        Equator
Port-
Gentil  Lambaréné
    Koulamoutou    Moanda
 Mouila        Franceville
        Tchibanga
ATLANTIC      CONGO
 OCEAN     12°
0   100 km
0   100 miles
```

500m/1640ft
200m/656ft
Sea Level

FACTFILE

OFFICIAL NAME: Gabonese Republic
DATE OF FORMATION: 1960
CAPITAL: Libreville
POPULATION: 2 million
TOTAL AREA: 103,346 sq. miles (267,667 sq. km)
DENSITY: 20 people per sq. mile
LANGUAGES: Fang, French*, Punu, Sira, Nzebi, Mpongwe

RELIGIONS: Christian (mainly Roman Catholic) 55%, traditional beliefs 40%, other 4%, Muslim 1%
ETHNIC MIX: Fang 26%, Shira-punu 24%, other 24%, foreign residents 15%, Nzabi-duma 11%
GOVERNMENT: Presidential system
CURRENCY: CFA franc = 100 centimes

The Gambia

The Gambia is a narrow, riverbank state on the west coast of Africa. It was renowned for its stability until its government was overthrown in a coup in 1994.

GEOGRAPHY

Located on the narrow strip of land bordering the Gambia River. Long, sandy beaches are backed by mangrove swamps along the river. Savanna and tropical forests higher up.

CLIMATE

Subtropical, with wet, humid months July–October, and warm, dry season November–May.

PEOPLE & SOCIETY

Little tension between various ethnic groups. The largest group, the Mandinka, has traditionally held power. Islam is a strong social influence, though there is no official state religion. A small expatriate community from the UK lives on the coast. Seasonal migrants come from neighboring states to harvest groundnuts each year. Women are active as traders. Yahya Jammeh, who led the 1994 coup, held power for 23 years.

THE ECONOMY

Around 70% of the labor force is involved in agriculture. Groundnuts are the principal crop. Fish stocks declining. Eco-tourism is promoted, though most visitors come for the beaches. Banjul is one of west Africa's finest deepwater ports: significant re-export trade. Oil potential offshore. Smuggling problems.

◆ **INSIGHT:** *Overfishing in the waters off The Gambia and Senegal, mainly by foreign vessels, is a growing problem*

FACTFILE

OFFICIAL NAME: Republic of The Gambia
DATE OF FORMATION: 1965
CAPITAL: Banjul
POPULATION: 2.1 million
TOTAL AREA: 4363 sq. miles (11,300 sq. km)
DENSITY: 544 people per sq. mile

LANGUAGES: Mandinka, Fulani, Wolof, Jola, Soninke, English*
RELIGIONS: Sunni Muslim 90%, Christian 8%, traditional beliefs 2%
ETHNIC MIX: Mandinka 42%, Fulani 18%, Wolof 16%, Jola 10%, Serahuli 9%, other 5%
GOVERNMENT: Presidential system
CURRENCY: Dalasi = 100 butut

Georgia

Located on the eastern shore of the Black Sea, Georgia was torn by civil war and ethnic disputes after achieving independence from the Soviet Union in 1991.

GEOGRAPHY
Kura Valley lies between Caucasus Mountains in the north and Lesser Caucasus range in the south. Lowlands along the Black Sea coast.

CLIMATE
Subtropical along the coast, changing to continental extremes at high altitudes. Rainfall is moderate.

PEOPLE & SOCIETY
Paternalistic society, with strong family, cultural, and literary traditions. Georgia was converted to Christianity in 326 CE. Armenians in the south are the poorest group. Civil conflicts in the early 1990s against Abkhaz and Osset separatists displaced 300,000 people. Abkhazia and South Ossetia now effectively operate as separate states, backed up by Russian forces since the 2008 war. Russia opposes Georgian hopes of joining the EU and NATO.

THE ECONOMY
Transit revenues from pipelines taking oil to the West. Long-established and booming wine industry. Fast pace of reforms since 2003 Rose Revolution, at cost of high unemployment.

INSIGHT: *Western Georgia was the land of the legendary Golden Fleece of Greek mythology*

3000m/9843ft	
2000m/6562ft	
1000m/3281ft	
500m/1640ft	
200m/656ft	
Sea Level	

0   100 km
0   100 miles

FACTFILE

OFFICIAL NAME: Georgia
DATE OF FORMATION: 1991
CAPITAL: Tbilisi
POPULATION: 3.9 million
TOTAL AREA: 26,911 sq. miles (69,700 sq. km)
DENSITY: 145 people per sq. mile
LANGUAGES: Georgian*, Russian, Azeri, Armenian, Mingrelian, Ossetian, Abkhazian
RELIGIONS: Orthodox Christian 89%, Muslim 9%, Roman Catholic 1%, other 1%
ETHNIC MIX: Georgian 87%, Azeri 6%, Armenian 4%, other 2%, Russian 1%
GOVERNMENT: Mixed presidential–parliamentary system
CURRENCY: Lari = 100 tetri

Germany

Europe's strongest industrial power and its most populous nation, Germany was divided after military defeat in 1945 into a free-market west and a communist east, but reunified in 1990.

 GEOGRAPHY
Central European coastal plains in the north, rising to rolling hills of central region and Alps in the far south.

 CLIMATE
Damp, temperate in northern and central regions. Continental extremes in mountainous south.

PEOPLE & SOCIETY
Regionalism is strong. The north is mainly Protestant, while the south is staunchly Roman Catholic. Social and economic differences still exist between east and west. Turks are the largest single ethnic minority; many came as guest workers in the 1950s–1970s. Levels of immigration are high; rules now favor skilled workers. Feminism is strong.

◆ **INSIGHT:** *Germany's rivers and canals carry as much freight as its busy highways*

THE ECONOMY
Major exporter of electronics, heavy engineering, chemicals, and cars. Worst recession for 60 years in 2008–2009. Aging population.

FACTFILE

OFFICIAL NAME: Federal Republic of Germany

DATE OF FORMATION: 1871

CAPITAL: Berlin

POPULATION: 82.1 million

TOTAL AREA: 137,846 sq. miles (357,021 sq. km)

DENSITY: 608 people per sq. mile

LANGUAGES: German*, Turkish

RELIGIONS: Nonreligious 36%, Roman Catholic 29%, Protestant 26%, Muslim 5%, other 4%

ETHNIC MIX: German 81%, other European 10%, other 4%, Turkish 3%, Polish 2%

GOVERNMENT: Parliamentary system

CURRENCY: Euro = 100 cents

Ghana

The heartland of the ancient Ashanti kingdom, Ghana in west Africa was once known as the Gold Coast. It has experienced intermittent periods of military rule since independence in 1957.

GEOGRAPHY
Mostly low-lying. The west is covered by rainforest. One of the world's largest artificial lakes – Lake Volta – was created by damming the White Volta River.

CLIMATE
Tropical. There are two wet seasons in the south, but the north is drier, and has just one.

PEOPLE & SOCIETY
Around 75 cultural-linguistic groups. The largest is the Akan, who include the Ashanti and Fanti peoples. Southern peoples are richer and more urban than those of the north. Family ties are strong. Women play a major role in market trading. Since Ghana's first peaceful handover of power at the 2000 election, the country has become a stable democracy. Poverty levels have been significantly reduced.

THE ECONOMY
World's second-largest cocoa producer. Oil discovered in 2007: on stream from 2010. Hardwood trees such as maple and sapele. Gold mining.

 INSIGHT: *Ghana was the first colony in west Africa to gain independence*

FACTFILE

OFFICIAL NAME: Republic of Ghana
DATE OF FORMATION: 1957
CAPITAL: Accra
POPULATION: 28.8 million
TOTAL AREA: 92,100 sq. miles (238,540 sq. km)
DENSITY: 324 people per sq. mile
LANGUAGES: Twi, Fanti, Ewe, Ga, Adangbe, Gurma, Dagomba (Dagbani), English*
RELIGIONS: Christian 71%, Muslim 18%, nonreligious 5%, traditional beliefs 5%, other 1%
ETHNIC MIX: Akan 47%, Gurma 17%, Ga-Dangme 14%, other 9%, Ewe 7%, Guan 6%
GOVERNMENT: Presidential system
CURRENCY: Cedi = 100 pesewas

Greece

The Balkan state of Greece is bounded on three sides by the Mediterranean, Aegean, and Ionian seas. It has a strong seafaring tradition, with some of the world's richest shipowners.

 GEOGRAPHY
Mountainous peninsula and over 2000 islands. Large plain along the mainland's Aegean coast.

 CLIMATE
Mainly Mediterranean, with dry, hot summers. Alpine climate in northern mountain areas.

 PEOPLE & SOCIETY
Postwar industrial development altered the dominance of agriculture and seafaring. Rural exodus to cities has been stemmed but a third of the population lives in Athens. Age-old culture and Greek Orthodox Church balance social mobility. Civil marriage and divorce only legalized in 1982. There has been much recent civil unrest against severe austerity measures.

◆ **INSIGHT:** *The modern Olympics, first held in Athens in 1896, evolved from Olympia's ancient Greek games*

 THE ECONOMY
Public debt and budget deficit very high: EU bailouts to avoid bankruptcy. World's largest shipping fleet. One of Europe's top tourist destinations. Fruit, vegetables, olives. Large black economy.

FACTFILE

OFFICIAL NAME: Hellenic Republic
DATE OF FORMATION: 1829
CAPITAL: Athens
POPULATION: 11.2 million
TOTAL AREA: 50,942 sq. miles (131,940 sq. km)
DENSITY: 222 people per sq. mile

LANGUAGES: Greek*, Turkish, Macedonian, Albanian
RELIGIONS: Orthodox Christian 90%, nonreligious 4%, other 4%, Muslim 2%
ETHNIC MIX: Greek 98%, other 2%
GOVERNMENT: Parliamentary system
CURRENCY: Euro = 100 cents

Grenada

The southernmost of the Windward Islands, Grenada made world headlines in 1983 when the US and Caribbean allies mounted an invasion to sever links with Castro's Cuba.

GEOGRAPHY
Volcanic in origin, with densely forested central mountains. Its territory also includes the islands of Carriacou and Petite Martinique.

CLIMATE
Tropical, tempered by trade winds. Hurricanes are a hazard in the July–November wet season.

PEOPLE & SOCIETY
Grenadians are mainly of African origin; their traditions remain strong, especially on Carriacou. Inter-ethnic marriage has reduced tensions between the groups. Extended families, often headed by women, are the norm. Levels of poverty, highest in rural areas, are a key political issue.

◆ **INSIGHT:** *Known as "the spice island of the Caribbean," it is the world's second-largest nutmeg producer*

THE ECONOMY
Severe damage from Hurricane Ivan in 2004 to crops and 90% of buildings; reconstruction took years. Nutmeg, cocoa, bananas, and mace. Smuggling is a serious problem.

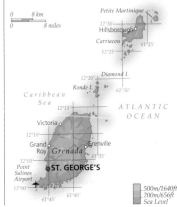

500m/1640ft
200m/656ft
Sea Level

FACTFILE

OFFICIAL NAME: Grenada
DATE OF FORMATION: 1974
CAPITAL: St. George's
POPULATION: 107,000
TOTAL AREA: 131 sq. miles (340 sq. km)
DENSITY: 817 people per sq. mile

LANGUAGES: English*, English Creole
RELIGIONS: Roman Catholic 68%, Anglican 17%, other 15%
ETHNIC MIX: Black African 82%, Mulatto (mixed race) 13%, East Indian 3%, other 2%
GOVERNMENT: Parliamentary system
CURRENCY: East Caribbean dollar = 100 cents

Guatemala

The largest and most populous nation on the Central American isthmus, Guatemala returned to civilian rule in 1986 after 32 years of violent and repressive military rule.

GEOGRAPHY
Narrow Pacific coastal plain. Central highlands with volcanoes. Short coast on the Caribbean Sea. Tropical rainforests in the north.

CLIMATE
Tropical: hot and humid in coastal regions and north. More temperate in the central highlands.

PEOPLE & SOCIETY
Amerindians, concentrated in the highlands, form a majority. Power, wealth, and land are controlled by *ladinos* (Westernized Amerindians and *mestizos*). Catholicism is predominant, mixed with Amerindian beliefs. Literacy is low. Over a tenth of the population live on less than $2 a day. Violent crime is a problem.

◆ INSIGHT: *Guatemala, which means "land of trees," was the center of the ancient Mayan civilization*

THE ECONOMY
Coffee, sugar, bananas, and textiles are top exports. Tourism. Damage from natural disasters. Marked wealth inequalities inhibit domestic market.

FACTFILE

OFFICIAL NAME: Republic of Guatemala

DATE OF FORMATION: 1838

CAPITAL: Guatemala City

POPULATION: 16.9 million

TOTAL AREA: 42,042 sq. miles (108,890 sq. km)

DENSITY: 404 people per sq. mile

LANGUAGES: Quiché, Mam, Cakchiquel, Kekchí, Spanish*

RELIGIONS: Roman Catholic 50%, Protestant 41%, nonreligious 6%, other 3%

ETHNIC MIX: Amerindian 60%, *Mestizo* (European–Amerindian) 30%, other 10%

GOVERNMENT: Presidential system

CURRENCY: Quetzal = 100 centavos

Guinea

Located on the west coast of Africa, Guinea was the first French colony in Africa to gain independence, in 1958. The country was under military rule in 1984–1995 and 2008–2010.

GEOGRAPHY

Coastal plains and mangrove swamps in the west rise to forested or savanna highlands in the south. Semidesert in the north.

CLIMATE

Tropical, with a wet season April–October. Conakry is especially rainy. The hot, dry *harmattan* wind blows from the Sahara during the dry season.

PEOPLE & SOCIETY

Peul and Malinké make up most of the population, but rivalries between them have allowed coastal peoples such as the Soussou to dominate politics. Daily life revolves around the extended family. Women acquired influence under Marxist party rule (1958–1984), but the Muslim revival since then has reversed the trend. Private enterprise has created a business class. A deadly Ebola outbreak hit the country in 2014–2015.

THE ECONOMY

Substantial iron, diamond, and especially bauxite reserves. Cash crops: bananas, coffee, pineapples, and palm oil. Poor infrastructure. Instability.

◆ **INSIGHT:** *The colors of Guinea's flag represent the three words of the country's motto: work (red), justice (yellow), and solidarity (green)*

1000m/3281ft
500m/1640ft
200m/656ft
Sea Level

0   100 km
0   100 miles

FACTFILE

OFFICIAL NAME: Republic of Guinea
DATE OF FORMATION: 1958
CAPITAL: Conakry
POPULATION: 12.7 million
TOTAL AREA: 94,925 sq. miles (245,857 sq. km)
DENSITY: 134 people per sq. mile

LANGUAGES: Pulaar, Malinké, Soussou, French*
RELIGIONS: Muslim 89%, Christian 7%, nonreligious 2%, traditional beliefs and other 2%
ETHNIC MIX: Peul 40%, Malinké 30%, Soussou 20%, other 10%
GOVERNMENT: Presidential system
CURRENCY: Guinea franc = 100 centimes

Guinea-Bissau

Known as Portuguese Guinea while a colony, Guinea-Bissau lies on Africa's west coast. Since 1994, its nascent democracy has been plagued by coups and rebellions.

GEOGRAPHY
Low-lying, apart from savanna highlands in northeast. Rainforests and swamps are found along coastal areas.

CLIMATE
Tropical, with wet season May–November and dry season December–April. Hot, dry *harmattan* desert wind blows during dry season.

PEOPLE & SOCIETY
The Balante in the south are the largest ethnic group. Though only around 1% of the population, the mixed race Portuguese–African *mestiços* dominate the government and bureaucracy. Most people live and work on small family farms, grouped in self-contained villages. The bulk of the urban population live in Bissau, where they face economic hardship. Narcotics trafficking took hold during instability in the 2000s; the state is still struggling to restore order.

THE ECONOMY
Mostly subsistence farming. Lack of sufficiency in rice staple. Main cash crop is cashew nuts. Major cocaine transit route from South America to Europe. Offshore oil potential. Fisheries and timber resources. Political instability.

◆ **INSIGHT:** *In 1974, Guinea-Bissau became the first Portuguese colony to gain independence*

FACTFILE

OFFICIAL NAME: Republic of Guinea-Bissau
DATE OF FORMATION: 1974
CAPITAL: Bissau
POPULATION: 1.9 million
TOTAL AREA: 13,946 sq. miles (36,120 sq. km)
DENSITY: 175 people per sq. mile

LANGUAGES: Portuguese Creole, Balante, Fulani, Malinké, Portuguese*
RELIGIONS: Muslim 54%, Christian 26%, traditional beliefs 18%, nonreligious 2%
ETHNIC MIX: Balante 30%, Fulani 20%, other 16%, Mandyako 14%, Mandinka 13%, Papel 7%
GOVERNMENT: Presidential system
CURRENCY: CFA franc = 100 centimes

Guyana

On the northeast coast of South America, Guyana is the continent's only English-speaking country. Independent since 1966, it has close ties with the anglophone Caribbean.

GEOGRAPHY

Mainly artificial coast, reclaimed by dikes and dams from swamps and tidal marshes. Forests cover 85% of the interior, rising to savanna uplands and mountains.

CLIMATE

Tropical. Coast cooled by sea breezes. Lowlands are hot, wet, and humid. Highlands are a little cooler.

PEOPLE & SOCIETY

Guyana is a complex multiracial society. Tension exists between the Afro-Guyanese, descended from slaves, and the Indo-Guyanese, descendants of laborers brought over after slavery was abolished. Politics is highly polarized around this split and has often spilled over into violence on the streets. Amerindian subsistence farmers are the poorest people in society and campaign for equal rights and representation.

THE ECONOMY

Diverse exports: gold, rice, shrimp, fish, bauxite, sugar, timber, rum. Debt relief granted. Narcotics transit zone.

INSIGHT: Guyana means "land of many waters," reflecting its dense network of rivers

FACTFILE

OFFICIAL NAME: Cooperative Republic of Guyana

DATE OF FORMATION: 1966

CAPITAL: Georgetown

POPULATION: 773,000

TOTAL AREA: 83,000 sq. miles (214,970 sq. km)

DENSITY: 10 people per sq. mile

LANGUAGES: English Creole, Hindi, Tamil, Amerindian languages, English*

RELIGIONS: Christian 57%, Hindu 28%, Muslim 10%, other 5%

ETHNIC MIX: East Indian 43%, Black African 30%, mixed race 17%, Amerindian 9%, other 1%

GOVERNMENT: Presidential system

CURRENCY: Guyanese dollar = 100 cents

Haiti

Formerly a French colony, Haiti shares the Caribbean island of Hispaniola with the Dominican Republic. At independence in 1804, it became the world's first black republic.

 GEOGRAPHY
Predominantly mountainous, with forests and fertile plains.

 CLIMATE
Tropical, with rain throughout the year. Humid in coastal areas, much cooler in the mountains.

 PEOPLE & SOCIETY
Most Haitians are of African descent. A few have European roots, primarily French. The rigid class structure maintains vast disparities of wealth. The majority of the population live in extreme poverty; Haiti is one of the poorest countries in the Americas. A combination of political oppression and a collapsing economy led thousands to seek asylum in the US or the Dominican Republic. Though most are Christians, many Haitians practice Voodoo, which was recognized as an official religion in 2003.

THE ECONOMY
Fragile: vulnerable to hurricane damage, shattered by 2010 earthquake. Political instability. Human and narcotics trafficking. High unemployment.

◆ **INSIGHT:** *A slave rebellion headed by Toussaint Louverture in 1791 led to Haiti's independence*

FACTFILE

OFFICIAL NAME: Republic of Haiti
DATE OF FORMATION: 1804
CAPITAL: Port-au-Prince
POPULATION: 11 million
TOTAL AREA: 10,714 sq. miles (27,750 sq. km)
DENSITY: 1034 people per sq. mile

LANGUAGES: French Creole*, French*
RELIGIONS: Roman Catholic 55%, Protestant 28%, other (including Voodoo) 16%, nonreligious 1%
ETHNIC MIX: Black African 95%, *Mulatto* (mixed race) and European 5%
GOVERNMENT: Presidential system
CURRENCY: Gourde = 100 centimes

Honduras

Straddling the Central American isthmus, Honduras returned to democratic rule in 1984, after a period of military government. Hurricane Mitch devastated the country in 1998.

GEOGRAPHY

Narrow plains along both coasts, with a mountainous interior, cut by river valleys. Tropical forests, swamps, and lagoons in the east.

CLIMATE

Tropical coastal lowlands are hot and humid, with May–October rains. Interior is cooler and drier.

PEOPLE & SOCIETY

The majority of the population is *mestizo* (mixed European–Amerindian). An English-speaking *garifuna* (black) community and Miskito Amerindians struggle to preserve their rights to land along the remote Caribbean coast. Women's status remains low. Wealth inequalities are large and poverty is at the root of social tension. Two-thirds of the population live in poverty. The army ousted the president in 2009. Violent crime is a major issue.

THE ECONOMY

Exports garments, coffee, bananas, and shellfish. Remittances account for almost a fifth of GDP. Debt relief from 2005. High underemployment and corruption. Mineral potential.

INSIGHT: *The Honduran currency is named after a Lenca Indian chief who was the main leader of resistance to the Spanish conquest in the 16th century*

FACTFILE

OFFICIAL NAME: Republic of Honduras

DATE OF FORMATION: 1838

CAPITAL: Tegucigalpa

POPULATION: 9.3 million

TOTAL AREA: 43,278 sq. miles (112,090 sq. km)

DENSITY: 215 people per sq. mile

LANGUAGES: Spanish*, Garifuna (Carib), English Creole

RELIGIONS: Roman Catholic 46%, Protestant 41%, nonreligious 10%, other 3%

ETHNIC MIX: *Mestizo* 90%, Black African 5%, Amerindian 4%, White 1%

GOVERNMENT: Presidential system

CURRENCY: Lempira = 100 centavos

Hungary

Landlocked in central Europe, Hungary was one of the twin centers of the once-great Habsburg Empire. It lost two-thirds of its historical territory for supporting Germany in WW I.

GEOGRAPHY

Landlocked. Fertile plains in the east and northwest; the west and north are hilly. The Danube River cuts through the country and the capital.

CLIMATE

Continental, with wet springs, late but very hot summers, and cold, cloudy winters. The transition between seasons tends to be sudden.

PEOPLE & SOCIETY

Hungary's population has been shrinking since the 1980s. Mostly ethnic Hungarian (Magyar), there are small minorities of Germans, Jews, and neighboring peoples. Roma face particular discrimination. The government is greatly concerned about the fate of ethnic Hungarians in Romania, Serbia, and Slovakia. Hungary joined the EU in 2004. Working hours are longer than in western Europe.

THE ECONOMY

Strong industrial base. Hard-hit by 2007–2009 global downturn: currency sank. IMF bailout to avoid meltdown: enforced spending cuts. Quick return to growth. Labor shortages. Low tax rates.

INSIGHT: *The Hungarian language originates from east of the Urals in Asia and is most closely related to Finnish*

FACTFILE

OFFICIAL NAME: Hungary

DATE OF FORMATION: 1918

CAPITAL: Budapest

POPULATION: 9.7 million

TOTAL AREA: 35,919 sq. miles (93,030 sq. km)

DENSITY: 272 people per sq. mile

LANGUAGES: Hungarian (Magyar)*

RELIGIONS: Roman Catholic 56%, nonreligious 21%, Presbyterian 13%, other (mostly Protestant) 10%

ETHNIC MIX: Magyar 92%, Roma 3%, other 3%, German 2%

GOVERNMENT: Parliamentary system

CURRENCY: Forint = 100 fillér

Iceland

Europe's westernmost country, Iceland's strategic ocean location straddles the Mid-Atlantic Ridge. Its spectacular landscape is largely uninhabited, aside from coastal towns.

GEOGRAPHY

Grassy coastal lowlands, with fjords in the north. Central plateau of cold lava desert, geothermal springs, and glaciers. Around 200 volcanoes, with numerous geysers and solfataras.

CLIMATE

Its location in the middle of the Gulf Stream moderates the climate. Mild winters and brief, cool summers.

PEOPLE & SOCIETY

Icelanders share a strong national identity. The language has changed little in 700 years, in part due to the country's isolation. There is high social mobility, free health care, and low-cost heating (geothermal and hydropower). Numbers of foreign residents are rising. Iceland's 2008 banking collapse and near financial ruin prompted it to apply for EU membership, but public opinion swung against joining so the bid was frozen.

THE ECONOMY

Once reliant on fish. Aluminum smelting. Banks overexposed in 2008 global downturn; króna depreciated 90%. Recovery led by tourism and exports.

◆ **INSIGHT:** *The word geyser is taken from Geysir (the "gusher") in southwest Iceland*

FACTFILE

OFFICIAL NAME: Republic of Iceland
DATE OF FORMATION: 1944
CAPITAL: Reykjavík
POPULATION: 334,000
TOTAL AREA: 39,768 sq. miles (103,000 sq. km)
DENSITY: 9 people per sq. mile

LANGUAGES: Icelandic*
RELIGIONS: Evangelical Lutheran 70%, other (mostly Christian) 10%, nonreligious 6%, Roman Catholic 4%
ETHNIC MIX: Icelandic 89%, other 7%, Polish 3%, Danish 1%
GOVERNMENT: Parliamentary system
CURRENCY: Icelandic króna = 100 aurar

India

India is the world's largest democracy. Its population, the world's second-highest, is still growing despite some success in reducing birth rates, and will exceed China's by around 2025.

GEOGRAPHY

India covers most of the south Asian subcontinent, separated from northern Asia by the Himalaya mountain range. From the foothills of the Himalayas, the Indo-Gangetic plain stretches south to the hills of the Vindhya range. Beyond the Vindhyas, the Deccan plateau covers much of central-southern India, fringed by the Western and Eastern Ghats and the narrow coastal plains.

CLIMATE

Varies greatly according to latitude, altitude, and season. Most of India has three seasons: hot, wet, and cool. Summer temperatures in the north can reach 104°F (40°C). Monsoon rains normally break in June, petering out in September to October. In the cool season, the weather is mainly dry. The climate in the warmer south is less variable than in the north.

PEOPLE & SOCIETY

Faced with cultural and religious factors encouraging large families, India's planners have long seen overpopulation as the main brake on economic development rather than environmental constraints. Birth control campaigns controversially included mass sterilizations mainly of men in the 1970s and more recently of women. Rural deprivation drives people to migrate to sprawling urban slums. Hinduism, the majority religion, underpins a caste system which determines social standing and even marriage; reforms can encounter violent opposition. Almost 30% of Indians – more in rural areas – are officially acknowledged to live in poverty. Tensions between Hindus and the Muslim minority, especially in Kashmir and Gujarat, sometimes flare up into intercommunal strife. Ethnic minorities in the northeast struggle for greater autonomy.

FACTFILE

OFFICIAL NAME: Republic of India
DATE OF FORMATION: 1947
CAPITAL: New Delhi
POPULATION: 1.34 billion
TOTAL AREA: 1,269,338 sq. miles
(3,287,590 sq. km)
DENSITY: 1167 people per sq. mile

LANGUAGES: Hindi*, English*, Urdu, Bengali, Marathi, Telugu, Tamil, Bihari, Gujarati, Kanarese
RELIGIONS: Hindu 81%, Muslim 13%, Christian 2%, Sikh 2%, Buddhist 1%, other 1%
ETHNIC MIX: Indo-Aryan 72%, Dravidian 25%, Mongoloid and other 3%
GOVERNMENT: Parliamentary system
CURRENCY: Indian rupee = 100 paise

THE ECONOMY

Among the world's fastest-growing economies since 1990s when free-market liberalization replaced protectionism. Tea, gems, textiles, cars, medicines exported. High-tech industries, digital services, outsourcing center. Cheap labor. Huge market. Success of "Bollywood" films.

INSIGHT: *India's national animal, the tiger, was depicted as early as 4000 years ago by the Mohenjo-Daro civilization*

5000m/16405ft
4000m/13124ft
3000m/9843ft
2000m/6562ft
1000m/3281ft
500m/1640ft
200m/656ft
Sea Level

A 'line of control' was agreed between India and Pakistan in 1972

35°

Aksai Chin - administered by China, claimed by India

Srīnagar
Jammu & Kashmir
Dēmqog/Demchok - administered by China, claimed by India

Amritsar
Jalandhar
Ludhiāna
Chandīgarh

Much of Arunāchal Pradesh is claimed by China

CHINA

Meerut

70°

PAKISTAN

Thar Desert

Delhi
Bareilly
NEPAL
Shiliguri
Assam
BHUTAN
Brahmaputra
MYANMAR
(BURMA)

NEW DELHI
Agra
Lucknow
Jodhpur
Jaipur
Kanpur
Patna
BANGLADESH
Imphāl

25°
Kota
Gwalior
Ganges

Rann of Kachchh
Vārānasi
Dhanbād
Kolkata
(Calcutta)

Gulf of Kachchh
Ahmadābād
Indore
Bhopāl
Jābalpur
Rānchī
Hāora
Mouths of the Ganges

Jāmnagar
Rājkot
Vadodara
Narmada
Nāgpur
Jamshedpur

Sūrat

20°

Gulf of Khambhāt
Kalyān
Nānded
Mahānadi
Cuttack

Mumbai
(Bombay)
Pune
Deccan
Godāvari
Visākhapatnam
Bay of Bengal

Arabian Sea
Solāpur
Hyderābād
Western Ghāts
Krishna

15°
Panaji
Hubbali

Eastern Ghāts

Chennai
(Madras)

INDIAN OCEAN

Andaman Islands
North Andaman
Middle Andaman

Mysūru (Mysore)
Bengalūru (Bangalore)
Salem
South Andaman
Port Blair
Little Andaman

Lakshadweep
(Laccadive Is.)
Coimbatore
Madurai

10°
Kochi (Cochin)

95°

Nicobar Islands

75°
80°
85°
90°

Indira Point
Great Nicobar

0   200 km
0   200 miles

Indonesia

Formerly called the Dutch East Indies, Indonesia is the world's largest archipelago, with 18,108 islands scattered across 3000 miles (5000 km). It is the world's fourth most populous nation.

GEOGRAPHY

Indonesia is highly mountainous, with numerous tropical swamps. The land is covered with dense rainforest, especially on New Guinea, where it remains largely unexplored. There are more than 200 volcanoes, many of which are still active. Earthquakes, eruptions, and tsunamis are hazards. The islands of Java, Bali, Lombok, Sumatra, and Borneo were once joined together by dry land, which has since been submerged by rising sea levels. Coastal lowland development distinguishes some of the large islands.

CLIMATE

The climate is predominantly tropical monsoon. Variations relate mainly to differences in latitude and altitude; hilly areas are cooler overall. Rain falls throughout the year, often in thunderstorms, but there is a relatively dry season from June to September.

PEOPLE & SOCIETY

The basic Melanesian–Malay ethnic division disguises a diverse society. Bahasa Indonesia, the national language, coexists with at least 250 other spoken languages or dialects. Attempts by the Javanese

FACTFILE

OFFICIAL NAME: Republic of Indonesia
DATE OF FORMATION: 1949
CAPITAL: Jakarta
POPULATION: 264 million
TOTAL AREA: 741,096 sq. miles (1,919,440 sq. km)
DENSITY: 381 people per sq. mile

LANGUAGES: Javanese, Sundanese, Madurese, Bahasa Indonesia*, Dutch
RELIGIONS: Sunni Muslim 87%, Protestant 7%, Roman Catholic 3%, Hindu 2%, Buddhist 1%
ETHNIC MIX: Javanese 40%, other 27%, Sundanese 16%, Coastal Malays 14%, Madurese 3%
GOVERNMENT: Presidential system
CURRENCY: Rupiah = 100 sen

political elite to suppress local cultures have been vigorously opposed, especially by the Aceh of northern Sumatra, and the Papuans. Religious and interethnic hostility is a problem, with clashes between Christians and Muslims in many areas, and discrimination against ethnic Chinese leading to mob attacks on their businesses. Gender equality is enshrined in law; women are active in public life.

$ THE ECONOMY

Varied resources, especially gas and coal. Large cheap, literate labor force. Growing market of middle-class consumers. Sizable state-owned sector. Price controls on basics. Bureaucracy and corruption damage business confidence, but recent policies are boosting foreign investment. 2004 tsunami devastated northern Sumatra, killing over 130,000 people. Regional conflicts, terrorist attacks, and piracy have deterred tourists.

4000m/13124ft
3000m/9843ft
2000m/6562ft
1000m/3281ft
500m/1640ft
Sea Level

0   500 km
0   500 miles

◆ **INSIGHT:** *Indonesia is home to the world's shortest men, on average just over 5 feet 2 inches (1.58 meters), and its largest lizard, the Komodo dragon.*

Iran

Since the 1979 Islamic fundamentalist revolution led by Ayatollah Khomeini, the Middle Eastern country of Iran has been the world's largest theocracy.

GEOGRAPHY
High desert plateau with large salt pans in the east. The west and north are mountainous. Coastal land bordering Caspian Sea is rainy and forested.

CLIMATE
Desert climate. Hot summers, and bitterly cold winters. Area around the Caspian Sea is more temperate.

PEOPLE & SOCIETY
Many ethnic groups, including Persians, Azaris (related to Azeris), Kurds. Militant Shi'a Islamism has dominated since the 1979 revolution. The mullahs' belief that adherence to religious values is more important than economic welfare has led to a fall in living standards. Female emancipation has been reversed. Student-backed demonstrations favoring greater liberalism have been suppressed. Years of harsh sanctions led to deal to limit Iran's uranium enrichment program.

THE ECONOMY
A leading oil producer: exports up since sanctions lifted. Government restricts contact with the West, blocking acquisition of vital technology. High unemployment, inflation. Black market.

◆ INSIGHT: *More than a hundred offenses carry the death penalty*

3000m/9843ft
2000m/6562ft
1000m/3281ft
500m/1640ft
200m/656ft
Sea Level

0   200 km
0   200 miles

FACTFILE

OFFICIAL NAME: Islamic Republic of Iran
DATE OF FORMATION: 1502
CAPITAL: Tehran
POPULATION: 81.2 million
TOTAL AREA: 636,293 sq. miles (1,648,000 sq. km)
DENSITY: 129 people per sq. mile

LANGUAGES: Farsi*, Azeri, Luri, Gilaki, Arabic, Mazanderani, Kurdish, Turkmen, Baluchi
RELIGIONS: Shi'a Muslim 90%, Sunni Muslim 9%, other 1%
ETHNIC MIX: Persian 51%, Azari 24%, other 10%, Lur and Bakhtiari 8%, Kurdish 7%
GOVERNMENT: Islamic theocracy
CURRENCY: Iranian rial = 100 dinars

Iraq

Oil-rich Iraq is situated in the central Middle East. The last five decades have been dominated by dictatorship, war, and civil strife. A US-led Coalition ousted Saddam Hussein in 2003.

GEOGRAPHY
Mainly desert. The Tigris and Euphrates rivers water fertile regions and create the southern marshland. Mountains along the northeast border.

CLIMATE
Southern deserts have hot, dry summers and mild winters. North has dry summers, but winters can be harsh in the mountains. Rainfall is low.

PEOPLE & SOCIETY
Carved out of remnants of the Ottoman Empire, Iraq is home to Arab Muslims (mainly Shi'a, some Sunni), northern Kurds (persecuted under Saddam), and smaller minorities. Since Saddam's removal, sectarian violence has overshadowed efforts to build democracy. US forces withdrew in 2011. By 2014 Islamic State jihadists had seized swathes of territory, but they have since been pushed back. Poverty is widespread.

THE ECONOMY
Economy and infrastructure have been destroyed. Given stability and aid for reconstruction, hopes of recovery would rest on massive oil reserves.

INSIGHT: As Mesopotamia, Iraq was the site where the Sumerians established the world's first civilization

FACTFILE

OFFICIAL NAME: Republic of Iraq
DATE OF FORMATION: 1932
CAPITAL: Baghdad
POPULATION: 38.3 million
TOTAL AREA: 168,753 sq. miles (437,072 sq. km)
DENSITY: 227 people per sq. mile

LANGUAGES: Arabic*, Kurdish*, Turkic languages, Armenian, Assyrian
RELIGIONS: Shi'a Muslim 60%, Sunni Muslim 35%, other (including Christian) 5%
ETHNIC MIX: Arab 80%, Kurdish 15%, Turkmen 3%, other 2%
GOVERNMENT: Parliamentary system
CURRENCY: New Iraqi dinar = 1000 fils

Ireland

In the Atlantic Ocean off the west coast of Britain, the Irish Republic governs about 85% of the island of Ireland, with the remainder (Northern Ireland) being part of the UK.

GEOGRAPHY
Low mountain ranges along an irregular coastline surround an inland plain punctuated by lakes, undulating hills, and peat bogs.

CLIMATE
The Gulf Stream accounts for the mild and wet climate. Snow is rare, except in the mountains.

PEOPLE & SOCIETY
Though homogeneous in ethnicity and Roman Catholic by religion, society has undergone a major generational change, liberalizing birth control, divorce, abortion, and general attitudes. Ireland's tradition as an emigrant nation has been reversed for most of the last two decades. Ireland and the UK signed a peace deal over Northern Ireland in 1998.

 INSIGHT: *About 30% of people can speak Irish, with 5% regular users*

THE ECONOMY
Efficient agriculture, electronics, and food-processing industries. Rapid growth until 2008: housing bubble burst, banks faltered, large EU bailouts. Growth has returned, but national debt is high.

1000m/3281ft
500m/1640ft
200m/656ft
Sea Level

FACTFILE

OFFICIAL NAME: Ireland
DATE OF FORMATION: 1922
CAPITAL: Dublin
POPULATION: 4.8 million
TOTAL AREA: 27,135 sq. miles (70,280 sq. km)
DENSITY: 180 people per sq. mile

LANGUAGES: English*, Irish*
RELIGIONS: Roman Catholic 86%, other Christian 6%, nonreligious 6%, Muslim 1%, other 1%
ETHNIC MIX: Irish 86%, other White 9%, Asian 2%, other 2%, Black 1%
GOVERNMENT: Parliamentary system
CURRENCY: Euro = 100 cents

Israel

Created as a new state in 1948, Israel lies on the eastern shore of the Mediterranean. Palestinian resistance to Israeli occupation has led to years of fierce violence.

GEOGRAPHY

Coastal plain. Desert in the south. In the east lie the Great Rift Valley and the Dead Sea – the lowest point on the Earth's land surface.

CLIMATE

Summers are hot and dry. Wet season, March–November, is mild.

PEOPLE & SOCIETY

Large numbers of Jews settled in Palestine before Israel was founded in 1948. After World War II, there was a massive increase in immigration. Sephardi Jews from the Middle East and Mediterranean are now in the majority, but Ashkenazi Jews from central Europe still dominate business and politics. Palestinians in Gaza and Jericho gained limited autonomy in 1994 but Israeli–Palestinian talks on a two-state solution, backed by most of the world, have repeatedly foundered.

THE ECONOMY

High-tech industries, modern infrastructure, and educated workforce, but hampered by conflict and boycotts.

INSIGHT: *All Jews worldwide have the right to Israeli citizenship*

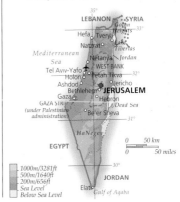

FACTFILE

OFFICIAL NAME: State of Israel

DATE OF FORMATION: 1948

CAPITAL: Jerusalem (not internationally recognized)

POPULATION: 8.3 million

TOTAL AREA: 8019 sq. miles (20,770 sq. km)

DENSITY: 1057 people per sq. mile

LANGUAGES: Hebrew*, Arabic*, Yiddish, German, Russian, Polish, Romanian, Persian

RELIGIONS: Jewish 81%, Muslim (mainly Sunni) 14%, Druze 2%, Christian 2%, other and nonreligious 1%

ETHNIC MIX: Jewish 81%, Arab 18%, other 1%

GOVERNMENT: Parliamentary system

CURRENCY: Shekel = 100 agorot

Italy

The Italian peninsula was home to the Roman Empire, one of the greatest ancient civilizations. The south has two famous volcanoes, Vesuvius (near Napoli) and Etna (on Sicily).

 ## GEOGRAPHY
The Appennines form the backbone of a rugged peninsula, extending from the Alps into the Mediterranean Sea. Alluvial plain in the north.

 ## CLIMATE
Mediterranean in the south. Seasonal extremes in the mountains and on the northern alluvial plain.

 ## PEOPLE & SOCIETY
Ethnically homogeneous, but with a gulf between the prosperous, industrial north and the poorer, agricultural south. Strong regional identities persist, especially on Sicily and Sardinia. Family ties remain strong, though the influence of the Roman Catholic Church has lessened.

◆ **INSIGHT:** *Italy was a collection of dukedoms, monarchies, and city-states before unification in the 1860s*

$ THE ECONOMY
World leader in industrial and product design, fashion, and textiles. Strong tourism, agriculture. Large public debt: austerity packages. Three recessions in the last decade. High youth unemployment.

```
3000m/9843ft
2000m/6562ft
1000m/3281ft
500m/1640ft
200m/656ft
Sea Level
```

FACTFILE

OFFICIAL NAME: Italian Republic
DATE OF FORMATION: 1861
CAPITAL: Rome
POPULATION: 59.4 million
TOTAL AREA: 116,305 sq. miles (301,230 sq. km)
DENSITY: 523 people per sq. mile
LANGUAGES: Italian*, German, French, Rhaeto-Romanic, Sardinian
RELIGIONS: Roman Catholic 90%, non-religious 6%, Muslim 2%, other Christian 2%
ETHNIC MIX: Italian 92%, other European 5%, other 2%, North African (mainly Moroccan) 1%
GOVERNMENT: Parliamentary system
CURRENCY: Euro = 100 cents

Jamaica

First colonized by the Spanish and then by the English, the Caribbean island of Jamaica achieved independence in 1962. It remains an influential force in Caribbean politics.

GEOGRAPHY

Mainly mountainous, with lush tropical vegetation. Inaccessible limestone area in the northwest. Low, irregular coastal plains are broken by hills and plateaus.

CLIMATE

Tropical. Hot and humid at sea level, with temperate mountain areas. Hurricanes are likely June–November.

PEOPLE & SOCIETY

Social tensions result from vast disparities in wealth, rather than race. Economic and political life is dominated by a few wealthy, long-established families. Many women hold senior positions in public life. Armed crime, much of it narcotics-related, is a problem. Large areas of Kingston, which have their own patois, are ruled by violent gangs. Jamaican music styles are influential worldwide.

THE ECONOMY

Major bauxite producer, though sector vulnerable to changes in world prices. Tourism and light industry. Sugar, bananas, coffee, and rum are exported. Debt burden dominates budget. High underemployment.

INSIGHT: *Jamaica's Rastafarians revere the late emperor of Ethiopia, Haile Selassie, as their spiritual leader, and see Africa as their spiritual home*

2000m/6562ft	
1000m/3281ft	
500m/1640ft	
200m/656ft	
Sea Level	

0   40 km

0   40 miles

FACTFILE

OFFICIAL NAME: Jamaica

DATE OF FORMATION: 1962

CAPITAL: Kingston

POPULATION: 2.9 million

TOTAL AREA: 4243 sq. miles (10,990 sq. km)

DENSITY: 694 people per sq. mile

LANGUAGES: English Creole, English*

RELIGIONS: Church of God 26%, non-religious 22%, other Christian 21%, Seventh-day Adventist 12%, Pentecostal 11%, other 8%

ETHNIC MIX: Black African 92%, *Mulatto* (mixed race) 6%, East Indian 1%, other 1%

GOVERNMENT: Parliamentary system

CURRENCY: Jamaican dollar = 100 cents

Japan

Japan is located off the east Asian coast and comprises four principal islands and over 3000 smaller ones. A powerful economy, it has an emperor as ceremonial head of state.

GEOGRAPHY

The terrain is predominantly mountainous, with fertile coastal plains; over two-thirds is woodland. There is no single continuous mountain range; the mountains divide into many small land blocks separated by lowlands and dissected by numerous river valleys. The islands lie on the Pacific "Ring of Fire," and earthquakes and volcanic eruptions are frequent. The Pacific coast is vunerable to tsunamis. There are numerous hot springs.

CLIMATE

Generally temperate–oceanic. Spring is warm and sunny, while summer is hot and humid, with high rainfall. In western Hokkaido and northwest Honshu, winters are very cold, with heavy snowfall. Freak storms and damaging floods in recent years have raised concern over global climate changes.

PEOPLE & SOCIETY

One of the most racially homogeneous societies in the world. A sense of order and social structure was founded on a strongly ingrained respect for elders and social superiors. In business, this underpinned the now much-diluted "lifetime employer" concept, where company allegiance determined social life as well as career. There is little tradition of generational rebellion, but the youth market is powerful and current fashions focus on teenagers. The education system is highly pressurized. Nongraduates have difficulty reaching management-level jobs, so competition for university places is intense. Long-term jobs for women are now the norm. One of the world's best healthcare systems and increased longevity have led to an aging population, with one in three people already over 60. The cost of living is high, especially in Tokyo.

FACTFILE

OFFICIAL NAME: Japan
DATE OF FORMATION: 1590
CAPITAL: Tokyo
POPULATION: 128 million
TOTAL AREA: 145,882 sq. miles (377,835 sq. km)
DENSITY: 877 people per sq. mile

LANGUAGES: Japanese*, Korean, Chinese
RELIGIONS: Buddhist 50%, nonreligious 23%, Shinto 16%, Christian 10%, Muslim 1%
ETHNIC MIX: Japanese 99%, other (mainly Korean) 1%
GOVERNMENT: Parliamentary system
CURRENCY: Yen = 100 sen

THE ECONOMY

World's third-largest economy. A market leader in high-tech electronics and cars. Global spread of business. Once-revolutionary management and production methods. Long-term research and development. Talent for developing ideas from abroad. Protectionism in domestic economy. Reform of financial sector delayed by traditional economic power brokers. Major coal importer. Retreat from nuclear power after massive damage caused by 2011 earthquake and tsunami: resulting energy imports bill ended 30 years of trade surpluses.

INSIGHT: *Despite high internet usage, the Japanese remain avid newspaper readers, with daily sales still approaching 40 million copies*

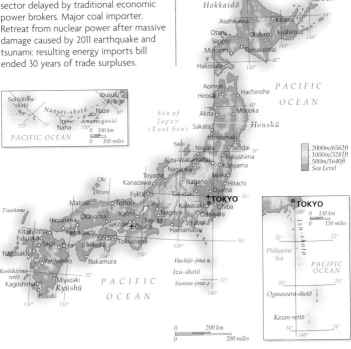

Jordan

The Kingdom of Jordan lies east of Israel, and borders the Palestinian West Bank. Usually pro-Western in outlook, Jordan fears the militant Islamists in Syria and Iraq.

GEOGRAPHY
Mostly desert plateaus, with occasional salt pans. The lowest parts lie along the eastern shores of the Dead Sea and the Jordan River.

CLIMATE
Hot, dry summers. Cool, wet winters. Areas below sea level very hot in summer, and warm in winter.

PEOPLE & SOCIETY
Jordanians are mainly Muslim with a strong national identity, but with Bedouin roots. The monarchy's power base lies among the rural tribes, which also provide the backbone of the army. Protests since 2011 have elicited gradual political reform, with greater powers for parliament. Jordan ceded its claim to the West Bank to the aspiring Palestinian state in 1988. Jordan hosts nearly three million refugees, most from Palestine, but more recently from Iraq and Syria.

THE ECONOMY
Lack of water. Exports garments, potash, fertilizers, and phosphates. Tourism hit by regional instability.

INSIGHT: *The Nabataean ruins of the ancient city of Petra attract thousands of tourists every year*

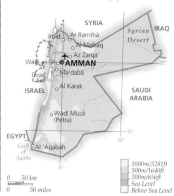

FACTFILE

OFFICIAL NAME: Hashemite Kingdom of Jordan

DATE OF FORMATION: 1946

CAPITAL: Amman

POPULATION: 9.7 million

TOTAL AREA: 35,637 sq. miles (92,300 sq. km)

DENSITY: 283 people per sq. mile

LANGUAGES: Arabic*

RELIGIONS: Sunni Muslim 92%, Christian 6%, other 2%

ETHNIC MIX: Arab 98%, Circassian 1%, Armenian 1%

GOVERNMENT: Monarchy

CURRENCY: Jordanian dinar = 1000 fils

Kazakhstan

Kazakhstan was the last of the former Soviet republics to declare independence. Foreign investment in the oil and natural gas sector is strengthening its regional power.

GEOGRAPHY

Mainly steppe. Volga Delta and Caspian Sea in the west. Central plateau. Inhospitable Altai Mountains in the east. Semidesert in the south.

CLIMATE

Dry continental. Temperature variations between desert south and northern steppes are large. Winters are mildest near the Caspian Sea.

PEOPLE & SOCIETY

Kazakhstan's ethnic diversity arose mainly from forced settlements there during Soviet times. Since independence, the proportion of ethnic Russians has dropped. Many emigrated, while ethnic Kazakhs arrived from neighboring states. Very few Kazakhs maintain a traditional nomadic lifestyle, but Islam and loyalty to clans remain strong. There are significant regional disparities of wealth.

THE ECONOMY

Vast mineral resources: natural gas, oil, bismuth, uranium, and cadmium. Oil pipelines to Russia, China, and Black Sea. Many Western investors. Wheat exports. Sale of farmland legal only since 2003.

INSIGHT: *The Soviet-built Baykonyr space center is still an important launch site for international missions*

FACTFILE

OFFICIAL NAME: Republic of Kazakhstan

DATE OF FORMATION: 1991

CAPITAL: Astana

POPULATION: 18.2 million

TOTAL AREA: 1,049,150 sq. miles (2,717,300 sq. km)

DENSITY: 17 people per sq. mile

LANGUAGES: Kazakh*, Russian, Ukrainian, German, Uzbek, Tatar, Uighur

RELIGIONS: Muslim (mainly Sunni) 71%, Orthodox Christian 26%, nonreligious 3%

ETHNIC MIX: Kazakh 63%, Russian 24%, other 6%, Uzbek 3%, Ukrainian 2%, Uighur 1%, Tatar 1%

GOVERNMENT: Presidential system

CURRENCY: Tenge = 100 tiyn

Kenya

Kenya straddles the equator on Africa's east coast. After nearly 40 years in power, the KANU party was soundly defeated in elections in 2002. Corruption is a serious issue.

GEOGRAPHY

A central plateau is divided by the Great Rift Valley. North of the equator is mainly semidesert. To the east lies a fertile coastal belt.

CLIMATE

The coast and the Great Rift Valley are hot and humid. The plateau interior is temperate. The northeastern desert is hot and dry. Rain usually falls April–May and October–November.

PEOPLE & SOCIETY

70 ethnic groups share about 40 languages. Strong clan and family links in rural areas are being weakened by urban migration. Poverty, severe drought, and years of high population growth exacerbate ethnic tensions.

◆ **INSIGHT:** *Kenya has around 60 national parks, game reserves, and marine reservations*

THE ECONOMY

Tourism, hurt by terrorist attacks. Flowers, tea, and coffee. Sizable informal economy. Diversified manufacturing sector. Reliant on food aid, as recurrent drought causes famines. Oil exploration.

5000m/16405ft
4000m/13124ft
3000m/9843ft
2000m/6562ft
1000m/3281ft
500m/1640ft
200m/656ft
Sea Level

0   100 km
0   100 miles

FACTFILE

OFFICIAL NAME: Republic of Kenya
DATE OF FORMATION: 1963
CAPITAL: Nairobi
POPULATION: 49.7 million
TOTAL AREA: 224,961 sq. miles (582,650 sq. km)
DENSITY: 227 people per sq. mile
LANGUAGES: Kiswahili*, English*, Kikuyu, Luo, Kalenjin, Kamba
RELIGIONS: Other Christian 60%, Roman Catholic 23%, Muslim 11%, other 4%, nonreligious 2%
ETHNIC MIX: Other 35%, Kikuyu 17%, Luhya 14%, Kalenjin 13%, Luo 11%, Kamba 10%
GOVERNMENT: Presidential system
CURRENCY: Kenya shilling = 100 cents

Kiribati

Situated in the mid-Pacific, the islands adopted the name Kiribati (pronounced "Keer-ee-bus," a corruption of their former name "Gilberts") upon independence from Britain in 1979.

GEOGRAPHY
Kiribati consists of three groups of tiny, very low-lying coral atolls scattered across 1,930,000 sq. miles (5 million sq. km) of ocean. Most of the 33 atolls have central lagoons.

CLIMATE
Central islands have a maritime equatorial climate. Those to north and south are tropical, with constant high temperatures. There is little rainfall.

PEOPLE & SOCIETY
Officially I-Kiribati, many local people still refer to themselves as Gilbertese. Almost all are Micronesian, apart from the inhabitants of the island of Banaba, who employed anthropologists to establish their racial distinction. Most people are poor subsistence farmers and many travel abroad to work. The islands are effectively ruled by traditional chiefs.

THE ECONOMY
Since exhaustion of Banaba's phosphate deposits in 1980, copra (dried coconut) and fish have become the main exports. Foreign aid and remittances are vital to compensate for Kiribati's isolation and lack of resources.

◆ **INSIGHT:** *In 1981, the UK paid A$10 million to Banabans to compensate for the destruction of their island by mining*

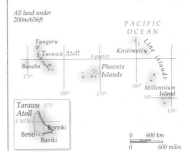

All land under 200m/656ft

PACIFIC OCEAN

Tungaru
Tarawa Atoll
Banaba
170°
Equator
Kiritimati
Line Islands
Phoenix Islands
180°   170°
160°   Millennium Island
10°
150°

Tarawa Atoll 173°
1°30'N
Betio   Bonriki
Bairiki

0   600 km
0   600 miles

FACTFILE

OFFICIAL NAME: Republic of Kiribati
DATE OF FORMATION: 1979
CAPITAL: Tarawa Atoll (Bairiki serves as administrative center)
POPULATION: 114,000
TOTAL AREA: 277 sq. miles (717 sq. km)
DENSITY: 416 people per sq. mile

LANGUAGES: English*, Kiribati
RELIGIONS: Roman Catholic 56%, Kiribati Protestant Church 34%, Mormon 5%, Baha'i 2%, Seventh-day Adventist 2%, other 1%
ETHNIC MIX: Micronesian 99%, other 1%
GOVERNMENT: Presidential system
CURRENCY: Australian dollar = 100 cents

North Korea

Separated from the democratic South by the world's most heavily defended border, the Stalinist North Korean state has been isolated from the outside world since 1948.

GEOGRAPHY

Mostly mountainous, with fertile plains in the southwest.

CLIMATE

Continental. Warm summers and cold winters, especially in the north, where snow is common.

PEOPLE & SOCIETY

Life is heavily regulated. Cult of personality is more powerful than the state-controlled religions, which include Korea's own Chondogyo. Women are expected to work and to run the home. Children are looked after in state-run crèches. The Korean Worker's Party is the sole party. Its elite have a privileged lifestyle. Globally condemned for its nuclear weapons tests, the regime's grip on power perpetuates its pariah status.

 INSIGHT: *Internet access is limited, and restricted to the political elite*

THE ECONOMY
Minerals are only resource. Vital aid streams lost with global collapse of communism after 1989. Decades of economic mismanagement have led to chronic food shortages. Lack of fuel. Disproportionate defense budget.

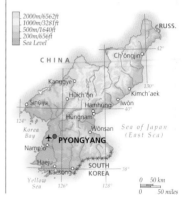

FACTFILE

OFFICIAL NAME: Democratic People's Republic of Korea

DATE OF FORMATION: 1948

CAPITAL: Pyongyang

POPULATION: 25.5 million

TOTAL AREA: 46,540 sq. miles (120,540 sq. km)

DENSITY: 549 people per sq. mile

LANGUAGES: Korean*

RELIGIONS: Government-controlled religions include Chondogyo, Buddhism, and Christianity

ETHNIC MIX: Korean 100%

GOVERNMENT: One-party state

CURRENCY: North Korean won = 100 chon

South Korea

South Korea occupies the southern half of the Korean peninsula. Under US sponsorship, it was separated from the communist North in 1948 and is now a capitalist economy.

GEOGRAPHY

Over 80% is mountainous and two-thirds is forested. The flattest and most populous parts lie along the west coast and in the extreme south.

CLIMATE

There are four distinct seasons. Winters are dry, and bitterly cold. Summers are hot and humid.

PEOPLE & SOCIETY

Inhabited for the last 2000 years by a single ethnic group. The nuclear family is replacing traditional extended households. Since the 1953 armistice, the Koreas have remained technically at war. Reunification is the ultimate goal, but the two sides fluctuate between harsh rhetoric or belligerence and conciliation, allowing cross-border family reunions.

◆ **INSIGHT:** *Half of all Koreans are named Kim, Lee, Park, or Choi*

THE ECONOMY

One of the world's leading shipbuilders. High-tech goods and cars: rising demand from China. Strong regional competition. Aging population.

FACTFILE

OFFICIAL NAME: Republic of Korea
DATE OF FORMATION: 1948
CAPITALS: Seoul; Sejong City (administrative)
POPULATION: 51 million
TOTAL AREA: 38,023 sq. miles (98,480 sq. km)
DENSITY: 1338 people per sq. mile

LANGUAGES: Korean*
RELIGIONS: Nonreligious 47%, Mahayana Buddhist 23%, other Christian 18%, Roman Catholic 11%, other 1%
ETHNIC MIX: Korean 100%
GOVERNMENT: Presidential system
CURRENCY: South Korean won = 100 chon

Kosovo (not internationally recognized)

Once part of the former Yugoslav state, Kosovo seceded from Serbia in 2008. International recognition, mainly from Western countries, is strongly opposed by Serbia and Russia.

GEOGRAPHY
Landlocked and mountainous, with two plains in the east and west.

CLIMATE
Continental, with warm, sunny summers and cold, snowy winters.

PEOPLE & SOCIETY
The balance of Albanians to Serbs in Kosovo has changed dramatically over centuries, both groups suffering interethnic violence at various times. Attacks against Albanians in the late 1990s caused a million to flee. After NATO stepped in, many Serbs left: Albanians now form a 92% majority. Most Albanians are Muslim. Serbs dominate three northern provinces, which have threatened to secede.

◆ **INSIGHT:** *The UN administered Kosovo in 1999–2008 after NATO intervention to stop Serb ethnic cleansing*

THE ECONOMY
One of the poorest countries in Europe. Inefficient agriculture. Lignite deposits. Aid and remittances cover a large trade deficit. Uncertain status deters foreign investors. Organized crime: narcotics and organ trafficking. High unemployment. Use of euro has helped fight inflation.

FACTFILE

OFFICIAL NAME: Republic of Kosovo
DATE OF FORMATION: 2008
CAPITAL: Prishtinë/Priština
POPULATION: 1.9 million
TOTAL AREA: 4212 sq. miles (10,908 sq. km)
DENSITY: 451 people per sq. mile

LANGUAGES: Albanian*, Serbian*, Bosniak, Gorani, Roma, Turkish
RELIGIONS: Muslim 92%, Roman Catholic 4%, Orthodox Christian 4%
ETHNIC MIX: Albanian 92%, Serb 4%, Bosniak and Gorani 2%, Turkish 1%, Roma 1%
GOVERNMENT: Parliamentary system
CURRENCY: Euro = 100 cents

Kuwait

Kuwait lies at the northwest tip of the Gulf, dwarfed by its neighbors Iraq, Iran, and Saudi Arabia. It was a British protectorate until 1961, when full independence was granted.

GEOGRAPHY
Terrain is low-lying desert. The lowest land is in the north. Cultivation is only possible along the coast.

CLIMATE
Summers are very hot and dry. Winters are cooler, with some rain and occasional frost at night.

PEOPLE & SOCIETY
Oil-rich monarchy, ruled by the al-Sabah family. It is a conservative Sunni Muslim society, but women are relatively free. Nonetheless, a 1999 decree giving women the vote was blocked for six years in parliament by Islamic traditionalists. Immigrant workers, from other Arab states, India, and Pakistan, now outnumber native citizens. US-led forces rescued Kuwait after the 1990 Iraqi invasion, and later used it as a launchpad for the 2003 invasion to oust Saddam Hussein.

THE ECONOMY
Oil and natural gas dominate the economy. Skilled workforce, raw materials, and food are imported. High standard of living. Financial services sector diversifies economy.

INSIGHT: *During the 1991 Gulf War, Iraq deliberately set fire to 800 of Kuwait's 950 oil wells*

FACTFILE

OFFICIAL NAME: State of Kuwait
DATE OF FORMATION: 1961
CAPITAL: Kuwait City
POPULATION: 4.1 million
TOTAL AREA: 6880 sq. miles (17,820 sq. km)
DENSITY: 596 people per sq. mile

LANGUAGES: Arabic*, English
RELIGIONS: Sunni Muslim 45%, Shi'a Muslim 40%, Christian, Hindu, and other 15%
ETHNIC MIX: Asian 39%, Kuwaiti 37%, other Arab 21%, African 2%, other 1%
GOVERNMENT: Monarchy
CURRENCY: Kuwaiti dinar = 1000 fils

Kyrgyzstan

A small and mountainous landlocked state in central Asia, Kyrgyzstan is one of the least urbanized ex-Soviet republics, and was slow to develop its own sense of cultural identity.

 GEOGRAPHY
The mountainous spurs of the Tien Shan range contain glaciers, alpine meadows, forests, and narrow valleys. Semidesert in the west.

 CLIMATE
Varies from permanent snow and cold deserts at high altitudes, to hot deserts in low regions.

PEOPLE & SOCIETY
Ethnic Kyrgyz have only been in the majority since the late 1980s – due to a high birth rate and the emigration of ethnic Russians. Wary of losing skills vital to the economy, the government has attempted to deter Russians from leaving; concessions include making Russian an official language. There are some tensions between Kyrgyz and Uzbeks, and a trend toward greater Islamization, particularly in the poorer south.

THE ECONOMY
Mainly still under state control; corruption issues. Agriculture employs under a third of the labor force. Cotton, wool, meat, and tobacco exports. Mercury, gold, and antimony are mined. Great potential for hydroelectric power.

INSIGHT: *Kyrgyz folklore is based around the 1000-year-old poem, Manas, which takes a week to recite*

4000m/13124ft
3000m/9843ft
2000m/6562ft
1000m/3281ft
500m/1640ft

FACTFILE

OFFICIAL NAME: Kyrgyz Republic
DATE OF FORMATION: 1991
CAPITAL: Bishkek
POPULATION: 6 million
TOTAL AREA: 76,641 sq. miles (198,500 sq. km)
DENSITY: 78 people per sq. mile
LANGUAGES: Kyrgyz*, Russian*, Uzbek, .

Tatar, Ukrainian
RELIGIONS: Muslim (mainly Sunni) 70%, Orthodox Christian 30%
ETHNIC MIX: Kyrgyz 71%, Uzbek 14%, Russian 8%, other 4%, Dungan 1%, Uighur 1%, Tajik 1%
GOVERNMENT: Mixed presidential–parliamentary system
CURRENCY: Som = 100 tyiyn

Laos

A French colony prior to 1953, Laos lies landlocked in southeast Asia. Heavily bombed during the Vietnam War, it fell in 1975 to communist insurgents, whose regime remains in power.

GEOGRAPHY
Largely forested mountains, broadening in the north to a plateau. Lowlands along the Mekong Valley.

CLIMATE
Monsoon rains September–May. The rest of the year is hot and dry.

PEOPLE & SOCIETY
There are over 60 ethnic groups. Lowland Laotians (Lao Loum) live along the Mekong River and are rice farmers. Upland and highland Laotians (Lao Theung and Lao Soung) traditionally employ environmentally damaging slash-and-burn farming, and grow illegal cash crops (notably opium). Government efforts to reform these practices are resisted.

◆ INSIGHT: *Three small Laotian kingdoms were unified under French control in 1899*

THE ECONOMY
One of world's least developed nations. Strong GDP growth. Copper, gold, electricity, garments, and coffee are exported. Illegal timber trade is a problem. Poor infrastructure. Levels of foreign investment are rising.

```
          0      100 km
          0      100 miles
```

2000m/6562ft
1000m/3281ft
500m/1640ft
200m/656ft
Sea Level

FACTFILE

OFFICIAL NAME: Lao People's Democratic Republic
DATE OF FORMATION: 1953
CAPITAL: Vientiane
POPULATION: 6.9 million
TOTAL AREA: 91,428 sq. miles (236,800 sq. km)
DENSITY: 77 people per sq. mile

LANGUAGES: Lao*, Mon-Khmer, Yao, Vietnamese, Chinese, French
RELIGIONS: Buddhist 67%, other 31%, Christian 2%
ETHNIC MIX: Lao Loum 66%, Lao Theung 30%, Lao Soung 2%, other 2%
GOVERNMENT: One-party state
CURRENCY: Kip = 100 at

Latvia

Latvia lies on the east coast of the Baltic Sea. Like its Baltic neighbors, it regained independence from Moscow in 1991, and joined the EU and NATO in 2004.

GEOGRAPHY

A flat coastal plain which is deeply indented by the Gulf of Riga. Poor drainage creates many bogs and swamps in the forested interior.

CLIMATE

Temperate, with warm summers and cold winters. There is steady rainfall throughout the year.

PEOPLE & SOCIETY

Latvians make up just under two-thirds of the population and are mostly Lutheran or Roman Catholic. They have been officially favored by the state since 1991 over the largely Orthodox Christian Russian minority. Latvian was declared the only official language in 2000 and, since 2004, has been used exclusively in schools. This discrimination has strained relations with Russia. Women enjoy full equality. The divorce rate is high, though down from the Soviet era peak.

THE ECONOMY

Service-led economy. After fast growth, global credit crunch brought Latvia to verge of bankruptcy in 2008: banks bailed out, and stringent austerity imposed. Worst recession in EU ensued. Quick return to growth: fastest in EU in 2012–2014. Adopted euro in 2014.

◆ **INSIGHT:** *In Latvia, life expectancy for men is ten years less than for women*

200m/656ft Sea Level

0   50 km

0   50 miles

FACTFILE

OFFICIAL NAME: Republic of Latvia

DATE OF FORMATION: 1991

CAPITAL: Riga

POPULATION: 1.9 million

TOTAL AREA: 24,938 sq. miles (64,589 sq. km)

DENSITY: 76 people per sq. mile

LANGUAGES: Latvian*, Russian

RELIGIONS: Orthodox Christian 31%, Roman Catholic 23%, nonreligious 21%, Lutheran 19%, other 6%

ETHNIC MIX: Latvian 62%, Russian 27%, Belarussian 3%, other 3%, Polish 2%, Ukrainian 2%, Lithuanian 1%

GOVERNMENT: Parliamentary system

CURRENCY: Euro = 100 cents

Lebanon

Once a vibrant cultural hotspot, Lebanon suffered 14 years of civil war and occupation until a 1989 peace deal. It now fears spillover from neighboring Syria's own civil war.

GEOGRAPHY
Behind a narrow Mediterranean coastal plain, two parallel mountain ranges run the length of the country, separated by the fertile Beqaa Valley.

CLIMATE
Winters are mild and summers are hot, with high coastal humidity. Snow falls on high ground in winter.

PEOPLE & SOCIETY
Huge gulf exists between the poor and a small, rich elite. Politics reflects divisions between the traditional ruling Maronite Christians and Sunni and Shi'a Muslims. A 1989 power-sharing deal ended civil war. Syria acted as power broker until made to withdraw in 2005. Political crises add to instability. Israel attacked in 2006 in a botched bid to crush Iran-backed Hezbollah militants. Lebanon hosts over a million Syrian refugees and 450,000 from Palestine.

THE ECONOMY
Wine and fruit. Much infrastructure destroyed. Instability undermines Beirut's role as regional financial center. High public debt. Refugee influx.

INSIGHT: *The Cedar of Lebanon has been the nation's symbol for more than 2000 years*

3000m/9843ft	
2000m/6562ft	
1000m/3281ft	
500m/1640ft	
200m/656ft	
Sea Level	

FACTFILE

OFFICIAL NAME: Republic of Lebanon
DATE OF FORMATION: 1941
CAPITAL: Beirut
POPULATION: 6.1 million
TOTAL AREA: 4015 sq. miles (10,400 sq. km)
DENSITY: 1544 people per sq. mile

LANGUAGES: Arabic*, French, Armenian, Assyrian
RELIGIONS: Muslim 60%, Christian 39%, other 1%
ETHNIC MIX: Arab 95%, Armenian 4%, other 1%
GOVERNMENT: Parliamentary system
CURRENCY: Lebanese pound = 100 piastres

Lesotho

The landlocked Kingdom of Lesotho is entirely surrounded by – and economically dependent on – South Africa, which even sent in troops to restore calm after rioting in 1998.

GEOGRAPHY
A high mountainous plateau, cut by valleys and ravines. The Maluti Range runs through the center. The Drakensberg Range lies to the east.

CLIMATE
Temperate. Summers are hot with torrential rain storms. Snow is frequent in the mountains in winter.

PEOPLE & SOCIETY
The overwhelming majority of people are Sotho, though there are some South Asians, Europeans, and Chinese. A strong sense of national identity has tended to minimize ethnic tensions. Many men work as migrant laborers in South Africa, leaving women to run households.

◆ INSIGHT: *One in four people live with HIV/AIDS and life expectancy is just 50 years – only Swaziland suffers worse rates*

THE ECONOMY
Dependent on South Africa. Water and energy exported from Highlands Water Scheme. Subsistence farming. Garment exports struggle to compete. HIV/AIDS is depleting workforce.

SOUTH AFRICA
Caledon
Hlotse
Teyateyaneng
Mokhotlong
MASERU
Maluti
Morija
Mantsonyane
Mafeteng
Drakensberg
Orange River
Mohales Hoek
SOUTH AFRICA

3000m/9843ft
2000m/6562ft
1000m/3281ft

0   50 km
0   50 miles

FACTFILE

OFFICIAL NAME: Kingdom of Lesotho
DATE OF FORMATION: 1966
CAPITAL: Maseru
POPULATION: 2.2 million
TOTAL AREA: 11,720 sq. miles (30,355 sq. km)
DENSITY: 188 people per sq. mile

LANGUAGES: English*, Sesotho*, isiZulu
RELIGIONS: Christian 90%, traditional beliefs 10%
ETHNIC MIX: Sotho 99%, European and Asian 1%
GOVERNMENT: Parliamentary system
CURRENCY: Loti = 100 lisente (or SA rand)

Liberia

Liberia, on Africa's Atlantic coast, was founded as a republic of freed slaves. A brutal coup in 1980 and years of civil war have left a legacy of gang violence and looting.

GEOGRAPHY
A coastline of beaches and mangrove swamps rises to forested plateaus and highlands inland.

CLIMATE
High temperatures. There is only one wet season, from May to October, except in the extreme southeast.

PEOPLE & SOCIETY
The key social distinction used to be between Americo-Liberians – descendants of freed slaves – and the indigenous tribal peoples. However, political assimilation and intermarriage have eased tensions. Intertribal tension is now a much more serious problem, fueling the 1990–2003 civil war. An Ebola outbreak hit the country in 2014–2015.

◆ **INSIGHT:** *Liberia is named for the people liberated from slavery who arrived from the US in the 1800s*

THE ECONOMY
War caused economic collapse. Rubber is key export. Bans now lifted on timber and diamond exports. Revenue from merchant shipping licenses. Debt burden. Vast iron ore reserves. Shutdown in 2014 due to Ebola.

FACTFILE

OFFICIAL NAME: Republic of Liberia
DATE OF FORMATION: 1847
CAPITAL: Monrovia
POPULATION: 4.7 million
TOTAL AREA: 43,000 sq. miles (111,370 sq. km)
DENSITY: 126 people per sq. mile
LANGUAGES: Kpelle, Vai, Bassa, Kru, Grebo, Kissi, Gola, Loma, English*
RELIGIONS: Christian 86%, Muslim 12%, nonreligious 1%, traditional beliefs and other 1%
ETHNIC MIX: Indigenous tribes (12 groups) 50%, Kpellé 20%, Bassa 14%, Gio 8%, Krou 6%, other 2%
GOVERNMENT: Presidential system
CURRENCY: Liberian dollar = 100 cents

Libya

Situated on north Africa's Mediterranean coast, Libya was declared a revolutionary state in 1969 by Colonel Gaddafi. Civil war, launched in the 2011 "Arab Spring," ousted his regime.

GEOGRAPHY
Apart from the coastal strip and a mountain range in the south, Libya is desert or semidesert.

CLIMATE
Hot and arid. The coastal area has a temperate climate, with mild, wet winters and hot, dry summers.

PEOPLE & SOCIETY
Once a nation of nomads and livestock herders, it is almost 80% urban. Gaddafi's revolution wiped out private enterprise and the middle classes, and promoted Islam and African unity. Sanctions were lifted after Libya offered compensation for terrorist bombings and ended its Weapons of Mass Destruction (WMD) program. In 2011, rebels from the east took power with international help, but failed to unite the country. Tripoli is in the sway of Islamist militias, while rival parliaments vie for political control.

THE ECONOMY
Oil is key export. Dates, olives, and fruit grow in oases, but most food is imported. Ongoing instability. Corruption and mismanagement.

◆ **INSIGHT:** 90% of Libya is still desert, despite grand irrigation projects

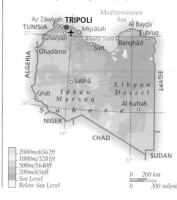

2000m/6562ft
1000m/3281ft
500m/1640ft
200m/656ft
Sea Level
Below Sea Level

0   200 km
0   200 miles

FACTFILE

OFFICIAL NAME: Libya

DATE OF FORMATION: 1951

CAPITAL: Tripoli

POPULATION: 6.4 million

TOTAL AREA: 679,358 sq. miles (1,759,540 sq. km)

DENSITY: 9 people per sq. mile

LANGUAGES: Arabic*, Tuareg

RELIGIONS: Muslim (mainly Sunni) 97%, other 3%

ETHNIC MIX: Arab and Berber 97%, other 3%

GOVERNMENT: Transitional regime

CURRENCY: Libyan dinar = 1000 dirhams

Liechtenstein

Perched in the Alps between Switzerland and Austria, the state of Liechtenstein became an independent principality of the Holy Roman Empire in 1719. It has close links with Switzerland.

GEOGRAPHY
The upper Rhine Valley covers the western third of the country. The mountains and narrow valleys of the eastern Alps make up the remainder.

CLIMATE
Warm, dry summers. Winters are cold, with heavy snow in the mountains from December to March.

PEOPLE & SOCIETY
The principality's role as a financial center accounts for its many foreign residents (a third of the population). Just over half of the workforce are cross-border commuters. Living standards are high, with few social tensions. Linked by a customs union since 1924, Switzerland handles Liechtenstein's foreign affairs and defense issues.

INSIGHT: *Women in Liechtenstein obtained the vote only in 1984*

THE ECONOMY
Banking secrecy (now modified) and low taxes help attract foreign investment. Anti-money-laundering rules are recent. Diversified exports include precision instruments, dental products, and chemicals.

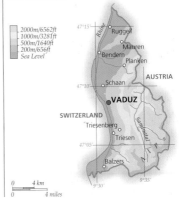

2000m/6562ft	
1000m/3281ft	
500m/1640ft	
200m/656ft	
Sea Level	

FACTFILE

OFFICIAL NAME: Principality of Liechtenstein

DATE OF FORMATION: 1719

CAPITAL: Vaduz

POPULATION: 38,000

TOTAL AREA: 62 sq. miles (160 sq. km)

DENSITY: 613 people per sq. mile

LANGUAGES: German*, Alemannish dialect, Italian

RELIGIONS: Roman Catholic 78%, Protestant 9%, Muslim 6%, nonreligious 5%, other 2%

ETHNIC MIX: Liechtensteiner 66%, other 12%, Swiss 10%, Austrian 6%, German 3%, Italian 3%

GOVERNMENT: Parliamentary system

CURRENCY: Swiss franc = 100 rappen/centimes

Lithuania

Lying on the eastern coast of the Baltic Sea, Lithuania is the largest of the Baltic states. The first Soviet republic to declare independence from Moscow in 1991, it joined the EU in 2004.

GEOGRAPHY
Mostly flat with moors, bogs, and an intensively farmed central lowland. Numerous lakes and forested sandy ridges in the east.

CLIMATE
Coastal location moderates continental extremes. Cold winters, cool summers, and steady rainfall.

PEOPLE & SOCIETY
Homogeneous population, with Lithuanians forming a large majority. Only 1200 Jews, known as Litvaks, remain in Lithuania. Strong Roman Catholic tradition and historic links with Poland. There are better relations among ethnic groups than in other Baltic states and interethnic marriages are fairly common. However, ethnic Russians and Poles see a threat from "Lithuanianization." A large income gap has grown since independence.

THE ECONOMY
High-tech and heavy industries: engineering, shipbuilding, food processing. Bounced back from deep recession in 2009; strong growth from 2011. Adopted euro in 2015. Russia has restricted trade.

INSIGHT: *The "amber coast" of Lithuania produces most of the world's amber – fossilized resin*

FACTFILE

OFFICIAL NAME: Republic of Lithuania
DATE OF FORMATION: 1991
CAPITAL: Vilnius
POPULATION: 2.9 million
TOTAL AREA: 25,174 sq. miles (65,200 sq. km)
DENSITY: 115 people per sq. mile

LANGUAGES: Lithuanian*, Russian
RELIGIONS: Roman Catholic 75%, Christian 14%, nonreligious 6%, Orthodox Christian 3%, other 2%
ETHNIC MIX: Lithuanian 85%, Polish 7%, Russian 6%, Belarussian 1%, other 1%
GOVERNMENT: Parliamentary system
CURRENCY: Euro = 100 cents

Luxembourg

Part of the plateau of the Ardennes in western Europe, Luxembourg is one of Europe's richest states. A tax haven and banking center, it is also home to key EU institutions.

GEOGRAPHY
Dense Ardennes forests in the north, with a low, open plateau to the south. Undulating terrain throughout.

CLIMATE
The climate is moist, with warm summers and mild winters. Snow is common only in the Ardennes.

PEOPLE & SOCIETY
Ethnic tensions are rare, despite a large proportion of foreigners (over a third of residents). Integration has been straightforward; most are fellow western Europeans and Catholics, mainly from Italy and Portugal. Low unemployment and high salaries promote stability. Divorce rates have risen over the last 50 years and marriage is less common.

◆ INSIGHT: *Luxembourg's capital is home to around 4000 investment funds and 150 banks*

THE ECONOMY
Traditional industries such as steelmaking have given way to the banking and service sectors. Low taxes and banking secrecy laws attract foreign investors.

FACTFILE

OFFICIAL NAME: Grand Duchy of Luxembourg

DATE OF FORMATION: 1867

CAPITAL: Luxembourg

POPULATION: 583,000

TOTAL AREA: 998 sq. miles (2586 sq. km)

DENSITY: 584 people per sq. mile

LANGUAGES: Luxembourgish*, German*, French*

RELIGIONS: Roman Catholic 97%, Protestant, Orthodox Christian, and Jewish 3%

ETHNIC MIX: Luxembourger 62%, foreign residents 38%

GOVERNMENT: Parliamentary system

CURRENCY: Euro = 100 cents

Macedonia

Landlocked Macedonia, formerly part of Yugoslavia, was hit hard in the 1990s by sanctions on its northern trading partners, and in 2001 by conflict with its Albanian minority.

GEOGRAPHY
Mainly mountainous or hilly, with deep river basins in the center. Plains in the northeast and southwest.

CLIMATE
Continental climate with wet springs and dry autumns. Heavy snowfalls in northern mountains.

PEOPLE & SOCIETY
Slav Macedonians are mostly Orthodox Christians, with some Muslims. Officially, Muslim Albanians account for 25% of the population, but they claim to number a third. Albanian militants fought a bitter war against the state in 2001. A peace deal offered greater equality, such as Albanian as an official language, but parts remain unfulfilled. A stumbling block to EU/NATO accession is Greece's objection to the name Macedonia, fearing possible claims to historic "Macedonian" lands in north Greece.

THE ECONOMY
Steel, minerals, clothing, shoes, and tobacco exported. High unemployment. Organized crime and large gray economy. Progress with reforms. EU candidate status. Ongoing political instability.

INSIGHT: *Ohrid is the deepest lake in Europe at 964 ft (294 m)*

FACTFILE

OFFICIAL NAME: Republic of Macedonia
DATE OF FORMATION: 1991
CAPITAL: Skopje
POPULATION: 2.1 million
TOTAL AREA: 9781 sq. miles (25,333 sq. km)
DENSITY: 212 people per sq. mile
LANGUAGES: Macedonian*, Albanian*, Turkish, Romani, Serbian
RELIGIONS: Orthodox Christian 65%, Muslim 33%, other 2%
ETHNIC MIX: Macedonian 64%, Albanian 25%, Turkish 4%, Roma 3%, Serb 2%, other 2%
GOVERNMENT: Mixed presidential–parliamentary system
CURRENCY: Macedonian denar = 100 deni

Madagascar

Lying off east Africa in the Indian Ocean, the former French colony of Madagascar is the world's fourth-largest island. Power struggles erupted onto the streets in 2002 and 2009.

GEOGRAPHY

More than two-thirds is a savanna-covered plateau, which drops in the east through rainforests to the coast.

CLIMATE

Tropical and often hit by cyclones. Monsoons affect the east coast. The southwest is much drier.

PEOPLE & SOCIETY

People are Malay-Indonesian in origin, intermixed with later migrants from Africa. The main ethnic division is between the Merina of the central plateau and the poorer *côtier* (coastal) peoples. The Merina, who have ruled historically, remain the social elite. The 2009 unrest led to a four-year transition, but politics remains unstable.

INSIGHT: *80% of Madagascar's plants and many of its animal species are found nowhere else*

THE ECONOMY

Most people are farmers. Cash crops are vanilla, coffee, and cloves. Garments and shrimp also exported. Political crises deter investors.

FACTFILE

OFFICIAL NAME: Republic of Madagascar
DATE OF FORMATION: 1960
CAPITAL: Antananarivo
POPULATION: 25.6 million
TOTAL AREA: 226,656 sq. miles (587,040 sq. km)
DENSITY: 114 people per sq. mile

LANGUAGES: Malagasy*, French*, English
RELIGIONS: Traditional beliefs 52%, Christian (mainly Roman Catholic) 41%, Muslim 7%
ETHNIC MIX: Other Malay 46%, Merina 26%, Betsimisaraka 15%, Betsileo 12%, other 1%
GOVERNMENT: Mixed presidential–parliamentary system
CURRENCY: Ariary = 5 iraimbilanja

Malawi

A former colony of the UK, Malawi lies landlocked in southeast Africa, following the Great Rift Valley. Its name means "the land where the sun is reflected in the water like fire."

GEOGRAPHY
Lake Nyasa takes up one-fifth of the landscape. Highlands lie west of the lake. Much of the land is covered by forests and savanna.

CLIMATE
Mainly subtropical. The south is hot and humid. Highlands are cooler.

PEOPLE & SOCIETY
Most Malawians share a common Bantu origin. Protestant Chewa live in central regions, while Muslim Yao live along the lake and in the south. Unlike neighboring states, ethnicity has not been exploited for political ends. Multiparty elections in 1994 ended the 30-year dictatorship of Dr. Banda. Half of the population lives in poverty.

◆ INSIGHT: *Lake Nyasa is 353 miles (568 km) in length and contains at least 500 species of fish*

THE ECONOMY
Mainly subsistence farming. Tobacco accounts for over half of export earnings. Tea and sugar are grown. Drought, floods, and corruption are problems.

FACTFILE

OFFICIAL NAME: Republic of Malawi

DATE OF FORMATION: 1964

CAPITAL: Lilongwe

POPULATION: 18.6 million

TOTAL AREA: 45,745 sq. miles (118,480 sq. km)

DENSITY: 512 people per sq. mile

LANGUAGES: Chewa, Lomwe, Yao, Ngoni, English*

RELIGIONS: Christian (mainly Protestant) 83%, Muslim 13%, nonreligious 2%, other 2%

ETHNIC MIX: Bantu 99%, other 1%

GOVERNMENT: Presidential system

CURRENCY: Malawi kwacha = 100 tambala

Malaysia

Malaysia stretches 1240 miles (2000 km) across southeast Asia from the Malay peninsula to Sabah in eastern Borneo. Federated in 1963, it included Singapore for two years.

GEOGRAPHY
The Malay Peninsula has central mountains, an eastern coastal belt, and fertile western plains. Swampy coastal plains rise to mountains on Borneo.

CLIMATE
Warm equatorial. Rainfall always heavy, but with distinct rainy seasons.

INSIGHT: *Malaysia is southeast Asia's second-biggest tourist destination, with over 26 million visitors a year*

PEOPLE & SOCIETY
The key distinction is between Malays (Bumiputras, literally "sons of the soil") and the Chinese, who traditionally controlled most economic activity. Since the 1970s, Malays have been favored for education and jobs, in order to address this imbalance.

THE ECONOMY
Successful industrial base includes electronics, manufacturing, and heavy industry. Tourism is a major earner. Leading producer of palm oil, tin, and tropical hardwoods.

2000m/6562ft
1000m/3281ft
500m/1640ft
200m/656ft
Sea Level

THAILAND
Kangar
Kota Bharu
George Town
Taiping
Malay Peninsula
Kuala Terengganu
South China Sea
KUALA LUMPUR
PUTRAJAYA
Klang
Mersing
Kepulauan Natuna
Natuna Sea
SINGAPORE
INDONESIA
Kudat
Kota Kinabalu
Sandakan
Sulu Sea
Keningau
BRUNEI
Miri
Sabah
Bintulu
Borneo
Sibu
Sarawak
Kuching
Sri Aman
INDONESIA
INDONESIA

0   100 km
0   100 miles

FACTFILE

OFFICIAL NAME: Malaysia
DATE OF FORMATION: 1963
CAPITALS: Kuala Lumpur; Putrajaya (administrative)
POPULATION: 31.6 million
TOTAL AREA: 127,316 sq. miles (329,750 sq. km)
DENSITY: 249 people per sq. mile

LANGUAGES: Bahasa Malaysia*, Malay, Chinese, Tamil, English
RELIGIONS: Muslim 62%, Buddhist 20%, Christian 9%, Hindu 6%, other 3%
ETHNIC MIX: Malay 50%, Chinese 22%, indigenous tribes 12%, other 9%, Indian 7%
GOVERNMENT: Parliamentary system
CURRENCY: Ringgit = 100 sen

Maldives

Set in the Indian Ocean, southwest of Sri Lanka, the Maldives is an archipelago of 1191 small coral islands, or atolls. 200 are inhabited. The word atoll comes from the Dhivehi word "atolu."

GEOGRAPHY
Consists of low-lying islands and coral atolls. The larger ones are covered in lush, tropical vegetation.

CLIMATE
Tropical. Rain falls throughout the year, but is heaviest June–November, during the monsoon. Violent storms occasionally hit the northern islands.

PEOPLE & SOCIETY
Maldivians, who are mostly Sunni Muslim, are descended from Sinhalese, Dravidian, Arab, and black ancestors. A third of the population live on Male'. Tourism has grown on separate resort islands away from residents. Politics was controlled by a group of influential families until young reformers pushed for parties to be legalized in 2005. However, legislative stalemate followed, and a controversial presidential election in 2013 returned the former elite to power.

THE ECONOMY
Luxury tourist industry is the economic mainstay. Fish, especially tuna, are the main export. Tsunami damage in 2004. Strong economic growth.

INSIGHT:
The islands, which all lie below 4 ft (1.2 m), are threatened by rising sea levels, brought about by global warming and climatic changes

Ihavandippolhu Atoll

Faadhippolhu Atoll

Horsburgh Atoll

Male' Atoll

Ari Atoll

●MALE

Felidhu Atoll

Mulakatho Atoll

Kolhumadulu Atoll

Hadhdhunmathi Atoll

One and Half Degree Channel

North Huvadhu Atoll

South Huvadhu Atoll

Addu Atoll

Gan

INDIAN OCEAN

Equator

☐ Sea Level

0   100 km
0   100 miles

FACTFILE

OFFICIAL NAME: Republic of Maldives
DATE OF FORMATION: 1965
CAPITAL: Male
POPULATION: 417,000
TOTAL AREA: 116 sq. miles (300 sq. km)
DENSITY: 3595 people per sq. mile

LANGUAGES: Dhivehi* (Maldivian), Sinhala, Tamil, Arabic
RELIGIONS: Sunni Muslim 94%, Hindu 3%, Christian 2%, Buddhist 1%
ETHNIC MIX: All Maldivians are of Arab–Sinhalese–Malay descent
GOVERNMENT: Presidential system
CURRENCY: Rufiyaa = 100 laari

A former French colony, Mali is landlocked in the heart of west Africa. The 1991 coup ended the 23-year dictatorship of Moussa Traoré and ushered in multiparty elections from 1992.

GEOGRAPHY
The northern half lies in the Sahara. The inland delta of the Niger River flows through grassy savanna in the south.

CLIMATE
In the south, intensely hot, dry weather precedes the westerly rains. The north is almost rainless.

PEOPLE & SOCIETY
Most people live in the south and are farmers, herders, or river fishermen. Nomadic Fulani and Tuareg herders travel the northern plains. Rebellion broke out there in 2012, initially Tuareg-led, but Islamist insurgents soon seized key towns. They were pushed back with international help, but low-level conflict continues. Women have little status.

INSIGHT: *Tombouctou (Timbuktu) was the center of the 14th-century Malinké trading empire*

THE ECONOMY
Widespread poverty. Less than 2% of land can be cultivated. Vulnerable to drought. Gold, high-quality cotton, and livestock account for 90% of exports. Tourism held back by instability and kidnappings by Al-Qaeda in the Maghreb.

0   200 km
0   200 miles

500m/1640ft
200m/656ft
Sea Level

FACTFILE

OFFICIAL NAME: Republic of Mali
DATE OF FORMATION: 1960
CAPITAL: Bamako
POPULATION: 18.5 million
TOTAL AREA: 478,764 sq. miles (1,240,000 sq. km)
DENSITY: 39 people per sq. mile

LANGUAGES: Bambara, Fulani, Senufo, Soninke, French*
RELIGIONS: Muslim (mainly Sunni) 90%, traditional beliefs 6%, Christian 4%
ETHNIC MIX: Bambara 52%, other 18%, Fulani 11%, Saracolé 7%, Soninka 7%, Tuareg 5%
GOVERNMENT: Presidential system
CURRENCY: CFA franc = 100 centimes

Malta

The densely populated Maltese archipelago lies between Africa and Europe. Controlled throughout its history by successive colonial powers, it gained independence from the UK in 1964.

GEOGRAPHY
The main island of Malta has low hills and a ragged coastline with numerous harbors, bays, sandy beaches, and rocky coves. The island of Gozo is more densely vegetated.

CLIMATE
Mediterranean climate. There are many hours of sunshine all year round, with very little rainfall.

PEOPLE & SOCIETY
Over the centuries, the Maltese have been subject to Arab, Sicilian, Spanish, French, and British influences. Today, the population is socially conservative and devoutly Roman Catholic – Malta only legalized divorce in 2011, the last European country except the Vatican to do so. Population density is among the highest in the world. Illegal migration from Africa has increased since Malta joined the EU in 2004.

THE ECONOMY
Tourism provides over 25% of GDP. Joined eurozone in 2008. Developing offshore banking, and high-tech industry. Semiconductors exported. Most goods have to be imported.

INSIGHT: *Malta is the only country to receive the George Cross for gallantry, in 1942 for national resilience to relentless German bombardment*

FACTFILE

OFFICIAL NAME: Republic of Malta
DATE OF FORMATION: 1964
CAPITAL: Valletta
POPULATION: 437,000
TOTAL AREA: 122 sq. miles (316 sq. km)
DENSITY: 3524 people per sq. mile

LANGUAGES: Maltese*, English*
RELIGIONS: Roman Catholic 98%, other and nonreligious 2%
ETHNIC MIX: Maltese 96%, other 4%
GOVERNMENT: Parliamentary system
CURRENCY: Euro = 100 cents

Marshall Islands

Under US rule as part of the UN Trust Territory of the Pacific Islands until independence in 1986, the Marshall Islands comprises a group of 34 widely scattered atolls.

GEOGRAPHY
Narrow coral rings with sandy beaches enclosing lagoons. Those in the south have thicker vegetation. Kwajalein is the world's largest atoll.

CLIMATE
Tropical oceanic, cooled year round by northeast trade winds.

PEOPLE & SOCIETY
Around half the poplulation live in Majuro, the capital and commercial center. Life on the outlying islands is still traditional, based around subsistence agriculture and fishing. Tensions are high due to poor living conditions, especially in periods of drought or flooding. Society is matrilineal, with land and titles handed down through the mother's clan.

◆ **INSIGHT:** *In 1954, Bikini Atoll was the site for the testing of the largest US H-bomb – the 18–22 megaton Bravo*

THE ECONOMY
Almost totally dependent on US aid and the rent paid by the US for its missile base on Kwajalein Atoll. High unemployment. Revenue from licenses to fish in Marshallese waters for tuna. Copra and coconut oil are the only significant agricultural exports.

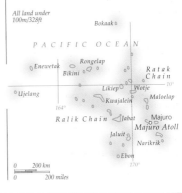

All land under 100m/328ft

Bokaak

PACIFIC OCEAN

Enewetak Rongelap Bikini Ratak Chain Likiep Wotje 10° Maloelap Ujelang Kwajalein 164° Majuro Ralik Chain Jabat Majuro Atoll Jaluit Narikrik Ebon 170°

0   200 km
0   200 miles

FACTFILE

OFFICIAL NAME: Republic of the Marshall Islands

DATE OF FORMATION: 1986

CAPITAL: Majuro Atoll

POPULATION: 53,000

TOTAL AREA: 70 sq. miles (181 sq. km)

DENSITY: 757 people per sq. mile

LANGUAGES: Marshallese*, English*, Japanese, German

RELIGIONS: Protestant 81%, other 11%, Roman Catholic 8%

ETHNIC MIX: Micronesian 90%, other 10%

GOVERNMENT: Presidential system

CURRENCY: US dollar = 100 cents

Mauritania

Two-thirds of Mauritania's territory is desert – the only productive land is that drained by the Senegal River. The country has taken a strongly Arab direction since 1964.

GEOGRAPHY
The Sahara, barren except for some scattered oases, covers the north. Savanna lands lie to the south.

CLIMATE
The climate is generally hot and dry, aggravated by the dusty *harmattan* wind. Summer rain in the south, and virtually none in the north.

PEOPLE & SOCIETY
The Maures control political and economic life. Family solidarity among nomadic peoples is particularly strong. Ethnic tension centers on the oppression of the black minority. Tens of thousands of blacks are estimated to be in illegal slavery. Coups have interrupted civilian rule in recent years.

INSIGHT: *Slavery officially became illegal in Mauritania in 1980, but de facto slavery still persists*

THE ECONOMY
Agriculture and herding. Iron, copper, and gold mining. World's largest gypsum deposits. Offshore oil from 2006. Rich fishing grounds.

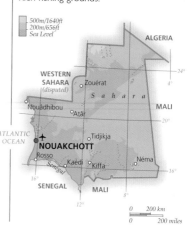

500m/1640ft
200m/656ft
Sea Level

ALGERIA

WESTERN SAHARA (disputed)
Zouérat

Sahara

MALI

Nouâdhibou   Atâr

ATLANTIC OCEAN
NOUAKCHOTT
Rosso   Tidjikja
Senegal   Kaédi   Kiffa   Néma

SENEGAL

MALI

0   200 km
0   200 miles

FACTFILE

OFFICIAL NAME: Islamic Republic of Mauritania
DATE OF FORMATION: 1960
CAPITAL: Nouakchott
POPULATION: 4.4 million
TOTAL AREA: 397,953 sq. miles (1,030,700 sq. km)

DENSITY: 11 people per sq. mile
LANGUAGES: Arabic*, Hassaniyah Arabic, Wolof, French
RELIGIONS: Sunni Muslim 100%
ETHNIC MIX: Maure 81%, Wolof 7%, Tukolor 5%, other 4%, Soninka 3%
GOVERNMENT: Presidential system
CURRENCY: Ouguiya = 5 khoums

Mauritius

The islands that make up Mauritius lie in the Indian Ocean east of Madagascar. They have enjoyed considerable economic success following recent industrial diversification and expansion.

GEOGRAPHY
The volcanic main island of Mauritius is ringed by coral reefs, and rises from the coast to a fertile central plateau. The outer islands – Rodrigues, the Agalega Islands, and the Cargados Carajos Shoals – lie some 300 miles (500 km) to the north.

CLIMATE
Warm and humid. Tropical storms are frequent December–March, the hottest and wettest months.

PEOPLE & SOCIETY
Most people are descendants of laborers brought over from India in the 19th century. A small minority of French descent form the wealthiest group. Creoles (descendants of African slaves) complain of discrimination. Literacy is high. Health care is free. Crime rates are low. Less-developed Rodrigues has been self-governing since 2001.

THE ECONOMY
Clothing manufacture, tourism, and sugar. Loss of preferential trade terms for sugar and textiles. Offshore financial center. Growing outsourcing and ICT industries. Most food is imported.

◆ **INSIGHT:** *The islands form part of the Mascarene Archipelago – once a land bridge between Asia and Africa*

500m/1640ft
200m/656ft
Sea Level

Ile Plate

Rodrigues
Port Mathurin

Triolet   Grand Baie
Pamplemousses
PORT LOUIS

INDIAN OCEAN

Curepipe

Mahebourg

Bel Ombre   Souillac

0   10 km
0   10 miles

FACTFILE

OFFICIAL NAME: Republic of Mauritius
DATE OF FORMATION: 1968
CAPITAL: Port Louis
POPULATION: 1.3 million
TOTAL AREA: 718 sq. miles (1860 sq. km)
DENSITY: 1811 people per sq. mile
LANGUAGES: French Creole, Hindi, Urdu, Tamil, Chinese, English*, French

RELIGIONS: Hindu 48%, Roman Catholic 26%, Muslim 17%, other Christian 7%, other 2%
ETHNIC MIX: Indo-Mauritian 68%, Creole 27%, Sino-Mauritian 3%, Franco-Mauritian 2%
GOVERNMENT: Parliamentary system
CURRENCY: Mauritian rupee = 100 cents

Mexico

Mexico stretches from the US border southward into the ancient Aztec and Mayan heartlands. Independence from Spain came in 1836. One in six Mexicans lives in the sprawling capital.

GEOGRAPHY
Coastal plains along the Pacific and Atlantic seaboards rise to a high arid central plateau. To the east and west are the Sierra Madre mountain ranges. Limestone lowlands form the projecting Yucatan peninsula.

CLIMATE
The plateau and high mountains are warm for much of the year. Pacific coast is tropical: storms occur mostly March–December. Northwest is dry.

PEOPLE & SOCIETY
Most Mexicans are *mestizos* of Spanish–Amerindian descent. Rural Amerindians are largely segregated from Hispanic society and most live in poverty, though the state promotes their culture. The Zapatista movement backs indigenous rights. Male dominance of politics and business is being challenged. Narcotics-related violent crime is rising.

THE ECONOMY
Major oil producer. Corn, fruit, sugar, vegetables are cash crops. NAFTA boosts exports, but exposes farmers to subsidized US competition. Wealth disparity. Return to growth since 2009 recession, triggered by global downturn and swine flu crisis.

◆ **INSIGHT:** *More people cross the US–Mexican border each year – illegally or legally – than any other border in the world*

FACTFILE

OFFICIAL NAME: United Mexican States

DATE OF FORMATION: 1836

CAPITAL: Mexico City

POPULATION: 129 million

TOTAL AREA: 761,602 sq. miles (1,972,550 sq. km)

DENSITY: 175 people per sq. mile

LANGUAGES: Spanish*, Nahuatl, Mayan, Zapotec, Mixtec, Otomi, Totonac, Tzotzil

RELIGIONS: Roman Catholic 81%, Protestant 9%, nonreligious 7%, other 3%

ETHNIC MIX: *Mestizo* 60%, Amerindian 30%, European 9%, other 1%

GOVERNMENT: Presidential system

CURRENCY: Mexican peso = 100 centavos

Micronesia

The Federated States of Micronesia (FSM), situated in the western Pacific, comprise 607 islands and atolls grouped into four main island states: Pohnpei, Kosrae, Chuuk, and Yap.

GEOGRAPHY

Mixture of high volcanic islands with forested interiors, and low-lying coral atolls. Some of the islands have coastal mangrove swamps.

CLIMATE

Tropical, with high humidity. There is very heavy rainfall outside the January–March dry season.

◆ **INSIGHT:** *Chuuk's lagoon contains the sunken wrecks of over 100 Japanese ships and 270 planes from World War II*

PEOPLE & SOCIETY

Micronesians are physically, culturally, and linguistically diverse. Melanesians live on Yap, Polynesians in Pohnpei. The supply of electricity and running water is limited. Society is based on matrilineal clans.

THE ECONOMY

Dependent on US aid. Fishing licenses are a key source of foreign revenue. Tourism, fishing, betel nuts, copra are economic mainstays. Trust fund created to reduce aid reliance.

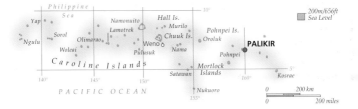

FACTFILE

OFFICIAL NAME: Federated States of Micronesia

DATE OF FORMATION: 1986

CAPITAL: Palikir (Pohnpei Island)

POPULATION: 105,000

TOTAL AREA: 271 sq. miles (702 sq. km)

DENSITY: 387 people per sq. mile

LANGUAGES: Trukese, Pohnpeian, Kosraean, Yapese, English*

RELIGIONS: Roman Catholic 53%, Protestant 43%, other 3%, nonreligious 1%

ETHNIC MIX: Chuukese 49%, Pohnpeian 24%, other 14%, Kosraean 6%, Yapese 5%, Asian 2%

GOVERNMENT: Nonparty system

CURRENCY: US dollar = 100 cents

Moldova

The most densely populated of the former Soviet republics, Moldova has strong ethnic, linguistic, and cultural links with Romania, but relations with Russia remain paramount.

GEOGRAPHY
Steppes and hilly plains are drained by the Dniester and Prut rivers.

CLIMATE
Warm summers and relatively mild winters. Moderate rainfall is evenly spread throughout the year.

PEOPLE & SOCIETY
A shared heritage with Romania defines national identity, though in 1994 Moldovans voted against possible reunification with Romania. Most of the population is engaged in intensive agriculture. Transnistria is a breakaway state along the east bank of the Dniester, home to a largely ethnic Slav population. The Gagauz, in the south, have accepted autonomy.

◆ **INSIGHT:** *Vast underground wine vaults contain entire "streets" of bottles built into rock quarries*

THE ECONOMY
Poorest country in Europe. Mainly agricultural: produces wine, tobacco, and fruit. Food processing and textiles. Depends on Russia for raw materials, fuel, and exports. Political instability.

FACTFILE

OFFICIAL NAME: Republic of Moldova
DATE OF FORMATION: 1991
CAPITAL: Chisinau
POPULATION: 4.1 million
TOTAL AREA: 13,067 sq. miles (33,843 sq. km)
DENSITY: 315 people per sq. mile
LANGUAGES: Moldovan (Romanian)*, Ukrainian, Russian
RELIGIONS: Orthodox Christian 92%, other 6%, nonreligious 2%
ETHNIC MIX: Moldovan 76%, Ukrainian 9%, Russian 6%, Gagauz 4%, Romanian 2%, Bulgarian 2%, other 1%
GOVERNMENT: Parliamentary system
CURRENCY: Moldovan leu = 100 bani

Monaco

Monaco is a tiny principality on the Côte d'Azur. Its destiny changed radically when the casino was opened in 1863. Today, it promotes its image as an upmarket, glamorous destination.

GEOGRAPHY

A rocky promontory overlooking a narrow coastal strip that has been enlarged through land reclamation.

CLIMATE

Mediterranean. Summers are hot and dry; days with 12 hours of sunshine are not uncommon. Winters are mild and sunny.

PEOPLE & SOCIETY

Less than 20% of residents are Monégasques. Almost half are French, the rest Italian, American, British, Belgian, and others. Nationals enjoy considerable privileges, including housing subsidies to protect them from Monaco's high property prices, and the right of first refusal before a job can be offered to a foreigner. Women have equal status, but only acquired the vote in 1962. Prince Albert married South African swimmer Charlene Wittstock in 2011.

THE ECONOMY

Tourism, gambling, and financial services. Banking secrecy laws and tax-haven conditions attract foreign investment. Close links and customs union with France (but not in EU). No resources: depends on imports.

INSIGHT: *High-profile social and sporting events attract large crowds each spring, including the Rose Ball, Tennis Open, and Grand Prix*

FACTFILE

OFFICIAL NAME: Principality of Monaco

DATE OF FORMATION: 1861

CAPITAL: Monaco

POPULATION: 38,000

TOTAL AREA: 0.75 sq. miles (1.95 sq. km)

DENSITY: 50,667 people per sq. mile

LANGUAGES: French*, Italian, Monégasque, English

RELIGIONS: Roman Catholic 89%, Protestant 6%, other 5%

ETHNIC MIX: French 47%, other 21%, Italian 16%, Monégasque 16%

GOVERNMENT: Mixed monarchical–parliamentary system

CURRENCY: Euro = 100 cents

Mongolia

Landlocked between Russia and China, Mongolia is a huge, isolated, and sparsely populated nation. Over two-thirds of the country is part of the Gobi Desert.

GEOGRAPHY

A mountainous steppe plateau in the north, with lakes in the north and west. The desert region of the Gobi dominates the south.

CLIMATE

Continental. Mild summers and long, dry, very cold winters, with heavy snowfall. Temperatures can drop as low as −22°F (−30°C).

PEOPLE & SOCIETY

Mongolia was unified in 1206 by Genghis Khan and was later absorbed into Manchu China. Most ethnic Mongolians live within China in Inner Mongolia. Tibetan Buddhism is the main religion. The traditional, nomadic way of life has been eroded as urban migration continues, spurred by zud (ferocious winters), which can devastate the rural economy. Agriculture employs less than a third of the workforce now.

THE ECONOMY

Rich mineral deposits – oil, coal, copper, uranium – are largely untapped. State involvement in mining is an issue. Cashmere exports. Democracy, from 1990, brought market reforms, but also rising wealth inequality. Boom in early 2010s burst by low global mineral prices and reduced demand from China.

◆ INSIGHT: *Horseracing, wrestling, and archery are the national sports*

RUSSIA

Ölgiy · Hovd · Mörön · Erdenet · Darhan · Sühbaatar

Altay

Altai Mountains

ULAANBAATAR

Kerulen

Choybalsan

Saynshand

Gobi

Dalandzadgad

CHINA

3000m/9843ft
2000m/6562ft
1000m/3281ft
500m/1640ft

0   400 km
0   400 miles

FACTFILE

OFFICIAL NAME: Mongolia
DATE OF FORMATION: 1924
CAPITAL: Ulaanbaatar
POPULATION: 3.1 million
TOTAL AREA: 604,247 sq. miles (1,565,000 sq. km)
DENSITY: 5 people per sq. mile
LANGUAGES: Khalkha Mongolian*, Kazakh

RELIGIONS: Tibetan Buddhist 53%, nonreligious 38%, Muslim 3%, Shamanist 3%, Christian 2%, other 1%
ETHNIC MIX: Khalkh 82%, other 9%, Kazakh 4%, Dorvod 3%, Bayad 2%
GOVERNMENT: Mixed presidential–parliamentary system
CURRENCY: Tugrik (tögrög) = 100 möngö

Montenegro

Perched on the Adriatic coast, this tiny republic became a separate state in 2006, after 88 years of federation with its neighbors in various forms of the state of Yugoslavia.

GEOGRAPHY
A narrow coastal strip on the Adriatic. Fertile lowland plains around Lake Scutari. Mountainous interior with deep canyons.

CLIMATE
The lowlands have hot, dry summers and mild winters. Heavy snow in winter in the mountains.

PEOPLE & SOCIETY
Most Montenegrins are Orthodox Christians. They speak a language closely related to Serbian, but that now mainly uses Latin alphabet. Albanians, who make up 70% of the population of the south's Ulcinj region, supported independence. Foreigners, particularly Russians, British, and Serbs, are buying Adriatic real estate.

◆ **INSIGHT:** *Dark forests once cloaked Montenegro's mountains; its name means "Black Mountain"*

THE ECONOMY
Tourism (along Adriatic) and construction industry drive growth. Bauxite reserves, and aluminum industry. Crackdown on cigarette smuggling, black market, and corruption led to approval in 2010 as candidate for EU membership. Uses euro, though not part of eurozone.

FACTFILE

OFFICIAL NAME: Montenegro

DATE OF FORMATION: 2006

CAPITAL: Podgorica

POPULATION: 623,000

TOTAL AREA: 5332 sq. miles (13,812 sq. km)

DENSITY: 117 people per sq. mile

LANGUAGES: Montenegrin*, Serbian, Albanian, Bosniak, Croatian

RELIGIONS: Orthodox Christian 74%, Muslim 20%, Roman Catholic 4%, nonreligious 1%, other 1%

ETHNIC MIX: Montenegrin 43%, Serb 32%, other 12%, Bosniak 8%, Albanian 5%

GOVERNMENT: Parliamentary system

CURRENCY: Euro = 100 cents

Morocco

Morocco is a former French colony in northwest Africa.
Since 1975, it has occupied the territory of Western Sahara, the future
of which is yet to be determined by UN-supervised referendum.

GEOGRAPHY
Fertile coastal plain is interrupted in the east by the Rif Mountains. Atlas Mountain ranges to the south. Beyond lies the outer fringe of the Sahara.

CLIMATE
Ranges from temperate and warm in the north, to semiarid in the south. Cooler in the mountains.

PEOPLE & SOCIETY
The Berber minority descend from north Africa's original inhabitants, and live mainly in mountain villages. The Arab majority inhabits the lowlands. Morocco is unusual among Arab states in granting Jews religious freedom and civil rights. The king is spiritual leader and head of state, but reduced his powers in response to the 2011 "Arab Spring" protests. Islamists have gained influence in politics. Islamist militancy is a concern, notably the emergence of terrorist cells.

THE ECONOMY
Major exporter of phosphates. Investment in tourism and agriculture. Fishing. Relations with EU strained over illegal immigrants and cannabis trade.

INSIGHT: *Karueein University in Fès, founded in 859 CE, is the world's oldest existing educational institution*

FACTFILE

OFFICIAL NAME: Kingdom of Morocco
DATE OF FORMATION: 1956
CAPITAL: Rabat
POPULATION: 35.7 million
TOTAL AREA: 172,316 sq. miles (446,300 sq. km)
DENSITY: 207 people per sq. mile
LANGUAGES: Arabic*, Tamazight* (Berber),
French, Spanish
RELIGIONS: Muslim (mainly Sunni) 99%, other (mostly Christian) 1%
ETHNIC MIX: Arab 70%, Berber 29%, European 1%
GOVERNMENT: Mixed monarchical–parliamentary system
CURRENCY: Mor. dirham = 100 centimes

Mozambique

Mozambique lies on the southeast African coast. It was torn apart by a savage and devastating civil war between the Marxist government and a rebel faction between 1977 and 1992.

GEOGRAPHY

Largely a savanna-covered plateau. The coast is fringed by coral reefs and lagoons. The Zambezi River bisects the country.

CLIMATE

Tropical. Temperatures are hottest on the coast. Extremes of rainfall: drought and flood.

PEOPLE & SOCIETY

Tensions exist between north and south, rather than between ethnic groups. Life is centered on the extended family. Polygamy is fairly common. The country is struggling with the legacy of a war that killed around a million people, and the effects of frequent floods and droughts. Half the population lives in abject poverty.

INSIGHT: *Maputo's busy port serves Zimbabwe and South Africa*

THE ECONOMY

Extremely dependent on aid. Coal, aluminum, cashew nuts, shrimp, cotton exported. Mineral reserves. Debt relief.

FACTFILE

OFFICIAL NAME: Republic of Mozambique

DATE OF FORMATION: 1975

CAPITAL: Maputo

POPULATION: 29.7 million

TOTAL AREA: 309,494 sq. miles (801,590 sq. km)

DENSITY: 98 people per sq. mile

LANGUAGES: Makua, Xitsonga, Sena, Lomwe, Portuguese*

RELIGIONS: Roman Catholic 28%, nonreligious 19%, Muslim 18%, traditional beliefs 16%, Pentecostal 11%, other 8%

ETHNIC MIX: Makua Lomwe 47%, Tsonga 23%, Malawi 12%, Shona 11%, Yao 4%, other 3%

GOVERNMENT: Presidential system

CURRENCY: New metical = 100 centavos

Myanmar (Burma)

Forming the eastern shores of the Bay of Bengal and the Andaman Sea in southeast Asia, Myanmar has suffered from isolation, political repression, and ethnic conflict.

GEOGRAPHY

Mostly tropical rainforest. Fertile Irrawaddy basin lies between mountains in the west, and Shan plateau in the east.

CLIMATE

Tropical. Hot summers, with high humidity, and warm winters.

PEOPLE & SOCIETY

The military, in power from 1962, paid little regard to human rights, and suppressed opposition. The National League for Democracy (NLD) won polls in 1990 but was kept from power until 2016. Conflicts with ethnic minorities are ongoing, despite 2015 peace deal with eight rebel groups. Over 600,000 Rohingya fled to Bangladesh in 2017 escaping "ethnic cleansing" by the army.

◆ **INSIGHT:** *Myanmar is one of the world's biggest teak exporters, though reserves are diminishing rapidly*

THE ECONOMY

Corrupt, mismanaged. Gas, teak, and gems are exported. One of world's largest illegal opium producers. Prone to natural disasters. Black market goods carry high prices. Strong GDP growth since 1992.

Map showing Myanmar with neighboring INDIA, CHINA, LAOS, THAILAND, Bay of Bengal, Andaman Sea. Cities include Myitkyina, Monywa, Mandalay, Pakokku, Sagaing, Sittwe, Taunggyi, Shan Plateau, NAY PYI TAW, Taungoo, Thandwe, Pyay, Hinthada, Bago, Thaton, Patheinn, Insein, Mawlamyine, Yangon (Rangoon), Kyaikkami, Mouths of the Irrawaddy, Dawei, Myeik, Mergui Archipelago, Isthmus of Kra.

```
4000m/13124ft
2000m/6562ft
1000m/3281ft
500m/1640ft
200m/656ft
Sea Level
```

0   200 km
0   200 miles

FACTFILE

OFFICIAL NAME: Republic of the Union of Myanmar

DATE OF FORMATION: 1948

CAPITAL: Nay Pyi Taw

POPULATION: 53.4 million

TOTAL AREA: 261,969 sq. miles (678,500 sq. km)

DENSITY: 210 people per sq. mile

LANGUAGES: Burmese (Myanmar)*, Shan, Karen, Rakhine, Chin, Yangbye, Kachin, Mon

RELIGIONS: Buddhist 88%, Christian 6%, Muslim 4%, Animist 1%, other 1%

ETHNIC MIX: Burman (Bamah) 68%, other 12%, Shan 9%, Karen 7%, Rakhine 4%

GOVERNMENT: Presidential system

CURRENCY: Kyat = 100 pyas

Located in southwestern Africa, Namibia gained independence from South Africa in 1990, after 24 years of armed struggle. It regained the territory of Walvis Bay in 1994.

GEOGRAPHY
The Namib Desert stretches along the coastal strip. Inland, a ridge of mountains rises to 8000 ft (2500 m). The Kalahari Desert lies in the east.

CLIMATE
Almost rainless. The coast is usually shrouded in thick fog, unless the hot, dry *berg* wind is blowing.

PEOPLE & SOCIETY
The Ovambo, the main ethnic group, live mainly in the more populous north. Some 100,000 whites, many of German descent, are centered around Windhoek and still control the economy. The minority San and Khoi bushmen are among the oldest human communities in the world. Homosexual rights are restricted.

◆ **INSIGHT:** *The Namib is the Earth's oldest, and one of its driest, deserts*

THE ECONOMY
Varied mineral resources, notably uranium and diamonds. Rich offshore fishing grounds. High unemployment. HIV/AIDS epidemic. One of Africa's most skewed distributions of wealth.

FACTFILE

OFFICIAL NAME: Republic of Namibia
DATE OF FORMATION: 1990
CAPITAL: Windhoek
POPULATION: 2.5 million
TOTAL AREA: 318,694 sq. miles (825,418 sq. km)
DENSITY: 8 people per sq. mile
LANGUAGES: Ovambo, Kavango, English*, Bergdama, German, Afrikaans
RELIGIONS: Christian 90%, traditional beliefs 10%
ETHNIC MIX: Ovambo 50%, other tribes 22%, Kavango 9%, Damara 7%, Herero 7%, other 5%
GOVERNMENT: Presidential system
CURRENCY: Namibian dollar = 100 cents; SA rand is also legal tender

Nauru

Nauru lies in the Pacific, northeast of Australia.
Phosphate deposits gave its inhabitants huge temporary wealth,
but economic mismanagement has left them facing ruin.

GEOGRAPHY
A single low-lying coral atoll, with a fertile coastal belt. Coral cliffs encircle an elevated interior plateau.

CLIMATE
Equatorial, moderated by sea breezes. Occasional long droughts.

PEOPLE & SOCIETY
Native Nauruans are of mixed Micronesian and Polynesian origin. Most live in simple, traditional houses and spend their money on luxury cars and consumer goods. Welfare and education are free. A diet of imported processed foods has caused widespread obesity and diabetes. Mining was left to imported laborers, mainly from Kiribati, who lived in enclaves of male-only barracks and had few rights. Many young Nauruans leave to seek a better life in Australia or New Zealand.

THE ECONOMY
Phosphate revenues diminished. Sale of fishing rights. Revenue from hosting Australian refugee detention center. Offshore banking facilities closed. State trust fund invested badly overseas.

INSIGHT: *Phosphate mining has left 80% of the island uninhabitable*

FACTFILE

OFFICIAL NAME: Republic of Nauru
DATE OF FORMATION: 1968
CAPITAL: None (Yaren *defacto* capital)
POPULATION: 13,000
TOTAL AREA: 8.1 sq. miles (21 sq. km)
DENSITY: 1605 people per sq. mile

LANGUAGES: Nauruan*, Kiribati, Chinese, Tuvaluan, English*
RELIGIONS: Nauruan Congregational Church 60%, Roman Catholic 35%, other 5%
ETHNIC MIX: Nauruan 93%, Chinese 5%, other Pacific islanders 1%, European 1%
GOVERNMENT: Nonparty system
CURRENCY: Australian dollar = 100 cents

Nepal

Nepal, lying between India and China on the southern shoulder of the Himalayas, is one of the world's poorest countries. Its agricultural economy is heavily dependent on the monsoon.

GEOGRAPHY
Mainly mountainous. The area includes some of the highest mountains in the world, including Mount Everest. Flat, fertile river plains form the south.

CLIMATE
Warm monsoon season from July to October. The rest of the year is dry, sunny, and mild. Winter temperatures in the Himalayas average 14°F (–10°C).

PEOPLE & SOCIETY
Tensions are few between the diverse ethnic groups. Buddhist women, including Sherpas, face fewer social restrictions than Hindus. Trafficking of women and child labor are problems. Human rights violations rose during the 1999–2006 Maoist insurgency. The peace deal led to the abolition of the monarchy and the Maoists joining the political mainstream, but fractious coalitions mean instability continues.

THE ECONOMY
Agriculture employs three-quarters of workforce. Crops include rice and wheat. Tourism and investment affected by instability. Reliant on aid and overseas remittances. Hydropower potential.

INSIGHT: *Southern Nepal was the birthplace of Buddha (Prince Siddhartha Gautama) in 563 BCE*

FACTFILE
OFFICIAL NAME: Federal Democratic Republic of Nepal
DATE OF FORMATION: 1769
CAPITAL: Kathmandu
POPULATION: 29.3 million
TOTAL AREA: 54,363 sq. miles (140,800 sq. km)
DENSITY: 555 people per sq. mile

LANGUAGES: Nepali*, Maithili, Bhojpuri
RELIGIONS: Hindu 82%, Buddhist 9%, other (including Christian) 5%, Muslim 4%
ETHNIC MIX: Other 52%, Chhetri 17%, Hill Brahman 12%, Magar 7%, Tharu 7%, Tamang 6%
GOVERNMENT: Parliamentary system
CURRENCY: Nepalese rupee = 100 paisa

Netherlands

Astride the delta of five major rivers in northwest Europe, the Netherlands built its historic wealth on maritime trade. Rotterdam is Europe's largest port.

GEOGRAPHY
Mainly flat, with 27% of the land below sea level and protected by dunes, dikes, and canals. There are a few low hills in the south and east.

CLIMATE
Mild, rainy winters and cool summers. Gales from the North Sea are common in fall and winter.

PEOPLE & SOCIETY
The Dutch have a long history of welcoming immigrants from former colonies and refugees seeking asylum. However, lack of integration is now raising fears about the failing asylum system, immigrant crime, and militant Islam. Population is mostly urban and the density is high. The state does not try to impose a particular morality on its citizens. Laws concerning sexuality, narcotics-taking, and euthanasia are among the world's most liberal.

THE ECONOMY
Major trading hub. High-profile multinationals. Diverse industrial base: chemicals, machinery, electronics, and metals. Costly social welfare system.

◆ **INSIGHT:** *In 2002, the Netherlands became the first country in the world to legalize euthanasia*

FACTFILE

OFFICIAL NAME: Kingdom of the Netherlands
DATE OF FORMATION: 1648
CAPITALS: Amsterdam; The Hague (administrative)
POPULATION: 17 million
TOTAL AREA: 16,033 sq. miles (41,526 sq. km)

DENSITY: 1298 people per sq. mile
LANGUAGES: Dutch*, Frisian
RELIGIONS: Roman Catholic 36%, other 34%, Protestant 27%, Muslim 3%
ETHNIC MIX: Dutch 82%, other 12%, Turkish 2%, Surinamese 2%, Moroccan 2%
GOVERNMENT: Parliamentary system
CURRENCY: Euro = 100 cents

New Zealand

Lying in the South Pacific, 990 miles (1600 km) southeast of Australia, New Zealand comprises North and South Islands, separated by the Cook Strait, and many smaller islands.

GEOGRAPHY

North Island, noted for hot springs and geysers, has the bulk of the population. South Island is mostly mountainous, with eastern lowlands.

CLIMATE

Generally temperate and damp. The far north is almost subtropical, whereas southern winters are cold.

PEOPLE & SOCIETY

Maoris were the first settlers, 1200 years ago. Today's majority European population is descended mainly from British migrants who settled after 1840. Maoris' living and education standards are generally lower than average. The government is continuing to negotiate the settlement of Maori land claims.

 INSIGHT: *New Zealand was the first country to give women the vote (1893)*

THE ECONOMY

Modern agricultural sector; world's top exporter of dairy products. Dairy vies with tourism as the biggest foreign-exchange earner. High-tech manufacturing. Open economy. Strong trade links.

2000m/6562ft
1000m/3281ft
500m/1640ft
200m/656ft
Sea Level

North Island

Auckland
Hamilton · Tauranga
New Plymouth · Rotorua
Palmerston · Hastings
Tasman North
Sea Blenheim · **WELLINGTON**
Greymouth · Cook Strait
South Island Christchurch
Timaru
Queenstown · *PACIFIC OCEAN*
Dunedin
Invercargill
Stewart Island

0   200 km
0   200 miles

FACTFILE

OFFICIAL NAME: New Zealand

DATE OF FORMATION: 1947

CAPITAL: Wellington

POPULATION: 4.7 million

TOTAL AREA: 103,737 sq. miles (268,680 sq. km)

DENSITY: 45 people per sq. mile

LANGUAGES: English*, Maori*

RELIGIONS: Nonreligious 36%, other Christian 16%, Anglican 15%, Roman Catholic 14%, Presbyterian 11%, other 8%

ETHNIC MIX: European 60%, other 19%, Maori 14%, Chinese 4%, Samoan 3%

GOVERNMENT: Parliamentary system

CURRENCY: New Zealand dollar = 100 cents

Nicaragua

Nicaragua lies at the heart of Central America. The
Sandinista revolution of 1978 led to 11 years of civil war between
the left-wing Sandinistas and the right-wing US-backed Contras.

GEOGRAPHY
Extensive forested plains in the
east. Central mountain region with many
active volcanoes. The Pacific coastlands
are dominated by lakes.

CLIMATE
Tropical. The lowlands are hot all
year round. The mountains are cooler.
Prone to occasional hurricanes.

PEOPLE & SOCIETY
Most people are *mestizo* (mixed
Spanish–Amerindian), and there is a large
white elite. Caribbean regions are home
to communities of Miskito Amerindians
and blacks, who gained autonomy in 1987.
The revolution improved the status of
women, but these gains have been
undone by rampant poverty.

◆ **INSIGHT:** *Lake Nicaragua is the
only freshwater lake in the world
to contain marine animals*

THE ECONOMY
One of poorest countries in the
Americas. Textiles, coffee, meat, tobacco
are main exports: affected by world price
fluctuations. Remittances from abroad.
Substantial debt relief. Corruption.

1000m/3281ft
500m/1640ft
200m/656ft
Sea Level

HONDURAS

Coco

14°

Ocotal

Estelí Matagalpa

Chinandega Matiguas

León ◆MANAGUA Juigalpa Bluefields

12° Granada

San Rafael del Sur Rivas *Lago de
Nicaragua*
(Lake Nicaragua)

86° COSTA RICA San Juan 84°

Caribbean
Sea

Mosquito Coast

0 ___ 100 km
0 ___ 100 miles

FACTFILE

OFFICIAL NAME: Republic of Nicaragua

DATE OF FORMATION: 1838

CAPITAL: Managua

POPULATION: 6.2 million

TOTAL AREA: 49,998 sq. miles
(129,494 sq. km)

DENSITY: 135 people per sq. mile)

LANGUAGES: Spanish*, English Creole,
Miskito

RELIGIONS: Roman Catholic 50%,
Protestant 40%, nonreligious 7%, other 3%

ETHNIC MIX: Mestizo 69%, White 17%,
Black 9%, Amerindian 5%

GOVERNMENT: Presidential system

CURRENCY: Córdoba oro = 100 centavos

Niger lies in west Africa, upstream from Nigeria on the Niger River. One of the world's poorest states, it was ruled by one-party or military regimes until multipartyism was allowed in 1992.

GEOGRAPHY

The north and northeast regions are part of the Sahara. The Air Mountains in the center rise high above the desert. Savanna lies to the south.

CLIMATE

High temperatures persist for most of the year at around 95°F (35°C). The north is virtually rainless.

PEOPLE & SOCIETY

Tuareg nomads in the north feel excluded from politics and the benefits of their area's uranium resources. An early 1990s rebellion reignited briefly in 2007–2009. In the south, egalitarianism and a sense of community help to combat economic difficulties. Almost the entire urban population lives in slum conditions. Two-thirds of the population is under 25. Women have limited rights and girls often lack access to education. The army seized power briefly in 2010.

THE ECONOMY

Vast uranium reserves. Oil producer from 2011. Frequent droughts and food shortages. Banditry. Expansion of Sahara.

◆ **INSIGHT:** *The name Niger comes from the Tuareg word* n'eghirren, *which means "flowing water"*

FACTFILE

OFFICIAL NAME: Republic of Niger
DATE OF FORMATION: 1960
CAPITAL: Niamey
POPULATION: 21.5 million
TOTAL AREA: 489,188 sq. miles (1,267,000 sq. km)
DENSITY: 44 people per sq. mile

LANGUAGES: Hausa, Djerma, Fulani, Tuareg, Teda, French*
RELIGIONS: Muslim 99%, other (including Christian) 1%
ETHNIC MIX: Hausa 55%, Djerma and Songhai 21%, Tuareg 9%, Peul 9%, Kanuri 5%, other 1%
GOVERNMENT: Presidential system
CURRENCY: CFA franc = 100 centimes

Nigeria

West Africa's biggest nation, Nigeria is a federation of 36 states and the capital, Abuja. Dominated by military governments since 1966, democracy returned in 1999.

GEOGRAPHY
Coastal area of beaches, swamps, and lagoons gives way to rainforest, and then to savanna on the high plateaus. Semidesert to the north.

CLIMATE
The south is hot, rainy, and humid for most of the year. The arid north has one very humid wet season. The Jos Plateau and highlands are cooler.

PEOPLE & SOCIETY
Some 250 ethnic groups: tensions threaten national unity, with sporadic intercommunal violence. The mainly Muslim north has introduced *sharia* (Islamic law); Boko Haram militants use bombings, assassinations, and abductions to fight for an Islamic state. Women have more economic independence in the south. Militants in the oil-rich Niger Delta demand a share in the oil wealth for the region's impoverished population.

THE ECONOMY
Overdependent on oil, principal export since 1970s. Mismanagement and corruption. Debt relief. Instability.

INSIGHT: *Nigeria is Africa's most populous state – one in every six Africans is Nigerian*

FACTFILE

OFFICIAL NAME: Federal Republic of Nigeria

DATE OF FORMATION: 1960

CAPITAL: Abuja

POPULATION: 191 million

TOTAL AREA: 356,667 sq. miles (923,768 sq. km)

DENSITY: 543 people per sq. mile

LANGUAGES: Hausa, English*, Yoruba, Ibo

RELIGIONS: Muslim 50%, Christian 40%, traditional beliefs 10%

ETHNIC MIX: Other 29%, Hausa 21%, Yoruba 21%, Ibo 18%, Fulani 11%

GOVERNMENT: Presidential system

CURRENCY: Naira = 100 kobo

Norway

The Kingdom of Norway traces the rugged western coast of Scandinavia. Settlements are largely restricted to southern and coastal areas. Vast oil and natural gas revenues bring prosperity.

GEOGRAPHY

The western coast is indented with numerous fjords and features tens of thousands of islands. Mountains and plateaus cover most of the country.

CLIMATE

Mild coastal climate. Inland, the weather is more extreme, with warmer summers and cold, snowy winters.

PEOPLE & SOCIETY

Fairly homogeneous, but has welcomed refugees from Iraq, Somalia, Bosnia, Sri Lanka, and elsewhere. Strong family tradition, but divorce is common. Fair-minded consensus promotes female equality, boosted by the generous childcare provision. Wealth is more evenly distributed than in most countries. Voted against joining the EU in 1994.

 INSIGHT: *Near Narvik, mainland Norway is only 4 miles (7 km) wide*

THE ECONOMY

Western Europe's top oil and natural gas producer: trust fund saves for post-oil future. Metal, chemical, and engineering industries. Generous aid donor. High cost of living.

2000m/6562ft
1000m/3281ft
500m/1640ft
200m/656ft
Sea Level

Hammerfest
70°
RUSSIA
Tromsø
FINLAND
68°
Narvik
24°
28°
Bodø
20°
Arctic Circle
Norwegian
Sea
66°
SWEDEN
Trondheim
64°
Ålesund
62°
Lillehammer
Bergen
Hønefoss
60°
North
Sea
OSLO
Stavanger
Moss
Kristiansand
58°
Skagerrak
8°

0   200 km
0   200 miles

FACTFILE

OFFICIAL NAME: Kingdom of Norway

DATE OF FORMATION: 1905

CAPITAL: Oslo

POPULATION: 5.3 million

TOTAL AREA: 125,181 sq. miles (324,220 sq. km)

DENSITY: 45 people per sq. mile

LANGUAGES: Norwegian* (*Bokmål* "book language" and *Nynorsk* "new Norsk"), Sámi

RELIGIONS: Evangelical Lutheran 88%, other and nonreligious 8%, Muslim 2%, Pentecostal 1%, Roman Catholic 1%

ETHNIC MIX: Norwegian 93%, other 6%, Sámi 1%

GOVERNMENT: Parliamentary system

CURRENCY: Norwegian krone = 100 øre

Oman

Oman occupies a strategic position on the Arabian Peninsula, at the entrance to the Persian Gulf. It is the least developed Gulf state, despite modest oil exports.

GEOGRAPHY
Mostly gravelly desert, with mountains in the north and south. Some narrow fertile coastal strips.

CLIMATE
Blistering heat in the west. Summer temperatures often climb above 113°F (45°C). Southern uplands receive rains June–September.

PEOPLE & SOCIETY
Urban drift has seen most Omanis move to northern towns. Around half are Ibadi Muslims who follow an appointed leader, the imam. Ibadism is not opposed to freedom for women; a few women hold positions of authority. Numbers of foreign workers, mostly from South Asia, have risen to almost half of population.

◆ INSIGHT: Until the late 1980s, Oman was closed to all but business or official visitors

THE ECONOMY
Oil and natural gas account for almost all export revenue. Commercially extractable reserves are limited. Other exports include fish, animals, and dates. Foreigners work in all sectors.

2000m/6562ft
1000m/3281ft
500m/1640ft
200m/656ft
Sea Level

Strait of Hormuz
Al Khaşab
Gulf
Musandam of
Peninsula Oman
UAE Şuḩār
MUSCAT
24° Al Qābil Ar Rustāq
Bahlah Şamad
SAUDI Sūr
ARABIA 60°
Arabian
Sea
20° Duqm
Ar Rub' al Khāli INDIAN
OCEAN
Şawqirah
YEMEN
52° Şalālah
56°

0   100 km
0   100 miles

FACTFILE
OFFICIAL NAME: Sultanate of Oman
DATE OF FORMATION: 1951
CAPITAL: Muscat
POPULATION: 4.6 million
TOTAL AREA: 82,031 sq. miles (212,460 sq. km)
DENSITY: 56 people per sq. mile
LANGUAGES: Arabic*, Baluchi, Farsi, Hindi, Punjabi

RELIGIONS: Other Muslim 50%, Ibadi Muslim 25%, Hindu 17%, other 8%
ETHNIC MIX: Arab 54%, Bangladeshi 15%, Indian 15%, African and other 11%, Pakistani 5%
GOVERNMENT: Monarchy
CURRENCY: Omani rial = 1000 baisa

Pakistan

Once a part of British India, Pakistan was created in 1947 in response to demands for an independent Muslim state. In 1971, Bangladesh (former East Pakistan) became a separate state.

GEOGRAPHY

Indus floodplain across east and south. Hindu Kush mountains in north. Semidesert plateau, mountains in west.

CLIMATE

Temperatures can soar to 122°F (50°C) in south and west, and fall to −4°F (−20°C) in the Hindu Kush.

PEOPLE & SOCIETY

Punjabis dominate government and the army. Tensions with minority groups, exacerbated by the vast gap between rich and poor. Strong family ties permeate politics and business. Relations with India are tense over Kashmir and terrorism. Islamist *taliban* insurgency in tribal areas on Afghan border: fighting has displaced millions.

◆ INSIGHT: *In 1988, Pakistan elected Benazir Bhutto as the first female prime minister in the Muslim world*

THE ECONOMY

Major cotton and rice producer, but unpredictable weather conditions often affect crop. Textiles. Instability. Corruption. Aid to fight terrorism and for earthquake reconstruction.

5000m/16405ft	
4000m/13124ft	
3000m/9843ft	
2000m/6562ft	
1000m/3281ft	
500m/1640ft	
200m/656ft	
Sea Level	

FACTFILE

OFFICIAL NAME: Islamic Republic of Pakistan

DATE OF FORMATION: 1947

CAPITAL: Islamabad

POPULATION: 197 million

TOTAL AREA: 310,401 sq. miles (803,940 sq. km)

DENSITY: 662 people per sq. mile

LANGUAGES: Punjabi, Sindhi, Pashtu, Urdu*, Baluchi, Brahui

RELIGIONS: Sunni Muslim 77%, Shi'a Muslim 20%, Hindu 2%, Christian 1%

ETHNIC MIX: Punjabi 56%, Pathan (Pashtun) 15%, Sindhi 14%, Mohajir 7%, Baluchi 4%, other 4%

GOVERNMENT: Parliamentary system

CURRENCY: Pakistani rupee = 100 paisa

Palau

The 300-island Palau archipelago (known locally as Belau) lies in the western Pacific Ocean. It achieved independence in 1994, and is gradually reducing its aid dependence.

GEOGRAPHY
Terrain varies from thickly forested mountains to limestone and coral reefs. Babeldaob, the largest island, is volcanic, with many rivers and waterfalls.

CLIMATE
Hot and wet. Little variation in daily and seasonal temperatures. February–April is the dry season.

PEOPLE & SOCIETY
Native Palauans are a mix of the original Southeast Asian migrants and Pacific settlers. A modern influx from Asia, particularly the Philippines, China, and Bangladesh, has led to tension. As two-thirds of the population live on the island-city of Koror, a new capital was constructed recently on Babeldaob. Native culture is preserved on outer islands despite strong influence from the US and Japan. Modekngei is a blend of Christianity and local beliefs.

THE ECONOMY
Tourism and fishing licenses are main earners. Coconuts, bananas, and taro. New 15-year US aid plan to 2024.

INSIGHT: *Palau's reefs contain 1500 species of fish and 700 types of coral*

FACTFILE
OFFICIAL NAME: Republic of Palau
DATE OF FORMATION: 1994
CAPITAL: Ngerulmud
POPULATION: 22,000
TOTAL AREA: 177 sq. miles (458 sq. km)
DENSITY: 112 people per sq. mile
LANGUAGES: Palauan*, English*, Japanese, Angaur, Tobi, Sonsorolese

RELIGIONS: Roman Catholic 49%, Protestant 33%, Modekngei 9%, other 8%, nonreligious 1%
ETHNIC MIX: Palauan 73%, Filipino 16%, other Asian 7%, other Micronesian 3%, other 1%
GOVERNMENT: Nonparty system
CURRENCY: US dollar = 100 cents

Panama

A Spanish colony until 1821, Panama is the southernmost country in Central America. The colossal Panama Canal (which was under US control until 2000) links the Pacific and Atlantic oceans.

GEOGRAPHY

Lowlands along both coasts, with savanna-covered plains and rolling hills. Mountainous interior. Swamps and rainforests in the east.

CLIMATE

Hot and humid, with heavy rainfall in the May–December wet season. Cooler at high altitudes.

PEOPLE & SOCIETY

A multiethnic society, dominated by people of mixed Spanish–Amerindian origin (mestizo). Amerindians live in remote areas. The Panama Canal and former US military bases (the last of which closed in 1999) have given society a cosmopolitan outlook, but Catholicism and the extended family remain strong. Wealth is unevenly divided. Money-laundering, narcotics trafficking, and corruption are rife.

THE ECONOMY

Colón Free Trade Zone: world's second-largest. Revenue from canal up since expansion opened in 2016. Income from merchant ships sailing under flag of Panama. Banana and shrimp exports.

INSIGHT: *The Panama Canal shortens the sea route between the east coast of the US and Japan by 3000 miles (4800 km)*

FACTFILE

OFFICIAL NAME: Republic of Panama

DATE OF FORMATION: 1903

CAPITAL: Panama City

POPULATION: 4.1 million

TOTAL AREA: 30,193 sq. miles (78,200 sq. km)

DENSITY: 140 people per sq. mile

LANGUAGES: English Creole, Spanish*, Amerindian languages, Chibchan languages

RELIGIONS: Roman Catholic 70%, Protestant 19%, nonreligious 7%, other 4%

ETHNIC MIX: Mestizo 70%, Black 14%, White 10%, Amerindian 6%

GOVERNMENT: Presidential system

CURRENCY: Balboa = 100 centésimos; US dollar is also legal tender

Papua New Guinea

A former Australian colony, Papua New Guinea (PNG) occupies the eastern section of the island of New Guinea and several other island groups. Much of the country is isolated.

GEOGRAPHY
Mountainous and forested mainland, with broad, swampy river valleys. 40 active volcanoes in the north. Around 600 outer islands.

CLIMATE
Hot and humid in lowlands, cooling toward highlands, where snow can fall on highest peaks.

PEOPLE & SOCIETY
Around 800 language groups and even more tribes. The main social distinction is between lowlanders, who have frequent contact with the outside world, and the very isolated, but increasingly threatened, highlanders. Great tensions exist between highland tribes, and vendettas can often last several generations. The island of Bougainville has been granted autonomy and promised a referendum on independence by 2020.

THE ECONOMY
Minerals: gold, copper, oil, and natural gas. High government spending almost led to national bankruptcy in 2002. Strong GDP growth in 2007–2015.

INSIGHT: *PNG is home to the only known poisonous birds; contact with the feathers of some species of pitohui produces skin blisters*

FACTFILE

OFFICIAL NAME: Independent State of Papua New Guinea

DATE OF FORMATION: 1975

CAPITAL: Port Moresby

POPULATION: 8.3 million

TOTAL AREA: 178,703 sq. miles (462,840 sq. km)

DENSITY: 47 people per sq. mile

LANGUAGES: Tok Pisin* (Pidgin English), Papuan, English*, Hiri Motu*, c.800 others

RELIGIONS: Protestant 60%, Roman Catholic 37%, other 3%

ETHNIC MIX: Melanesian or mixed race 100%

GOVERNMENT: Parliamentary system

CURRENCY: Kina = 100 toea

Paraguay

Landlocked in central South America, and once a
Spanish colony, Paraguay's post independence history has
included periods of military rule. Free elections held since 1993.

GEOGRAPHY
The Paraguay River divides the hilly
and forested east from a flat alluvial
plain, with marsh and semidesert scrub
land in the west.

CLIMATE
Subtropical. The Gran Chaco is
generally hotter and drier. All areas
experience floods and droughts.

PEOPLE & SOCIETY
The population is mainly *mestizo*
(mixed Spanish and native Guaraní origin).
Most people are bilingual, though in rural
areas Guaraní is more widely used. Cattle
ranchers populate the Chaco, along
with communities of the German-origin
Mennonite Church. Right-wing Colorados
in power for decades, except 2008–2013.

◆ **INSIGHT:** *The War of the Triple*
Alliance (1864–1870) killed almost 90%
of Paraguay's male population

THE ECONOMY
Agriculture: soybeans are the
main export. Electricity exported from
massive hydroelectric dams, including
Itaipú (world's second-largest, jointly run
with Brazil). Large informal economy.
Corruption and smuggling.

1000m/3281ft
500m/1640ft
200m/656ft
Sea Level

FACTFILE

OFFICIAL NAME: Republic of Paraguay

DATE OF FORMATION: 1811

CAPITAL: Asunción

POPULATION: 6.8 million

TOTAL AREA: 157,046 sq. miles
(406,750 sq. km)

DENSITY: 44 people per sq. mile

LANGUAGES: Guaraní*, Spanish*, German

RELIGIONS: Roman Catholic 89%,
Protestant (including Mennonite) 7%,
other 3%, nonreligious 1%

ETHNIC MIX: *Mestizo* 91%, other 7%,
Amerindian 2%

GOVERNMENT: Presidential system

CURRENCY: Guaraní = 100 céntimos

Peru

Once the heart of the Inca Empire, before the Spanish conquest in the 16th century, Peru lies on the Pacific coast of South America, just south of the equator.

GEOGRAPHY
Coastal plain rises to the Andes Mountains. Uplands, dissected by fertile valleys, lie east of the Andes. Tropical forest in the extreme east.

CLIMATE
Coast is mainly arid. Middle slopes of the Andes are temperate; higher peaks are snow-covered. East is hot, humid, and very wet.

PEOPLE & SOCIETY
Though most people are Amerindians or mixed-race *mestizos*, society is dominated by a small group of Spanish descendants. Amerindians, and the small black community, suffer discrimination in towns, but access to information and political power are growing; the first Amerindian president was elected in 2001–2006. Clashes with left-wing militants killed almost 70,000 people between 1980 and 2000.

THE ECONOMY
Abundant minerals: notably copper and gold. Rich Pacific fish stocks. World's second-largest cocaine producer.

INSIGHT: *Lake Titicaca is the world's highest navigable lake*

FACTFILE

OFFICIAL NAME: Republic of Peru
DATE OF FORMATION: 1824
CAPITAL: Lima
POPULATION: 32.2 million
TOTAL AREA: 496,223 sq. miles (1,285,200 sq. km)
DENSITY: 65 people per sq. mile

LANGUAGES: Spanish*, Quechua*, Aymara*
RELIGIONS: Roman Catholic 76%, Protestant 17%, Nonreligious 4%, Other 3%
ETHNIC MIX: Amerindian 45%, *Mestizo* (European–Amerindian) 37%, White 15%, other 3%
GOVERNMENT: Presidential system
CURRENCY: New sol = 100 céntimos

Philippines

Lying in the western Pacific Ocean, the Philippines is the world's second-largest archipelago, with 7107 islands, of which 4600 are named but only around 1000 inhabited.

GEOGRAPHY
Larger islands are forested and mountainous. Over 20 active volcanoes. Frequent earthquakes.

CLIMATE
Tropical. Warm and humid all year round. Typhoons occur in the rainy season: June–October.

PEOPLE & SOCIETY
Over 100 ethnic groups, most of which are of Malay origin. The Catholic Church is a dominant cultural force; it opposes family-planning, despite high population growth. The Chinese minority has been established for over 400 years. Women play a prominent part in society. High literacy levels. Islamist separatists and communist insurgents undermine stability.

◆ INSIGHT: *Mass "People Power" demonstrations have brought down two presidents, in 1986 and 2001*

THE ECONOMY
Coconuts, bananas, and pineapples exported. Growing outsourcing center. Remittances from abroad. Corruption and poor infrastructure limit growth.

2000m/6562ft
1000m/3281ft
500m/1640ft
200m/656ft
Sea Level

Babuyan Is.
PACIFIC
OCEAN
Luzon
Philippine Sea
Cabanatuan
Angeles
MANILA
Batangas
Legazpi City
Mindoro
Calbayog
Samar
South China Sea
Panay
Iloilo
Bacolod City
Cebu
Palawan
Puerto Princesa
Negros
Butuan
Iligan
Sulu Sea
Zamboanga
Davao
Mindanao
General Santos
Sulu Archipelago
Celebes Sea
Balabac Strait

0   200 km
0   200 miles

FACTFILE
OFFICIAL NAME: Republic of the Philippines
DATE OF FORMATION: 1946
CAPITAL: Manila
POPULATION: 105 million
TOTAL AREA: 115,830 sq. miles (300,000 sq. km)
DENSITY: 911 people per sq. mile

LANGUAGES: Filipino*, English*, Tagalog, Cebuano, Ilocano, Hiligaynon, many others
RELIGIONS: Roman Catholic 81%, other Christian 11%, Muslim 5%, other 3%
ETHNIC MIX: other 34%, Tagalog 28%, Cebuano 13%, Ilocano 9%, Hiligaynon 8%, Bisaya 8%
GOVERNMENT: Presidential system
CURRENCY: Philippine peso = 100 centavos

Poland

Located in the heart of Europe, Poland has undergone massive social, economic, and political change since the collapse of communism in 1989. It joined the EU in 2004.

GEOGRAPHY
Lowlands, part of the North European Plain, cover most of the country. The Tatra Mountains run along the southern border.

CLIMATE
Rainfall peaks during the hot summers. Cold winters with snow, especially in the mountains.

PEOPLE & SOCIETY
Ethnic homogeneity masks social tensions. Secular liberals criticize the semiofficial status of the Roman Catholic Church, though its influence is now waning. Abortion is banned, except for special cases. Growing wealth disparities are resented. The German minority in the west is becoming more assertive.

◆ **INSIGHT:** *Wild wisent (European bison) live in the Bialowieza Forest straddling the Poland–Belarus border*

THE ECONOMY
Switching from heavy industries to services. Foreign investment reflects big potential market. Rapid privatization. Only EU state to avoid recession in 2007–2009 global downturn. Not adopting euro yet.

1000m/3281ft
500m/1640ft
200m/656ft
Sea Level

0   100 km
0   100 miles

FACTFILE

OFFICIAL NAME: Republic of Poland

DATE OF FORMATION: 1918

CAPITAL: Warsaw

POPULATION: 38.2 million

TOTAL AREA: 120,728 sq. miles (312,685 sq. km)

DENSITY: 325 people per sq. mile

LANGUAGES: Polish*

RELIGIONS: Roman Catholic 87%, nonreligious 7%, other 5%, Orthodox Christian 1%

ETHNIC MIX: Polish 97%, Silesian 2%, other 1%

GOVERNMENT: Parliamentary system

CURRENCY: Zloty = 100 groszy

Portugal

Portugal, with its long Atlantic coast, lies on the western side of the Iberian Peninsula, which it shares with Spain. It is the most westerly country on the European mainland.

GEOGRAPHY

The Tagus River bisects the country roughly east to west, dividing the mountainous north from the lower and more undulating south.

CLIMATE

North is cool and moist. South is warmer, with dry, mild winters.

PEOPLE & SOCIETY

A homogeneous and stable society, which is losing some of its conservative traditions. History of immigration from former colonies, and recently from eastern Europe. Urban areas and the south are more socially liberal. The north is more responsive to traditional Roman Catholic values. Family ties remain important.

◆ **INSIGHT:** *Portugal is the world's leading producer of cork, which comes from the bark of the cork oak*

THE ECONOMY

Tourism. Exports of vegetables, fruit, wine, cars, and clothing. Mounting debt forced EU bailout in 2011; rejection of austerity from 2014; recovery by 2017.

FACTFILE

OFFICIAL NAME: Portuguese Republic

DATE OF FORMATION: 1139

CAPITAL: Lisbon

POPULATION: 10.3 million

TOTAL AREA: 35,672 sq. miles (92,391 sq. km)

DENSITY: 290 people per sq. mile

LANGUAGES: Portuguese*

RELIGIONS: Roman Catholic 88%, non-religious 7%, other Christian 4%, other 1%

ETHNIC MIX: Portuguese 98%, African and other 2%

GOVERNMENT: Parliamentary system

CURRENCY: Euro = 100 cents

Qatar

Qatar projects from the Arabian Peninsula into the Persian Gulf. A founding member of OPEC, it is one of the world's wealthiest states due to oil and natural gas exports.

GEOGRAPHY
Flat, semiarid desert with dunes and salt pans. Vegetation is limited to small patches of scrub.

CLIMATE
Hot and humid. Temperatures in summer can soar to over 104°F (40°C). Rainfall is rare.

PEOPLE & SOCIETY
Only one in five residents is native-born; the rest are guest workers from across the Middle East, the Indian subcontinent, Southeast Asia, and north Africa. Qataris were once nomadic Bedouins, but since the advent of oil wealth, most now live in Doha and its suburbs, leaving the north dotted with abandoned villages. Women enjoy relative freedom; most wear the veil.

 INSIGHT: *There are three times as many men as women in Qatar*

THE ECONOMY
Steady supply of crude oil and huge natural gas reserves, plus related industries. All other raw materials and most foods are imported. Economy is heavily dependent on foreign workforce. Strong GDP growth in 2004–2011; steady growth since.

FACTFILE

OFFICIAL NAME: State of Qatar
DATE OF FORMATION: 1971
CAPITAL: Doha
POPULATION: 2.6 million
TOTAL AREA: 4416 sq. miles
(11,437 sq. km)
DENSITY: 612 people per sq. mile

LANGUAGES: Arabic*
RELIGIONS: Muslim (mainly Sunni) 78%, other 14%, Christian 8%
ETHNIC MIX: Qatari 20%, other Arab 20%, Indian 20%, Nepalese 13%, Filipino 10%, other 10%, Pakistani 7%
GOVERNMENT: Monarchy
CURRENCY: Qatar riyal = 100 dirhams

Romania

Once dominated by Poles, Hungarians, and Ottomans, Romania has been slowly converting to a market economy since the 1989 overthrow of its communist regime. It joined the EU in 2007.

GEOGRAPHY

Carpathian Mountains encircle the Transylvanian plateau. Wide plains to the south and east. Danube River forms the southern border.

CLIMATE
Continental. Summers are hot and humid, winters are cold and snowy. Very heavy spring rains.

PEOPLE & SOCIETY
Romanians are ethnically distinct from their Slav and Hungarian (Magyar) neighbors. Hungarians are the largest minority, living mainly in Transylvania. They are protected by the influence of Hungary, unlike the Roma, who suffer discrimination. Net emigration (since EU membership) is slowing. Low birth rate.

◆ **INSIGHT:** *In 2001, Romania became the last country in Europe to lift its ban on homosexuality*

THE ECONOMY
Polluting, outdated heavy industry. Unmechanized agriculture. High budget deficits exposed economy in 2007–2009 global downturn: IMF bailout, austerity measures. Returned to strong growth. Low wages (for Europe) attracts foreign investment. Will not join euro before 2022.

2000m/6562ft	
1000m/3281ft	
500m/1640ft	
200m/656ft	
Sea Level	

0   100 km
0   100 miles

FACTFILE

OFFICIAL NAME: Romania

DATE OF FORMATION: 1878

CAPITAL: Bucharest

POPULATION: 19.7 million

TOTAL AREA: 91,699 sq. miles (237,500 sq. km)

DENSITY: 222 people per sq. mile

LANGUAGES: Romanian*, Hungarian (Magyar), Romani, German

RELIGIONS: Orthodox Christian 86%, other 8%, Roman Catholic 5%, nonreligious 1%

ETHNIC MIX: Romanian 89%, Magyar 7%, Roma 3%, other 1%

GOVERNMENT: Mixed presidential–parliamentary system

CURRENCY: New Romanian leu = 100 bani

Russia

Russia was the core of the old Soviet Union, which broke up in 1991. Russia is still the world's largest state. Its diversity is a source of both strength and problems.

GEOGRAPHY
The Ural Mountains divide the European steppes and forests from the tundra and forests of Siberia. South-central deserts and mountains.

CLIMATE
Continental in European Russia, with warm summers and freezing winters. Elsewhere climate ranges from sub-arctic to Mediterranean and hot desert.

PEOPLE & SOCIETY
57 "nationalities" and 95 minorities in addition to ethnic Russians. Separatism suppressed. Population decrease has slowed. HIV/AIDS rising. Crime is rife.

THE ECONOMY
Vast resources (oil, gas, metals, timber). Inefficient industry, agriculture. Tax evasion. Black market, organized crime. Wealth disparities. Sanctions.

INSIGHT: *The Trans-Siberian Railroad, running 5578 miles (9297 km) from Moscow to Vladivostok, is the longest in the world, traversing eight time zones*

3000m/9843ft
2000m/6562ft
1000m/3281ft
500m/1640ft
200m/656ft
Sea Level
Below Sea Level

0   1000 km
0   1000 miles

FACTFILE

OFFICIAL NAME: Russian Federation or Russia

DATE OF FORMATION: 1480

CAPITAL: Moscow

POPULATION: 144 million

TOTAL AREA: 6,592,735 sq. miles (17,075,200 sq. km)

DENSITY: 22 people per sq. mile

LANGUAGES: Russian*, Tatar, Ukrainian, other

RELIGIONS: Orthodox Christian 71%, nonreligious 15%, Muslim 11%, other 3%

ETHNIC MIX: Russian 81%, other 11%, Tatar 4%, Ukrainian 1%, Bashkir 1%, Chavash 1%, Chechen 1%

GOVERNMENT: Mixed presidential–parliamentary system

CURRENCY: Russian rouble = 100 kopeks

Rwanda

Rwanda lies just south of the equator in east central Africa, far from the nearest sea port. Since independence from France in 1962, ethnic tensions have dominated politics.

GEOGRAPHY
A series of plateaus descend from the ridge of volcanic peaks in the west to the Akagera River on the eastern border. The Great Rift Valley also passes through this region.

CLIMATE
Tropical, though tempered by the altitude. Two wet seasons are separated by a dry season, from June to August. Heaviest rain in the west.

PEOPLE & SOCIETY
For over 500 years the cattle-owning Tutsi minority were politically dominant over the land-owning Hutu. In 1959, violent revolt led to a reversal of the roles. Ethnic tensions are fierce; in the most recent violence, in 1994, over 800,000 people, mostly Tutsi, were massacred in an act of state-backed genocide; trials finally ended in 2015. Most people live at subsistence level.

THE ECONOMY
Reliant on aid. Production of tea and speciality coffee is booming. Strong GDP growth from 2004. Exports tin, coltan, and iron ore. Oil and gas reserves. Ecotourism is growing. Landlocked: high transportation costs.

INSIGHT: *Rwanda's parliament in 2008 was the first in the world to have more women members than men*

FACTFILE

OFFICIAL NAME: Republic of Rwanda
DATE OF FORMATION: 1962
CAPITAL: Kigali
POPULATION: 12.2 million
TOTAL AREA: 10,169 sq. miles (26,338 sq. km)
DENSITY: 1266 people per sq. mile
LANGUAGES: Kinyarwanda*, French*, Kiswahili, English*
RELIGIONS: Roman Catholic 44%, Protestant 38%, Seventh-day Adventist 12%, other and nonreligious 4%, Muslim 2%
ETHNIC MIX: Hutu 85%, Tutsi 14%, other (including Twa) 1%
GOVERNMENT: Presidential system
CURRENCY: Rwanda franc = 100 centimes

St. Kitts & Nevis

A popular Caribbean tourist destination, St. Kitts and Nevis lies in the northern part of the Leeward Island chain. Nevis is the smaller and less developed of the two islands.

GEOGRAPHY
Volcanic in origin, with forested, mountainous interiors. Nevis has hot and cold springs.

CLIMATE
Tropical, tempered by trade winds. Little seasonal variation in temperature. Moderate rainfall.

PEOPLE & SOCIETY
Most people are descended from former African slaves. There are small numbers of Europeans, and South Asians, and a community of Lebanese. Levels of emigration are high; overseas remittances are an important source of national income. Workers from the closed sugar industry were paid compensation in 2015. Native professionals and civil servants have largely replaced the former expatriate elite. Nevis's secessionist movement has subsided given its greater political representation on the mainland.

THE ECONOMY
Successful tourist industry is vulnerable to downturns in US market. Financial services. Once-key sugar industry closed down in 2005.

INSIGHT: *Nevis has been renowned as a spa since the 18th century, and is known as the "Queen of the Caribbean"*

FACTFILE

OFFICIAL NAME: Federation of Saint Christopher and Nevis
DATE OF FORMATION: 1983
CAPITAL: Basseterre
POPULATION: 55,000
TOTAL AREA: 101 sq. miles (261 sq. km)
DENSITY: 396 people per sq. mile

LANGUAGES: English*, English Creole
RELIGIONS: Anglican 33%, Methodist 29%, other 22%, Moravian 9%, Roman Catholic 7%
ETHNIC MIX: Black 95%, mixed race 3%, White 1%, other and Amerindian 1%
GOVERNMENT: Parliamentary system
CURRENCY: East Caribbean dollar = 100 cents

St. Lucia

St. Lucia is one of the most beautiful of the Caribbean Windward Islands. Ruled by France and the UK at different times in its past, the island retains the influences of both.

GEOGRAPHY
Volcanic and mountainous, with some broad fertile valleys. The Pitons, ancient lava cones, rise from the sea on the forested west coast.

CLIMATE
Tropical, moderated by trade winds. May–October wet season brings daily warm showers. Rainfall is highest in the mountains.

PEOPLE & SOCIETY
The population is a tension-free mixture of descendants of Africans, Caribs, and Europeans. Family life and the Roman Catholic Church are important to most St. Lucians. In rural areas, women often head the households and run much of the farming. Plantation and hotel owners are the richest group. New hotels create jobs, but there is resistance to overdevelopment and fears for local culture and nature.

THE ECONOMY
Banana production fluctuates; exports struggle to compete since loss of preferential access to EU market. Successful tourism. Offshore banking.

INSIGHT: *St. Lucia has two Nobel laureates, the most per capita in the world*

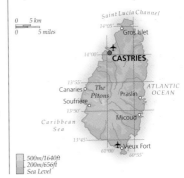

FACTFILE

OFFICIAL NAME: Saint Lucia
DATE OF FORMATION: 1979
CAPITAL: Castries
POPULATION: 178,000
TOTAL AREA: 239 sq. miles (620 sq. km)
DENSITY: 754 people per sq. mile
LANGUAGES: English*, French Creole

RELIGIONS: Roman Catholic 68%, Seventh-day Adventist 9%, other Christian 9%, Pentecostal 6%, nonreligious 5%, Rastafarian 2%, other 1%
ETHNIC MIX: Black 84%, Mulatto (mixed race) 12%, Asian 3%, other 1%
GOVERNMENT: Parliamentary system
CURRENCY: East Caribbean dollar = 100 cents

St. Vincent & the Grenadines

The islands of St. Vincent and the Grenadines form part of the Windward group in the Caribbean. St. Vincent is mostly volcanic, while the Grenadines are flat, mainly bare, coral reefs.

GEOGRAPHY
St. Vincent is mountainous and forested, with one of two active volcanoes in the Caribbean, La Soufrière. The Grenadines are 32 islands and cays, fringed by beaches.

CLIMATE
Tropical, with constant trade winds. Hurricanes are likely during the wet season in July–November.

PEOPLE & SOCIETY
Population is racially diverse; intermarriage has reduced tensions. Society is informal and relaxed, but family life is strongly influenced by the Christian Church. Locals fear that their traditional lifestyle is being threatened by the expanding tourist industry.

◆ **INSIGHT:** *The islands' precolonial inhabitants, the Carib, named them "Harioun" – home of the blessed*

THE ECONOMY
Dependent on agriculture and tourism. Bananas are the main cash crop. Tourism, targeted at the jet-set and cruise-ship markets, is concentrated on the Grenadines.

FACTFILE

OFFICIAL NAME: Saint Vincent and the Grenadines

DATE OF FORMATION: 1979

CAPITAL: Kingstown

POPULATION: 110,000

TOTAL AREA: 150 sq. miles (389 sq. km)

DENSITY: 840 people per sq. mile

LANGUAGES: English*, English Creole

RELIGIONS: other Christian 37%, Anglican 18%, Pentecostal 18%, Methodist 11%, nonreligious 9%, other 7%

ETHNIC MIX: Black 73%, Mulatto (mixed race) 20%, Carib 4%, Asian 2%, Other 1%

GOVERNMENT: Parliamentary system

CURRENCY: East Caribbean dollar = 100 cents

Samoa

The Pacific islands of Samoa gained independence from New Zealand in 1962. Four of the nine volcanic islands are inhabited – Apolima, Manono, Savai'i, and Upolu.

GEOGRAPHY

Comprises two large islands and seven smaller ones. The two largest islands have rainforested, mountainous interiors surrounded by coastal lowlands and coral reefs.

CLIMATE

Tropical, with high humidity. Cooler in May–November. Cyclone season is December–March.

PEOPLE & SOCIETY

Ethnic Samoans are the world's second-largest Polynesian group, after the Maoris. Their way of life is communal and formalized. Extended family groups own 80% of the land. Each family has an elected chief, who looks after its political and social interests. Large-scale migration to the US and New Zealand reflects the country's lack of jobs and the attractions of a Western lifestyle.

THE ECONOMY

Exports fish, coconut products (oil, cream, and copra), and nonu fruit. Dependent on aid and expatriate remittances. Growth of tourism and offshore banking. Loss of Japanese car parts factory in 2016. Rainforests are increasingly exploited for timber.

◆ **INSIGHT:** *Samoa was named for the sacred (sa) chickens (moa) of Lu, son of Tagaloa, the god of creation*

FACTFILE

OFFICIAL NAME: Independent State of Samoa

DATE OF FORMATION: 1962

CAPITAL: Apia

POPULATION: 195,000

TOTAL AREA: 1104 sq. miles (2860 sq. km)

DENSITY: 178 people per sq. mile

LANGUAGES: Samoan*, English*

RELIGIONS: other Christian 78%, Roman Catholic 20%, other 2%

ETHNIC MIX: Polynesian 91%, Euronesian (mixed European and Polynesian) 7%, other 2%

GOVERNMENT: Parliamentary system

CURRENCY: Tala = 100 sene

San Marino

Perched on the slopes of Monte Titano in the Italian Appennines, San Marino has maintained its independence since the 4th century CE, but Italy effectively controls most of its affairs.

GEOGRAPHY

Distinctive limestone outcrop of Monte Titano dominates wooded hills and pastures near Italy's Adriatic coast.

CLIMATE

High altitude and sea breezes moderate a Mediterranean climate. Hot summers and cool, wet winters.

PEOPLE & SOCIETY

Territory is divided into nine "castles," or districts. Tightly knit society, with 16 centuries of tradition. Strict immigration rules require 30-year residence before applying for citizenship. Living standards are similar to those in northern Italy. Over 13,000 Sammarinesi live abroad, most in Italy. Almost two million tourists a year visit San Marino.

◆ **INSIGHT:** *Sales of postage stamps and coins contribute around 10% of the national income*

THE ECONOMY
Tourism, banking, manufacturing, and investment all hit by 2008–2009 global downturn. Banking transparency has improved. Lower tax rates than Italy. Wine, cheese, olive oil, textiles, and ceramics are exported. Also relies on Italian subsidy and infrastructure.

Dogana
Serravalle
Fiorina
Cailungo
Gualdicciolo
Borgo Maggiore
ITALY
Monte Titano 2424ft (739m) ▲ ● SAN MARINO
Faetano
Murata
ITALY
Chiesanuova
A p p e n n i n o
Montegiardino

500m/1640ft
200m/656ft
Sea Level

0   4 km
0   4 miles

FACTFILE

OFFICIAL NAME: Republic of San Marino

DATE OF FORMATION: 1631

CAPITAL: San Marino

POPULATION: 33,000

TOTAL AREA: 23.6 sq. miles (61 sq. km)

DENSITY: 1375 people per sq. mile

LANGUAGES: Italian*

RELIGIONS: Roman Catholic 93%, other and nonreligious 7%

ETHNIC MIX: Sammarinese 88%, Italian 10%, other 2%

GOVERNMENT: Parliamentary system

CURRENCY: Euro = 100 cents

Sao Tome & Principe

A former Portuguese colony, Sao Tome and Principe comprises two main islands and surrounding islets, off the west coast of Africa. Elections in 1991 ended 15 years of Marxism.

GEOGRAPHY
Islands scattered across the equator. Sao Tome and Principe are heavily forested and mountainous.

CLIMATE
Hot and humid, but cooled by the Benguela Current. Plentiful rainfall.

PEOPLE & SOCIETY
Population is mostly black, though Portuguese culture pre-dominates. Blacks are high-profile in political leadership. Society is well integrated and free from racial prejudice. Príncipe assumed autonomous status in 1995. There is a growing business class. The extended family offers the main form of social security. Africa's highest aid-to-population ratios.

◆ INSIGHT: *The population is entirely of immigrant descent: the islands were uninhabited when colonized in 1470*

THE ECONOMY
Cocoa earns almost 70% of export revenue. Coconuts, pepper, coffee also farmed. Tourism. Reliant on aid. Offshore oil reserves, not commercially viable yet.

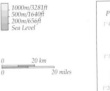

FACTFILE

OFFICIAL NAME: Democratic Republic of Sao Tome and Principe

DATE OF FORMATION: 1975

CAPITAL: São Tomé

POPULATION: 200,000

TOTAL AREA: 386 sq. miles (1001 sq. km)

DENSITY: 539 people per sq. mile

LANGUAGES: Portuguese Creole, Portuguese*

RELIGIONS: Roman Catholic 56%, non-religious 21%, other Christian 15%, other 8%

ETHNIC MIX: Black 90%, Portuguese and Creole 10%

GOVERNMENT: Mixed presidential–parliamentary system

CURRENCY: Dobra = 100 céntimos

Saudi Arabia

Occupying most of the Arabian Peninsula, Saudi Arabia covers an area the size of western Europe. It is one of the world's largest oil producers and has a major petrochemicals industry.

GEOGRAPHY
Mostly desert or semidesert plateau. Mountain ranges in the west run parallel to the Red Sea and drop steeply to a coastal plain.

CLIMATE
In summer, temperatures often soar above 118°F (48°C), but in winter they may fall below freezing. Rainfall is rare.

PEOPLE & SOCIETY
Most Saudis are Sunni Muslims who embrace *sharia* (Islamic law) and follow the strictly orthodox Wahhabi interpretation of Islam in their daily lives. Women are obliged to wear the veil, and have no role in public life; restrictions on driving eased in 2017. The al-Sa'ud family rules with absolute power. Backed by the religious establishment, it controls all political life and makes few concessions to calls for wider public participation.

THE ECONOMY
Vast oil and natural gas reserves. 11 million workers are foreign: new policy means firms must employ more Saudis.

INSIGHT: *Two million Muslims a year make the hajj (pilgrimage) to the holy city of Mecca. Only practicing Muslims are allowed inside the city*

FACTFILE

OFFICIAL NAME: Kingdom of Saudi Arabia
DATE OF FORMATION: 1932
CAPITAL: Riyadh
POPULATION: 32.9 million
TOTAL AREA: 756,981 sq. miles (1,960,582 sq. km)
DENSITY: 40 people per sq. mile

LANGUAGES: Arabic*
RELIGIONS: (Native population) Sunni Muslim 85%, Shi'a Muslim 15%
ETHNIC MIX: Arab 72%, foreign residents (mostly south or southeast Asian) 20%, Afro-Asian 8%
GOVERNMENT: Monarchy
CURRENCY: Saudi riyal = 100 halalat

Senegal

Senegal's capital, Dakar, stands on the westernmost cape of Africa. After independence from France, Senegal became a single-party state, but it has had multiparty elections since 1981.

GEOGRAPHY

Arid semidesert in the north. The south is mainly savanna bushland. Plains in the southeast.

CLIMATE

Tropical, with humid rainy conditions June–October, and a drier season December–May. The coast is cooled by northern trade winds.

PEOPLE & SOCIETY

Interethnic marriage has reduced ethnic tensions. Groups can be identified regionally. Dakar is a Wolof area, with the Serer to the east and southeast of Dakar. The Senegal River is dominated by the Peul and Toucouleur. The Diola (Jola) in Casamance have felt excluded, causing a long secessionist struggle; a 2014 cease-fire may end the conflict, though plans to mine the region's resources are controversial. A large diaspora spreads Senegalese culture and music.

THE ECONOMY

Good infrastructure, particularly port at Dakar. Fishing (though stocks diminishing). Remittances. Phosphate mining. Groundnuts. Development of tourism. Oil reserves off Casamance.

◆ **INSIGHT:** *Senegal's name derives from the Muslim Zenega Berbers who invaded in the 1300s*

FACTFILE

OFFICIAL NAME: Republic of Senegal
DATE OF FORMATION: 1960
CAPITAL: Dakar
POPULATION: 15.9 million
TOTAL AREA: 75,749 sq. miles
(196,190 sq. km)
DENSITY: 214 people per sq. mile

LANGUAGES: Wolof, Pulaar, Serer, Diola, Mandinka, Malinké, Soninké, French*
RELIGIONS: Sunni Muslim 95%, Christian (mainly Catholic) 4%, traditional beliefs 1%
ETHNIC MIX: Wolof 43%, Serer 15%, other 14%, Peul 14%, Toucouleur 9%, Diola 5%
GOVERNMENT: Presidential system
CURRENCY: CFA franc = 100 centimes

Serbia

The central and eastern region of what was once Yugoslavia, Serbia was a pariah state until Slobodan Milosevic was ousted in 2000. Montenegro broke away in 2006, and Kosovo in 2008.

GEOGRAPHY

Landlocked since secession of Montenegro. Fertile Danube plain in the north, rolling uplands in the center and southeast. Mountains in the southwest.

CLIMATE

Continental in the north, with wet springs and warm summers. Colder winters with heavy snow in the south.

PEOPLE & SOCIETY

Serbs are Orthodox Christian and use the Cyrillic script. Catholic Magyars (Hungarians) in Vojvodina have some autonomy. Society was severely shaken in the 1990s by interethnic conflict. After Serbia's cooperation in apprehending suspected war criminals, it was granted EU candidate status, but the issue of Kosovo is a major obstacle to accession.

 INSIGHT: *The medieval Serbian Empire reached into northern Greece*

THE ECONOMY

Recovery from sanctions and 1999 NATO bombing: GDP only returned to pre-1990 level by 2006. Reserves of coal, and oil. Strong industrial base. Privatization ongoing. Foreign investment growing. Danube is a key transportation link.

FACTFILE

OFFICIAL NAME: Republic of Serbia
DATE OF FORMATION: 2006
CAPITAL: Belgrade
POPULATION: 8.8 million
TOTAL AREA: 29,905 sq. miles (77,453 sq. km)
DENSITY: 294 people per sq. mile

LANGUAGES: Serbian*, Hungarian (Magyar)
RELIGIONS: Orthodox Christian 88%, Roman Catholic 4%, nonreligious 4%, Muslim 2%, other 2%
ETHNIC MIX: Serb 87%, Magyar 4%, other 3%, Roma 2%, Bosniak 2%, Croat 1%, Slovak 1%
GOVERNMENT: Parliamentary system
CURRENCY: Serbian dinar = 100 para

Seychelles

Formerly a UK colony, the Seychelles comprises 115 islands in the Indian Ocean. After 14 years as a one-party state, multiparty elections were introduced in 1993.

GEOGRAPHY
Mostly low-lying coral atolls, but 40, including the largest, Mahé, are mountainous and are the only granitic midocean islands in the world.

CLIMATE
Tropical oceanic climate. Hot and humid. Rainy season December–May.

PEOPLE & SOCIETY
The islands were uninhabited when French settlers arrived in the 18th century. Today, the population is homogeneous – a result of inter-marriage between ethnic groups. Almost 90% of people live on Mahé. Living standards are among Africa's highest, but poverty has risen. The welfare system caters to all.

◆ **INSIGHT:** *The Seychelles' unique species include the coco-de-mer palm, which produces the world's largest seeds*

THE ECONOMY
Tourism is main sector, based on appeal of beaches and exotic wildlife. Tuna is fished and canned for export. Offshore financial services growing. Most domestic requirements are imported. Re-export trade. Virtually no mineral resources. High debt-servicing burden.

VICTORIA
55°30'
Mahé
0   5 km
0   5 miles
4°45'
Inner Islands
54°
Grand'Anse   Praslin
Mahé
50°
6°
Amirante
Islands
I N D I A N
I s l a n d s
O C E A N
Aldabra
Group   O u t e r
Farquhar
Group
10°

500m/1640ft
200m/656ft
Sea Level

0   100 km
0   100 miles

FACTFILE

OFFICIAL NAME: Republic of Seychelles

DATE OF FORMATION: 1976

CAPITAL: Victoria

POPULATION: 95,000

TOTAL AREA: 176 sq. miles (455 sq. km)

DENSITY: 913 people per sq. mile

LANGUAGES: French Creole*, English*, French*

RELIGIONS: Roman Catholic 84%, Anglican 6%, other Christian 5%, Hindu 2%, other and nonreligious 2%, Muslim 1%

ETHNIC MIX: Creole 89%, Indian 5%, other 4%, Chinese 2%

GOVERNMENT: Presidential system

CURRENCY: Seychelles rupee = 100 cents

Sierra Leone

The west African state of Sierra Leone achieved independence from the UK in 1961. Today, trying to recover from a brutal civil war in the 1990s, it is one of the world's poorest nations.

GEOGRAPHY
Flat plain, running the length of the coast, stretches inland for 83 miles (133 km). Beyond, forests rise to highlands near neighboring Guinea in the northeast.

CLIMATE
Hot tropical weather, with very high rainfall and humidity. The dusty, northeastern *harmattan* wind blows November–April.

PEOPLE & SOCIETY
Mende and Temne are the major ethnic groups. Freetown's citizens are largely descended from slaves freed from Britain and the US, resulting in a strongly Anglicized Creole culture in the capital. The countryside is less developed. A devastating civil war broke out in 1991 and was not properly resolved until a 2001 peace agreement; two million had been displaced. A deadly Ebola outbreak hit the country in 2014–2015.

THE ECONOMY
Aid is vital: reconstruction is taking years. Diamond exports, but smuggling is rife. Rutile and bauxite are also mined. Coffee, cocoa, and palm fruits are cash crops, but most farming is subsistence.

◆ **INSIGHT:** *The British philanthropist Granville Sharp set up a settlement for freed slaves in Freetown in 1787*

FACTFILE

OFFICIAL NAME: Republic of Sierra Leone
DATE OF FORMATION: 1961
CAPITAL: Freetown
POPULATION: 7.6 million
TOTAL AREA: 27,698 sq. miles (71,740 sq. km)
DENSITY: 275 people per sq. mile

LANGUAGES: Mende, Temne, Krio, English*
RELIGIONS: Muslim 60%, Christian 30%, traditional beliefs 10%
ETHNIC MIX: Mende 35%, Temne 32%, other 21%, Limba 8%, Kuranko 4%
GOVERNMENT: Presidential system
CURRENCY: Leone = 100 cents

Singapore

Linked to the southernmost tip of the Malay peninsula by a causeway, Singapore was established as a trading settlement in 1819. It is now one of Asia's most important commercial centers.

GEOGRAPHY
Little remains of the original vegetation on Singapore Island. The other 54 much smaller islands are little more than swampy jungle.

CLIMATE
Equatorial. Hot and humid, with heavy rainfall all year round.

PEOPLE & SOCIETY
Chinese majority includes old-established English-speaking Straits Chinese and more recent immigrants. Median income is highest in Indian households and lowest in Malay households. Significant expatriate workforce. Aging population: cash incentives and longer parental leave aim to boost birth rate. Society is highly regulated; official campaigns aim to improve public behavior. Crime is low; punishment can be severe. Living standards are among world's highest.

THE ECONOMY
Wealth from success as entrepôt and center of high-tech industries, such as electronics and pharmaceuticals. Leads research in new biotechnologies. Most food, energy, and water imported. Worst-ever recession in 2008–2009.

INSIGHT: *Chewing gum was banned outright from 1992 to 2004*

Urban areas
Open areas
Nature reserves

FACTFILE

OFFICIAL NAME: Republic of Singapore

DATE OF FORMATION: 1965

CAPITAL: Singapore

POPULATION: 5.7 million

TOTAL AREA: 250 sq. miles (648 sq. km)

DENSITY: 24,153 people per sq. mile

LANGUAGES: Mandarin*, Malay*, Tamil*, English*

RELIGIONS: Christian 31%, Buddhist 28%, nonreligious 14%, Muslim 13%, Taoist 9%, Hindu 4%, other 1%

ETHNIC MIX: Chinese 74%, Malay 14%, Indian 9%, other 3%

GOVERNMENT: Parliamentary system

CURRENCY: Singapore dollar = 100 cents

Slovakia

Landlocked in central Europe, Slovakia became a separate state in 1993, splitting ex-communist Czechoslovakia in two. It joined the EU in 2004 and the eurozone five years later.

GEOGRAPHY
The Tatra Mountains stretch along the northern border with Poland. Southern lowlands include the fertile Danube plain.

CLIMATE
Continental. Moderately warm summers and steady rainfall. Cold winters with heavy snowfalls.

PEOPLE & SOCIETY
Slovaks are the dominant group. Magyars (Hungarians) seek to protect their language and culture, backed by Hungary. Magyar parties exist in the political mainstream, on occasion joining the ruling coalition. A 2010 law banning dual citizenship other than by birth or marriage mostly affects Czechs and Germans, not Hungarians. Roma are unrepresented and face significant discrimination. Rural eastern regions are least developed.

THE ECONOMY
Heavy industry, especially cars. Exports hit by 2007–2009 global downturn. High unemployment. Budget deficit has been brought down. Successful privatizations.

INSIGHT: *From 1526 to 1784 Bratislava, then known as Pozsony, served as the capital of Hungary*

2000m/6562ft
1000m/3281ft
500m/1640ft
200m/656ft
Sea Level

FACTFILE

OFFICIAL NAME: Slovak Republic
DATE OF FORMATION: 1993
CAPITAL: Bratislava
POPULATION: 5.4 million
TOTAL AREA: 18,859 sq. miles (48,845 sq. km)
DENSITY: 285 people per sq. mile
LANGUAGES: Slovak*, Hungarian (Magyar),
Czech

RELIGIONS: Roman Catholic 69%, nonreligious 15%, other Christian 11%, Greek Catholic (Uniate) 4%, other 1%
ETHNIC MIX: Slovak 87%, Magyar 9%, Roma 2%, other 1%, Czech 1%
GOVERNMENT: Parliamentary system
CURRENCY: Euro = 100 cents

Slovenia

Lying at the junction of central Europe and the Balkans, Slovenia seceded from socialist Yugoslavia in 1991. In 2004, it became the first former Yugoslav state to join the EU.

GEOGRAPHY
Alpine terrain with hills and mountains. Forests cover almost half the country's area. There is a short coastline on the Adriatic Sea.

CLIMATE
Mediterranean climate on the small coastal strip. The alpine interior has continental extremes.

PEOPLE & SOCIETY
Long historical association with western Europe accounts for the "Alpine" rather than "Balkan" outlook of Slovenia's people, despite close similarities to other former Yugoslavs. The absence of sizable Serb or Croat minorities made for a relatively peaceful secession from Yugoslavia. There are small communities of Italians and Magyars (Hungarians) in the southwest and east respectively.

THE ECONOMY
First new EU member to join eurozone (in 2007). Export-oriented, so vulnerable to global economic trends. Competitive manufacturing industry. Sizable state-owned sector remains.

INSIGHT: *A wheel found in a marsh in 2003 is claimed to be the world's oldest, pre-dating 3000 BCE*

FACTFILE

OFFICIAL NAME: Republic of Slovenia
DATE OF FORMATION: 1991
CAPITAL: Ljubljana
POPULATION: 2.1 million
TOTAL AREA: 7820 sq. miles (20,253 sq. km)
DENSITY: 269 people per sq. mile

LANGUAGES: Slovenian*
RELIGIONS: Roman Catholic 75%, nonreligious 18%, Muslim 3%, Orthodox Christian 3%, other (mostly Protestant) 1%
ETHNIC MIX: Slovene 92%, other 3%, Serb 2%, Croat 2%, Bosniak 1%
GOVERNMENT: Parliamentary system
CURRENCY: Euro = 100 cents

Solomon Islands

The Solomons archipelago comprises several hundred coral reef islands scattered in the southwestern Pacific. Most of the population live on the six largest islands.

GEOGRAPHY
The six largest islands are volcanic, mountainous, and thickly forested. Flat coastal plains provide the only cultivable land.

CLIMATE
Northern islands are hot and humid all year round; farther south a cool season develops. November–April wet season brings cyclones.

PEOPLE & SOCIETY
Almost all islanders are Melanesian. Animist beliefs sit alongside Christianity. Tensions are regional; Guadalcanal natives (Isatabu) fought immigrant Malaitan workers in the 1998–2000 conflict, displacing 35,000 and ruining the economy. From 2003, Australian-led peacekeepers tried to restore stability. A new devolved "state system" has granted outlying islands more autonomy, but politics remains volatile.

THE ECONOMY
Subsistence farming and fishing sustain about 75% of people. Main cash crops are copra, cocoa, palm oil. Gold deposits, but main mine has been closed on and off. Civil conflict bankrupted the government. Forests have been depleted.

◆ **INSIGHT:** *The battle for Japanese-held Guadalcanal was the first major US offensive in the Pacific War during World War II*

FACTFILE

OFFICIAL NAME: Solomon Islands
DATE OF FORMATION: 1978
CAPITAL: Honiara
POPULATION: 599,000
TOTAL AREA: 10,985 sq. miles (28,450 sq. km)
DENSITY: 55 people per sq. mile
LANGUAGES: English*, Pidgin English, Melanesian Pidgin, 120 (est.) native languages

RELIGIONS: Church of Melanesia (Anglican) 34%, Roman Catholic 19%, other 19%, South Seas Evangelical Church 17%, Methodist 11%
ETHNIC MIX: Melanesian 93%, Polynesian 4%, Micronesian 2%, other 1%
GOVERNMENT: Parliamentary system
CURRENCY: Solomon Is. dollar = 100 cents

Somalia

A semiarid state occupying the Horn of Africa, Somalia was formed from the Italian and British colonies of Somaliland. Conflict has left it without effective government since 1991.

GEOGRAPHY
Highlands in the north, flatter scrub-covered land to the south. Coastal areas are more fertile.

CLIMATE
Very dry, except for the north coast, which is hot and humid. The interior has among the world's highest average annual temperatures.

PEOPLE & SOCIETY
The clan system forms the basis of commercial, political, and social life. The minority Bantu are traditionally seen as socially inferior to Somalis. Since the 1991 coup, Somalia has lacked strong central authority. Somaliland claims independence, and Puntland autonomy. Islamist militias controlled rump Somalia by 2009; al-Shabab has been pushed out of key towns but remains a threat. A new federal structure was formulated in 2012, but national governments are short-lived.

THE ECONOMY
Ongoing war. All goods, except arms, are in short supply. Piracy, banditry. Few natural resources. Prone to drought, causing food insecurity, recurrent famine. Somaliland is more stable, but its trade is hampered by lack of global recognition.

INSIGHT: *Until 1973, Somali was an unwritten language*

DJIBOUTI

Gulf of Aden

Berbera

SOMALILAND
(not internationally
recognized)

Hargeysa

Burco

Garoowe

ETHIOPIA

Gaalkacyo

Beledweyne

KENYA

Baydhabo

MOGADISHU

Marka

INDIAN
OCEAN

Jilib   *Equator*

Kismaayo

0	200 km
0	200 miles

1000m/3281ft
500m/1640ft
200m/656ft
Sea Level
Below Sea Level

Raas Caseyr

Puntland

FACTFILE

OFFICIAL NAME: Federal Republic of Somalia

DATE OF FORMATION: 1960

CAPITAL: Mogadishu

POPULATION: 14.7 million

TOTAL AREA: 246,199 sq. miles (637,657 sq. km)

DENSITY: 61 people per sq. mile

LANGUAGES: Somali*, Arabic*, English, Italian

RELIGIONS: Sunni Muslim 99%, Christian 1%

ETHNIC MIX: Somali 85%, other 15%

GOVERNMENT: Nonparty system

CURRENCY: Somali shilin = 100 senti

South Africa

After 80 years of white minority rule, South Africa held its first multiracial, multiparty elections in 1994. Victory for the blacks marked the symbolic overturning of long years of apartheid.

GEOGRAPHY
Much of the interior is grassy *veld*. Desert in the west and far north. Mountains in the east, south, and west.

CLIMATE
Warm, temperate, and dry. Cape Town has a Mediterranean climate. Semiarid in the west.

PEOPLE & SOCIETY

The majority black population now dominates politically, but the minority white community still controls the economy. A small black middle class is growing, but unemployment among blacks remains high. Seven million people are HIV-positive, but the fight against AIDS is hampered by social attitudes. Violent crime is a problem.

◆ INSIGHT: *Over the last century, South Africa has produced over half of the world's gold*

THE ECONOMY
Africa's largest, most developed economy. Leading mineral producer, notably metals, diamonds, coal. Tourism is also key. Wealth gap has widened: jobs, housing, and better access to basic services are needed to fight poverty.

■	2000m/6562ft
■	1000m/3281ft
■	500m/1640ft
	Sea Level

ZIMBABWE
BOTSWANA
MOZAMBIQUE
Limpopo
PRETORIA · Middelburg
SWAZILAND
NAMIBIA
Kalahari Vryburg · Soweto · Johannesburg
Desert Upington Piet Retief
Orange Vaal Kroonstad
Kimberley
BLOEMFONTEIN Pietermaritzburg
Northern Karoo Middelburg LESOTHO
Durban
CAPE *Great Karoo* INDIAN
TOWN Beaufort-West OCEAN
George East London
Cape of Port Elizabeth
Good Hope

0 ——— 400 km
0 ——— 400 miles

FACTFILE
OFFICIAL NAME: Republic of South Africa
DATE OF FORMATION: 1934
CAPITALS: Pretoria; Cape Town; Bloemfontein
POPULATION: 56.7 million
TOTAL AREA: 471,008 sq. miles (1,219,912 sq. km)
DENSITY: 120 people per sq. mile

LANGUAGES: English*, isiZulu*, isiXhosa*, Afrikaans*, 7 other official languages*
RELIGIONS: Christian 81%, nonreligious 15%, Muslim 2%, Hindu 1%, other 1%
ETHNIC MIX: Black 80%, White 9%, Coloured 9%, Asian 2%
GOVERNMENT: Presidential system
CURRENCY: Rand = 100 cents

South Sudan

A long civil war in Sudan led to independence in 2011 for the mainly Christian southern part. The landlocked new state is poor and lacks vital infrastructure, despite its oil reserves.

GEOGRAPHY
The White Nile flows through South Sudan, from remote forest areas into the world's largest swamp, the Sudd.

CLIMATE
Tropical South Sudan's long, heavy rains result in some areas getting cut off. January to March is drier.

PEOPLE & SOCIETY
Most people are subsistence farmers. Village life is based on extended families; arranged marriages involve the payment of bride-price. There are over 60 language groups. The common cause of independence engendered ethnic unity. The Sudanese People's Liberation Movement, whose armed wing led the fighting, holds power in the new country, but a fallout between president and vice president in 2013 has spiraled into civil war, exposing ethnic divisions between Dinka and Nuer.

THE ECONOMY
Needs aid for humanitarian crisis and development. Drought and famine. Unresolved issues over oil revenue and borders with Sudan, which controls oil export pipeline. Foreign debt. Instability.

INSIGHT: *Decades of fighting from 1983 left over four million internally displaced*

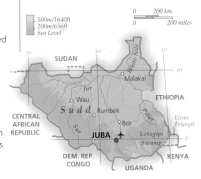

500m/1640ft
200m/656ft
Sea Level

0   200 km
0   200 miles

SUDAN
White Nile
Malakal
Jur
Wau
Sudd   Rumbek
Sue   Bor
Pibor
JUBA
Lotagipi Swamp
Eleni Triangle
CENTRAL AFRICAN REPUBLIC
ETHIOPIA
DEM. REP. CONGO
UGANDA
KENYA

FACTFILE

OFFICIAL NAME: Republic of South Sudan

DATE OF FORMATION: 2011

CAPITAL: Juba

POPULATION: 12.6 million

TOTAL AREA: 248,777 sq. miles (644,329 sq. km)

DENSITY: 51 people per sq. mile

LANGUAGES: Arabic, Dinka, Nuer, Zande, Bari, Shilluk, Lotuko, English*

RELIGIONS: Over half of the population follow Christian or traditional beliefs

ETHNIC MIX: Dinka 40%, Nuer 15%, Bari 10%, Azande 10%, Shilluk 10%, Arab 10%, other 5%

GOVERNMENT: Transitional regime

CURRENCY: South Sudan pound = 100 piastres

Spain

At its unification under Ferdinand and Isabella in 1492, Spain occupied a pivotal position between Europe, Africa, the North Atlantic, and the Mediterranean.

GEOGRAPHY

Mountain ranges in the north, center, and south, with a huge central plateau. Mediterranean lowlands. Verdant valleys in the northwest.

CLIMATE

Maritime in the north. Hotter and drier in the south. The central plateau has an extreme climate.

PEOPLE & SOCIETY

A vigorous ethnic regionalism, suppressed under Franco's fascist regime, now flourishes. Catalonia voted unofficially for independence in 2017. People remain churchgoing, though Roman Catholic teachings on social issues are often flouted. Spanish women are increasingly emancipated, with strong political representation.

◆ **INSIGHT:** *Over 3000 festivals and feasts take place each year in Spain*

THE ECONOMY

Exports food, and wine. Few natural resources. Large fishing fleet. A target for economic migrants from Africa. 2008 – 2009 global downturn hit motor industry and tourism and ended the construction boom: high unemployment followed. Decade of austerity to cut debt, deficits.

FACTFILE

OFFICIAL NAME: Kingdom of Spain

DATE OF FORMATION: 1492

CAPITAL: Madrid

POPULATION: 46.4 million

TOTAL AREA: 194,896 sq. miles (504,782 sq. km)

DENSITY: 241 people per sq. mile

LANGUAGES: Spanish*, Catalan*, Galician*, Basque*

RELIGIONS: Roman Catholic 71%, nonreligious 26%, other 3%

ETHNIC MIX: Castilian Spanish 72%, Catalan 17%, Galician 6%, Basque 2%, other 2%, Roma 1%

GOVERNMENT: Parliamentary system

CURRENCY: Euro = 100 cents

Sri Lanka

The teardrop-shaped island of Sri Lanka is separated from India by the Palk Strait. Ethnic Tamil rebels – the Tamil Tigers – were defeated in 2009, after a brutal 26-year civil war.

GEOGRAPHY

The main island is dominated by rugged central highlands. Fertile northern plains are dissected by rivers. Much of the land is tropical jungle.

CLIMATE

Tropical, with breezes on the coast and cooler air in the highlands. Northeast is driest and hottest.

PEOPLE & SOCIETY

The Sinhalese are mostly Buddhist, while Tamils are mostly Hindu, and Moors are the Muslim descendants of Arab traders. Tamils were the minority group favored by the British colonists. Majority-Sinhalese power since independence in 1948 fueled tensions, erupting into civil war in 1983. The eventual government victory in 2009 made this the only rebel insurgency ever defeated in modern times.

THE ECONOMY

Garment industry. Remittances. Major tea exporter, also rubber and coconuts. End of costly civil war; return of foreign investment and tourists.

INSIGHT: *Sri Lanka elected the world's first woman prime minister, Sirimavo Bandaranaike, in 1960*

FACTFILE

OFFICIAL NAME: Democratic Socialist Republic of Sri Lanka

DATE OF FORMATION: 1948

CAPITAL: Colombo / Sri Jayewardenapura Kotte

POPULATION: 20.9 million

TOTAL AREA: 25,332 sq. miles (65,610 sq. km)

DENSITY: 836 people per sq. mile

LANGUAGES: Sinhala*, Tamil*, English

RELIGIONS: Buddhist 70%, Hindu 13%, Muslim 10%, Christian (mainly Roman Catholic) 7%

ETHNIC MIX: Sinhalese 75%, Tamil 15%, Moor 9%, Other 1%

GOVERNMENT: Mixed presidential–parliamentary system

CURRENCY: Sri Lanka rupee = 100 cents

Sudan

The secession of the black African south in 2011 left Sudan as Africa's third-largest country. Darfur in the west is suffering a terrible humanitarian crisis.

GEOGRAPHY
Lies within the upper Nile basin. Mostly arid plains. Highlands border the Red Sea in the northeast.

CLIMATE
North is hot, arid desert with constant dry winds. Rainy season lasting a few months in the south.

PEOPLE & SOCIETY
About two million people are nomads. There are many ethnic groups. Islamic law, imposed by the Arab majority, restricts women's freedoms and alienated the non-Muslim south, which finally seceded in 2011 after prolonged conflict. Ethnic violence by Arab militias in Darfur since 2003 has killed 400,000 people and created a huge refugee crisis within Sudan and in neighboring Chad and CAR. President Bashir faces an international arrest warrant for crimes against humanity.

THE ECONOMY
Oil reserves reduced by secession of South. Violence and drought hamper farming. Sesame, gum arabic, groundnuts. Millions of people displaced. Large debt.

INSIGHT: *Sudan has more pyramids than Egypt: over 200 structures remain from ancient Nubian kingdoms on the Nile*

2000m/6562ft	
1000m/3281ft	
500m/1640ft	
200m/656ft	
Sea Level	

0   400 km

0   400 miles

FACTFILE

OFFICIAL NAME: Republic of the Sudan

DATE OF FORMATION: 1956

CAPITAL: Khartoum

POPULATION: 40.5 million

TOTAL AREA: 718,722 sq. miles (1,861,481 sq. km)

DENSITY: 56 people per sq. mile

LANGUAGES: Arabic*, Nubian, Beja, Fur, English*

RELIGIONS: Almost all Muslim (mainly Sunni)

ETHNIC MIX: Arab 60%, other 18%, Nubian 10%, Beja 8%, Fur 3%, Zaghawa 1%

GOVERNMENT: Presidential system

CURRENCY: New Sudanese pound = 100 piastres

Suriname

Suriname is a former Dutch colony on the north coast of South America. Democracy was restored in 1991, after almost 11 years of military rule. The Netherlands is still a major donor of aid.

GEOGRAPHY
Mostly covered by tropical rainforest. Coastal plain rises to central plateaus and the Guiana Highlands.

CLIMATE
Tropical. Hot and humid, but cooled by trade winds. High rainfall, especially in the interior.

PEOPLE & SOCIETY
The Dutch brought laborers from South Asia and Java. Independence saw mass emigration: around 450,000 Surinamese live in the Netherlands. Of those left, over 85% live near the coast, the rest in scattered rainforest communities. Indigenous Amerindians account for just under 4% of the population. Bosnegers – descended from runaway African slaves – fought the military government in the late 1980s. Under civilian rule, each group has had a political party representing its interests.

THE ECONOMY
Alumina and gold are the key exports. Rice and bananas are main cash crops. Oil production and tourism are growing. Excessive bureaucracy.

◆ **INSIGHT:** *In a 1667 Anglo-Dutch deal, Holland gained Suriname but lost New Amsterdam (now New York)*

ATLANTIC OCEAN
Nieuw Nickerie
PARAMARIBO Nieuw Amsterdam
Kwakoegron
Coranyne
Brokopondo
Maroni
W. J. van Blommesteinmeer
FRENCH GUIANA
GUYANA
Guiana Highlands
BRAZIL

1000m/3281ft
500m/1640ft
200m/656ft
Sea Level

0   200 km
0   200 miles

FACTFILE

OFFICIAL NAME: Republic of Suriname
DATE OF FORMATION: 1975
CAPITAL: Paramaribo
POPULATION: 558,000
TOTAL AREA: 63,039 sq. miles (163,270 sq. km)
DENSITY: 9 people per sq. mile
LANGUAGES: Sranan (Creole), Dutch*,

Javanese, Sarnami Hindi, Saramaccan, Carib
RELIGIONS: Christian 50%, Hindu 23%, Muslim 14%, other 13%
ETHNIC MIX: E Indian 27%, Creole 18%, Black 15%, Javanese 15%, mixed race 13%, other 12%
GOVERNMENT: Mixed presidential–parliamentary system
CURRENCY: Surinamese dollar = 100 cents

Swaziland

The tiny southern African kingdom of Swaziland is crippled with HIV/AIDS and economically dependent on South Africa. Vocal demands for multiparty democracy have been ignored.

GEOGRAPHY

Mainly high plateaus and mountains. Rolling grasslands and low scrub plains to the east. Pine forests on western border.

CLIMATE

Temperatures rise and rainfall declines as the land descends eastward, from high to low grassy *veld*.

PEOPLE & SOCIETY

One of Africa's most conservative states, though there is pressure from urban-based modernizers. Political system promotes Swazi tradition and is dominated by powerful monarchy. Women face discrimination. Swaziland has the world's highest prevalence of HIV/AIDS: education, testing, and access to treatment have cut infection rates.

◆ INSIGHT: *Polygamy is practiced in Swaziland – when King Sobhuza died in 1982, he left 100 widows*

THE ECONOMY

Sugarcane is the main cash crop. Wood pulp and soft drink concentrates are also exported. Loss of workforce to HIV/AIDS, and high cost of health care.

FACTFILE

OFFICIAL NAME: Kingdom of Swaziland
DATE OF FORMATION: 1968
CAPITALS: Mbabane; Lobamba
POPULATION: 1.4 million
TOTAL AREA: 6704 sq. miles (17,363 sq. km)
DENSITY: 211 people per sq. mile

LANGUAGES: English*, siSwati*, isiZulu, Xitsonga
RELIGIONS: Traditional beliefs 40%, other 30%, Roman Catholic 20%, Muslim 10%
ETHNIC MIX: Swazi 97%, other 3%
GOVERNMENT: Monarchy
CURRENCY: Lilangeni = 100 cents

Sweden

The largest Scandinavian country by both population and area, Sweden has one of the world's most extensive welfare systems and is among the leading proponents of equal rights for women.

GEOGRAPHY

Heavily forested, with many lakes. Northern plateau extends beyond the Arctic Circle. Southern lowlands are widely cultivated.

CLIMATE
Southern coasts warmed by Gulf Stream. Northern areas have more extreme continental climate.

PEOPLE & SOCIETY

The nuclear family forms the basis of society, and marriage rates have improved since the 1980s, but over half of babies are born outside marriage. The model welfare system is paid for by a high tax burden. Women are well represented at all levels. A minority of about 30,000 Sámi lives in the far north. Most industries and the bulk of people are based in and around the southern cities. An EU member since 1995, Sweden has voted not to join the euro.

THE ECONOMY
Companies of global importance, including Volvo, Saab, SKF, Ericsson, IKEA. Highly developed infrastructure. Up-to-date technology. Skilled workforce.

INSIGHT: *Sweden has maintained a position of armed neutrality since 1815*

FACTFILE

OFFICIAL NAME: Kingdom of Sweden
DATE OF FORMATION: 1523
CAPITAL: Stockholm
POPULATION: 9.9 million
TOTAL AREA: 173,731 sq. miles (449,964 sq. km)
DENSITY: 62 people per sq. mile
LANGUAGES: Swedish*, Finnish, Sámi

RELIGIONS: Evangelical Lutheran 75%, other 13%, other Protestant 5%, Muslim 5%, Roman Catholic 2%
ETHNIC MIX: Swedish 86%, foreign-born or first-generation immigrant 12%, Finnish and Sámi 2%
GOVERNMENT: Parliamentary system
CURRENCY: Swedish krona = 100 öre

Switzerland

One of the world's most prosperous countries, Switzerland sits at the center of Europe. It has retained its neutral status through every major European conflict since 1815.

GEOGRAPHY

Mostly mountainous, with river valleys. The Alps cover 60% of its area; the Jura in the west cover 10%. Lowlands lie along the east–west axis.

CLIMATE

Most rain falls in the warm summer months. Winters are snowy, but milder and foggy away from the mountains. Avalanches are a problem.

PEOPLE & SOCIETY

Switzerland is composed of distinct German-Swiss, French-Swiss, and Italian-Swiss linguistic groups. In the east, a 40,000-strong minority speaks Romansch. The country is divided into 26 autonomous cantons (states), each with control over health care, education, housing, and taxation. Public referenda are widely used to decide policy. Society is conservative; marriage and divorce rates are above the EU averages.

THE ECONOMY

Diversified economy relies on services – the banking sector manages over a quarter of the world's offshore private wealth – and specialized industries (engineering, watches, etc).

INSIGHT: *Famed for its neutrality, Switzerland only joined the UN in 2002, and remains outside the EU*

	3000m/9843ft
	2000m/6562ft
	1000m/3281ft
	500m/1640ft
	200m/656ft

0   50 km

0   50 miles

FACTFILE

OFFICIAL NAME: Swiss Confederation

DATE OF FORMATION: 1291

CAPITAL: Bern

POPULATION: 8.5 million

TOTAL AREA: 15,942 sq. miles (41,290 sq. km)

DENSITY: 554 people per sq. mile

LANGUAGES: German*, Swiss-German, French*, Italian*, Romansch*

RELIGIONS: Roman Catholic 39%, other Christian 34%, nonreligious 21%, Muslim 5%, other 1%

ETHNIC MIX: German 64%, French 20%, other 9.5%, Italian 6%, Romansch 0.5%

GOVERNMENT: Parliamentary system

CURRENCY: Swiss franc = 100 rappen/centimes

Syria

Stretching from the eastern Mediterranean to the Tigris River, Syria's borders are regarded as an artificial creation of French colonial rule by many Syrians. Civil war erupted in 2011.

GEOGRAPHY
A short stretch of coastal plain is backed by a low range of hills. The Euphrates River cuts through a vast interior desert plateau.

CLIMATE
Mediterranean coastal climate. Inland areas are arid. In winter, snow is common on the mountains.

PEOPLE & SOCIETY
Towns tend to lie near the coast. Most Syrians are Sunni Muslim, but the Shi'a Alawis control politics. Assad's authoritarian regime, in power since 1970, fiercely repressed pro-democracy "Arab Spring" protests in 2011: brutal conflict soon broke out. 500,000 have died and 11 million are displaced, including Iraqis and Palestinians formerly sheltering in Syrian refugee camps. Islamic State (IS) jihadists controlled the Euphrates Valley by 2014, but have now been pushed back.

THE ECONOMY
Conflict has destroyed economy. Oil fields recaptured from IS, production down. Sanctions limit exports. Lack of food, medicines. Infrastructure bombed.

INSIGHT: *Syria is an ancient land; there are at least 3500 as yet unexcavated archaeological sites*

FACTFILE

OFFICIAL NAME: Syrian Arab Republic
DATE OF FORMATION: 1941
CAPITAL: Damascus
POPULATION: 18.3 million
TOTAL AREA: 71,498 sq. miles (184,180 sq. km)
DENSITY: 258 people per sq. mile

LANGUAGES: Arabic*, French, Kurdish, Armenian, Circassian, Assyrian, Aramaic
RELIGIONS: Sunni Muslim 74%, Alawi (Shi'a sect) 12%, Christian 10%, Druze 3%, other 1%
ETHNIC MIX: Arab 90%, Kurdish 9%, Armenian, Turkmen, and Circassian 1%
GOVERNMENT: Presidential system
CURRENCY: Syrian pound = 100 piastres

Taiwan

The republic of Taiwan (formerly Formosa) is on an island 80 miles (130 km) off the southeast coast of mainland China, which still considers it to be a renegade province.

GEOGRAPHY
Mountain region covers two-thirds of the island. Highly fertile lowlands and coastal plains.

CLIMATE
Tropical monsoon. Hot and humid. Typhoons July–September. Snow falls in the mountains in winter.

PEOPLE & SOCIETY
Most Taiwanese are Han Chinese, descendants of the 1644 migration of the Ming dynasty from the mainland. The modern republic was created in 1949, when the nationalist Kuomintang was expelled from the mainland following Communist victory in the civil war. 100,000 emigrés established themselves as a ruling class. Initial resentment has subsided as a new Taiwan-born generation has taken over the reins of power. The aboriginal minority suffers discrimination.

THE ECONOMY
Successful economy of small, adaptable companies. High-tech goods: TVs, computers, and semiconductors. Rising trade, and investment with China.

INSIGHT: *Taiwan lost its seat at the UN to Beijing in 1971: both claim to represent "China"*

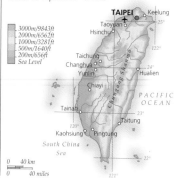

3000m/9843ft
2000m/6562ft
1000m/3281ft
500m/1640ft
200m/656ft
Sea Level

TAIPEI
Keelung
Taoyuan
Hsinchu
Taichung
Changhua
Yunlin
Chiayi
Tainan
Kaohsiung
Pingtung
Hualien
Taitung
Chianang Shanmo
PACIFIC OCEAN
South China Sea

0   40 km
0   40 miles

FACTFILE

OFFICIAL NAME: Republic of China (ROC)
DATE OF FORMATION: 1949
CAPITAL: Taipei
POPULATION: 23.5 million
TOTAL AREA: 13,892 sq. miles (35,980 sq. km)
DENSITY: 1887 people per sq. mile
LANGUAGES: Amoy Chinese, Mandarin Chinese*, Hakka Chinese
RELIGIONS: Buddhist, Confucianist, and Taoist 93%, Christian 5%, other 2%
ETHNIC MIX: Han Chinese (pre-20th-century migration) 84%, Han Chinese (20th-century migration) 14%, Aboriginal 2%
GOVERNMENT: Presidential system
CURRENCY: Taiwan dollar = 100 cents

Tajikistan

Tajikistan lies landlocked on the western slopes of the Pamirs in central Asia. Soon after the breakup of the USSR in 1991, civil war erupted between ruling communists and Islamists.

GEOGRAPHY

Mainly mountainous: bare slopes of the Pamir ranges, with fast-flowing rivers, cover most of the country. Small but fertile Fergana Valley in the northwest.

CLIMATE

Continental extremes in the valleys. Bitterly cold winters in the mountains. Rainfall is low.

PEOPLE & SOCIETY

Unlike the other former Soviet republics of central Asia, Tajikistan is dominated by a people of Persian (Iranian) rather than Turkic origin. The main ethnic conflict is with the Turkic Uzbek minority. Russians are discriminated against; most fled in the 1992–1997 civil war, and standards of living fell dramatically. A third of the population lives in poverty. Recession in Russia has brought many of Tajikistan's 1.2 million migrant workers home.

THE ECONOMY

Remittances falling. Cotton: expanding textile industry. Also exports aluminum. Uranium deposits. Corruption. Transit route for illicit Afghan opium. China leads in foreign investment.

◆ **INSIGHT:** *Carpet-making, an ancient tradition learned from Persia, is still a major source of revenue*

FACTFILE

OFFICIAL NAME: Republic of Tajikistan
DATE OF FORMATION: 1991
CAPITAL: Dushanbe
POPULATION: 8.9 million
TOTAL AREA: 55,251 sq. miles (143,100 sq. km)
DENSITY: 161 people per sq. mile

LANGUAGES: Tajik*, Uzbek, Russian
RELIGIONS: Sunni Muslim 95%, Shi'a Muslim 3%, other 2%
ETHNIC MIX: Tajik 84%, Uzbek 12%, other 2%, Kyrgyz 1%, Russian 1%
GOVERNMENT: Presidential system
CURRENCY: Somoni = 100 diram

Tanzania

The east African state of Tanzania was formed in 1964 by the union of Tanganyika and the Zanzibar islands. A third of its area is game reserve or national park.

GEOGRAPHY
The mainland is mostly a high plateau lying to the east of the Great Rift Valley. Forested coastal plain. Highlands in the north and south.

CLIMATE
Tropical on the coast and Zanzibar. Semiarid on the central plateau, semitemperate in the highlands. March–May rains.

PEOPLE & SOCIETY
99% of people belong to one of 120 small ethnic Bantu groups. Arabs, Asians, and Europeans make up the remaining population. Use of Kiswahili as the lingua franca has eliminated ethnic rivalries. The majority of Tanzanians are subsistence farmers.

◆ **INSIGHT:** *At 19,340 ft (5895 m), Kilimanjaro in northeast Tanzania is Africa's highest mountain*

THE ECONOMY
Reliant on agriculture, including forestry and cattle. Coffee, cotton, tea, cashew nuts, sisal, and cloves are cash crops. Gold, diamonds, and gems mined. Safari and beach tourism. Debt relief.

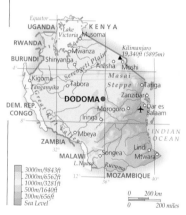

FACTFILE

OFFICIAL NAME: United Republic of Tanzania
DATE OF FORMATION: 1964
CAPITAL: Dodoma
POPULATION: 57.3 million
TOTAL AREA: 364,898 sq. miles (945,087 sq. km)
DENSITY: 167 people per sq. mile

LANGUAGES: Kiswahili*, Sukuma, Chagga, Nyamwezi, Hehe, Makonde, Yao, English*
RELIGIONS: Christian 63%, Muslim 35%, other 2%
ETHNIC MIX: Native African (over 120 tribes) 99%, European, Asian, and Arab 1%
GOVERNMENT: Presidential system
CURRENCY: Tanzanian shilling = 100 cents

Thailand

Thailand lies at the heart of mainland southeast Asia.
Continuing rapid industrialization has resulted in massive congestion
in the capital and a serious depletion of natural resources.

GEOGRAPHY

One-third is low plateau, drained by tributaries of the Mekong River. The central plain is the most fertile area.

CLIMATE

Tropical. Hot, humid March–May; monsoon rains May–October; cooler season November–March.

PEOPLE & SOCIETY

Buddhism is a national binding force. 800,000 hill tribes-people live in the north and northeast. The Chinese minority is the most assimilated in the region. Malay Islamists fight for secession in the undeveloped far south. Politics has been unstable since the fall of populist Prime Minister Thaksin in 2006. The army stepped in again in 2014: polls are due.

◆ INSIGHT: *Thailand, meaning "land of the free," is the only SE Asian nation never to have been colonized*

THE ECONOMY

Successful manufacturing. Natural gas reserves. Leading exporter of rice and rubber. Political turmoil. Southeast Asis's top tourism destination. Damage from natural disasters.

FACTFILE

OFFICIAL NAME: Kingdom of Thailand

DATE OF FORMATION: 1238

CAPITAL: Bangkok

POPULATION: 69 million

TOTAL AREA: 198,455 sq. miles (514,000 sq. km)

DENSITY: 350 people per sq. mile

LANGUAGES: Thai*, Chinese, Malay, Khmer, Mon, Karen, Miao

RELIGIONS: Buddhist 94%, Muslim 5%, other (including Christian) 1%

ETHNIC MIX: Thai 83%, Chinese 12%, Malay 3%, Khmer and other 2%

GOVERNMENT: Transitional regime

CURRENCY: Baht = 100 satang

Togo

Togo lies sandwiched between Ghana and Benin in west Africa. General Eyadema ruled from 1967–2005; his son succeeded him. Lomé port is an important entrepôt for regional trade.

GEOGRAPHY

Central forested region bounded by savanna lands to the north and south. Mountain range stretches southwest to northeast.

CLIMATE

Coast hot and humid; drier inland. Rainy season March–July, with heaviest falls in the west.

PEOPLE & SOCIETY

Harsh resentment between Ewe in the south and Kabye in the north. Kabye control the government and the military, but the north is less developed than the south. Extended family is important. Tribalism and nepotism are key factors in everyday life. Some ethnic groups, such as the Mina, have matriarchal societies.

INSIGHT: *The "Nana Benz," the entrepreneurial market-women of Lomé, control Togo's retail trade*

THE ECONOMY

Most people are farmers; many lack access to electricity and clean water. Main cash crops are cotton, coffee, and cocoa. Togo's phosphate deposits are the most mineral-rich in the world, but the sector suffered from mismanagement in 1997–2007, and has only recently secured foreign investment.

BURKINA FASO

Dapaong

BENIN

Sansanné-Mango

Kara

Tchamba

GHANA

Mono

Atakpamé

500m/1640ft
200m/656ft
Sea Level

Kpalimé
Tsévié
Aného

0   50 km
0   50 miles

LOMÉ

ATLANTIC OCEAN

FACTFILE

OFFICIAL NAME: Republic of Togo

DATE OF FORMATION: 1960

CAPITAL: Lomé

POPULATION: 7.8 million

TOTAL AREA: 21,924 sq. miles (56,785 sq. km)

DENSITY: 371 people per sq. mile

LANGUAGES: Ewe, Kabye, Gurma, French*

RELIGIONS: Christian 47%, traditional beliefs 33%, Muslim 14%, other 6%

ETHNIC MIX: Ewe 46%, other African 41%, Kabye 12%, European 1%

GOVERNMENT: Presidential system

CURRENCY: CFA franc = 100 centimes

Tonga

Tonga is a South Pacific archipelago of 170 islands; only 45 of these islands are inhabited. The king retains significant powers though some democratic reforms were introduced in 2011.

GEOGRAPHY
Easterly islands are generally low and fertile. Those in the west are higher and volcanic in origin.

CLIMATE
Tropical oceanic. Temperatures range between 68°F (20°C) and 86°F (30°C) all year round. Heavy rainfall, especially February–March.

PEOPLE & SOCIETY
Tonga is the last remaining Polynesian monarchy. All land belongs to the crown, but is administered by nobles who allot it to the common people. Respect for traditional values is high, though younger, Westernized Tongans are starting to question some attitudes. The first elected commoner became prime minister in 2006.

 INSIGHT: *Tonga was never brought under foreign rule*

THE ECONOMY
Remittances. Squashes and vanilla exported. Tourism growing. Struggling to repay large debt to China, for rebuilding capital's business district after 2006 prodemocracy riots. Fisheries potential.

Niuatoputapu
Tafahi
17°

0   100 km
0   100 miles
18°

'Uta Vava'u
Vava'u Group
Neiafu
19°

PACIFIC
OCEAN
Tofua   Pangai
Ha'apai Group
Kotu Group
20°
174°

Nomuka Group
Otu Tolu Group

NUKU'ALOFA
Tongatapu
21°
'Eua   Ohonua
Tongatapu Group
175°

200m/656ft Sea Level

FACTFILE

OFFICIAL NAME: Kingdom of Tonga
DATE OF FORMATION: 1970
CAPITAL: Nuku'alofa
POPULATION: 107,000
TOTAL AREA: 289 sq. miles (748 sq. km)
DENSITY: 385 people per sq. mile
LANGUAGES: English*, Tongan*

RELIGIONS: Free Wesleyan 38%, Church of Jesus Christ of Latter-day Saints 17%, Roman Catholic 16%, other Christian 16%, Free Church of Tonga 12%, other 1%
ETHNIC MIX: Tongan 98%, other 2%
GOVERNMENT: Monarchy
CURRENCY: Pa'anga (Tongan dollar) = 100 seniti

Trinidad & Tobago

The two islands of the former UK colony of Trinidad and Tobago are the most southerly of the Caribbean Windward Islands, lying just 9 miles (15 km) off the coast of Venezuela.

GEOGRAPHY
Both islands are hilly and wooded. Trinidad has rugged mountains in north, and swamps on its east and west coasts.

CLIMATE
Tropical, with July–December wet season. Escapes the region's hurricanes, which pass to the north.

PEOPLE & SOCIETY
Trinidad's East Indian community is the Caribbean's largest and holds onto its Muslim and Hindu heritage. There are tensions with the mainly Christian blacks; political parties are divided along race lines. Blacks form a majority on Tobago. A high murder rate and gang violence are problems. The islands are the birthplace of steel bands and Calypso music.

 INSIGHT: *Trinidad has the world's largest pitch lake; it was mined to build the world's first asphalt roads*

THE ECONOMY
Oil and natural gas: major provider of liquefied natural gas to US, but reserves are declining fast. Associated industries: second-largest producer of methanol. Tourism on wildlife-rich Tobago.

FACTFILE

OFFICIAL NAME: Republic of Trinidad and Tobago

DATE OF FORMATION: 1962

CAPITAL: Port of Spain

POPULATION: 1.4 million

TOTAL AREA: 1980 sq. miles (5128 sq. km)

DENSITY: 707 people per sq. mile

LANGUAGES: English Creole, English*, Hindi, French, Spanish

RELIGIONS: Protestant 38%, Roman Catholic 24%, Hindu 20%, other 12%, Muslim 6%,

ETHNIC MIX: East Indian 38%, Black 36%, mixed race 24%, White, Chinese, and other 2%

GOVERNMENT: Parliamentary system

CURRENCY: Trin. & Tob. dollar = 100 cents

Tunisia

A French north African colony until 1956, Tunisia was relatively liberal in social terms, but in 2011 protesters ousted the dictatorial president, triggering the "Arab Spring" across the region.

GEOGRAPHY

Mountains in the north are surrounded by plains. Vast, low-lying salt pans in the center. To the south lies the Sahara Desert.

CLIMATE

Summer temperatures are high. The north is often wet and windy in winter. Far south is arid.

PEOPLE & SOCIETY

The population is almost entirely of Arab-Berber descent, with Jewish and Christian minorities. The extended family remains socially important. Women have better rights than in most other Arab countries and make up over a quarter of the workforce. Tunisia has mainland Africa's lowest birth rate, the result of a long-standing family planning policy. The Islamist En-Nahda party has been in and out of government since 2011, sometimes working in coalition with secular parties.

THE ECONOMY

Diversified. Exports olives, dates, citrus fruit, and phosphates. Terror attacks affecting tourism. High unemployment, basic prices, and debt. Free trade with EU.

INSIGHT: *Tunisia was the center of trading empires from the 9th century BCE*

FACTFILE

OFFICIAL NAME: Republic of Tunisia

DATE OF FORMATION: 1956

CAPITAL: Tunis

POPULATION: 11.5 million

TOTAL AREA: 63,169 sq. miles (163,610 sq. km)

DENSITY: 192 people per sq. mile

LANGUAGES: Arabic*, French

RELIGIONS: Muslim (mainly Sunni) 98%, Christian 1%, Jewish 1%

ETHNIC MIX: Arab and Berber 98%, Jewish 1%, European 1%

GOVERNMENT: Mixed presidential–parliamentary system

CURRENCY: Tunisian dinar = 1000 millimes

Turkey

Lying partly in the region of eastern Thrace in Europe, but mostly in Asia, Turkey's position gives it significant influence in the Mediterranean, the Black Sea, and the Middle East.

GEOGRAPHY

Asian Turkey (Anatolia) is dominated by two mountain ranges, separated by a high, semidesert plateau. Coastal regions are fertile.

CLIMATE

Coast has a Mediterranean climate. Interior has cold, snowy winters and hot, dry summers.

PEOPLE & SOCIETY

Despite racial diversity, Turkey has a strong sense of national identity, and close links with other Turkic states. Kurds, the largest minority, based in the southeast, have waged a violent campaign for greater autonomy intermittently since 1984. The current political dominance of Islamists challenges Turkey's cherished identity as a secular state. It has applied to join the EU, but progress will be slow.

THE ECONOMY

Liberalized economy, boosted by self-sufficient agriculture, and textiles, tourism, and manufacturing sectors. Route of Asian oil pipelines to Europe.

◆ INSIGHT: Turkey had two of the seven wonders of the ancient world: the tomb of King Mausolus at Halicarnassus (now Bodrum), and the temple of Artemis at Ephesus

FACTFILE

OFFICIAL NAME: Republic of Turkey

DATE OF FORMATION: 1923

CAPITAL: Ankara

POPULATION: 80.7 million

TOTAL AREA: 301,382 sq. miles (780,580 sq. km)

DENSITY: 272 people per sq. mile

LANGUAGES: Turkish*, Kurdish, Arabic, Circassian, Armenian, Greek, Georgian, Ladino

RELIGIONS: Muslim (mainly Sunni) 99%, other 1%

ETHNIC MIX: Turkish 70%, Kurdish 20%, other 8%, Arab 2%

GOVERNMENT: Parliamentary system

CURRENCY: Turkish lira = 100 kurus

Turkmenistan

Stretching from the Caspian Sea into the central Asian desert, Turkmenistan has had less upheaval than most ex-Soviet states, under President Niyazov's dictatorial rule (1991–2006).

GEOGRAPHY
Low Garagum Desert covers 80% of the country. Mountains on the southern border with Iran. Fertile Amu Darya Valley in the north.

CLIMATE
Arid desert climate with extreme summer heat, but sub-freezing winter temperatures.

PEOPLE & SOCIETY
The Turkmen were once largely nomadic, and the tribal unit remains strong, with population clustered around desert oases. "Turkmenization" of government, education, and religion has strained relations with Uzbek and Russian minorities. Political reform since Niyazov's sudden death in 2006 led to multiparty elections in 2013, though all seats were won by the former sole party and Niyazov's successor runs a similarly authoritarian regime.

THE ECONOMY
State-controlled, though there is some private investment. Natural gas and oil are main resources. Overintensive farming of cotton. Black market.

◆ **INSIGHT:** *President Niyazov created an elaborate personality cult, styling himself as Turkmenbashi – "head" of all Turkmen*

FACTFILE

OFFICIAL NAME: Turkmenistan

DATE OF FORMATION: 1991

CAPITAL: Asgabat

POPULATION: 5.8 million

TOTAL AREA: 188,455 sq. miles (488,100 sq. km)

DENSITY: 31 people per sq. mile

LANGUAGES: Turkmen*, Uzbek, Russian, Kazakh, Tatar

RELIGIONS: Sunni Muslim 89%, Orthodox Christian 9%, other 2%

ETHNIC MIX: Turkmen 85%, other 6%, Uzbek 5%, Russian 4%

GOVERNMENT: Presidential system

CURRENCY: New manat = 100 tenge

Tuvalu

One of the world's smallest, most isolated states, Tuvalu lies in the central Pacific. The nine islands were linked to the Gilbert Islands (Kiribati) as a UK colony until independence.

GEOGRAPHY

A series of coral atolls, none more than 15 ft (4.6 m) above sea level. Poor soils restrict vegetation to bush, coconut palms, and breadfruit trees.

CLIMATE

Hot all year round. Heavy annual rainfall. Hurricane season brings many violent storms.

PEOPLE & SOCIETY

People are mostly Polynesian. Around half the population lives on Funafuti, where government jobs are based. Life is communal and traditional. Most people live by subsistence farming, digging pits out of the coral to grow crops. Fresh water is precious, due to frequent droughts.

◆ INSIGHT: *Low-lying Tuvalu, like the Maldives, is set to disappear with rising sea levels*

THE ECONOMY

World's smallest economy; top aid per capita. Remittances from Tuvaluan seafarers. Sale of fishing licenses. Copra, stamps, coins exported. Income from trust fund and lease of .tv Internet suffix.

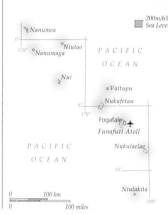

PACIFIC OCEAN

Nanumea
Niutao
Nanumaga
Nui
Vaitupu
Nukufetau
Fogafale
Funafuti Atoll
Nukulaelae
Niulakita

200m/656ft
Sea Level

PACIFIC OCEAN

0   100 km
0   100 miles

FACTFILE

OFFICIAL NAME: Tuvalu
DATE OF FORMATION: 1978
CAPITAL: Funafuti Atoll
POPULATION: 11,000
TOTAL AREA: 10 sq. miles (26 sq. km)
DENSITY: 1100 people per sq. mile
LANGUAGES: Tuvaluan*, Kiribati, English*

RELIGIONS: Church of Tuvalu 91%, other (mostly Protestant) 5%, Baha'i 2%, Seventh-day Adventist 2%
ETHNIC MIX: Polynesian 96%, Micronesian 4%
GOVERNMENT: Nonparty system
CURRENCY: Australian dollar and Tuvaluan dollar = 100 cents each

Uganda

Landlocked in east Africa, Uganda has a history of ethnic strife. Under President Museveni, steps have been taken to restore peace and to rebuild the economy and democracy.

GEOGRAPHY

Predominantly a large plateau with the Ruwenzori mountain range and the Great Rift Valley in the west. Lake Victoria lies to the southeast. Vegetation is of savanna type.

CLIMATE

Altitude and the influence of the lakes modify the equatorial climate. Rain falls throughout the year; spring is the wettest period.

PEOPLE & SOCIETY

Mostly rural population comprising 13 main ethnic groups. President Museveni has worked hard to break down ethnic animosities, but a noticeable north–south divide persists, with most development in the south and more income inequality in the north. After two decades of brutal clashes (1987–2008), the army pursued remnants of the Lord's Resistance Army across the DRC, South Sudan, and CAR.

THE ECONOMY

Resource-rich, but undeveloped and poor. Exports coffee, fish, tea, and flowers. Hydroelectric power. Oil production to come onstream soon. Great potential from mining. Debt relief.

INSIGHT: *Lake Victoria is the world's third-largest lake*

3000m/9843ft	
2000m/6562ft	
1000m/3281ft	
500m/1640ft	

SOUTH SUDAN
KENYA
Arua
Gulu
Albert Nile
DEM. REP. CONGO
Lake Albert
Lake Kyoga
Victoria Nile
Mbale
Kabarole
Jinja
Tororo
Kasese
Mubende
KAMPALA
Entebbe
Equator
Lake Edward
Masaka
Sese Is.
Mbarara
Lake Victoria
Kabale
TANZANIA
RWANDA

0   100 km
0   100 miles

FACTFILE

OFFICIAL NAME: Republic of Uganda
DATE OF FORMATION: 1962
CAPITAL: Kampala
POPULATION: 42.9 million
TOTAL AREA: 91,135 sq. miles (236,040 sq. km)
DENSITY: 557 people per sq. mile
LANGUAGES: Luganda, Nkole, Chiga, Lango,

Acholi, Teso, Lugbara, English*
RELIGIONS: Roman Catholic 42%, Protestant 42%, Muslim (mainly Sunni) 12%, other 3%, nonreligious 1%
ETHNIC MIX: Other 50%, Baganda 17%, Banyakole 10%, Basoga 9%, Iteso 7%, Bakiga 7%
GOVERNMENT: Presidential system
CURRENCY: Uganda shilling = 100 cents

Ukraine

The former "breadbasket of the Soviet Union," Ukraine lies on the Black Sea. Divisions between pro-Russian sentiments and pro-European nationalism erupted into civil war in 2014.

GEOGRAPHY
Mainly fertile steppes and forests. Carpathian Mountains in the west, Crimean chain in the south. Pripet Marshes in the northwest.

CLIMATE
Mainly continental climate, with distinct seasons. Southern Crimea has Mediterranean climate.

PEOPLE & SOCIETY
The population is shrinking: the death rate has exceeded the birth rate since the end of the Soviet era. Divorce rates are high. Over 90% of people in the west are Ukrainian, but in cities in the east and south Russians form a majority. Pro-Russian president Yanukovych's refusal to sign an EU deal provoked protests that ousted him from power in 2014. Russia responded by backing eastern rebels and annexing Crimea. Fighting continues in the east.

THE ECONOMY
Minerals: 5% of global reserves. Political instability, and conflict in the east. Slow reform of land laws, holding back agriculture. Oil/natural gas transit from Russia and the Caspian to Europe: natural gas price disputes with Russia.

◆ INSIGHT: *Ukraine means "on the border," referring to its position on the edge of the old Russian Empire*

(since 2014 the Ukrainian territory of Crimea has been annexed by Russia)

FACTFILE

OFFICIAL NAME: Ukraine

DATE OF FORMATION: 1991

CAPITAL: Kyiv

POPULATION: 44.2 million

TOTAL AREA: 223,089 sq. miles (603,700 sq. km)

DENSITY: 190 people per sq. mile

LANGUAGES: Ukrainian*, Russian, Tatar

RELIGIONS: Orthodox Christian 78%, Roman Catholic 10%, nonreligious 7%, other 5%

ETHNIC MIX: Ukrainian 78%, Russian 17%, other 4%, Belarussian 1%

GOVERNMENT: Mixed presidential–parliamentary system

CURRENCY: Hryvna = 100 kopiykas

United Arab Emirates

Bordering the Gulf on the northern coast of the Arabian Peninsula, the seven states of the UAE are Abu Dhabi, Dubai, Sharjah, Ajman, Umm al Qaywayn, Ras al Khaymah, and Fujayrah.

GEOGRAPHY
Mostly flat, semiarid desert with dunes, salt pans, and occasional oases. Cities are watered by extensive irrigation systems.

CLIMATE
Summers are humid, despite minimal rainfall. Sand-laden *shamal* winds blow in winter and spring.

PEOPLE & SOCIETY

Emirians, who make up just a quarter of the population, are mostly Sunni Muslims of Bedouin descent, and largely city dwellers. In theory, women enjoy equal rights with men. Poverty is rare and there is no income tax. The 1970s oil boom encouraged the immigration of workers, mostly from Asia. Western expatriates are permitted a virtually unrestricted lifestyle. Dubai boasts the world's tallest tower, luxury shopping facilities, and superb hotels.

THE ECONOMY
Major oil and natural gas exporter; plentiful reserves. Diversifying economy. Dynamic Dubai: free trade zone and financial center. Sales tax introduced in 2018. Water is scarce. Imports most food. Some emirates are less developed.

 INSIGHT: *Mina Jabal Ali, in Dubai, is the largest man-made port in the world*

500m/1640ft
200m/656ft
Sea Level

FACTFILE

OFFICIAL NAME: United Arab Emirates
DATE OF FORMATION: 1971
CAPITAL: Abu Dhabi
POPULATION: 9.4 million
TOTAL AREA: 32,000 sq. miles (82,880 sq. km)
DENSITY: 291 people per sq. mile

LANGUAGES: Arabic*, Farsi, Indian and Pakistani languages, English
RELIGIONS: Muslim (mainly Sunni) 96%, Christian, Hindu, and other 4%
ETHNIC MIX: Asian 60%, Emirian 25%, other Arab 12%, European 3%
GOVERNMENT: Monarchy
CURRENCY: UAE dirham = 100 fils

United Kingdom

Separated from continental Europe by the English Channel, the UK consists of Great Britain (England, Wales, and Scotland), several smaller islands, and Northern Ireland.

GEOGRAPHY

Rugged uplands dominate the landscape of Scotland, Wales, and northern England. All of the peaks in the United Kingdom over 4000 ft (1219 m) are in highland Scotland. The Pennine mountains, known as the "backbone of England," run the length of northern England. Lowland England rises into several ranges of rolling hills, and there is an interconnected system of rivers and canals. Over 600 islands, many uninhabited, lie west and north of the Scottish mainland.

CLIMATE

Generally mild, temperate, and highly changeable. Rain is fairly well distributed throughout the year. The west is generally wetter than the east, and the south is warmer than the north. Winter snow is common in upland areas.

PEOPLE & SOCIETY

Scotland, Wales, and Northern Ireland have devolved government and a sense of separate identity, but Scotland's 2014 referendum rejected independence. The UK was divided by the referendum decision in 2016 to end European Union membership; younger voters mostly opposed this, leaving many resentful. Ethnically, the 2011 census recorded the population as over 87% White or White British, almost 7% Asian or Asian British, and 3% Black or Black British. Income inequality has widened since 1884, when records began. Minorities suffer more from unemployment, social stress, and deprivation, with isolation particularly affecting Asian women, but disaffection and underachievement among white working-class youths is also of growing concern. One in four families have single parents, usually the mothers, and half of all babies are now born outside marriage, though mostly to cohabiting couples.

FACTFILE

OFFICIAL NAME: United Kingdom of Great Britain and Northern Ireland

DATE OF FORMATION: 1707

CAPITAL: London

POPULATION: 66.2 million

TOTAL AREA: 94,525 sq. miles (244,820 sq. km)

DENSITY: 710 people per sq. mile

LANGUAGES: English*, Welsh, Scottish Gaelic

RELIGIONS: Christian 64%, nonreligious 28%, Muslim 5%, other 2%, Hindu 1%

ETHNIC MIX: White 87%, Indian and Pakistani 4%, other 3%, Black 3%, other Asian 1%, Bengali 1%, Chinese 1%

GOVERNMENT: Parliamentary system

CURRENCY: Pound sterling = 100 pence

THE ECONOMY

World leader in financial services. Home to strong multinational companies. High-tech industries include biotechnology, telecommunications, and innovative computer software development. Earnings from tourism. Entrepreneurial culture and flexible employment practices. Service sector dominates, also pharmaceuticals, defense industries, precision engineering, but long-term decline of manufacturing, particularly heavy industries and car manufacture. Energy sector based on diminishing North Sea oil and natural gas resources. High levels of public, corporate, and consumer debt. Spending cuts to reduce government deficit put pressure on social and welfare programs and infrastructure. Nonparticipant in euro. Decision to leave European Union by 2019 implies major changes, notably in trading relationships, creating uncertainty for business and investment.

INSIGHT: *The UK has no formal written constitution, but a stable government system based on Parliament, which originated as a check on royal power in the 13th century*

1000m/3281ft
500m/1640ft
200m/656ft
Sea Level

0   100 km

0   100 miles

United States of America

Stretching across the most temperate part of North America, the US is rich in resources, has the world's third-largest population, and remains its leading economic power.

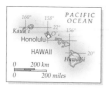

GEOGRAPHY

The US has a varied topography. Forested mountains stretch from New England in the far northeast, giving way to lowlands and swamps in the extreme south. The central plains are dominated by the Mississippi–Missouri River system and the Great Lakes on the Canadian border. The Rocky Mountains in the west contain active volcanoes and drop to the coast across the earthquake-prone San Andreas Fault. The southwest is arid desert. Mountainous Alaska is mostly Arctic tundra.

CLIMATE

There are four main climatic zones. The north and east are continental and temperate, with heavy rainfall, warm summers, and cold winters. Florida and the Deep South are tropical and prone to hurricanes. The southwest is arid desert, with searing summer heat and low rainfall. Southern California is Mediterranean, with hot summers and mild winters.

◆ **INSIGHT:** *The United States of America has the world's oldest constitution. Drafted in 1787, it has operated continuously ever since, albeit with numerous amendments*

	3000m/9843ft
	2000m/6562ft
	1000m/3281ft
	500m/1640ft
	200m/656ft
	Sea Level

0   400 km

0   400 miles

United States of America

◆ **INSIGHT:** *By law, the original records collected in a United States census must remain confidential for 72 years*

PEOPLE & SOCIETY

After over 400 years of settlement, White Americans are an economically dominant majority, but the ethnic balance is shifting. The fast-growing Hispanic community is predicted to top 30% of the population by 2050. African-Americans, a community originally uprooted by the slave trade, are less numerous but have a strong consciousness; in 2009 Barack Obama, whose father was African, became the first non-White US president. Native Americans, dispossessed in the 19th century, are now among the poorest people. Overall, living standards are high, but bad diet and insufficient exercise have left over a third of Americans obese. Religion and state are constitutionally separated, but Conservative Christianity is a powerful force. In gender politics, women still struggle for pay equality and against sexual harassment.

THE ECONOMY

World's largest economy, biggest importer, second-biggest exporter. Huge resource base. Established high-tech, engineering, entertainment industries. Global spread of US culture. Decline of manufacturing as jobs lost to low-wage economies. The bursting of a "bubble" of excessively risky mortgage lending in 2008 triggered global financial and stock market crisis. US government debt, already high, escalated as anti-recession incentives combined tax cuts with increased public spending. Obama's government struggled to maintain a social agenda to address widening inequalities; by contrast, Trump's post-2017 administration scaled welfare programs back, while focusing tax cuts on business. The resulting boost to growth, at least short term, backed Trump's populist claims to be finally putting "America First". This also included hostility to international free trade agreements if their impact did not sufficiently favor US interests.

FACTFILE

OFFICIAL NAME: United States of America
DATE OF FORMATION: 1776
CAPITAL: Washington, D.C.
POPULATION: 324 million
TOTAL AREA: 3,717,792 sq. miles (9,626,091 sq. km)
DENSITY: 92 people per sq. mile

LANGUAGES: English*, Spanish, other
RELIGIONS: Protestant 47%, nonreligious 23%, R. Catholic 21%, other 6%, Jewish 2%, Muslim 1%
ETHNIC MIX: White 60%, Hispanic 17%, African American 14%, Asian 6%, Native American 2%, Hawaiian or Pacific Islander 1%
GOVERNMENT: Presidential system
CURRENCY: US dollar = 100 cents

Uruguay

Situated in southeastern South America, Uruguay returned to civilian government in 1985, after 12 years of military rule. Most land is used for farming: Uruguay is a major wool exporter.

GEOGRAPHY
Low, rolling grasslands cover 80% of the country. Narrow coastal plain. Alluvial floodplain in southwest. Five rivers flow westward and drain into the Uruguay River.

CLIMATE
Temperate throughout the country. Warm summers, mild winters, and moderate rainfall.

PEOPLE & SOCIETY
Uruguayans are largely second- or third-generation Italians or Spaniards. Cattle-ranching wealth funded South America's first welfare state. Decades of emigration (peaking during the 1960s economic decline, the period of military rule, and the 1999–2002 economic crisis) plus a low birth rate mean the population is aging rapidly. Though many people are Roman Catholic, attitudes are liberal and all forms of religion are tolerated.

THE ECONOMY
Exports wool, meat, hides, rice, wood, and soy. Well-educated workforce. Banking services. Mineral potential.

INSIGHT: *Uruguay's rich pastures are ideal for raising livestock; animal products bring in over 40% of export earnings*

FACTFILE

OFFICIAL NAME: Oriental Republic of Uruguay

DATE OF FORMATION: 1828

CAPITAL: Montevideo

POPULATION: 3.5 million

TOTAL AREA: 68,039 sq. miles (176,220 sq. km)

DENSITY: 52 people per sq. mile

LANGUAGES: Spanish*

RELIGIONS: Roman Catholic 42%, Protestant 15%, nonreligious 37%, other 6%

ETHNIC MIX: White 87%, Black 7%, *Mestizo* (European–Amerindian) 5%, other 1%

GOVERNMENT: Presidential system

CURRENCY: Uruguayan peso = 100 centésimos

Uzbekistan

Sharing what is left of the Aral Sea with neighboring Kazakhstan, Uzbekistan lies on the ancient Silk Road between Asia and Europe. It is the most populous central Asian republic.

GEOGRAPHY

Arid and semiarid plains in much of the west. Fertile, irrigated farmland in the east lies below the peaks of the western Pamirs.

CLIMATE

Harsh continental climate. Summers can be extremely hot and dry; winters are cold.

PEOPLE & SOCIETY

Complex ethnic makeup. Most people live in the fertile east. Birth rates are high, and the status of women is still low. Ex-Communists are in firm control, but traditional social patterns based on religion, clan, and region have reemerged. Islam Karimov ruled from 1991 until his death in 2016. Constitutional measures aim to control the influence of Islam: activities against Islamists have drawn international condemnation.

THE ECONOMY

Highly regulated. Reserves of natural gas, oil, coal, gold (has one of the world's largest gold mines), and other minerals. Cash crop is cotton: requires much irrigation. Grain imports necessary.

INSIGHT: *The Aral Sea holds just a tenth of its former volume of water, due to diversion of rivers for irrigation*

FACTFILE

OFFICIAL NAME: Republic of Uzbekistan
DATE OF FORMATION: 1991
CAPITAL: Tashkent
POPULATION: 31.9 million
TOTAL AREA: 172,741 sq. miles (447,400 sq. km)
DENSITY: 185 people per sq. mile

LANGUAGES: Uzbek*, Russian, Tajik, Kazakh
RELIGIONS: Sunni Muslim 88%, Orthodox Christian 9%, other 3%
ETHNIC MIX: Uzbek 80%, other 6%, Russian 6%, Tajik 5%, Kazakh 3%
GOVERNMENT: Presidential system
CURRENCY: Som = 100 tiyin

Vanuatu

An archipelago of 82 islands and islets in the South
Pacific, Vanuatu was ruled jointly by the UK and France from 1906
until independence in 1980. Politics is democratic but volatile.

GEOGRAPHY
Mountainous and volcanic, with
coral beaches and dense rainforest.
Cultivated land along the coasts.

CLIMATE
Tropical. Temperatures and rainfall
decline from north to south.

PEOPLE & SOCIETY
Indigenous Melanesians form a
majority. Ni-Vanuatu culture is traditional;
local social and religious customs are
strong, despite centuries of missionary
influence. Subsistence farming and
fishing are the main activities. 80%
of the population lives on the 12 main
islands. Women have lower social
status than men and payment of
bride-price is common.

◆ **INSIGHT:** *With 112 indigenous tongues,
Vanuatu has the world's highest per
capita density of languages*

THE ECONOMY
Reliant on aid. Main exports are
copra (dried coconut), kava, cocoa, and
beef. Tourism. Offshore banking: rules
tightened after international pressure.

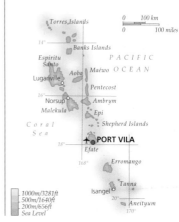

FACTFILE
OFFICIAL NAME: Republic of Vanuatu
DATE OF FORMATION: 1980
CAPITAL: Port Vila
POPULATION: 270,000
TOTAL AREA: 4710 sq. miles
(12,200 sq. km)
DENSITY: 57 people per sq. mile

LANGUAGES: Bislama (Melanesian pidgin)*,
English*, French*, other indigenous languages
RELIGIONS: Other 33%, Presbyterian 28%,
Anglican 15%, Seventh-day Adventist 12%,
Roman Catholic 12%
ETHNIC MIX: Ni-Vanuatu 99%, other 1%
GOVERNMENT: Parliamentary system
CURRENCY: Vatu = 100 centimes

Vatican City

The Vatican City, or Holy See, the seat of the Roman Catholic Church, is a walled enclave in the Italian city of Rome. It is the world's smallest fully independent state.

 GEOGRAPHY
The Vatican's territory includes 10 other buildings in Rome, plus the papal residence. The Vatican Gardens cover half the City's area.

 CLIMATE
Mild winters with regular rainfall. Hot, dry summers with occasional thunderstorms.

 PEOPLE & SOCIETY
The Vatican has about 800 permanent inhabitants, including over 100 lay persons. Thousands of lay staff are also employed. Citizenship can be acquired through long-term residence and holding a position within the City. The reigning pope has supreme legislative and judicial powers, and holds office for life. Though the Vatican City is officially neutral, papal opinion has a great influence on the world's 1.3 billion Roman Catholics.

THE ECONOMY
Investments and voluntary contributions made by Catholics worldwide (known as Peter's Pence) are backed up by tourist revenue and the issue of Vatican stamps and coins.

◆ **INSIGHT:** *The Vatican City is the spiritual center for one in six of the world's population*

FACTFILE

OFFICIAL NAME: Vatican City State
DATE OF FORMATION: 1929
CAPITAL: Vatican City
POPULATION: 800
TOTAL AREA: 0.17 sq. miles (0.44 sq. km)
DENSITY: 4706 people per sq. mile

LANGUAGES: Italian*, Latin*
RELIGIONS: Roman Catholic 100%
ETHNIC MIX: Cardinals are from many nationalities, but Italians form the largest group. Most resident lay persons are Italian. The current pope is from Argentina.
GOVERNMENT: Papal state
CURRENCY: Euro = 100 cents

Venezuela

On the southern shores of the Caribbean, Venezuela was the first of Spain's colonies to seek independence. Despite its oil wealth, the economy is in crisis and many live in poverty.

GEOGRAPHY

Andes Mountains and the Maracaibo lowlands in the northwest. Central grassy plains are drained by the Orinoco River system. Forested Guiana Highlands in the southeast.

CLIMATE
Tropical. Hot and humid. Uplands are cooler. Orinoco plains are alternately parched or flooded.

PEOPLE & SOCIETY
Venezuela has one of the most urbanized societies in the region, with most people living in the northern cities. Historically, it is a "melting pot," with immigrants from Europe and all over Latin America. The few indigenous Amerindians live in remote areas. Left-wing President Hugo Chávez (1999–2013) pushed populist policies, funded by oil wealth; his successor inherited a drained economy, unrest, and political turmoil.

THE ECONOMY
World's largest oil reserves. Minerals. Nationalizations deter foreign investors. Corruption-prone state sector. Economic crisis: GDP down 30% since 2013. Lack of basic goods, hyperinflation.

INSIGHT: *Venezuela's Angel Falls is the world's tallest waterfall, with a total drop of 3210 ft (979 m)*

2000m/6562ft
1000m/3281ft
500m/1640ft
200m/656ft
Sea Level

FACTFILE

OFFICIAL NAME: Bolivarian Republic of Venezuela

DATE OF FORMATION: 1830

CAPITAL: Caracas

POPULATION: 32 million

TOTAL AREA: 352,143 sq. miles (912,050 sq. km)

DENSITY: 94 people per sq. mile

LANGUAGES: Spanish*, Amerindian languages

RELIGIONS: Roman Catholic 73%, Protestant 17%, nonreligious 7%, other 3%

ETHNIC MIX: *Mestizo* (European–Amerindian) 69%, White 20%, Black 9%, Amerindian 2%

GOVERNMENT: Presidential system

CURRENCY: Bolívar fuerte = 100 céntimos

Vietnam

French rule of Vietnam ended in 1954. Divided at 17°N, the US-backed South fought the Communist North. Reunified after the North's 1975 victory, it is run as a single-party state.

GEOGRAPHY
A heavily forested mountain range separates the northern Red River delta lowlands from the Mekong Delta in the south.

CLIMATE
Cool winters in the north; the south is tropical with even temperatures.

PEOPLE & SOCIETY
Ethnic Vietnamese dominate; the Chinese minority was viewed as a corrupt bourgeoisie by the victorious Communists after the war. Mountain-based minorities (montagnards) were also sidelined; tensions persist over the settling of highlands by lowlanders. Women play an active role in society. There is no political or press freedom.

◆ **INSIGHT:** *Intense US bombing and defoliant spraying in the 1962–1975 Vietnam War has scarred the landscape*

THE ECONOMY
Liberal economic policy (*doi moi*) from 1986: now one of fastest-growing economies. Major rice exporter. Cheap labor. Strong manufacturing: textiles, and electrical goods. Diverse resource base.

FACTFILE

OFFICIAL NAME: Socialist Republic of Vietnam

DATE OF FORMATION: 1976

CAPITAL: Hanoi

POPULATION: 95.5 million

TOTAL AREA: 127,243 sq. miles (329,560 sq. km)

DENSITY: 760 people per sq. mile

LANGUAGES: Vietnamese*, Chinese, Thai, Khmer, Muong, Nung, Miao, Yao, Jarai

RELIGIONS: Nonreligious 81%, Buddhist 9%, Roman Catholic 7%, Cao Dai 1%, other 2%

ETHNIC MIX: Vietnamese 86%, other 8%, Tay 2%, Thai 2%, Muong 1%, Khome 1%

GOVERNMENT: One-party state

CURRENCY: Dông = 10 hao = 100 xu

Yemen

Located in southern Arabia, Yemen was formerly two countries: the People's Democratic Republic of Yemen (south and east) and the Yemen Arab Republic (northwest) were united in 1990.

GEOGRAPHY
Mountainous west with a fertile strip along the Red Sea. Arid desert and mountains elsewhere.

CLIMATE
Desert climate, modified by altitude, which affects temperatures by as much as 54°F (30°C).

PEOPLE & SOCIETY
Yemenis are almost entirely of Arab and Bedouin descent. In rural areas, tribalism and Islamic orthodoxy are strong and most women wear the veil. Popular protests that began in the 2011 "Arab Spring" ended President Saleh's 33-year rule. In 2014, Houthi rebels advanced on Sana from the north, triggering a civil war that has displaced 2 million. Three-quarters of Yemenis need humanitarian assistance. A Saudi-led coalition is assisting the army.

THE ECONOMY
Conflict has destroyed the economy. Hyperinflation; lack of basic goods. Oil and natural gas reserves. Qat (mild narcotic), coffee, cotton grown.

INSIGHT: *Mokha, on the Red Sea, gave its name to the first coffee beans exported to Europe in the 1600s*

3000m/9843ft
2000m/6562ft
1000m/3281ft
500m/1640ft
200m/656ft
Sea Level

0   100 km
0   100 miles

FACTFILE

OFFICIAL NAME: Republic of Yemen
DATE OF FORMATION: 1990
CAPITAL: Sanaa
POPULATION: 28.3 million
TOTAL AREA: 203,849 sq. miles (527,970 sq. km)
DENSITY: 130 people per sq. mile

LANGUAGES: Arabic*
RELIGIONS: Sunni Muslim 55%, Shi'a Muslim 42%, Christian, Hindu, and Jewish 3%
ETHNIC MIX: Arab 99%, Afro-Arab, Indian, Somali, and European 1%
GOVERNMENT: Transitional regime
CURRENCY: Yemeni rial = 100 fils

Zambia

Bordered to the south by the Zambezi River, Zambia lies at the heart of southern Africa. In 1991, it made a peaceful transition from single-party rule to multiparty democracy.

GEOGRAPHY

A high savanna plateau, broken by mountains in the northeast. Vegetation mainly trees and scrub.

CLIMATE

Tropical, with three seasons: cool and dry, hot and dry, and wet. Southwest is prone to drought.

PEOPLE & SOCIETY

There are more than 70 different ethnic groups, but there are fewer tensions than in many African states. Major groups are the Bemba (in the northeast), Tonga (south), Nyanja (east), and Lozi (west). There are also thousands of refugees, mostly from the DRC and Angola. Zambia's National Gender Policy aims to redress inequalities between the sexes. One in seven adults is infected with HIV/AIDS. Nevertheless, Zambia has a high population growth rate. Nearly half of Zambians live in extreme poverty.

THE ECONOMY

Copper: output has risen since 2000, when decades of falling global prices ended. New agricultural exports, notably flowers. Debt relief.

INSIGHT: *Spray from Musi-o-Tunya (Victoria Falls) can be seen up to 20 miles (35 km) away*

FACTFILE

OFFICIAL NAME: Republic of Zambia
DATE OF FORMATION: 1964
CAPITAL: Lusaka
POPULATION: 17.1 million
TOTAL AREA: 290,584 sq. miles (752,614 sq. km)
DENSITY: 60 people per sq. mile
LANGUAGES: Bemba, Tonga, Nyanja, Lozi, Lala-Bisa, Nsenga, English*

RELIGIONS: Protestant 75%, Roman Catholic 20%, other (including Muslim) 3%, nonreligious 2%
ETHNIC MIX: Bemba 34%, other African 26%, Tonga 16%, Nyanja 14%, Lozi 9%, European 1%
GOVERNMENT: Presidential system
CURRENCY: New Zamb. kwacha = 100 ngwee

Zimbabwe

Situated in southern Africa, Zimbabwe achieved independence from the UK in 1980. President Robert Mugabe then ruled for 37 years, and became increasingly authoritarian.

GEOGRAPHY
High plateaus in center bordered by Zambezi River in the north and Limpopo in the south. Rivers crisscross central area.

CLIMATE
Tropical, though moderated by the high altitude. Wet season November–March. Drought is common in the eastern highlands.

PEOPLE & SOCIETY
Two main ethnic groups: Shona in the north and east, and Ndebele in the south. Shona outnumber Ndebele by four to one. Whites are generally far more affluent than blacks. Official efforts to redress this imbalance (such as land redistribution) have become increasingly aggressive. Rising opposition to Mugabe's regime and the state of the economy prompted the army to intervene in 2017 and his own party demanded he step down.

THE ECONOMY
Undermined by mismanagement, corruption, and international isolation. Abandoned own currency in 2009 after hyperinflation. Needs reform, investment.

INSIGHT: *The ruins of the 1000-year-old city of Great Zimbabwe, after which the country is named, are near modern-day Masvingo*

FACTFILE

OFFICIAL NAME: Republic of Zimbabwe

DATE OF FORMATION: 1980

CAPITAL: Harare

POPULATION: 16.5 million

TOTAL AREA: 150,803 sq. miles (390,580 sq. km)

DENSITY: 111 people per sq. mile

LANGUAGES: Shona, isiNdebele, English*

RELIGIONS: Syncretic 50%, Christian 25%, traditional beliefs 24%, other 1%

ETHNIC MIX: Shona 71%, Ndebele 16%, other African 11%, White 1%, Asian 1%

GOVERNMENT: Presidential system

CURRENCY: US $, S. African rand, euro, UK £, Botswanan pula, Australian $, Chinese yuan, Indian rupee, Japanese yen all legal tender

Overseas territories

Despite the rapid process of global decolonization since World War II, around eight million people in more than 50 territories around the world continue to live under the protection of Australia, Denmark, France, the Netherlands, New Zealand, Norway, the UK, or the USA. These remnants of former colonial empires may have persisted for economic, strategic, or political reasons and are administered by the protecting country in a variety of ways.

AUSTRALIA

Australia's overseas territories have not been an issue since Papua New Guinea became independent in 1975. Consequently, there is no overriding policy toward them.

Ashmore & Cartier Is. *Ref: 124 A3*
STATUS: External territory
CLAIMED: 1931
POPULATION: None
AREA: 2 sq miles (5.2 sq km)

Christmas Island *Ref: 123 E5*

STATUS: External territory
CLAIMED: 1958
CAPITAL: The Settlement
POPULATION: 2205
AREA: 52 sq miles (135 sq km)

Cocos Islands *Ref: 123 D5*
STATUS: External territory
CLAIMED: 1955
CAPITAL: West Island
POPULATION: 596
AREA: 5.5 sq miles (14 sq km)

Coral Sea Islands *Ref: 126 B4*
STATUS: External territory
CLAIMED: 1969
POPULATION: below 10 (scientists)
AREA: 1.2 sq miles (3 sq km)

Heard & McDonald Is. *Ref: 123 C7*
STATUS: External territory
CLAIMED: 1947
POPULATION: None
AREA: 161 sq miles (417 sq km)

Norfolk Island *Ref: 124 D4*

STATUS: External territory
CLAIMED: 1774
CAPITAL: Kingston
POPULATION: 1748
AREA: 13 sq miles (34 sq km)

DENMARK

The Faroes and Greenland have had home rule since 1948 and 1979 respectively.

Faroe Islands *Ref: 65 F5*

STATUS: External territory
CLAIMED: 1380
CAPITAL: Tórshavn
POPULATION: 49,117
AREA: 540 sq miles (1399 sq km)

Greenland *Ref: 64 D3*

STATUS: External territory
CLAIMED: 1380
CAPITAL: Nuuk
POPULATION: 56,190
AREA: 836,109 sq miles (2,166,086 sq km)

Overseas territories

FRANCE

France's relations with *L'Outre-Mer* stress interdependence rather than independence. *Départements* have their own governments. *Collectivités* have some autonomy.

Clipperton Island *Ref: 135 F3*
STATUS: Dependency of French Polynesia
CLAIMED: 1935
POPULATION: None
AREA: 3.4 sq miles (9 sq km)

French Guiana *Ref: 41 H3*
STATUS: Overseas department
CLAIMED: 1817
CAPITAL: Cayenne
POPULATION: 276,000
AREA: 35,135 sq miles (91,000 sq km)

French Polynesia *Ref: 127 H4*
STATUS: Overseas collectivity
CLAIMED: 1843
CAPITAL: Papeete ,
POPULATION: 280,210
AREA: 1608 sq miles (4165 sq km)

French Southern & Antarctic Lands
Ref: 123 B6
STATUS: Overseas territory
CLAIMED: 1772, 1840, 1843, 1924
CAPITAL: Port-aux-Français
POPULATION: 150
AREA: 169,800 sq miles (439,781 sq km)

Guadeloupe *Ref: 37 G4*
STATUS: Overseas department
CLAIMED: 1635
CAPITAL: Basse-Terre
POPULATION: 400,187
AREA: 629 sq miles (1628 sq km)

Martinique *Ref: 37 G4*
STATUS: Overseas department
CLAIMED: 1635
CAPITAL: Fort-de-France
POPULATION: 396,000
AREA: 425 sq miles (1100 sq km)

Mayotte *Ref: 61 G2*
STATUS: Overseas department
CLAIMED: 1843
CAPITAL: Mamoudzou
POPULATION: 212,645
AREA: 144 sq miles (374 sq km)

New Caledonia *Ref: 126 D5*
STATUS: Self-governing territory
CLAIMED: 1853
CAPITAL: Nouméa
POPULATION: 278,000
AREA: 7347 sq miles (19,100 sq km)

Réunion *Ref: 61 H4*
STATUS: Overseas department
CLAIMED: 1638
CAPITAL: Saint-Denis
POPULATION: 867,000
AREA: 970 sq miles (2500 sq km)

St. Barthélemy *Ref: 37 G3*
STATUS: Overseas collectivity
CLAIMED: 1878
CAPITAL: Gustavia
POPULATION: 7184
AREA: 8 sq miles (21 sq km)

St. Martin *Ref: 37 E5*
STATUS: Overseas collectivity
CLAIMED: 1648
CAPITAL: Marigot
POPULATION: 31,950
AREA: 20 sq miles (53 sq km)

Overseas territories

St. Pierre & Miquelon *Ref: 21 G4*
STATUS: Overseas collectivity
CLAIMED: 1604
CAPITAL: Saint-Pierre
POPULATION: 5533
AREA: 93 sq miles (242 sq km)

Wallis & Futuna *Ref: 127 E4*
STATUS: Overseas collectivity
CLAIMED: 1842
CAPITAL: Mata'Utu
POPULATION: 15,714
AREA: 106 sq miles (274 sq km)

NETHERLANDS
These islands were once part of the Dutch West Indies. They are now self-governing.

Aruba *Ref: 37 E5*
STATUS: Constituent country
CLAIMED: 1636
CAPITAL: Oranjestad
POPULATION: 104,822
AREA: 75 sq miles (194 sq km)

Bonaire *Ref: 37 E5*
STATUS: Special municipality
CLAIMED: 1816
CAPITAL: Kralendijk
POPULATION: 19,400
AREA: 113 sq miles (294 sq km)

Curaçao *Ref: 37 E5*
STATUS: Constituent country
CLAIMED: 1815
CAPITAL: Willemstad
POPULATION: 160,000
AREA: 171 sq miles (444 sq km)

Saba *Ref: 37 G3*
STATUS: Special municipality
CLAIMED: 1816
CAPITAL: The Bottom
POPULATION: 1846
AREA: 5 sq miles (13 sq km)

Sint-Eustatius *Ref: 37 G3*
STATUS: Special municipality
CLAIMED: 1784
CAPITAL: Oranjestad
POPULATION: 3200
AREA: 8 sq miles (21 sq km)

Sint-Maarten *Ref: 37 G3*
STATUS: Constituent country
CLAIMED: 1648
CAPITAL: Phillipsburg
POPULATION: 40,010
AREA: 13 sq miles (34 sq km)

NEW ZEALAND

New Zealand remains responsible for its territories' foreign policy and defense.

Cook Islands *Ref: 127 G4*
STATUS: Associated territory
CLAIMED: 1901
CAPITAL: Avarua
POPULATION: 11,700
AREA: 91 sq miles (235 sq km)

Niue *Ref: 127 F5*
STATUS: Associated territory
CLAIMED: 1901
CAPITAL: Alofi
POPULATION: 1618
AREA: 102 sq miles (264 sq km)

Overseas territories

Tokelau *Ref: 127 F3*
STATUS: Dependent territory
CLAIMED: 1926
CAPITAL: None
POPULATION: 1285
AREA: 4 sq miles (10 sq km)

NORWAY

There is a NATO base on Jan Mayen.
Bouvet Island is a nature reserve.

Bouvet Island *Ref: 49 D7*
STATUS: Dependency
CLAIMED: 1928
POPULATION: None
AREA: 22 sq miles (58 sq km)

Jan Mayen *Ref: 65 F3*
STATUS: Dependency
CLAIMED: 1929
POPULATION: 18 (Meteorologists)
AREA: 147 sq miles (381 sq km)

Peter I. Island *Ref: 136 A3*
STATUS: Dependency
CLAIMED: 1931
POPULATION: None
AREA: 69 sq miles (180 sq km)

Svalbard *Ref: 65 F2*
STATUS: Dependency
CLAIMED: 1920
CAPITAL: Longyearbyen
POPULATION: 2752
AREA: 24,289 sq miles (62,906 sq km)

UNITED KINGDOM

UK overseas territories are locally governed
by a mix of elected and appointed officials.

Anguilla *Ref: 37 G3*

STATUS: Overseas territory
CLAIMED: 1650
CAPITAL: The Valley
POPULATION: 17,087
AREA: 37 sq miles (96 sq km)

Ascension Island *Ref: 49 C5*
STATUS: Overseas territory
CLAIMED: 1673
CAPITAL: Georgetown
POPULATION: 806
AREA: 34 sq miles (88 sq km)

Bermuda *Ref: 17 E6*

STATUS: Overseas territory
CLAIMED: 1612
CAPITAL: Hamilton
POPULATION: 65,331
AREA: 20 sq miles (53 sq km)

British Indian Ocean Territory
Ref: 122 C4 STATUS: Overseas territory

CLAIMED: 1814
CAPITAL: Diego Garcia
POPULATION: 4200
AREA: 23 sq miles (60 sq km)

British Virgin Islands *Ref: 37 F3*

STATUS: Overseas territory
CLAIMED: 1672
CAPITAL: Road Town
POPULATION: 30,661
AREA: 59 sq miles (153 sq km)

Cayman Islands *Ref: 36 B3*

STATUS: Overseas territory
CLAIMED: 1670
CAPITAL: George Town
POPULATION: 60,765
AREA: 100 sq miles (259 sq km)

Overseas territories

Falkland Islands *Ref: 47 D7*

STATUS: Overseas territory
CLAIMED: 1832
CAPITAL: Stanley
POPULATION: 3198
AREA: 4699 sq miles (12,173 sq km)

Gibraltar *Ref: 74 D5*

STATUS: Overseas territory
CLAIMED: 1713
CAPITAL: Gibraltar
POPULATION: 34,410
AREA: 2.5 sq miles (6.5 sq km)

Guernsey *Ref: 71 D8*

STATUS: Crown Dependency
CLAIMED: 1066
CAPITAL: St. Peter Port
POPULATION: 66,502
AREA: 25 sq miles (65 sq km)

Isle of Man *Ref: 71 C5*

STATUS: Crown Dependency
CLAIMED: 1765
CAPITAL: Douglas
POPULATION: 83,740
AREA: 221 sq miles (572 sq km)

Jersey *Ref: 71 D8*

STATUS: Crown Dependency
CLAIMED: 1066
CAPITAL: St. Helier
POPULATION: 98,840
AREA: 45 sq miles (116 sq km)

Montserrat *Ref: 37 G4*

STATUS: Overseas territory
CLAIMED: 1632
CAPITAL: Brades *(de facto)*
POPULATION: 5292
AREA: 40 sq miles (102 sq km)

Pitcairn Group of Is. *Ref: 125 G4*

STATUS: Overseas territory
CLAIMED: 1887
CAPITAL: Adamstown
POPULATION: 54
AREA: 18 sq miles (47 sq km)

Saint Helena *Ref: 49 D5*

STATUS: Overseas territory
CLAIMED: 1673
CAPITAL: Jamestown
POPULATION: 4800
AREA: 47 sq miles (122 sq km)

South Georgia & the South Sandwich Islands *Ref: 49 C7*

STATUS: Overseas territory
CLAIMED: 1775
POPULATION: None
AREA: 1387 sq miles (3592 sq km)

Tristan da Cunha *Ref: 49 D6*

STATUS: Overseas territory
CLAIMED: 1612
CAPITAL: Edinburgh
POPULATION: 293
AREA: 38 sq miles (98 sq km)

Turks & Caicos Islands *Ref: 37 E2*

STATUS: Overseas territory
CLAIMED: 1766
CAPITAL: Cockburn Town
POPULATION: 34,900
AREA: 166 sq miles (430 sq km)

UNITED STATES

Commonwealth territories are self-governing and an integral part of the US. Unincorporated territories have varying degrees of autonomy.

Overseas territories

American Samoa *Ref: 127 F4*
STATUS: Unincorp. territory
CLAIMED: 1900
CAPITAL: Pago Pago
POPULATION: 55,600
AREA: 75 sq miles (195 sq km)

Baker & Howland Islands *Ref: 127 E2*
STATUS: Unincorporated territory
CLAIMED: 1856
POPULATION: None
AREA: 0.5 sq miles (1.4 sq km)

Guam *Ref: 126 B1*

STATUS: Unincorp. territory
CLAIMED: 1898
CAPITAL: Hagåtña
POPULATION: 162,900
AREA: 212 sq miles (549 sq km)

Jarvis Island *Ref: 127 G2*
STATUS: Unincorporated territory
CLAIMED: 1856
POPULATION: None
AREA: 1.7 sq miles (4.5 sq km)

Johnston Atoll *Ref: 125 E1*
STATUS: Unincorporated territory
CLAIMED: 1858
POPULATION: None
AREA: 1 sq mile (2.8 sq km)

Kingman Reef *Ref: 127 F2*
STATUS: Unincorporated territory
CLAIMED: 1856
POPULATION: None
AREA: 0.4 sq miles (1 sq km)

Midway Islands *Ref: 134 D2*
STATUS: Unincorporated territory
CLAIMED: 1867
CAPITAL: None
POPULATION: 40
AREA: 2 sq miles (5.2 sq km)

Navassa Island *Ref: 36 D3*
STATUS: Unincorporated territory
CLAIMED: 1856
POPULATION: None
AREA: 2 sq miles (5.2 sq km)

Northern Mariana Islands *Ref: 124 C1*

STATUS: Comm. territory
CLAIMED: 1947
CAPITAL: Saipan
POPULATION: 55,020
AREA: 177 sq miles (457 sq km)

Palmyra Atoll *Ref: 127 G2*
STATUS: Incorporated territory
CLAIMED: 1898
POPULATION: None
AREA: 5 sq miles (12 sq km)

Puerto Rico *Ref: 37 F3*

STATUS: Comm. territory
CLAIMED: 1898
CAPITAL: San Juan
POPULATION: 3.7 million
AREA: 3515 sq miles (9104 sq km)

Virgin Islands *Ref: 37 F3*
STATUS: Unincorp. territory
CLAIMED: 1917
CAPITAL: Charlotte Amalie
POPULATION: 102,950
AREA: 137 sq miles (355 sq km)

Wake Island *Ref: 124 D1*
STATUS: Unincorporated territory
CLAIMED: 1898
CAPITAL: None
POPULATION: 150 (US air base)
AREA: 2.5 sq miles (6.5 sq km)

International organizations

This listing provides acronym definitions for the main international organizations concerned with worldwide economics, trade, and defense, plus an indication of membership.

ASEAN
Association of Southeast Asian Nations
ESTABLISHED: 1967
MEMBERS: Brunei, Cambodia, Indonesia, Laos, Malaysia, Myanmar, Philippines, Singapore, Thailand, Vietnam

CIS
Commonwealth of Independent States
ESTABLISHED: 1991
MEMBERS: Arm., Az., Belarus, Kaz., Kyrgy., Mold., Russia, Tajik., Turkmen.*, Ukraine*, Uzbek. *Associate members*

COMM   *The Commonwealth of Nations*
ESTABLISHED: 1931; evolved out of the British Empire. Formerly known as the British Commonwealth of Nations.
MEMBERS: 52   *(Fiji currently suspended)*

EU   *European Union*
ESTABLISHED: 1965; formerly known as EEC (European Economic Community) and EC (Economic Community)
MEMBERS: Austria, Belg., Bulg., Croatia, Cyprus, Czech Rep., Denmark, Est., Fin., Fr., Ger., Greece, Hung., Ireland, Italy, Lat., Lith., Lux., Malta, Neth., Pol., Port., Rom., Slvka., Slvna., Spain, Swed., UK *(in process of leaving)*

G8   *Group of 8*
ESTABLISHED: 1994
MEMBERS: Canada, France, Germany, Italy, Japan, Russia, UK, US

IMF   *International Monetary Fund*
(UN agency)
ESTABLISHED: 1945
MEMBERS: 188

NAFTA
North American Free Trade Agreement
ESTABLISHED: 1994
MEMBERS: Canada, Mexico, US

NATO
North Atlantic Treaty Organization
ESTABLISHED: 1949
MEMBERS: Albania, Belg., Bulg., Canada, Croatia, Czech Rep., Denmark, Est., Fr., Ger., Greece, Hung., Iceland, Italy, Lat., Lith., Lux., Mon., Neth., Norway, Poland, Port., Rom., Slovakia, Slovenia, Spain, Turkey, UK, US

OPEC   *Organization of Petroleum Exporting Countries*
ESTABLISHED: 1960
MEMBERS: Algeria, Angola, Ecuador, Gabon, Ind., Iran, Iraq, Kuwait, Libya, Nigeria, Qatar, Saudi Arabia, U.A.E., Ven.

UN   *United Nations*
ESTABLISHED: 1945
MEMBERS: 193; all nations are represented, except Taiwan and Kosovo. The Vatican City has "observer status" only. Palestine is a "non-member observer state."

WTO   *World Trade Organization*
ESTABLISHED: 1995
MEMBERS: 164 *(including EU, Hong Kong, Macao)*

Abbreviations

This glossary provides a comprehensive guide to abbreviations in this atlas.

abbrev. abbreviation
Afgh. Afghanistan
Amh. Amharic
anc. ancient
Ar. Arabic
Arm. Armenia/Armenian
Aus. Austria
Aust. Australia
Az. Azerbaijan

Bas. Basque
Bel. Belorussian
Belg. Belgium/Belgian
Bos. & Herz. Bosnia & Herzegovina
Bul. Bulgarian
Bulg. Bulgaria
Bur. Burmese

C Central
C. Cape
Cam. Cambodian
Cast. Castilian
Chin. Chinese
Comm. Commonwealth
Cord. Cordillera (Sp. mts.)
Cz. Czech
Czech Rep. Czech Republic

D.C. District of Columbia
Dan. Danish
Dominican Rep. Dominican Republic

E East
Emb. Embalse
Eng. English
Eq. Guinea Equatorial Guinea
Est. Estonia/Estonian

Faer. Faeroese
Fin. Finland/Finnish
Flem. Flemish
Fr. France/French

Geo. Georgia
Geor. Georgian
Ger. Germany/German
Gk. Greek

Heb. Hebrew
Hung. Hungary/Hungarian

I. Island
Ind. Indonesia, Indonesian
Is. Islands
It. Italian

Kaz. Kazakhstan/Kazakh
Kep. Kepulauan (Indonesian island group)
Kir. Kirghiz
Kor. Korean
Kos. Kosovo
Kurd. Kurdish
Kyrgy. Kyrgyzstan

L. Lake, Lago
Lat. Latvia
Latv. Latvian
Leb. Lebanon
Liech. Liechtenstein
Lith. Lithuania/Lithuanian
Lux. Luxembourg

Mac. Macedonia
Med. Sea Mediterranean Sea
Mon. Montenegro
Mold. Moldova
Mt. Mount/Mountain
Mts. Mountains

N North
N. Korea North Korea
Neth. Netherlands
NW Northwest
NZ New Zealand

P. Pulau (Ind. island)
Peg. Pegunungan (Ind. mountain range)
Per. Persian
Pol. Poland/Polish
Port. Portugal, Portuguese
prev. previously

R. River, Rio, Rio, Roman
Res. Reservoir
Rom. Romania/Romanian
Rus. Russian
Russ. Fed. Russian Federation

S South
S. Korea South Korea
SA South Africa
SCr. Serbian and Croatian
Serb. Serbia
Slvka. Slovakia
Slvna. Slovenia
Som. Somali
Sp. Spanish
St, St. Saint
Str. Strait
Swed. Swedish
Switz. Switzerland

Tajik. Tajikistan
Th. Thai
Turk. Turkish
Turkm. Turkmen
Turkmen. Turkmenistan

U.A.E. United Arab Emirates
UK United Kingdom
Ukr. Ukrainian
Uninhab. Uninhabitable
Unincorp. Unincorporated
Urug. Uruguayan
US United States of America
Uzb. Uzbek
Uzbek. Uzbekistan

var. variant
Vdkhr. Vodokhranilishche (Rus. reservoir)
Vdskh. Vodoskhovyshche (Ukr. reservoir)
Ven. Venezuela

W West
W. Sahara Western Sahara
Wel. Welsh
WW 1 World War One

Yugo. Yugoslavia

Zamb. Zambian

A

Al Baṣrah Iraq *var.* Basra 102 C4

Al Bayḍā' Libya 53 G2

Albert, Lake *lake* Uganda/Dem. Rep. Congo 59 E5

Alberta *province* Canada 19 E4

Albi France 73 C6

Albuquerque New Mexico, USA 28 D2

Alcácer do Sal Portugal 74 C4

Aldabra Group *island group* Seychelles 61 G2

Aleg Mauritania 56 C3

Aleksandriya *see* Oleksandriya

Aleksandropol' *see* Gyumri

Aleksinac Serbia 82 E4

Alençon France 72 B3

Aleppo *see* Ḥalab

Alessandria Italy 78 B2

Ålesund Norway 67 A5

Aleutian Basin *undersea feature* Bering Sea 134 D1

Aleutian Islands *islands* Alaska, USA 18 A3

Aleutian Trench *undersea feature* Pacific Ocean 134 D1

Alexander Island *island* Antarctica 136 A3

Alexandra New Zealand 133 B7

Alexandretta *see* İskenderun

Alexandria *see* Al Iskandarīyah

Alexandria Louisiana, USA 30 B3

Alexandroúpoli Greece 86 D3

Al Fāshir *see* El Fasher

Alföld *see* Great Hungarian Plain

Algarve *region* Portugal 74 C4

Algeciras Spain 74 D5

Alger *see* Algiers

Algeria *country* N Africa 52-53

Alghero Italy 79 A5

Al Ghurdaqah Egypt *var.* Hurghada 54 B2

Algiers *capital* of Algeria *var.* Alger 52 D1

Al Ḥasakah Syria 100 D2

Al Ḥudaydah Yemen 103 B7

Al Ḥufūf Saudi Arabia 103 C5

Alicante *see* Alicante/Alacant

Alicante/Alacant Spain *Sp.* Alicante, *Cat.* Alacant 75 F4

Alice Springs Australia 130 A4

Al Iskandarīyah Egypt *Eng.* Alexandria 54 B1

Al Ismā'īlīya Egypt *Eng.* Ismalia 54 B1

Al Jawf Saudi Arabia 102 B4

Al Jazīrah *region* Iraq/Syria 100 C2

Al Jīzah Egypt *var.* El Giza 54 B1

Al Karak Jordan 101 B6

Al Khalīl *see* Hebron

Al Khārijah Egypt *var.* El Khārga, Kharga 54 B2

Al Khums Libya 53 F2

Al Khurṭūm *see* Khartoum

Alkmaar Netherlands 68 C2

Al Kufrah Libya 53 H4

Al Lādhiqīyah Syria *Eng.* Latakia 100 B3

Allahābād India 117 E4

Allenstein *see* Olsztyn

Allentown Pennsylvania, USA 23 F4

Alma-Ata *capital* of Kazakhstan *Rus./Kaz.* Almaty 96 C5

Al Madīnah Saudi Arabia *Eng.* Medina 102 A5

Al Mafraq Jordan 101 B5

Almalyk Uzbekistan *Uzb.* Olmaliq 105 E2

Al Manāmah *see* Manama

Al Marj Libya 53 G2

Almaty *see* Alma-Ata

Al Mawṣil Iraq *Eng.* Mosul 102 B3

Almelo Netherlands 68 E3

Almería Spain 75 E5

Al Minyā Egypt 54 B2

Al Mukallā Yemen 103 C7

Alofi *capital* of Niue 127 F5

Alor, Kepulauan *island group* Indonesia 121 E5

Alps *mountain range* C Europe 62 D4

Al Qāhirah *see* Cairo

Al Qāmishlī Syria *var.* Kamishli 100 E1

Al Qunayṭirah Syria 100 B4

Altai Mountains *mountain range* C Asia 108 C2

Altamura Italy 79 E5

Altar, Desierto de *Desert* Mexico/USA *var.* Sonoran Desert 32 A1

Altay China 108 C2

Altay Mongolia 108 D2

Altun Shan *mountain range* China 108 C3

Alturas California, USA 26 B4

Al Uqṣur Egypt *Eng.* Luxor 54 B2

Alytus Lithuania *Pol.* Olita 89 B5

Amadeus, Lake *seasonal lake* Australia 129 E5

Amakusa-nada *island group* Japan 113 A6

Amami-Ō-shima *island* Japan 113 A8

Amarillo Texas, USA 29 E2

Amazon *river* South America 38 C3

Amazon Basin *region* C South America 42 D2

Ambanja Madagascar 61 G2

Ambarchik Russia 97 G2

Ambato Ecuador 40 A4

Amboasary Madagascar 61 F4

Ambon Indonesia 121 F4

Ambositra Madagascar 61 G3

Ambriz Angola 60 B1

Amdo China 108 C4

Ameland *island* Netherlands 68 D1

American Falls Reservoir *Reservoir* Idaho, USA 26 E4

American Samoa *unincorporated territory* USA, Pacific Ocean 127 F4

Amersfoort Netherlands 68 D3

Amga *river* Russia 95 F2

Amiens France 72 C3

Amīndīvi Islands *island group* India 114 C2

Amirante Islands *island group* Seychelles 61 H1

Amman *capital* of Jordan 101 B5

Ammassalik Greenland *var.* Angmagssalik 64 D4

Araguaia *river* Brazil 43 F3

Arāk Iran 102 C3

Araks *see* Aras

Arak's *see* Aras

Aral Sea *inland sea* Kazakhstan/Uzbekistan 94 C3

Araouane Mali 57 E2

Ararat, Mount *peak* Turkey *var.* Great Ararat, *Turk.* Büyükağrı Dağı 94 F3

Aras *river* SW Asia *Arm.* Arak's, *Per.* Rüd-e Aras, *Rus.* Araks, *Turk.* Aras Nehri 99 G3

Aras Nehri *see* Aras

Arauca Colombia 40 C2

Arauca *river* Colombia/ Venezuela 40 C2

Arbil Iraq *Kurd.* Hawlêr 102 B3

Archangel *var.* Arkhangel'sk

Arctic Ocean 18-19 137

Arda *river* Bulgaria/Greece 86 C3

Ardabil Iran 102 C3

Ardennes *region* W Europe 69 D7

Arendal Norway 67 A6

Arensburg *see* Kuressaare

Arequipa Peru 42 B4

Arezzo Italy 78 C3

Argentina *country* S South America 46-47

Argentine Basin *undersea feature* Atlantic Ocean 49 B7

Argun *river* China/Russia 95 E3

Arica Chile 46 B1

Arizona *state* USA 28 B2

Arkansas *state* USA 30 B1

Arkansas *river* C USA 17 C5

Arkhangel'sk Russia *var.* Archangel 92 C3

Arles France 73 D6

Arlington Texas, USA 29 G3

Arlington Virginia, USA 23 E4

Arlon Belgium 69 D8

Armenia *country* SW Asia 99 G2

Armenia Colombia 40 B3

Armidale Australia 131 D5

Arnhem Netherlands 68 D4

Arnhem Land *region* Australia 128 E2

Arno *river* Italy 78 B3

Arran *island* Scotland, UK 70 C4

Ar Raqqah Syria 100 C2

Arras France 72 C3

Ar Riyāḍ *see* Riyadh

Ar Rub 'al Khālī *desert* Asia *Eng.* Empty Quarter, Great Sandy Desert 103 C6

Ar Rustāq Oman *var.* Rostak 103 D5

Artesia New Mexico, USA 28 D3

Artigas Uruguay 44 B4

Aru, Kepulauan *island group* Indonesia 121 G5

Arua Uganda 55 B6

Aruba *self-governing territory* Netherlands, West Indies 37 E5

Arusha Tanzania 55 C7

Asad, Buḥayrat al *Lake* Syria *Eng.* Lake Assad 100 C2

Asadābād Afghanistan 105 E4

Asahikawa Japan 112 D2

Asamankese Ghana 57 E5

Ascension Island *overseas territory* UK, Atlantic Ocean 49 C5

Ascoli Piceno Italy 78 C4

'Aseb Eritrea *var.* Assab 54 D4

Ashburton New Zealand 133 C6

Asheville North Carolina, USA 31 E1

Aşgabat *capital of* Turkmenistan *prev.* Ashkhabad, Poltoratsk 104 C3

Ashkhabad *see* Aşgabat

Ashmore and Cartier Islands *Australian external territory* Indian Ocean 124 E4

Ash Shāriqah United Arab Emirates *Eng.* Sharjah 103 D5

Asia 94-95 106-107

Asmara *capital of* Eritrea *Amh.* Asmera 54 C4

Asmera *see* Asmara

Assab *see* 'Aseb

As Salt Jordan *var.* Salt 101 B5

Assamakka Niger 57 F2

Assen Netherlands 68 E2

Assad, Lake *see* Asad, Buḥayrat al

As Sulayyil Saudi Arabia 103 B6

As Suwaydā' Syria 101 B5

As Suways Egypt *Eng.* Suez 54 B1

Astana *country capital* Kazakhstan *prev.* Akmola, Akmolinsk, Tselinograd, Kaz. Aqmola. 96 C4

Astoria Oregon, USA 26 A2

Astrakhan' Russia 93 B7

Astypálaia *island* Greece 87 D6

Asunción *capital of* Paraguay 44 B3

Aswān Egypt 54 B2

Asyūṭ Egypt 54 B2

Atacama Desert *desert* Chile 46 B2

Atamyrat *prev.* Kerki. Turkmenistan 104 D3

Aṭār Mauritania 56 C2

Atbara Sudan 54 C3

Athabasca, Lake *lake* Canada 19 F4

Athens *capital of* Greece *Gk.* Athína, *prev.* Athínai 87 C5

Athens Georgia, USA 31 E2

Athina *see* Athens

Athínai *see* Athens

Athlone Ireland 71 B5

Ati Chad 58 C3

Atlanta Georgia, USA 30 D2

Atlantic City New Jersey, USA 23 F4

Atlantic Ocean 48-49

Atlantic-Indian Basin *undersea feature* Indian Ocean 136 B1

Atlantic-Indian Ridge *undersea feature* Atlantic Ocean 49 D7

Atlas Mountains *mountain range* Morocco 52 C3

Aṭ Ṭafīlah Jordan 101 B6

Aṭ Ṭā'if Saudi Arabia 102 B6

Attapu Laos 119 E5

Attawapiskat Canada 20 C3

Attawapiskat *river* Canada 20 B3

Attu Island *island* Alaska, USA 18 A2

Auch France 73 B6

Auckland New Zealand 132 D3

Auckland Islands *island group* New Zealand 124 D5

Augsburg Germany 77 C6

Augusta Australia 129 B7

Augusta Georgia, USA 31 E2

Augusta Maine, USA 23 G2

Aurillac France 73 C5

Aurora Colorado, USA 24 D4

Aurora Illinois, USA 22 B3

Aussig *see* Ústí nad Labem

Austin Texas, USA 29 G4

Australasia 124-125

Australes, Îles *island group* French Polynesia 125 F4

Austral Fracture Zone *tectonic feature* Pacific Ocean 125 H4

Australia *country* Pacific Ocean 124

Australian Alps Australia 131 D7

Australian Capital Territory *territory* Australia *abbrev.* A.C.T. 131 D6

Austria *country* C Europe 77

Auxerre France 72 C4

Avarua *capital of* Cook Islands 127 G5

Aveiro Portugal 74 C2

Avignon France 73 D6

Ávila Spain 74 D2

Avilés Spain 74 D1

Awbārī Libya 53 F3

Axel Heiberg Island *island* Canada 19 F1

Axiós *see* Vardar

Ayacucho Peru 42 B4

Aydarko'l Ko'li *lake* Uzbekistan *var.* Aydarkül 104 D2

Aydarkül *see* Aydarko'l Ko'li

Aydın Turkey 98 A3

Ayer's Rock *see* Uluru

Ayeyarwady *river* Myanmar *var.* Irrawaddy 118 B2

Ayr Scotland, UK 70 C4

Ayutthaya Thailand 119 C5

Ayvalık Turkey 98 A3

Azaouâd *desert* Mali 57 E2

A'zāz Syria 100 B2

Azerbaijan *country* SW Asia 99 G2

Azores *islands* Portugal, Atlantic Ocean 48 C3

Azov, Sea of Black Sea *Ukr.* Azovs'ke More, *Rus.* Azovskoye More 93 A6 91 G4

Azovs'ke More *see* Azov, Sea of

Azovskoye More *see* Azov, Sea of

Azul Argentina 46 D4

Azur, Côte d' *coastal region* France 73 E6

Az Zarqā' Jordan 101 B5

Az Zāwiyah Libya 53 F2

B

Baalbek Lebanon *var.* Ba'labakk 100 B4

Babeldaob *Island* Palau 124 B2

Babruysk/Bobruysk Belarus *Rus.* Bobruysk 89 D6

Babuyan Channel *channel* Philippines 121 E1

Bacan, Pulau *island* Indonesia 121 F4

Bačka Topola Serbia 82 D3

Bacău Romania 90 C4

Badajoz Spain 74 C4

Baden Switzerland 77 E6

Bādiyat ash Shām *see* Syrian Desert

Baffin Bay *sea feature* Atlantic Ocean 88 B1

Baffin Island *island* Canada 19 G2

Bafing *river* Africa 56 C3

Bafoussam Cameroon 58 B4

Bagdad *see* Baghdad

Bagé Brazil 44 C4

Baghdād *capital of* Iraq *var.* Bagdad, Baghdad 102 B3

Baghdad *see* Baghdad

Baghlān Afghanistan 105 E3

Bago Myanmar *prev.* Pegu 118 B4

Bagoé *river* Côte d'Ivoire/Mali 56 D4

Baguio Philippines 121 E1

Bahamas, The *country* West Indies, Atlantic Ocean 36

Baharden *see* Baharly

Baharly Turkmenistan *prev.* Baharden, Bäherden, Bakharden, Bakherden 104 B3

Bahawalpur Pakistan 116 C3

Bäherden *see* Baharly

Bahía Blanca Argentina 47 C5

Bahía, Islas de la *islands* Honduras 34 D2

Bahir Dar Ethiopia 54 C4

Bahrain *country* SW Asia 103 C5

Baia Mare Romania 90 B3

Baikal, Lake *see* Baykal, Ozero

Baishan China 110 E3

Baja Hungary 81 C7

Baja California *peninsula* Mexico *Eng.* Lower California 32 B2

Bajo Nuevo *island* Colombia 35 F2

Baker Oregon, USA 26 C3

Baker & Howland Islands *unincorporated territory* USA, Pacific Ocean 125 E2

Bakersfield California, USA 27 C7

Bakharden *see* Baharly

Bakherden *see* Baharly

Bākhtarān *see* Kermānshāh

Bakı *see* Baku

Baku *capital of* Azerbaijan *Az.* Bakı, *var.* Baky 99 H2

Baky *see* Baku

Balabac Strait *sea feature* South China Sea/Sulu Sea 120 D2

Ba'labakk *see* Baalbek

Balakovo Russia 93 C6

Bālā Murghāb Afghanistan 104 D4

Balaton *lake* Hungary *var.* Lake Balaton, *Ger.* Plattensee 81 C7

Balaton, Lake *see* Balaton

Balbina, Represa *Reservoir* Brazil 42 D2

Baleares, Islas *island group* Spain *Eng.* Balearic Islands 75 H3

Balearic Islands *see* Baleares, Islas

Bali *island* Indonesia 120 D5

Balıkesir Turkey 98 A3

Balikpapan Indonesia 120 D4

Balkanabat Turkmenistan *prev.* Nebitdag 104 B2

Balkan Mountains *mountain range* Bulgaria *Bul.* Stara Planina 86 C2

Balkhash Kazakhstan 96 C5

Balkhash, Lake *see* Balkhash, Ozero

Balkhash, Ozero *lake* Kazakhstan *Eng.* Lake Balkhash 94 C3

Ballarat Australia 131 C7

Balsas *river* Mexico 33 E5

Bălţi Moldova 90 D3

Baltic Port *see* Paldiski

Baltic Sea Atlantic Ocean 67 C7

Baltimore Maryland, USA 23 F4

Baltischport *see* Paldiski

Baltiski *see* Paldiski

Bamako *capital of* Mali 56 D3

Bambari Central African Republic 58 D4

Bamenda Cameroon 58 B4

Banaba *island* Kiribati *prev.* Ocean Island 127 E2

Bandaaceh Indonesia 120 A3

Banda, Laut *see* Banda Sea

Banda Sea *sea feature* Pacific Ocean *Ind.* Laut Banda 121 F4

Bandar-e ʿAbbās Iran 102 D4

Bandar-e Büshehr Iran 102 C4

Bandar Lampung Indonesia *prev.* Tanjungkarang 120 C4

Bandar Seri Begawan *capital of* Brunei 120 D3

Bandon Oregon, USA 26 A3

Bandundu Dem. Rep. Congo 59 C6

Bandung Indonesia 120 C5

Bangalore *see* Bengalūru

Banggai, Kepulauan *island group* Indonesia 121 E4

Banghāzī Libya *Eng.* Benghazi 53 G2

Bangka, Palau *island* Indonesia 120 C4

Bangkok *capital of* Thailand *Th.* Krung Thep 119 C5

Bangladesh *country* S Asia 117

Bangor Northern Ireland, UK 71 B5

Bangor Maine, USA 23 G2

Bangui *capital of* Central African Republic 59 C5

Bani *river* Mali 56 D3

Bani Suwayf Egypt *var.* Beni Suef 54 B1

Banja Luka Bosnia & Herzegovina 82 B3

Banjarmasin Indonesia 120 D4

Banjul *capital of* The Gambia 56 B3

Banks Island *island* Canada 19 E2

Banks Islands *island group* Vanuatu, Pacific Ocean 126 D4

Banks Peninsula *peninsula* New Zealand 133 C6

Banks Strait *sea feature* Tasman Sea 131 C7

Bantry Bay *sea feature* Ireland 71 A6

Banyo Cameroon 58 B4

Banzare Seamounts *undersea feature* Indian Ocean 123 C7

Baotou China 109 F3

Baranavichy/Baranovichi Belarus *Rus.* Baranovichi, *Pol.* Baranowicze 89 C6

Baranovichi *see* Baranavichy/Baranovichi

Baranowicze *see* Baranavichy/Baranovichi

Barbados *country* West Indies 37 H4

Barbuda *island* Antigua & Barbuda 37 G3

Barcaldine Australia 130 C4

Barcelona Spain 75 G2

Barcelona Venezuela 41 E1

Barcolod City Philippines 121 E2

Bareilly India 117 E3

Barentsburg Svalbard 65 F2

Barentsøya *island* Svalbard 65 G2

Barents Sea Arctic Ocean 137 H5

Bari Italy 79 E5

Barinas Venezuela 40 D2

Barisan, Pegunungan *mountains* Indonesia 120 B4

Barkly Tableland *plateau* Australia 130 B3

Barlavento, Ilhas de *island group* Cape Verde *var.* Windward Islands 56 A2

Bar-le-Duc France 72 D3

Barlee, Lake *lake* Australia 129 B 5

Barlee Range *mountain range* Australia 128 B4

Barnaul Russia 96 D4

Barnstaple England, UK 71 C7

Barquisimeto Venezuela 40 D2

Barra *island* Scotland, UK 70 B3

Barranquilla Colombia 40 B1

Barrier Range *mountain range* Australia 131 C5

Barrow *river* Ireland 71 B6

Barstow California, USA 27 C7

Bartang *river* Tajikistan 105 F3

Bartica Guyana 41 G2

Baruun-Urt Mongolia 109 E2

Barwon River *river* Australia 131 D5

Barysaw *see* Barysaw/Borisov

Barysaw/Borisov Belarus *Bel.* Barysaw, *Rus.* Borisov 89 D5

Basarabeasca Moldova 90 D4

Basel Switzerland 77 B6

Basra *see* Al Başrah

Bassein *see* Pathein

Basse-Terre *capital of* Guadeloupe 37 G4

Basseterre *capital of* St Kitts & Nevis 37 G3

Bass Strait *sea feature* Australia 131 C7

Bastia Corse, France 73 E7

Bastogne Belgium 69 D7
Bata Equatorial Guinea 58 A5
Batangas Philippines 121 E2
Bátdâmbâng see Battambang
Bath England, UK 71 D6
Bathurst Canada 21 F4
Bathurst Island island Australia 128 D2
Bathurst Island island Canada 19 F2
Bāṭin, Wādī al dry watercourse Asia 102 C4
Batman Turkey var. İluh 99 E4
Batna Algeria 53 E1
Baton Rouge Louisiana, USA 30 B3
Battambang Cambodia var. Bátdâmbâng 119 D5
Batticaloa Sri Lanka 115 E3
Batumi Georgia 99 F2
Bauru Brazil 44 D2
Bavarian Alps mountains Austria/Germany 77 C6
Bayamo Cuba 36 C2
Bayan Har Shan mountain range China 108 D4
Bayanhongor Mongolia 108 D2
Bay City Michigan, USA 22 C3
Baydhabo Somalia 55 D6
Baykal, Ozero lake Russia Eng. Lake Baikal 95 E3
Bayonne France 73 A6
Bayramaly Turkmenistan 104 C3
Bayrūt see Beirut
Beaufort Sea Arctic Ocean 137 F2
Beaufort West South Africa 60 D5
Beaumont Texas, USA 29 H4
Beauvais France 72 C3
Béchar Algeria 52 C2
Be'er Sheva' Israel 101 A6
Beijing capital of China var. Peking 110 C4
Beira Mozambique 61 E3
Beirut capital of Lebanon var. Beyrouth, Bayrūt 100 B4
Beja Portugal 74 C4

Béjaïa Algeria 53 E1
Bek-Budi see Karshi
Békéscsaba Hungary 81 D7
Belagāvi India prev. Belgaum 114 C1
Belarus country E Europe var. Belorusia 89
Belau see Palau
Belcher Islands islands Canada 20 C2
Beledweyne Somalia 55 D5
Belém Brazil 43 F2
Belfast Northern Ireland, UK 71 B5
Belfort France 72 E4
Belgaum see Belagāvi
Belgium country W Europe 69
Belgorod Russia 93 A5
Belgrade capital of Serbia SCr. Beograd 82 D3
Belitung, Pulau island Indonesia 120 C4
Belize country Central America 34
Belize City Belize 34 C1
Belle Île, island France 72 A4
Belle Isle, Strait of sea feature Canada 21 G3
Bellevue Washington, USA 26 B2
Bellingham Washington, USA 26 B1
Bellingshausen Sea Antarctica 136 A3
Bello Colombia 40 B2
Bellville South Africa 60 C5
Belmopan capital of Belize 34 C1
Belo Horizonte Brazil 45 F1
Belorussia see Belarus
Belostok see Białystok
Beloye More Arctic Ocean Eng. White Sea 63 F1
Belyy, Ostrov island Russia 137 H4
Bend Oregon, USA 26 B3
Bender Moldova var. Tighina 90 D4
Bendigo Australia 131 C7
Benevento Italy 79 D5

Bengal, Bay of sea feature Indian Ocean 122 D3
Bengalūru India prev. Bangalore 114 D2
Bengbu China 111 D5
Benghazi see Banghāzī
Bengkulu Indonesia 120 B4
Benguela Angola 60 B2
Beni river Bolivia 42 C4
Benidorm Spain 75 F4
Beni-Mellal Morocco 52 C2
Benin country N Africa prev. Dahomey 57
Benin, Bight of sea feature W Africa 57 F5
Benin City Nigeria 57 F5
Beni Suef see Banī Suwayf
Ben Nevis mountain Scotland, UK 70 C3
Benue river Cameroon/Nigeria 57 G4
Beograd see Belgrade
Berat Albania 83 D6
Berbera Somalia 54 D4
Berbérati Central African Republic 58 C5
Berdyans'k Ukraine 91 G4
Bereket Turkmenistan prev. Gazandzhyk, var. Kazandzhik, Turkm. Gazanjyk 104 B2
Berezina see Byerazino
Bergamo Italy 78 B2
Bergen Norway 67 A5
Bergse Maas river Netherlands 68 D4
Bering Sea Pacific Ocean 134 D1
Bering Strait sea feature Bering Sea/Chukchi Sea 134 D1
Berkeley California, USA 27 B6
Berlin capital of Germany 76 D3
Bermejo river Argentina 46 D2
Bermuda overseas territory UK, Atlantic Ocean 48 B3
Bern capital of Switzerland Fr. Berne 77 B7
Berne see Bern
Berner Alpen mountain range Switzerland 77 B7
Bertoua Cameroon 59 B5

Besançon France 72 D4

Besztercebánya *see* Banská Bystrica

Bethlehem West Bank 101 A5

Beyrouth *see* Beirut

Béziers France 73 C6

Bezmein *see* Abadan

Bhamo Myanmar 118 B2

Bhāvnagar India 116 C4

Bhōpal India 116 D4

Bhutan *country* S Asia 117

Biak, Pulau *island* Indonesia 121 G4

Białystok Poland *Rus.* Belostok 80 E3

Biel Switzerland 77 B7

Bielefeld Germany 76 B4

Bielitz-Biala *see* Bielsko-Biala

Bielsko-Biała Poland *Ger.* Bielitz-Biala 81 D5

Bié Plateau *upland* Angola 51 C6

Bighorn Mountains *mountains* C USA 24 C2

Bignona Senegal 56 B3

Big Spring Texas, USA 29 E3

Bihać Bosnia & Herzegovina 82 B3

Bihār *state* India 117 F3

Bijelo Polje Montenegro 82 D4

Bīkāner India 116 C3

Bila Tserkva Ukraine 91 E2

Bilbao Spain 75 E1

Billings Montana, USA 24 C2

Bilma, Grand Erg de *desert* Niger 57 G3

Biloela Australia 130 D4

Biloxi Mississippi, USA 30 C3

Biltine Chad 58 D3

Binghamton New York, USA 23 F3

Birāk Libya 53 F3

Birātnagar Nepal 117 F3

Birmingham England, UK 71 D6

Birmingham Alabama, USA 30 D2

Bîr Mogreïn Mauritania 56 C1

Birsen *see* Biržai

Biržai Lithuania *Ger.* Birsen 88 C4

Biscay, Bay of *sea feature* Atlantic Ocean 62 C4

Bishkek *capital of* Kyrgyzstan *prev.* Frunze, Pishpek 105 F2

Bishop California, USA 27 C6

Biskra Algeria 53 E2

Bismarck North Dakota, USA 25 E2

Bismarck Archipelago *island group* Papua New Guinea 126 B3

Bismarck Sea *sea* Pacific Ocean 124 B2

Bissau *capital of* Guinea-Bissau 56 B4

Bitola Macedonia 83 E6

Bitterroot Range *mountains* NW USA 26 D2

Biwa-ko *lake* Japan 113 C5

Bizerte Tunisia 53 E1

Bjelovar Croatia 82 B2

Bjørnøya *island* N Norway *Eng.* Bear Island 65 G3

Black Drin *river* Albania/Macedonia 83 D5

Black Forest *see* Schwarzwald

Black Hills *mountains* C USA 24 D3

Blackpool England, UK 71 D5

Black River *river* China/Vietnam 118 D3

Black Sea Asia/Europe 63 F4

Black Volta *river* Ghana/Côte d'Ivoire 57 E4

Blackwater *river* Ireland 71 A6

Blagoevgrad Bulgaria 86 C3

Blagoveshchensk Russia 97 G4

Blanca, Bahía *sea feature* Argentina 39 D5

Blanche, Lake *lake* Australia 131 B5

Blantyre Malawi 61 E2

Blenheim New Zealand 133 D5

Blida Algeria 53 E1

Bloemfontein *financial capital of* South Africa 60 D4

Blois France 72 C4

Bloomington Indiana, USA 22 C4

Bluefields Nicaragua 35 E3

Blue Mountains *mountains* W USA 26 C2

Blue Nile *river* Ethiopia/Sudan 54 C4

Blumenau Brazil 44 D3

Bo Sierra Leone 56 C4

Boa Vista Brazil 42 D1

Boa Vista *island* Cape Verde 56 A3

Bobo-Dioulasso Burkina Faso 56 D4

Bobruysk *see* Babruysk/Bobruysk

Boca de la Serpiente *see* Serpent's Mouth, The

Bochum Germany 76 B4

Bodø Norway 66 C3

Bodrum Turkey 98 A4

Bogor Indonesia 120 C5

Bogotá *capital of* Colombia 40 B3

Bo Hai *sea feature* Yellow Sea 110 D4

Bohemian Forest *region* Germany 77 D5

Bohol Sea *Sea* Philippines 121 E2

Boise Idaho, USA 26 D3

Boké Guinea 56 C4

Bokhara *see* Buxoro

Bol Chad 58 B3

Bolivia *country* C South America 42-43

Bologna Italy 78 C3

Bolton England, UK 71 D5

Bolzano Italy *Ger.* Bozen 78 C2

Boma Dem. Rep. Congo 59 B7

Bombay *see* Mumbai

Bomu *river* Central African Republic/Dem. Rep. Congo 59 D5

Bonaire *special municipality* Netherlands, West Indies 37 E5

Bongo, Massif des *upland* Central African Republic 58 D4

Bongor Chad 58 C3

Bonn Germany 76 B4

Boosaaso Somalia 54 E4

Borås Sweden 67 B7

Bordeaux France 73 B5

Borger Texas, USA 29 E2

Borisov see Barysaw

Borlänge Sweden 67 C6

Borneo island SE Asia 120-121

Bornholm island Denmark 67 C8

Bosanski Šamac Bosnia & Herzegovina 82 C3

Bosna river Bosnia & Herzegovina 82 C3

Bosne I Hercegovine, Federacija Admin. region republic Bosnia and Herzegovina 82 C4

Bosnia & Herzegovina country SE Europe 82-83

Bosporus sea feature Turkey Turk. İstanbul Boğazi 98 B2

Bossangoa Central African Republic 58 C4

Bosten Hu Lake China 108 C3

Boston Massachusetts, USA 23 G3

Bothnia, Gulf of sea feature Baltic Sea 67 C5

Botoşani Romania 90 C3

Botswana country southern Africa 60

Bouar Central African Republic 58 C4

Bougainville Island island Papua New Guinea 126 C3

Bougouni Mali 56 D4

Boulder Colorado, USA 24 C4

Boulogne-sur-Mer France 72 C2

Bourges France 72 C4

Bourgogne region France Eng. Burgundy 72 D4

Bourke Australia 131 C5

Bournemouth England, UK 71 D7

Bouvet Island external territory Norway, Atlantic Ocean 49 D7

Bowen Australia 130 D3

Bowling Green Kentucky, USA 28 C3

Bozeman Montana, USA 24 B2

Bozen see Bolzano

Brač island Croatia 82 B4

Brades de facto capital of Montserrat 37 G3

Bradford England, UK 71 D5

Braga Portugal 74 C2

Bragança Portugal 74 C2

Brahmaputra river Asia 117 G3

Brăila Romania 90 D4

Brainerd Minnesota, USA 25 F2

Brandon Canada 19 F5

Brasília capital of Brazil 43 F4

Braşov Romania 90 C4

Bratislava capital of Slovakia Ger. Pressburg, Hung. Pozsony 81 C6

Bratsk Russia 97 E4

Braunau am Inn Austria 77 D6

Braunschweig Germany Eng. Brunswick 76 C4

Brazil country South America 42-43

Brazil Basin undersea feature Atlantic Ocean 49 C5

Brazilian Highlands upland Brazil 43 G4

Brazos river SW USA 29 G3

Brazzaville capital of Congo 59 B6

Brecon Beacons hills Wales, UK 71 C6

Breda Netherlands 68 C4

Bregenz Austria 77 B7

Bremen Germany 76 B3

Bremerhaven Germany 76 B3

Brescia Italy 78 B2

Breslau see Wrocław

Brest Belarus Pol. Brześć nad Bugiem, prev. Brześć Litewski, Rus. Brest-Litovsk 89 B6

Brest France 72 A3

Brest-Litovsk see Brest

Bretagne region France Eng. Brittany 72 A3

Brezhnev see Naberezhnyye Chelny

Bria Central African Republic 58 D4

Bridgetown capital of Barbados 37 H4

Brig Switzerland 77 B5

Brighton England, UK 71 E7

Brindisi Italy 79 E5

Brisbane Australia 131 E5

Bristol England, UK 71 D6

British Columbia province Canada 18-19

British Indian Ocean Territory overseas territory UK, Indian Ocean 122 C4

British Isles islands W Europe 70-71

British Virgin Islands overseas territory UK, West Indies 37

Brittany see Bretagne

Brno Czech Republic (Czechia) Ger. Brünn 81 B5

Broken Arrow Oklahoma, USA 29 G1

Broken Hill Australia 131 B6

Broken Ridge undersea feature Indian Ocean 123 D6

Bromberg see Bydgoszcz

Brooks Range mountains Alaska, USA 18 D2

Brookton Australia 129 B6

Broome Australia 128 C3

Brownfield Texas, USA 29 E2

Brownsville Texas, USA 29 G5

Bruges see Brugge

Brugge Belgium Fr. Bruges 69 A5

Brunei country E Asia 120 D3

Brünn see Brno

Brunswick Georgia, USA 31 E3

Brunswick see Braunschweig

Brusa see Bursa

Brussel see Brussels

Brussels capital of Belgium Fr. Bruxelles, Flem. Brussel 69 C6

Brüx see Most

Bruxelles see Brussels

Bryan Texas, USA 29 G3

Bryansk Russia 93 A5 96 A2

Brześć Litewski see Brest

Brześć nad Bugiem see Brest

Bucaramanga Colombia 40 C2

Buchanan Liberia 56 C5

Bucharest capital of Romania 90 C5

Budapest *capital of* Hungary 81 C6

Budweis *see* České Budějovice

Buenaventura Colombia 40 B3

Buenos Aires *capital of* Argentina 46 D4

Buenos Aires, Lago *lake* Argentina/Chile 47 B6

Buffalo New York, USA 23 E3

Bug *river* E Europe 90 C1

Bujumbura *capital of* Burundi *prev.* Usumbura 55 B7

Bukavu Dem. Rep. Congo 59 E6

Bukhara *see* Buxoro

Bulawayo Zimbabwe 60 D3

Bulgan Mongolia 109 E2

Bulgaria *country* E Europe 86

Bumba Dem. Rep. Congo 59 D5

Bunbury Australia 129 B6

Bundaberg Australia 130 E4

Bunia Dem. Rep. Congo 59 E6

Buraydah Saudi Arabia 103 B5

Burē Ethiopia 54 C4

Burgas Bulgaria 86 E2

Burgos Spain 75 E2

Burgundy *see* Bourgogne

Burketown Australia 130 B3

Burkina Faso *country* W Africa 57

Burlington Iowa, USA 25 G4

Burlington Vermont, USA 23 F2

Burma *see* Myanmar

Burnie Tasmania 131 C8

Burns Oregon, USA 26 C3

Bursa Turkey *prev.* Brusa 98 B3

Būr Sa‘īd Egypt *Eng.* Port Said 54 B1

Burtnieku Ezers *lake* Latvia 88 C3

Buru, Pulau *island* Indonesia 121 E4

Burundi *country* C Africa 55

Busan South Korea *prev.* Pusan 110 E4

Busselton Australia 129 B7

Butembo Dem. Rep. Congo 59 E5

Buton, Pulau *Island* Indonesia 121 E4

Butuan Philippines 121 F2

Buxoro Uzbekistan *var.* Bokhara, *Rus.* Bukhara 104 D2

Büyükağrı Dağı *see* Ararat, Mount

Buzău Romania 90 C4

Büzmeýin *see* Abadan

Byaresina *river* Belarus *Rus.* Berezina 89 D6

Bydgoszcz Poland *Ger.* Bromberg 80 C3

Byzantium *see* İstanbul

C

Caazapá Paraguay 44 C3

Cabanatuan Philippines 121 E1

Cabimas Venezuela 40 C1

Cabinda *exclave* Angola 60 B1

Cabot Strait *sea feature* Atlantic Ocean 21 G4

Čačak Serbia 82 D3

Cáceres Spain 74 D3

Cachoeiro de Itapemirim Brazil 45 F1

Cadiz Philippines 121 E2

Cádiz Spain 74 D5

Caen France 72 B3

Cagayan de Oro Philippines 121 F2

Cagliari Italy 79 A5

Cahors France 73 B5

Cairns Australia 130 D3

Cairo *capital of* Egypt *Ar.* Al Qāhirah, *var.* El Qâhira 54 B1

Čakovec Croatia 82 B2

Calabar Nigeria 57 G5

Calabria *region* Italy 79 D6

Calafate *see* El Calafate

Calais France 72 C2

Calais Maine, USA 23 H1

Calama Chile 46 B2

Calbayog Philippines 121 F2

Calcutta *see* Kolkāta

Caldas da Rainha Portugal 74 B3

Caldwell Idaho, USA 27 C3

Caleta Olivia Argentina 47 C6

Calgary Canada 19 E5

Cali Colombia 40 A3

Calicut *see* Kozhikode

California *state* USA 26-27

California, Golfo de *sea feature* Pacific Ocean *Eng.* California, Gulf of 32 C2 123 F2

Callabonna, Lake *lake* Australia 131 B5

Callao Peru 42 A3

Caltanissetta Italy 79 C7

Camagüey Cuba 36 C2

Cambodia *country* SE Asia *Cam.* Kampuchea 119

Cambridge England, UK 71 E6

Cambridge New Zealand 132 D2

Cameroon *country* W Africa 58-59

Campbell Plateau *undersea feature* Pacific Ocean 134 C5

Campeche Mexico 33 G4

Campeche, Bahía de *sea feature* Mexico *Eng.* Gulf of Campeche 33 G4

Campina Grande Brazil 43 H3

Campinas Brazil 45 E2

Campo Grande Brazil 44 C1

Campos Brazil 45 F2

Canada *country* North America 16-17

Canada Basin *undersea feature* Arctic Ocean *var.* Laurentian Basin 137 F2

Canadian River *river* SW USA 29 E2

Çanakkale Turkey 98 A3

Çanakkale Boğazı *see* Dardanelles

Canarias, Islas *islands* Spain *Eng.* Canary Islands 50 A2

Canary Basin *undersea feature* Atlantic Ocean 48 C4

Canary Islands *see* Canarias, Islas

Canaveral, Cape *coastal feature* Florida, USA 31 F4

Canberra *capital of* Australia 131 D6

Cancún Mexico 33 H3

Caniapiscau *river* Canada 21 E2

Caniapiscau, Réservoir *Reservoir* Canada 21 E3

Canik Dağları *mountains* Turkey 98 D2

Çankırı Turkey 98 C2

Cannes France 73 D6

Canoas Brazil 44 D4

Canterbury England, UK 71 E6

Canterbury Bight *sea feature* Pacific Ocean 133 C6

Canterbury Plains *plain* New Zealand 133 B6

Cân Tho Vietnam 119 D6

Canton Ohio, USA 22 D4

Canton *see* Guangzhou

Cape Basin *undersea feature* Atlantic Ocean 49 D6

Cape Town *legislative capital of* South Africa 60 C5

Cape Verde *country* Atlantic Ocean 56 A2

Cape Verde Basin *undersea feature* Atlantic Ocean 48 C4

Cape York Peninsula *peninsula* Australia 124 B3

Cap-Haïtien Haiti 36 D3

Capri, Isola di *island* Italy 79 D5

Caquetá *river* Colombia 40 C4

CAR *see* Central African Republic

Caracas *capital of* Venezuela 40 D1

Carazinho Brazil 44 C3

Carbondale Illinois, USA 22 B5

Carcassonne France 73 C6

Cardiff Wales, UK 71 C6

Cardigan Bay *sea feature* Wales, UK 71 C6

Carey, Lake *lake* Australia 129 C5

Caribbean Sea Atlantic Ocean 36-37

Carlisle England, UK 70 D4

Carlsbad New Mexico, USA 28 D3

Carlsberg Ridge *undersea feature* Indian Ocean 122 B4

Carnavon Australia 128 A5

Carnegie, Lake *lake* Australia 129 C5

Carolina Brazil 43 F3

Caroline Island *see* Millennium Island

Caroline Islands *island group* Micronesia 126 B1

Caroni *river* Venezuela 41 F2

Carpathian Mountains *mountain range* E Europe *var.* Carpathians 63 E4

Carpathians *see* Carpathian Mountains

Carpaţii Meridionali *mountain range* Romania *Eng.* South Carpathians, Transylvanian Alps 90 B4

Carpentaria, Gulf of *sea feature* Australia 130 B2

Carson City Nevada, USA 27 B5

Cartagena Colombia 40 B1

Cartagena Spain 75 F4

Cartago Costa Rica 35 E4

Cartwright Canada 21 G2

Carúpano Venezuela 41 E1

Casablanca Morocco 52 C2

Casa Grande Arizona, USA 28 B3

Cascade Range *mountain range* Canada/USA 26 B2

Cascais Portugal 74 B3

Casper Wyoming, USA 24 C3

Caspian Sea *inland sea* Asia/Europe 94 B4

Castelló de la Plana *see* Castelló de la Plana/Castelló de la Plana

Castelló de la Plana *see* Castelló de la Plana/Castelló de la Plana

Castelló de la Plana/Castelló de la Plana Spain *Sp.* Castellón de la Plana, *Cat.* Castelló de la Plana 75 F3

Castelo Branco Portugal 74 C3

Castries *capital of* St Lucia 37 G4

Castro Chile 47 B6

Cat Island *island* The Bahamas 36 D1

Catania Italy 79 D7

Catanzaro Italy 79 D6

Cauca *river* Colombia 40 B2

Caucasus *mountains* Asia/Europe 93 A7

Caura *river* Venezuela 41 E2

Caviana, Ilha *island* Brazil 43 F1

Cawnpore *see* Kānpur

Caxias do Sul Brazil 44 D4

Cayenne *capital of* French Guiana 41 H3

Cayman Islands *overseas territory* UK, West Indies 36

Cebu Philippines 121 E2

Cedar Rapids Iowa, USA 25 G3

Cedros, Isla *island* Mexico 32 A2

Ceduna Australia 131 A6

Cefalù Italy 79 C6

Celebes *see* Sulawesi

Celebes Sea Pacific Ocean *Ind.* Laut Sulawesi 134 B3

Celje Slovenia 77 E7

Central African Republic *country* C Africa *abbrev.* CAR 58-59

Central, Cordillera *mountain range* Philippines 121 E1

Central Makran Range *mountains* Pakistan 116 A3

Central Pacific Basin *undersea feature* Pacific Ocean 125 E1

Central Russian Upland *upland* Russia 94 B3

Central Siberian Plateau *see* Srednesibirskoye Ploskogor'ye

Central Siberian Uplands *see* Srednesibirskoye Ploskogor'ye

Central, Sistema *mountain range* Spain 74 D3

Cephalonia *see* Kefalloniá

Ceram Sea *Sea* Indonesia 121 F4

Cernăuţi *see* Chernivtsi

Cēsis Latvia *Ger.* Wenden 88 C3

České Budějovice Czech Republic (Czechia) *Ger.* Budweis 81 B5

Ceuta *external territory* Spain, N Africa 52 C1

Cévennes *mountains* France 73 C6

Ceylon *see* Sri Lanka

Chona *river* Russia 95 E2

Chon Buri Thailand 119 C5

Ch'ŏngjin North Korea 110 E3

Chongqing *province* China *var.* Chungking 111 B5

Chonos, Archipiélago de los *island group* Chile 47 B6

Chornobyl' Ukraine *Rus.* Chernobyl' 91 E1

Choûm Mauritania 56 C2

Choybalsan Mongolia 109 E2

Christchurch New Zealand 133 C6

Christmas Island *external territory* Australia, Indian Ocean 122 D5

Christmas Island *see* Kiritimati

Christmas Ridge *undersea feature* Pacific Ocean 125 F1

Chuan *see* Sichuan

Chubut *river* Argentina 47 B6

Chudskoye Ozero *see* Peipus, Lake

Chui *see* Chuy

Chukchi Plain *undersea feature* Arctic Ocean 137 G2

Chukchi Sea Arctic Ocean *Rus.* Chukotskoye More 137 F1

Chukotskoye More *see* Chukchi Sea

Chula Vista California, USA 27 C8

Chulym *river* Russia 94 D3

Chumphon Thailand 119 C6

Chungking *see* Chongqing

Chuquicamata Chile 46 B2

Chur Switzerland 77 B7

Churchill Canada 19 G4

Chuuk Islands *island group* Micronesia 126 B1

Chuy Brazil *var.* Chui 44 C5

Cienfuegos Cuba 36 B2

Cieza Spain 75 F4

Cilacap Indonesia 120 C5

Cincinnati Ohio, USA 22 C4

Ciudad Bolívar Venezuela 41 E2

Ciudad del Este Paraguay 44 C3

Ciudad de México *see* Mexico City

Ciudad Guayana Venezuela 41 E2

Ciudad Juárez Mexico 32 C1

Ciudad Obregón Mexico 32 B2

Ciudad Ojeda Venezuela 40 C1

Ciudad Real Spain 75 E3

Ciudad Valles Mexico 33 E3

Ciudad Victoria Mexico 33 E3

Clarence *river* New Zealand 133 C5

Clarion Fracture Zone *tectonic feature* Pacific Ocean 125 G1

Clarksville Tennessee, USA 30 D1

Clearwater Florida, USA 31 E4

Clermont Australia 130 D4

Clermont-Ferrand France 73 C5

Cleveland Ohio, USA 22 D3

Clipperton Fracture Zone *tectonic feature* Pacific Ocean 125 G2

Clipperton Island *external territory* France, Pacific Ocean 135 F3

Cloncurry Australia 130 C3

Clovis New Mexico, USA 29 E2

Cluj-Napoca Romania 90 B3

Clutha *river* New Zealand 133 B7

Coast Ranges *mountain range* W USA 26 A5

Coats Island *island* Canada 20 C1

Coats Land *physical region* Antarctica 136 B2

Coatzacoalcos Mexico 33 G4

Cobán Guatemala 34 B2

Cochabamba Bolivia 42 C4

Cochin *see* Kochi

Cochrane Canada 20 C4

Cochrane Chile 47 B6

Coco *river* Honduras/Nicaragua 34 D2

Cocos Basin *undersea feature* Indian Ocean 122 D4

Cocos Islands *external territory* Australia, Indian Ocean 122 D5

Cod, Cape *coastal feature* NE USA 23 G3

Coeur d'Alene Idaho, USA 26 C2

Coffs Harbour Australia 131 E6

Coihaique Chile 47 B6

Coimbatore India 114 D3

Coimbra Portugal 74 C3

Colchester England, UK 71 E6

Colmar France 72 E4

Cologne *see* Köln

Colombia *country* N South America 40-41

Colombo *administrative capital* of Sri Lanka 115 E4

Colón Panama 35 F4

Colón, Archipiélago de *see* Galapagos Islands

Colorado *state* USA 24 C4

Colorado *river* USA 16 B5

Colorado *river* Argentina 47 C5

Colorado Plateau *upland region* S USA 28 B1

Colorado Springs Colorado, USA 24 D4

Columbia South Carolina, USA 31 F2

Columbia *river* NW USA 26 C1

Columbus Georgia, USA 30 D3

Columbus Mississippi, USA 30 C2

Columbus Nebraska, USA 25 E4

Columbus Ohio, USA 22 D4

Comayagua Honduras 34 C2

Comilla Bangladesh 117 G4

Communism Peak *peak* Tajikistan *Rus.* Pik Kommunizma, *prev.* Stalin Peak, Garmo Peak 105 F3

Como, Lago di *lake* Italy 78 B2

Comodoro Rivadavia Argentina 47 C6

Comoros *country* Indian Ocean 61

Conakry *capital of* Guinea 56 C4

D

Dacca see Dhaka

Daegu South Korea prev. Taegu 110 E4

Daejeon South Korea prev. Taejŏn 110 E4

Dagden see Hiiumaa

Dagö see Hiiumaa

Dagupan Philippines 121 E1

Da Hinggan Ling mountain range China Eng. Great Khingan Range 109 G1

Dahomey see Benin

Dakar capital of Senegal 56 B3

Đakovo Croatia 82 C3

Dalain Hob China 108 D3

Dalaman Turkey 98 B4

Dalandzadgad Mongolia 109 E3

Đa Lat Vietnam 119 E5

Dalby Australia 131 D5

Dalian China 110 D4

Dallas Texas, USA 29 G3

Dalmacija region Croatia 82 B4

Daly Waters Australia 128 E3

Damān India 116 C5

Damas see Damascus

Damascus Syria var. Esh Sham, Fr. Damas, Ar. Dimashq 100 B4

Dampier Australia 128 B4

Damxung China 108 C5

Đa Nẵng Vietnam 119 E4

Dandong China 110 D4

Daneborg Greenland 65 E3

Danghara Tajikistan 105 E3

Danmarksstraedet see Denmark Strait

Danube river C Europe 63 E4

Danville Virginia, USA 23 E5

Danzig see Gdańsk

Danzig, Gulf of see Gdańsk, Gulf of

Darä Syria 101 B5

Dardanelles sea feature Turkey Turk. Çanakkale Boğazı 98 A2

Dar es Salaam Tanzania 55 C7

Darfur Cultural region Sudan 54 A4

Darhan Mongolia 109 E2

Darien, Gulf of sea feature Caribbean Sea 35 G5

Darling river Australia 131 C6

Darmstadt Germany 77 B5

Darnah Libya 53 H2

Dartmoor region England, UK 71 C7

Dartmouth Canada 21 F4

Darwin Australia 128 D2

Dashhowuz see Daşoguz

Daşoguz Turkmenistan prev. Tashauz, Turkm. Dashhowuz 104 C2

Datong China 110 C4

Daugava see Western Dvina

Daugavpils Latvia Ger. Dünaburg, Rus. Dvinsk 88 D4

Dāvangere India 114 D2

Davao Philippines 121 F3

Davao Gulf gulf Philippines 121 F3

Davenport Iowa, USA 25 F3

David Panama 35 E5

Davie Ridge undersea feature Indian Ocean 123 A5

Davis Sea Indian Ocean 136 D3

Davis Strait sea feature Atlantic Ocean 64 C3

Dawei Myanmar prev. Tavoy 119 B5

Dayr az Zawr Syria 100 D3

Dayton Ohio, USA 22 C4

Daytona Beach Florida, USA 31 F4

Dead Sea salt lake SW Asia Ar. Al Baḥr al Mayyit, Baḥrat Lūṭ, Heb. Yam HaMelah 101 B5

Death Valley valley W USA 27 C6

Deatnu river Finland/Norway 66 D2

Debrecen Hungary prev. Debreczen, Ger. Debreczin 81 D6

Debreczen see Debrecen

Debreczin see Debrecen

Decatur Illinois, USA 22 B4

Deccan plateau India 106 B3 115 D1

Děčín Czech Republic (Czechia) Ger. Tetschen 80 B4

Dej Romania 90 B3

Delaware state USA 23 F4

Delémont Switzerland 77 A7

Delft Netherlands 68 C4

Delfzijl Netherlands 68 E1

Delhi India 116 D3

Del Rio Texas, USA 29 F4

Demchok see Dêmqog

Demopolis Alabama, USA 30 C2

Dêmqog disputed region China/India var. Demchok 108 B3

Denali see Mount McKinley

Denham Australia 129 A5

Den Helder Netherlands 68 C2

Denizli Turkey 98 B4

Denmark country NW Europe 67

Denmark Strait sea feature Greenland/Iceland var. Danmarksstraedet 65 D3

Denpasar Indonesia 120 D5

Denton Texas, USA 29 G2

Denver Colorado, USA 24 D4

Dera Ghazi Khan Pakistan 116 C2

Derby England, UK 71 D6

Derg, Lough lake Ireland 71 B6

Desē Ethiopia 54 C4

Deseado river Argentina 47 C6

Des Moines Iowa, USA 25 F3

Despoto Planina see Rhodope Mountains

Dessau Germany 76 D4

Detroit Michigan, USA 22 D3

Deutschendorf see Poprad

Deva Romania 90 B4

Deventer Netherlands 68 D3

Devollit, Lumi i river Albania 83 D6

Devon Island island Canada 19 F2

Devonport Tasmania, Australia 131 C8

Enderbury Island *atoll* Kiribati 136 C2

Enderby Land *region* Antarctica 136 C2

Enderby Plain *undersea feature* Indian Ocean 123 B7

England *national region* UK 70-71

English Channel *sea feature* Atlantic Ocean 71 D7

Enguri *river* Georgia *Rus.* Inguri 99 F1

Enid Oklahoma, USA 29 F1

Ennedi *plateau* Chad 58 D2

Enns *river* Austria 77 D6

Enschede Netherlands 68 E3

Ensenada Mexico 32 A1

Entebbe Uganda 55 B6

Enugu Nigeria 57 G5

Eolie, Isole *island group* Italy *Eng.* Lipari Islands, *var.* Aeolian Islands 79 D6

Eperies *see* Prešov

Eperjes *see* Prešov

Épinal France 72 E4

Equatorial Guinea *country* W Africa 59

Erdenet Mongolia 109 E2

Erechim Brazil 44 D3

Erenhot China 109 F2

Erevan *see* Yerevan

Ereğli Turkey 98 C4

Erfurt Germany 76 C4

Erie Pennsylvania, USA 22 D3

Erie, Lake *lake* Canada/USA 17 D5

Eritrea *country* E Africa 54

Erivan *see* Yerevan

Erlangen Germany 77 C5

Ernākulam India 114 D3

Er Rachidia Morocco 52 C2

Erzerum *see* Erzurum

Erzgebirge *mountain range* Czech Republic (Czechia)/ Germany *var* Krušné Hory 77 D5

Erzincan Turkey 99 E3

Erzurum Turkey *prev.* Erzerum 99 F3

Esbjerg Denmark 67 A7

Esch-sur-Alzette Luxembourg 69 D8

Escuintla Guatemala 34 B2

Eşfahān Iran 102 C3

Esh Sham *see* Damascus

Eskişehir Turkey 98 B3

Esmeraldas Ecuador 40 A4

Esperance Australia 129 C6

Espíritu Santo *island* Vanuatu 124 D3

Espoo Finland 67 D6

Esquel Argentina 47 B6

Essaouira Morocco 52 B2

Essen Germany 76 A4

Essequibo *river* Guyana 41 G3

Estelí Nicaragua 34 D3

Estevan Canada 19 F5

Estonia *country* E Europe 88 D2

Ethiopia *country* E Africa 54-55

Ethiopian Highlands *upland* E Africa 50 D4

Etna, Mount *peak* Sicily, Italy 79 D7

Etosha Pan *salt basin* Namibia 60 C3

Eucla Australia 129 D6

Eugene Oregon, USA 26 A3

Eugene Washington, USA 26 B1

Euphrates *river* SW Asia 102 C4

Europe 62-63

Evansville Indiana, USA 22 B5

Everest, Mount *peak* China/ Nepal 108 B3

Everett Washington, USA 26 B1

Everglades, The *wetlands* Florida, USA 31 F5

Évvoia *island* Greece 87 C5

Exeter England, UK 71 C7

Exmoor *region* England, UK 71 C7

Exmouth Australia 128 A4

Exmouth Gulf *gulf* Australia 128 A4

Exmouth Plateau *undersea feature* Indian Ocean 123 E5

Eyre North, Lake *salt lake* Australia131 B5

Eyre Peninsula *peninsula* Australia131 A6

Eyre South, Lake *salt lake* Australia131 B5

F

Fada-N'gourma Burkina Faso 57 E4

Faeroe Islands *see* Faroe Islands

Færøerne *see* Faroe Islands

Faguibine, Lac *lake* Mali 57 E3

Fairbanks Alaska, USA 18 D3

Fairlie New Zealand 133 B6

Faisalabad Pakistan 116 C2

Faīzābād Afghanistan *prev.* Feyzābād 105 E3

Falkland Islands *overseas territory* UK, Atlantic Ocean 47 D7

Fallon Nevada, USA 27 C5

Falun Sweden 67 C6

Famagusta *see* Gazimağusa

Fanning Island *see* Tabuaeran

Farafangana Madagascar 61 G4

Farāh Afghanistan 104 C4

Farasān, Jazā'ir *island group* Saudi Arabia 103 B6

Farewell, Cape *headland* New Zealand 132 C4

Farewell, Cape *see* Nunap Isua

Farghona *see* Farg'ona

Farg'ona Uzbekistan *prev.* Novyy Margilan, *Uzb.* Farghona 105 F2

Fargo North Dakota, USA 25 E2

Farkhor Tajikistan 105 E3

Farmington New Mexico, USA 28 C1

Faro Portugal 74 C4

Faroe Islands *self-governing territory* Denmark, Atlantic Ocean *Far.* Fóroyar, *Dan.* Færøerne, *var.* Faeroe Islands 65 F5

Farquhar Group *island group* Seychelles 51 F2

Farvel, Cap *see* Nunap Isua

Faxaflói *bay* Iceland 64 D5

Faya Chad 58 C2

Fayetteville Arkansas, USA 30 A1

Freetown *capital of* Sierra Leone 56 C4
Freiburg im Breisgau Germany 77 B6
Fremantle Australia 129 B6
French Guiana *overseas department* France, N South America 41
French Polynesia *overseas collectivity* France, Pacific Ocean 135 E3
French Southern and Antarctic Lands *French overseas territory* Indian Ocean *Fr.* Terres Australes et Antarctiques Françaises 123 C7
Fresnillo Mexico 32 D1
Fresno California, USA 27 B6
Fobisher Bay *see* Iqaluit
Frome, Lake *salt lake* Australia 131 B5
Frunze *see* Bishkek
Fu-chien *see* Fujian
Fuerte Olimpo Paraguay 44 B1
Fuerteventura *island* Spain 52 A3
Fuhkien *see* Fujian
Fujian *province* China *var.* Fu-chien, Fuhkien, Fukien, Min 111 D6
Fukien *see* Fujian
Fukui Japan 113 C5
Fukuoka Japan 113 A6
Fukushima Japan 112 D4
Fulda Germany 77 C5
Funafuti Atoll *capital of* Tuvalu 127 E3
Fünfkirchen *see* Pécs
Fushun China 110 D3
Furnas, Represa de *Reservoir* Brazil 45 E1
Fuxin China 110 D3
Fujian China *prev.* Linchuan 111 D6
FYR Macedonia *see* Macedonia

G

Gaalkacyo Somalia 55 E5
Gabès Tunisia 53 E2

Gabon *country* W Africa 59
Gaborone *capital of* Botswana 60 D4
Gabrovo Bulgaria 86 D2
Gadsden Alabama, USA 30 D2
Gaeta, Golfo di *sea feature* Italy 79 C5
Gafsa Tunisia 53 E2
Gagnoa Côte d'Ivoire 56 D5
Gagra Georgia 99 E1
Gairdner, Lake *lake* Australia 131 B6
Galapagos Fracture Zone *tectonic feature* Pacific Ocean 135 F3
Galapagos Islands *islands* Ecuador, Pacific Ocean *var.* Tortoise Islands, *Sp.* Archipiélago de Colón 135 G3
Galapagos Rise *undersea feature* Pacific Ocean 135 G3
Galaţi Romania 90 D4
Galesburg Illinois, USA 22 B4
Galicia *region* Spain 74 C1
Galilee, Sea of *see* Tiberias, Lake
Galle Sri Lanka 115 E4
Gallego Rise *undersea feature* Pacific Ocean 135 F3
Gallipoli Italy 79 E5
Gällivare Sweden 66 D3
Gallup New Mexico, USA 28 C2
Galveston Texas, USA 29 G4
Galway Ireland 71 A5
Gambia, The *country* W Africa 56
Gambia *River* Africa 56 C3
Gambier, Îles *island group* French Polynesia 135 E4
Gan *see* Gansu
Gan *see* Jiangxi
Gäncä Azerbaijan *Rus.* Gyandzha, *prev.* Kirovabad, Yelisavetpol 99 G2
Gand *see* Gent
Gander Canada 21 H3
Gāndhīdhām India 116 B4
Gandia Spain 75 F3
Ganges *river* S Asia 116 F4

Ganges Fan *Undersea feature* Bay of Bengal 122 D3
Ganges, Mouths of the *wetlands* Bangladesh/India 117 G4
Gangtok India 117 G3
Gansu *province* China *var.* Gan, Kansu 111 B5
Gao Mali 57 E3
Gaoual Guinea 56 C4
Gaoxiong *see* Kaohsiung
Gar China *var.* Shiquanhe 108 A4
Garagum Kanaly *canal* Turkmenistan *prev.* Karakumskiy Kanal 104 C3
Garagum *desert* Turkmenistan *var.* Kara Kum, Karakumy 104 C2
Garda, Lago di *lake* Italy 78 B2
Gardēz Afghanistan *prev.* Gardiz 105 E4
Gardīz *see* Gardēz
Garissa Kenya 55 C6
Garmo Peak *see* Communism Peak
Garonne *river* France 73 B5
Garoowe Somalia 55 E5
Garoua Cameroon 58 B4
Gary Indiana, USA 22 B3
Gaspé Canada 21 F4
Gastonia North Carolina, USA 31 E1
Gävle Sweden 67 C5
Gaya India 117 F4
Gaza Gaza Strip 101 A6
Gazandzhyk *see* Bereket
Gazanjyk *see* Bereket
Gaza Strip *disputed territory* SW Asia 101 A6
Gaziantep Turkey *prev.* Aintab 98 D4
Gazimağusa Cyprus *var.* Famagusta *Gk.* Ammochostos 98 C5
Gdańsk Poland *Ger.* Danzig 80 C2
Gdańsk, Gulf of *Gulf var.* Danzig, Gulf of Poland 80 C2
Gdingen *see* Gdynia
Gdynia Poland *Ger.* Gdingen 80 C2

Grand Canyon *valley* SW USA 28 B1

Grande, Rio *river* Brazil 45 E1

Grande, Rio *River* Mexico/ USA 17 B6

Grande Comore *island* Comoros 61 F2

Grande Prairie Canada 19 E4

Grand Erg Occidental *desert region* Algeria 52 D2

Grand Erg Oriental *desert region* Algeria/Tunisia 53 E3

Grand Falls Canada 21 G3

Grand Forks North Dakota, USA 25 E1

Grand Junction Colorado, USA 24 C4

Grand Rapids Michigan, USA 22 C3

Graudenz *see* Grudziądz

Graz Austria 77 E7

Great Abaco *island* The Bahamas 36 C1

Great Ararat *see* Ararat, Mount

Great Australian Bight *sea feature* Australia 129 D6

Great Barrier Island *island* N NZ 132 D2

Great Barrier Reef *coral reef* Coral Sea 130 C4

Great Basin *region* USA 26 D4

Great Bear Lake *lake* Canada 19 E3

Great Dividing Range *mountain range* Australia 130-131

Great Exhibition Bay *inlet* New Zealand 132 C1

Great Wall of China *ancient monument* China 110 C4

Greater Antilles *island group* West Indies 36 C3

Great Exuma Island *island* The Bahamas 36 C2

Great Falls Montana, USA 24 B1

Great Hungarian Plain *plain* SE Europe *Hung.* Alföld 81 D7

Great Inagua *island* The Bahamas 36 D2

Great Khingan Range *see* Da Hinggan Ling

Great Lakes, The *lakes* N America *see* Erie, Huron, Michigan, Ontario, Superior 17 C5

Great Nicobar *island* India 115 H3

Great Plain of China *region* China 106 E2

Great Plains *region* N America 16-17 C5

Great Rift Valley *valley* E Africa/SW Asia 55 C6

Great Salt Desert *see* Kavīr, Dasht-e

Great Salt Lake *salt lake* Utah, USA 24 B3

Great Sand Sea *desert region* Egypt/Libya 53 H3

Great Sandy Desert *desert* Australia 128 C4

Great Sandy Desert *see* Ar Rubʿ al Khali

Great Slave Lake *lake* Canada 19 E4

Great Victoria Desert *desert* Australia 129 C5

Greece *country* SE Europe 86-87

Green Bay Wisconsin, USA 22 B2

Greenland *self-governing territory* Denmark, Atlantic Ocean *var.* Grønland 64

Greenland Sea Atlantic Ocean 65 F2

Greenock Scotland, UK 70 C4

Greensboro North Carolina, USA 31 F1

Greenville South Carolina, USA 31 E2

Greifswald Germany 76 D2

Gregory Range *mountain range* Australia 130 C3

Grenada *country* West Indies 37 G5

Grenoble France 73 D5

Greymouth New Zealand 133 B5

Grey Range *mountain range* Australia 124 B4

Grimsby England, UK 71 E5

Grodno *see* Hrodna/Grodno

Groningen Netherlands 68 E1

Grønland *see* Greenland

Groote Eylandt *island* Australia 130 B2

Grootfontein Namibia 60 C3

Grosseto Italy 78 B4

Grosskanizsa *see* Nagykanizsa

Groznyy Russia 93 B7 96 A4

Grudziądz Poland *Ger.* Graudenz 80 C3

Grünberg in Schlesien *see* Zielona Góra

Guadalajara Mexico 32 D4

Guadalcanal Solomon Islands 124 C3

Guadalquivir *river* Spain 74 D4

Guadeloupe *overseas department* France, West Indies 37 G4

Guadiana *river* Portugal/Spain 74 C4

Gualeguaychú Argentina 46 D4

Guam *unincorporated territory* USA, Pacific Ocean 126 B1

Guanare Venezuela 40 D1

Guanare *river* Venezuela 40 D2

Guangdong *province* China *var.* Kuang-tung, Kwangtung, Yue 111 C6

Guangxi *autonomous region* China *var.* Kwangsi 111 B6

Guangzhou China *Eng.* Canton 111 C6

Guantánamo Cuba 36 D3

Guaporé *River* Bolivia/Brazil 32 D3

Guarapuava Brazil 44 D3

Guatemala *country* Central America 34

Guatemala Basin *undersea feature* Pacific Ocean 135 G3

Guatemala City *capital of* Guatemala 34 B2

Guaviare *river* Colombia 40 D3

Guayaquil Ecuador 40 A4

Guayaquil, Golfo do *sea feature* Ecuador/Peru 40 A5

Guernsey *British Crown Dependency* Channel Islands 71 D8

Güney Dogu Toroslar *mountain range* SE Turkey 99 F3

Guiana Highlands *upland* N South America 38 C2

Havana *capital of* Cuba *Sp.* La Habana 36 B2
Havelock North Carolina, USA 31 G1
Havre Montana, USA 24 C1
Havre-Saint-Pierre Canada 21 F3
Hawaii *state* USA 135 E2
Hawaiian Islands *islands* USA 125 F1
Hawaiian Ridge *undersea feature* Pacific Ocean 134 D2
Hawera New Zealand 132 D4
Hawke Bay *bay* New Zealand 132 E4
Hawlēr *see* Arbīl
Hawthorne Nevada, USA 27 C6
Hay River Canada 19 E4
Hays Kansas, USA 25 E4
Hazar Turkmenistan *prev.* Cheleken 104 A2
Heard & McDonald Islands *islands* Indian Ocean 123 C7
Hebei *province* China *var.* Hopeh, Hopei, Ji; *prev.* Chihli 110 C4
Hebron West Bank *var.* Al Khalīl, El Khalil, *Heb.* Ḥevron 101 D7
Heerenveen Netherlands 68 D2
Heerlen Netherlands 69 D6
Hefa Israel *prev.* Haifa 101 A5
Hefei China 111 D5
Hei *see* Heilongjiang
Heidelberg Germany 77 B5
Heilbronn Germany 77 B5
Heilongjiang *province* China *var.* Hei, Hei-lung-chiang 110 E3
Hei-lung-chiang *see* Heilongjiang
Helena Montana, USA 24 B2
Hells Canyon *valley* Idaho/ Oregon USA 26 C3
Helmand *river* Afghanistan 104 C5
Helmond Netherlands 69 D5
Helsingborg Sweden 67 B7
Helsinki *capital of* Finland 67 D6
Henan *province* China *var.* Honan, Yu 111 C5

Hengduan Shan *mountain range* China 111 A6
Hengelo Netherlands 68 E3
Hengyang China 111 C6
Henzada *see* Hinthada
Herāt Afghanistan 104 C4
Hermansverk Norway 67 A5
Hermosillo Mexico 32 B2
Herning Denmark 67 A7
Heywood Islands *island group* Australia 128 C3
Hiiumaa *island* Estonia *Ger.* Dagden, *Swed.* Dagö 88 C2
Hildesheim Germany 76 C4
Hilversum Netherlands 68 C3
Himalayas *mountain range* S Asia 106 B2
Himora Ethiopia 54 C4
Ḥimṣ Syria *var.* Homs 100 B3
Hinchinbrook Island *island* Australia 130 D3
Hindu Kush *mountain range* C Asia 105 E4
Hinthada Myanmar *prev.* Henzada 118 A4
Hiroshima Japan 113 B5
Hitachi Japan 112 D4
Hjørring Denmark 67 A7
Hlybokaye Belarus *Rus.* Glubokoye 89 D5
Hobart Tasmania 131 C8
Hobbs New Mexico, USA 29 E3
Hô Chi Minh Vietnam *var.* Ho Chi Minh City, *prev.* Saigon 119 E6
Ho Chi Minh City *see* Hô Chi Minh
Hodeida *see* Al Ḥudaydah
Hoek van Holland Netherlands 68 B4
Hoggar *see* Ahaggar
Hohe Tauern *mountain range* Austria 77 C7
Hohhot China 109 F3
Hokitika New Zealand 133 B5
Hokkaidō *island* Japan 112 D2
Holguín Cuba 36 C2
Holland *see* Netherlands
Hollabrunn Austria 77 E6
Holon Israel 101 A5

Holyhead Wales, UK 71 C5
Hombori Mopti, Mali 57 E3
Homs *see* Ḥimṣ
Homyel'/Gomel' Belarus *Rus.* Gomel' 89 E7
Honan *see* Henan
Honduras *country* Central America 34-35
Honduras, Gulf of *sea feature* Caribbean Sea 34 C2
Honefoss Norway 67 B6
Hông Gai *see* Ha Long
Hong Kong *special administrative region* China, E Asia 111 C6
Honiara *capital of* Solomon Islands 126 C3
Honshū *island* Japan 1 12 D3
Hoorn Netherlands 68 C2
Hopa Turkey 99 F2
Hopedale Canada 21 F2
Hopeh *see* Hebei
Hopei *see* Hebei
Hopkinsville Kentucky, USA 22 B5
Horki Belarus *Rus.* Gorki 89 E5
Horlivka Ukraine *Rus.* Gorlovka 90 G3
Horn, Cape *see* Hornos, Cabo
Hornos, Cabo *Eng* Cape Horn *coastal feature* Chile 47 C8
Horsham Australia 131 C7
Hospitalet *see* L'Hospitalet de Llobregat
Hot Springs Arkansas, USA 30 B2
Houston Texas, USA 29 G4
Hovd Mongolia 108 C2
Hövsgöl Nuur *lake* Mongolia 108 D1
Hpa-An Myanmar 118 B4
Hradec Králové Czech Republic (Czechia) *Ger.* Königgrätz 81 B5
Hrodna/Grodno Belarus *Rus.* Grodno 89 B5
Huacho Peru 42 A3
Huainan China 111 D5
Huambo Angola 60 B2
Huancayo Peru 42 B3

Ionian Sea Mediterranean Sea 87 A6

Íos island Greece 87 D6

Iowa state USA 25 F3

Ipoh Malaysia 120 B3

Ipswich England, UK 71 E6

Iqaluit Canada prev. Frobisher Bay 19 H3

Iquique Chile 46 B1

Iquitos Peru 42 B2

Irákleio Greece 87 D7

Iran country SW Asia 102-103

Iranian Plateau upland Iran 102 D4

Iraq country SW Asia 102

Irbid Jordan 101 B5

Ireland country W Europe 70-71

Irian Jaya see Papua

Irish Sea British Isles 71 C5

Irkutsk Russia 97 E4

Iron Mountain Michigan, USA 22 B2

Ironwood Michigan, USA 22 B1

Irrawaddy see Ayeyarwady

Irrawaddy, Mouths of the wetlands Myanmar 118 A4

Irtysh River Asia 94 C3

Iruña see Pamplona/Iruña

Ishim River Kazakhstan/Russia 94 C3

Isiro Dem. Rep. Congo 59 E5

İskenderun Turkey Eng. Alexandretta 98 D4

Iskür river Bulgaria 86 C1

Iskür, Yazovir Reservoir Bulgaria 86 C2

Islay island Scotland, UK 70 B4

Islamabad capital of Pakistan 116 C1

Ismaila see Al Ismā'īlīya

Isnā Egypt 54 B2

Isparta Turkey 98 B4

Israel country SW Asia 100-101

Issyk-Kul, Ozero lake Kyrgyzstan 105 G2

İstanbul Turkey var. Stambul, prev. Constantinople, Byzantium, Bul. Tsarigrad 98 B2

İstanbul Boğazı see Bosporus

Itabuna Brazil 43 G4

Itagüí Colombia 40 B2

Italy country S Europe 78-79

Ittoqqortoormiit Greenland 65 E3

Iturup island Japan/Russia (disputed) 112 E1

Ivanhoe Australia 131 C6

Ivano-Frankivs'k Ukraine 90 C2

Ivanovo Russia 92 B4

Ivittuut Greenland 64 B4

Ivory Coast see Côte d'Ivoire

Ivujivik Canada 20 D1

Iwaki Japan 112 D4

Izabal, Lago de lake Guatemala 34 C2

Izhevsk Russia 93 C5 96 B3

İzmir Turkey prev. Smyrna 98 A3

İzmit Turkey var. Kocaeli 98 B2

Izu-shotō island group Japan 113 D6

J

Jabal ash Shifā desert Saudi Arabia 102 A4

Jabalpur India 116 E4

Jackson Mississippi, USA 30 C2

Jacksonville Florida, USA 31 E3

Jacksonville Texas, USA 29 G3

Jacmel Haiti 36 D3

Jaén Spain 75 E4

Jaffna Sri Lanka 115 E3

Jagdaqi China 109 G1

Jiangxi province China 111 C6

Jaipur India 116 D3

Jajce Bosnia & Herzegovina 82 C4

Jakarta capital of Indonesia 120 C5

Jakobstad Finland 66 D4

Jakobstad see Jēkabpils

Jalālābād Afghanistan 105 E4

Jalal-Abad see Dzhalal-Abad

Jalandhar India 116 D2

Jalapa see Xalapa

Jamaame Somalia 55 D6

Jamaica country West Indies 36

Jamālpur Bangladesh 117 G4

Jambi Indonesia 120 B4

James Bay sea feature Canada 20 C4

Jammu & Kashmir disputed region India/Pakistan 116 D2

Jāmnagar India 116 B4

Jan Mayen external territory Norway, Arctic Ocean 65 F3

Japan country E Asia 112-113

Japan, Sea of Pacific Ocean 112 B3

Jarvis Island unincorporated territory USA, Pacific Ocean 125 F2

Java see Jawa

Java Sea Pacific Ocean var. Laut Jawa 122 D4

Java Trench undersea feature Indian Ocean 122 D4

Jawa island Indonesia var. Java 120 C5

Jawa, Laut see Java Sea

Jayapura Indonesia 121 H4

Jāzān Saudi Arabia 103 B6

Jaz Mūrīān, Hāmūn-e lake Iran 102 E4

Jedda see Jiddah

Jefferson City Missouri, USA 25 G4

Jeju-do island South Korea prev. Cheju-do 111 E5

Jeju Strait sea feature South Korea prev. Cheju Strait 111 E5

Jēkabpils Latvia Ger. Jakobstadt 88 C4

Jelgava Latvia Ger. Mitau 88 C3

Jember Indonesia 120 D5

Jena Germany 76 C4

Jenīn West Bank var. Janīn, Jinīn; anc. Engannim. West Bank 101 D6

Jérémie Haiti 36 D3

Jerevan see Yerevan

Jericho West Bank 101 B5

Jerid, Chott el salt lake Africa 84 D4

Jersey British Crown Dependency Channel Islands 71 D8

Jerusalem *capital of* Israel *(not internationally recognized)* 101 B5

Jhelum Pakistan 116 C2

Ji *see* Hebei

Ji *see* Jilin

Jiangsu *province* China *var.* Chiang-su, Kiangsu, Su 111 D5

Jiangxi *province* China *var.* Chiang-hsi, Gan, Kiangsi 111 C6

Jiaxing Zhejiang, China 111 D5

Jibuti *see* Djibouti

Jiddah Saudi Arabia *Eng.* Jedda 103 A5

Jiftlik Post West Bank 101 D7

Jihlava Czech Republic (Czechia) *Ger.* Iglau 81 B5

Jilin *province* China *var.* Chi-lin, Girin, Ji, Kirin 110 E3

Jilin China 110 E3

Jīma Ethiopia 55 C5

Jin *see* Shanxi

Jinan China 111 C4

Jingdezhen China 111 D5

Jinhua China 111 D5

Jining *see* Ulan Qab

Jinotega Nicaragua 34 D3

Jinsha Jiang *river* China 108 C3

Jinzhou China 110 D4

João Pessoa Brazil 43 H3

Jodhpur India 116 C3

Joensuu Finland 67 E5

Johannesburg South Africa 60 D4

Johnston Atoll *US unincorporated territory* Pacific Ocean 125 E1

Johor Bahru Malaysia 120 C3

Joinville Brazil 44 D3

Joliet Illinois, USA 22 B3

Jönköping Sweden 67 B7

Jonquière Canada 21 E4

Jordan *country* SW Asia 100-101

Jordan *river* SW Asia 101 B5

Joseph Bonaparte Gulf *gulf* Australia 128 D2

Jos Plateau *upland* Nigeria 57 G4

Juan Fernandez, Islas *islands* Chile 46 A4

Juàzeiro Brazil 43 G3

Juàzeiro do Norte Brazil 43 G3

Juba *capital of* South Sudan 55 B5

Júcar *river* Spain 75 E3

Judenburg Austria 77 D7

Juigalpa Nicaragua 34 D3

Juiz de Fora Brazil 43 G5 45 F2

Juneau Alaska, USA 18 D4

Junggar Pendi *desert* China 108 C2

Junín Argentina 46 D4

Jura *mountains* France/ Switzerland 77 A7

Jura *island* Scotland, UK 70 B4

Jurbarkas Lithuania *Ger.* Jurburg, *var.* Georgenburg 88 B4

Jurburg *see* Jurbarkas

Juruá *river* Brazil/Peru 42 C2

Juticalpa Honduras 34 D2

Jutland *see* Jylland

Juventud, Isla de la *island* Cuba 36 B2

Jylland *peninsula* Denmark *Eng.* Jutland 67 A7

Jyväskylä Finland 67 D5

K

K2 *peak* China/Pakistan *Eng.* Mount Godwin Austen 116 D1

Kaachka *see* Kaka

Kaakhka *see* Kaka

Kabale Uganda 55 B6

Kabinda Dem. Rep. Congo 59 D7

Kābol *see* Kabul

Kabul *capital of* Afghanistan *Per.* Kabol 105 E4

Kachch, Gulf of *sea feature* Arabian Sea 116 B4

Kachch, Rann of *wetland* India/ Pakistan *var.* Rann of Kutch 116 B4

Kadugli Sudan 54 B4

Kaduna Nigeria 57 G4

Kaédi Mauritania 56 C3

Kâghet *Physical region* Mauritania 56 D1

Kagoshima Japan 113 A6

Kahramanmaraş Turkey *var.* Marash, Maraş 98 D4

Kai, Kepulauan *island group* Indonesia 121 G4

Kaifeng China 111 C5

Kaikohe New Zealand 132 C2

Kaikoura New Zealand 133 C5

Kainji Reservoir *Reservoir* Nigeria 57 F4

Kairouan Tunisia 53 E1

Kaiserslautern Germany 77 B5

Kaitaia New Zealand 132 C2

Kajaani Finland 66 E4

Kaka Turkmenistan *prev.* Kaakhka, *var.* Kaachka 104 C3

Kakhovka Ukraine 91 F4

Kakhovs'ka Vodoskhovyshche *Reservoir* Ukraine 91 F3

Kalahari Desert *desert* southern Africa 60 C4

Kalamariá Greece 86 C3

Kalámata Greece 87 B6

Kalât *see* Qalât

Kalbarri Australia 129 A5

Kalemie Dem. Rep. Congo 59 E7

Kalgoorlie Australia 129 C6

Kalimantan *geopolitical region* Indonesia *Eng.* Indonesian Borneo 120 D4

Kaliningrad *external territory* Russia 96 A2

Kaliningrad Kaliningrad, Russia *prev.* Königsberg 88 A4

Kalinkavichy Belarus *Rus.* Kalinkovichi 89 D7

Kalinkovichi *see* Kalinkavichy

Kalisch *see* Kalisz

Kalispell Montana, USA 24 B1

Kalisz Poland *Ger.* Kalisch 80 C4

Kalmar Sweden 67 C7

Kalpeni Island *island* India 114 C3

Kama *river* Russia 92 D4

Kamchatka *peninsula* Russia 97 H3

Kamchiya *river* Bulgaria 86 E2

Kamina Dem. Rep. Congo 59 D7

Kamishli see Al Qāmishlī

Kamloops Canada 19 E5

Kampala capital of Uganda 55 B6

Kâmpóng Cham see Kampong Cham

Kampong Cham Cambodia var. Kâmpóng Cham 119 D6

Kâmpóng Chhnăng see Kampong Chhnang

Kampong Chhnang Cambodia var. Kâmpóng Chhnăng 119 D5

Kâmpôt see Kampot

Kampot Cambodia var. Kâmpôt 119 D6

Kampuchea see Cambodia

Kam"yanets'-Podil's'kyy Ukraine 90 C3

Kananga Dem. Rep. Congo 59 D7

Kanazawa Japan 112 C4

Kandahār Afghanistan var. Qandahār 104 D5

Kandi Benin 57 F4

Kanivs'ke Vodoskhovyshche Reservoir Ukraine 91 E2

Kandy Sri Lanka 115 E3

Kanestron, Ákra see Palioúri, Akrotírio

Kangaroo Island island Australia 131 B7

Kangertittivaq region Greenland 64 E3

Kangikajik headland Greenland 65 E4

Kanjiža Serbia 82 D2

Kankan Guinea 56 D4

Kano Nigeria 57 G4

Kānpur India prev. Cawnpore 117 E3

Kansas state USA 24-25

Kansas City Kansas, USA 25 F4

Kansas City Missouri, USA 25 F4

Kansk Russia 97 E4

Kansu see Gansu

Kaohsiung Taiwan var. Gaoxiong 111 D7

Kaolack Senegal 56 B3

Kapfenberg Austria 77 E7

Kaposvár Hungary 81 C7

Kapsukas see Marijampolė

Kapuas river Indonesia 120 D4

Kara-Balta Kyrgyzstan 105 F2

Karabük Turkey 98 C2

Karachi Pakistan 116 B4

Karaganda see Karagandy

Karagandy Kazakhstan prev. Karaganda 96 C4

Karakol Kyrgyzstan prev. Przheval'sk 105 G2

Kara Kum see Garagum

Karakumskiy Kanal see Garagum Kanaly

Karakumy see Garagum

Karamay China 108 C2

Karamea Bight gulf New Zealand 133 C5

Karasburg Namibia 60 C4

Kara Sea see Karskoye More

Karditsa Greece 86 B4

Kariba, Lake lake Zambia/ Zimbabwe 60 D3

Karimata, Selat strait Indonesia 120 C4

Karkinits'ka Zatoka sea feature Black Sea 91 E4

Karl-Marx-Stadt see Chemnitz

Karlovac Croatia 82 B3

Karlovy Vary Czech Republic (Czechia) Ger. Karlsbad 81 A5

Karlsbad see Karlovy Vary

Karlskrona Sweden 67 C7

Karlsruhe Germany 77 B5

Karlstad Sweden 67 B6

Karnātaka state India 114 D1

Kárpathos island Greece 87 E7

Kars Turkey 99 F2

Karshi Uzbekistan prev. Bek-Budi, Uzb. Qarshi 104 D3

Karskoye More Arctic Ocean Eng. Kara Sea 137 H3

Kasai river Dem. Rep. Congo 59 C6

Kasama Zambia 61 E2

Kaschau see Košice

Kāshān Iran 102 C3

Kashi China 108 A3

Kasongo Dem. Rep. Congo 59 E6

Kassa see Košice

Kassala Sudan 54 C4

Kassel Germany 76 B4

Kastamonu Turkey 98 C2

Katanning Australia 129 B6

Katerini Greece 86 B4

Katha Myanmar 118 B2

Katherine Australia 128 E2

Kathmandu capital of Nepal 117 F3

Katsina Nigeria 57 G3

Katowice Poland 81 C5

Kauen see Kaunas

Kaunas Lithuania Ger. Kauen, Pol. Kowno, Rus. Kovno 88 B4

Kavadarci Macedonia 82 E5

Kavála Greece 86 C3

Kavaratti Island island India 114 C3

Kavīr, Dasht-e Salt pan Iran 102 C3

Kawasaki Japan 113 D5

Kayan river Indonesia 120 D3

Kayes Mali 56 C3

Kayseri Turkey 98 D3

Kazakhstan country C Asia 96

Kazan' Russia 96 B3

Kazandzhik see Bereket

Kazanlŭk Bulgaria 86 D2

Kecskemét Hungary 81 D7

Kediri Indonesia 121 E4

Keetmanshoop Namibia 60 C4

Kefalloniá island Greece Eng. Cephalonia 87 A5

Keá see Tziá

Kelang see Klang

Kelmė Lithuania 88 B4

Kelowna Canada 19 E5

Kemerovo Russia 96 D4

Kemi Finland 66 D4

Kemi river Finland 66 D3

Kemijärvi Finland 66 D3

Kendari Indonesia 121 E4

Këneurgench see Köneürgench

Kénitra Morocco 52 C2

Kennewick Washington, USA 26 C2

Kenora Canada 20 A3

Kentucky state USA 22 C5

Kenya country E Africa 55

Kerala *state* India 114 D3

Kerch Ukraine 91 G4

Kerguelen *island group* Indian Ocean 123 C7

Kerguelen Plateau *undersea feature* Indian Ocean 123 C7

Kerki *see* Atamyrat

Kérkira *see* Kérkyra

Kérkyra Greece 86 A4

Kérkyra *island* Greece *prev.* Kérkira, *Eng.* Corfu 86 A4

Kermadec Islands *island group* Pacific Ocean 125 E4

Kermadec Trench *undersea feature* Pacific Ocean 125 E4

Kermān Iran *var.* Kirman 102 D4

Kermānshāh Iran *prev.* Bākhtarān 102 C3

Kerulen *river* China/Mongolia 109 E2

Kerýneia *see* Girne

Ketchikan Alaska, USA 18 D4

Key West Florida, USA 31 E5

Khabarovsk Russia 97 G4

Khanka, Lake *lake* China/Russia 110 E3

Khankendy *see* Xankändi

Kharga *see* Al Khārijah

Kharkiv Ukraine *Rus.* Khar'kov 91 G2

Khar'kov *see* Kharkiv

Khartoum *capital of* Sudan *var.* Al Khurtūm 54 B4

Khāsh Iran 102 E4

Khaskovo Bulgaria 86 D2

Khaydarkan Kyrgyzstan *var.* Khaydarken, Hajdarken 105 E2

Khaydarken *see* Khaydarkan

Kherson Ukraine 91 E4

Kheta *river* Russia 94 D2

Khíos *see* Chios

Khirbet el 'Aujā et Tahtā West Bank 101 D6

Khmel 'nyts'kyy Ukraine 90 D2

Khodzhent *see* Khŭjand

Khoi *see* Khūjand

Khokand *see* Qo'qon

Kholm *see* Khulm

Khon Kaen Thailand 118 C4

Khorog *see* Khorugh

Khorugh Tajikistan *Rus.* Khorog 105 F3

Khouribga Morocco 52 C2

Khrustal'nyy Ukraine *prev.* Krasnyy Luch 91 H3

Khudzhand *see* Khŭjand

Khŭjand Tajikistan *var.* Khodzheut, Khojend, *Rus.* Khudzhand *prev.* Leninabad 105 E2

Khulna Bangladesh 117 G4

Khulm Afghanistan *prev.* Kholm 105 E3

Khvoy Iran 102 B3

Kiangsi *see* Jiangxi

Kiangsu *see* Jiangsu

Kičevo Macedonia 83 D5

Kiel Germany 76 C2

Kielce Poland 80 D4

Kiev *see* Kyiv

Kiffa Mauritania 56 C3

Kigali *capital of* Rwanda 55 B6

Kigoma Tanzania 55 B7

Kikládhes *see* Kyklades

Kikwit Dem. Rep. Congo 59 C6

Kilimanjaro *peak* Tanzania 55 C7

Kilkis Greece 86 B3

Killarney Ireland 71 A6

Kimberley South Africa 60 D4

Kimberley Plateau *upland* Australia 128 D3

Kindia Guinea 56 C4

Kindu Dem. Rep. Congo 59 D6

King Island *island* Australia 131 C7

Kingisepp *see* Kuressaare

Kingman Reef *unincorporated territory* USA, Pacific Ocean 125 F2

King Sound *sound* Australia 128 C3

Kingsport Tennessee, USA 31 E1

Kingsville Texas, USA 29 G5

Kingston Canada 20 C5

Kingston *capital of* Jamaica 36 C3

Kingston upon Hull England, UK *var.* Hull 71 E5

Kingstown St Vincent & The Grenadines 36 G4

King William Island *island* Canada 19 F3

Kinneret, Yam *see* Tiberius, Lake

Kinshasa *capital of* Dem. Rep. Congo *prev.* Léopoldville 59 B6

Kirghizia *see* Kyrgyzstan

Kiribati *country* Pacific Ocean 127

Kirin *see* Jilin

Kiritimati *island* Kiribati *prev.* Christmas Island 127 G2

Kirkenes Norway 66 E2

Kirklareli Turkey 98 A2

Kirksville Missouri, USA 25 F4

Kirkūk Iraq 102 B3

Kirkwall Scotland, UK 70 C2

Kirman *see* Kermān

Kirov Russia 92 C4 96 B3

Kirovabad *see* Gäncä

Kirovakan *see* Vanadzor

Kirovohrad *see* Kropyvnyts'kyy

Kiruna Sweden 66 C3

Kisangani Dem. Rep. Congo *prev.* Stanleyville 59 D5

Kishinev *see* Chişinău

Kismaayo Somalia 55 D6

Kisumu Kenya 55 C6

Kitakyūshū Japan 113 A5

Kitami Japan 112 D2

Kitchener Canada 20 C5

Kitwe Zambia 60 D2

Kivu, Lake *lake* Rwanda/Dem. Rep. Congo 55 B6 59 E6

Kızıl Irmak *river* Turkey 98 C2

Kizyl-Arvat *see* Serdar

Kladno Czech Republic (Czechia) 81 A5

Klagenfurt Austria 77 D7

Klaipėda Lithuania *Ger.* Memel 88 B4

Klamath Falls Oregon, USA 26 B4

Khang Malaysia *var.* Kelang 120 B2

Ključ Bosnia & Herzegovina 82 B3

Knin Croatia 82 B4

Knoxville Tennessee, USA
31 E1
Knud Rasmussen Land *region*
Greenland 64 D1
Kōbe Japan 113 C5
Koblenz Germany 77 B5
Kobrin *see* Kobryn/Kobrin
Kobryn *see* Kobryn/Kobrin
Kobryn/Kobrin Belarus *Bel.*
Kobryn, *Rus.* Kobrin 89 B6
Kocaeli *see* İzmit
Kočani Macedonia 83 E5
Kōchi Japan 113 B6
Kochi India *prev.* Cochin
114 D3
Kodiak Alaska, USA 18 C3
Kodiak Island *island* Alaska,
USA 18 C3
Koedoes *see* Kudus
Kohīma India 117 H3
Kohtla-Järve Estonia 88 D2
Kokand *see* Qo'qon
Kokchetav Kazakhstan 96 C4
Kokkola Finland 66 D4
Koko Nor *see* Qinghai
Koko Nor *see* Qinghai Hu
Kokshaal-Tau *mountain range*
Kyrgyzstan 105 G2
Kola Peninsula *see* Kol'skiy
Poluostrov
Kolguyev, Ostrov *island* Russia
92 D2
Kolhumadulu Atoll *island*
Maldives 114 C5
Kolka Latvia 88 C3
Kolkāta India *prev.* Calcutta
117 F4
Köln Germany *Eng.* Cologne
76 B4
Kol'skiy Poluostrov *peninsula*
Russia *Eng.* Kola Peninsula
63 F1 92 C2
Kolwezi Dem. Rep. Congo
59 D8
Kolyma *river* Russia 95 G2
Kommunizma, Pik *see*
Communism Peak
Komoé *river* Côte d'Ivoire 57 E4
Komotini Greece 86 D3
Komsomol'sk-na-Amure Russia
97 G4

Kondoz *see* Kunduz
Konduz *see* Kunduz
Köneürgenç Turkmenistan
prev. Kunya-Urgench,
prev. Këneurgench 104 C2
Kong Christian IX Land *region*
Greenland 64 D4
Kong Christian X Land *region*
Greenland 64 E3
Kong Frederik VI Kyst *region*
Greenland 64 C4
Kong Frederik VIII Land *region*
Greenland 64 E2
Kong Frederik IX Land *region*
Greenland 64 D3
Kong Karls Land *island group*
Svalbard 65 G2
Kong Oscar Fjord *fjord*
Greenland 65 E3
Konia *see* Konya
Königgrätz *see* Hradec Králové
Königsberg *see* Kaliningrad
Konispol Albania 83 D7
Konjic Bosnia & Herzegovina
82 C4
Konya Turkey *prev.* Konia
98 C4
Kopaonik *mountains* Serbia
83 D4
Koper Slovenia 77 D8
Koprivnica Croatia 82 B2
Korçë Albania 83 D6
Korčula *island* Croatia 82 B4
Korea Bay *bay* China/North
Korea 110 D4
Korea Strait *sea feature* Japan/
South Korea
110-111 E5
Korinthiakós Kólpos *sea
feature* Greece *Eng.* Gulf of
Corinth 87 B5
Kórinthos Greece *Eng.* Corinth
87 B5
Kōriyama Japan 113 D4
Korla China 108 C3
Korosten' Ukraine 90 D1
Kortrijk Belgium 69 A6
Kos *island* Greece 87 E6
Kosciusko, Mount *peak*
Australia 131 D7
Košice Slovakia *Ger.* Kaschau,
Hung. Kassa 81 D6

Köslin *see* Koszalin
Kosovo *country (not
internationally recognised)*
SE Europe 83 D5
Kosovska Mitrovica *see*
Mitrovicë/Mitrovica
Kosrae *island* Micronesia 126 C2
Kossou, Lac de *lake* Côte
d'Ivoire 56 D4
Kostanay Kazakhstan *var.*
Kustanay 96 C4
Kostyantynivka Ukraine 91 G3
Koszalin Poland *Ger.* Köslin
80 B2
Kota India 116 D4
Kota Bharu Malaysia 120 B3
Kota Kinabalu Malaysia 120 D3
Kotka Finland 67 E5
Kotlas NW Russia 92 C4
Kotuy *river* Russia 95 E2
Koudougou Burkina Faso 57 E4
Kourou French Guiana 41 H2
Kousséri Cameroon 58 B3
Kouvola Finland 67 E5
Kovel' Ukraine 90 C1
Kovno *see* Kaunas
Kowno *see* Kaunas
Kozáni Greece 86 B4
Kozhikode India *prev.* Calicut
114 D2
Kra, Isthmus of *coastal feature*
Myanmar/Thailand 119 B6
Kragujevac Serbia 82 D4
Krakau *see* Kraków
Kraków Poland *Eng.* Cracow,
Ger. Krakau 81 D5
Kralendijk Bonaire 37 E5
Kraljevo Serbia 82 D4
Kranj Slovenia 77 D7
Krasnodar Russia 93 A6
Krasnovodsk *see* Türkmenbaşy
Krasnoyarsk Russia 96 D4
Krasnyy Luch *see* Khrustal'nyy
Kremenchuk Ukraine 91 F2
**Kremenchuts'ke
Vodoskhovyshche** *Reservoir*
Ukraine 91 E2
Krems an der Donau Austria
77 E6
Kretinga Lithuania *Ger.*
Krottingen 88 B3

L

Levkás *see* Lefkáda
Lewis *island* Scotland, UK 70 B2
Lewiston Idaho, USA 26 C2
Lewiston Maine, USA 23 G2
Lexington Kentucky, USA 22 C5
Lezhë Albania 83 D5
Lhasa China 108 C5
Lhazê China 108 C4
L'Hospitalet de Llobregat *var.* Hospitalet. Spain 75 G2
Liao *see* Liaoning
Liaoning *province* China *var.* Liao, Shengking; *hist.* Fengtien, Shenking. Admin. region 110 D3
Libau *see* Liepāja
Liberec Czech Republic (Czechia) *Ger.* Reichenberg 80 B4
Liberia *country* W Africa 56
Liberia Costa Rica 34 D4
Libreville *capital of* Gabon 59 A5
Libya *country* N Africa 53
Libyan Desert *desert* N Africa 50 C3
Lichuan China 111 B5
Liechtenstein *country* C Europe 77 B7
Liège Belgium 69 D6
Liegnitz *see* Legnica
Lienz Austria 77 D7
Linz Austria 77 D7
Liepāja Latvia *Ger.* Libau 88 B3
Liffey *river* Ireland 71 B5
Ligurian Sea Mediterranean Sea 78 A3
Likasi Dem. Rep. Congo 59 E8
Lille France 72 D2
Lillehammer Norway 67 B5
Lilongwe *capital of* Malawi 61 E2
Lima *capital of* Peru 42 B4
Limassol *see* Lemesós
Limerick Ireland 71 A6
Limnos *island* Greece *var.* Lemnos 86 D4
Limoges France 72 C5

Limón Costa Rica 35 E4
Limpopo *river* southern Africa 60 D3
Linares Chile 46 B4
Linares Spain 75 E4
Linchuan *see* Fuzhou
Lincoln England, UK 71 D5
Lincoln Nebraska, USA 25 F4
Lincoln Sea Arctic Ocean 64 E1
Linden Guyana 41 G2
Lindi Tanzania 55 C8
Line Islands *island group* Kiribati 127 G2
Linköping Sweden 67 C6
Linz Austria 77 D6
Lion, Golfe du *sea feature* Mediterranean Sea 73 D6
Lipari, Isola *island* Italy 79 D6
Lipari Islands *see* Isole Eolie
Lira Uganda 55 B6
Lisbon *capital of* Portugal *Port.* Lisboa 74 B3
Litani *river* SW Asia 91 B4
Lithuania *country* E Europe 88–89
Little Andaman *island* India 115 G2
Little Minch *sea feature* Scotland, UK 70 B3
Little Rock Arkansas, USA 30 B2
Liuzhou China 111 C6
Liverpool England, UK 71 D5
Livingstone Zambia 60 D3
Livno Bosnia & Herzegovina 82 B4
Livorno Italy 78 B3
Ljubljana *capital of* Slovenia 77 D7
Ljusnan *river* Sweden 67 B5
Llanos *region* Colombia/Venezuela 41 E2
Lleida Spain *Cast.* Lérida 75 F2
Lobamba *royal and legislative capital of* Swaziland 61 E4
Lobatse Botswana 60 D4
Lobito Angola 60 B2
Locarno Switzerland 77 B7
Lodja Dem. Rep. Congo 59 D6
Łódź Poland *Rus.* Lodz 80 D4

Lofoten *island group* Norway 66 B3
Logroño Spain 75 E2
Loire *river* France 72 B4
Loja Ecuador 40 A5
Lokitaung Kenya 55 C5
Loksa Estonia *Ger.* Loxa 88 D2
Lombok, Pulau *island* Indonesia 120 D5
Lomé *capital of* Togo 57 E5
Lomond, Loch *lake* Scotland, UK 70 C4
London Canada 20 C5
London *capital of* UK 71 E6
Londonderry Northern Ireland, UK 70 B4
Londonderry, Cape *coastal feature* Australia 128 D2
Londrina Brazil 44 D2
Long Beach California, USA 27 C8
Long Island *island* The Bahamas 34 D2
Long Island *island* NE USA 23 G3
Longreach Australia 130 C4
Long Strait *Strait* Russia 95 H2
Longview Texas, USA 29 G3
Longview Washington, USA 26 B2
Longyearbyen Svalbard 65 F2
Lop Nur *lake* China 108 C3
Lorca Spain 75 E4
Lord Howe Island *island* Australia 124 C4
Lord Howe Rise *undersea feature* Pacific Ocean 124 D4
Lorient France 72 A4
Los Alamos New Mexico, USA 28 D1
Los Angeles California, USA 27 C7
Loslau *see* Wodzisław Śląski
Los Mochis Mexico 32 C3
Losonc *see* Lučenec
Losontz *see* Lučenec
Lot *river* France 73 B5
Louangphrabang Laos 118 C3
Loubomo Congo 59 B6
Louisiana *state* USA 30 B3
Louisville Kentucky, USA 22 C5

Louisville Ridge *undersea feature* Pacific Ocean 125 E4

Lovech Bulgaria 86 C2

Lower California *see* Baja California

Lower Hutt New Zealand

Loxa *see* Loksa

Loyauté, Îles *island group* New Caledonia 126 D5

Loznica Serbia 82 C3

Lu *see* Shandong

Luanda *capital of* Angola 60 B1

Luanshya Zambia 60 D2

Lubango Angola 60 B2

Lubbock Texas, USA 29 E2

Lübeck Germany 76 C3

Lublin Poland *Rus.* Lyublin 80 E4

Lubny Ukraine 91 F2

Lubumbashi Dem. Rep. Congo 59 E8

Lucapa Angola 60 C1

Lucena Philippines 120 E2

Lučenec Slovakia *Hung.* Losonc, *Ger.* Losontz 81 D6

Lucerne *see* Luzern

Lucknow India 117 E3

Lüderitz Namibia 60 C4

Ludhiāna India 116 D2

Lugano Switzerland 77 B7

Lugo Spain 74 C1

Luhans'k Ukraine 91 H3

Luleå Sweden 66 D4

Lumsden New Zealand 133 A7

Lüneburg Germany 76 C3

Luninets *see* Luninets/Luninets

Luninyets *see* Luninyets/Luninets

Luninyets/Luninets Belarus *Bel.* Luninyets, *Rus.* Luninets 89 C6

Luoyang *var.* Honan, Lo-yang. China 110 C4

Lusaka *capital of* Zambia 60 D2

Lushnjë Albania 83 D6

Lût, Baḥrat *see* Dead Sea

Luts'k Ukraine 90 C1

Luxembourg *country* W Europe 69 D8

Luxembourg *capital of* Luxembourg 69 D8

Luxor *see* Al Uqşur

Luzern Switzerland *Fr.* Lucerne 77 B7

Luzon *island* Philippines 121 E1

Luzon Strait *sea feature* Philippines/Taiwan 107 E3

L'viv Ukraine *Rus.* L'vov 90 C2

L'vov *see* L'viv

Lyepyel' Belarus *Rus.* Lepel' 89 D5

Lyon France 73 D5

Lyublin *see* Lublin

M

Maale *see* Male

Ma'ān Jordan 101 B6

Maas *see* Meuse

Maastricht Netherlands 69 D6

Macao *special administrative region* China, E Asia *var.* Macau 111 C7

Macapá Brazil 43 F1

Macau *see* Macao

Macdonnell Ranges *mountains* Australia 130 A4

Macedonia *country* SE Europe officially Former Yugoslav Republic of Macedonia, *abbrev.* FYR Macedonia 83

Maceió Brazil 43 H3

Machala Ecuador 40 A5

Mackay Australia 130 D4

Mackay, Lake *lake* Australia 128 D4

Mackenzie *river* Canada 19 E4

Mackenzie Bay *sea feature* Atlantic Ocean 136 D3

Macleod, Lake *lake* Australia 128 A4

Mâcon France 72 D5

Macon Georgia, USA 31 E2

Madagascar *country* Indian Ocean 61

Madagascar Basin *undersea feature* Indian Ocean 123 B5

Madagascar Plateau *undersea feature* Indian Ocean 123 A6

Madang Papua New Guinea 126 B3

Madeira *river* Bolivia/Brazil 42 D2

Madeira *island group* Portugal 52 A2

Madhya Pradesh *state* India 117 E4

Madison Wisconsin, USA 22 B3

Madiun *prev.* Madioen. Indonesia 120 D5

Madona Latvia *Ger.* Modohn 88 D3

Madras *see* Chennai

Madre de Dios *river* Bolivia/Peru 42 C3

Madrid *capital of* Spain 75 E3

Madurai India 114 D3

Magadan Russian Fed. 97 G3

Magallanes *see* Punta Arenas

Magallanes, Estrecho de *see* Magellan, Strait of

Magdalena *river* Colombia 40 B2

Magdeburg Germany 76 C4

Magelang Indonesia 120 C5

Magellan, Strait of *sea feature* S South America *Sp.* Estrecho de Magallanes 47 B8

Maggiore, Lake *lake* Italy/Switzerland 78 B2

Mahajanga Madagascar 61 G3

Mahalapye Botswana 60 D4

Mahanādi *river* India 117 F5

Mahārashtra *state* India 116 D5

Mahé *island* Seychelles 61 H1

Mahilyow *see* Mahilyow/Mogilëv

Mahilyow/Mogilëv Belarus *Bel.* Mahilyow, *Rus.* Mogilëv 89 E6

Mährisch-Ostrava *see* Ostrava

Maicao Colombia 40 C1

Maiduguri Nigeria 57 H4

Maïmanah Afghanistan *prev.* Meymaneh 104 D4

Maine *state* USA 23 G1

Maine, Gulf of *gulf* USA 23 G2

Mainz Germany 77 B5
Maio *Island* Cape Verde 56 A3
Maíz, Islas del *islands* Nicaragua 35 E3
Majorca *see* Mallorca
Majuro Atoll *capital of* Marshall Islands *island* Marshall Islands 126 D1
Makarska Croatia 82 B4
Makarov Basin *undersea feature* Arctic Ocean 137 G3
Makassar Indonesia *prev.* Ujungpandang 121 E4
Makassar Strait *strait* Indonesia 120 D4
Makeyevka *see* Makiyivka
Makhachkala Russia 93 B7 96 A4
Makiyivka Ukraine *Rus.* Makeyevka 91 G5
Makkah Saudi Arabia *Eng.* Mecca 103 A5
Makkovik Canada 21 F2
Malabo *capital of* Equatorial Guinea 59 A5
Malacca, Strait of *sea feature* Indonesia/ Malaysia 106 C4 119 C8 120 B3
Maladzyechna Belarus *Rus.* Molodechno, *Pol.* Molodeczno 89 C5
Málaga Spain 74 D5
Malakal South Sudan 55 B5
Malang Indonesia 120 D5
Malanje Angola 60 C2
Malatya Turkey 99 E3
Malawi *country* southern Africa 61
Malay Peninsula *peninsula* Malaysia/Thailand 119 D8
Malaysia *country* Asia 120
Malden Island *atoll* Kiribati 125 F2
Maldives *country* Indian Ocean 114 C4
Male *capital of* Maldives *var.* Maale 114 C4
Malekula *island* Vanuatu 124 D3
Mali *country* W Africa 57
Malindi Kenya 55 C7

Mallorca *island* Spain *Eng.* Majorca 75 H3
Malmö Sweden 67 B7
Malta *country* Mediterranean Sea 79 C8
Malta Montana, USA 24 C1
Malta Channel *sea feature* Mediterranean Sea 79 C7
Maluku *island group* Indonesia *var.* Moluccas 107 E4 121 F4
Maluku, Laut Pacific Ocean *Eng.* Molucca Sea 121 F4
Mamberamo *river* Indonesia 121 H4
Mamoudzou *capital of* Mayotte 61 G2
Man, Isle of *British Crown Dependency* UK 71 C5
Manado Indonesia 121 F3
Managua *capital of* Nicaragua 34 D3
Manama *capital of* Bahrain *Ar.* Al Manāmah 103 C5
Mananjary Madagascar 61 G3
Manaus Brazil 42 D2
Manchester England, UK 71 D5
Manchester New Hampshire, USA 23 G2
Manchurian Plain *plain* E Asia 107 E1
Mandalay Myanmar 118 B3
Mangalia Romania 90 D5
Mangalore *see* Mangalūru
Mangalūru India *prev.* Mangalore 114 C2
Manicouagan, Réservoir *Reservoir* Canada 21 E3
Manihiki *atoll* Cook Islands 125 F3
Maniitsoq Greenland 64 C3
Manila *capital of* Philippines 121 E1
Manisa Turkey *prev.* Saruhan 98 A3
Manitoba *province* Canada 19 G4
Manizales Colombia 40 B3
Manjimup Australia 129 B7
Mannar Sri Lanka 115 E3

Mannar, Gulf of *sea feature* Indian Ocean 114 D3
Mannheim Germany 77 B5
Manono Dem. Rep. Congo 59 E7
Mansel Island *island* Canada 20 C1
Mansfield Ohio, USA 22 D4
Manta Ecuador 40 A4
Mantes-la-Jolie France 72 C3
Mantova Italy *Eng.* Mantua 78 B2
Mantua *see* Mantova
Manurewa New Zealand 132 D3
Manzhouli China 109 F1
Mao Chad 58 B3
Maoke, Pegunungan *mountains* Indonesia 121 H4
Maputo *capital of* Mozambique 61 E4
Mar, Serra do *mountains* Brazil 38 D4
Maracaibo Venezuela 40 C1
Maracaibo, Lago de *inlet* Venezuela 40 C1
Maracay Venezuela 40 D1
Maradi Niger 57 F3
Marāgheh Iran 102 C3
Marajó, Ilha de *island* Brazil 43 F2
Marañón *river* Peru 42 B2
Maraş *see* Kahramanmaraş
Marash *see* Kahramanmaraş
Marbella Spain 74 D5
Marble Bar Australia 128 B4
Mar Chiquita, Laguna *salt lake* Argentina 46 C3
Mardan Pakistan 116 C1
Mar del Plata Argentina 47 D5
Mardin Turkey 99 E4
Margarita, Isla de *island* Venezuela 41 E1
Mārgow, Dasht-e- *desert* Afghanistan 104 C5
Mariana Trench *undersea feature* Pacific Ocean 124 B1 126 B1
Marías, Islas *islands* Mexico 32 C4
Maribor Slovenia 77 E7

Marie Byrd Land *region*
Antarctica 136 B4

Mariehamn Finland 67 D6

Marijampolė Lithuania *prev.*
Kapsukas 88 B4

Marília Brazil 44 D2

Maringá Brazil 44 D2

Marion, Lake *lake* South
Carolina, USA 31 F2

Mariscal Estigarribia Paraguay
44 B2

Maritsa *river* SE Europe 86 D3

Mariupol' Ukraine *prev.*
Shdanov 91 G3

Marka Somalia 55 D6

Marmara, Sea of *see* Marmara
Denizi

Marmara Denizi Turkey *Eng.*
Sea of Marmara 98 B2

Marne *river* France 72 D3

Marotiri *Island group* French
Polynesia 125 F4

Maroua Cameroon 58 B3

Marowijne *river* French
Guiana/Suriname 41 H3

Marquesas Fracture Zone
tectonic feature Pacific Ocean
125 G3

Marquesas Islands *island group*
French Polynesia *Fr.* Îles
Marquises 125 G3

Marquette Michigan, USA
22 B1

Marquisas, Îles *see* Marquesas
Islands

Marrakech Morocco *Eng.*
Marrakesh 52 C2

Marrawah Australia 131 C8

Marree Australia 131 B5

Marsala Italy 79 C6

Marseille France 73 D6

Marshall Islands *country* Pacific
Ocean 126-127

Martin Slovakia *prev.*
Turčiansky Svätý Martin, *Ger.*
Sankt Martin, *Hung.*
Turócszentmárton 81 C5

Martinique *overseas
department* France, West
Indies 37

Mary Turkmenistan *prev.* Merv
104 C3

Maryborough Australia 131 E5

Maryland *state* USA 23 F4

Masai Steppe *grassland*
Tanzania 55 C7

Mascarene Basin *undersea
feature* Indian Ocean 123 B5

Mascarene Islands *island group*
Indian Ocean 61 H4

Mascarene Plain *undersea
feature* Indian Ocean 123 B5

Mascarene Plateau *undersea
feature* Indian Ocean 123 B5

Maseru *capital of* Lesotho
60 D4

Mas-ha Bank 101 D6

Mashhad Iran *var.* Meshed
100 E3

Masindi Uganda 55 B6

Maşīrah, Jazīrat *Island* Oman
103 E6

Maşīrah, Khalīj *bay* Oman
103 E6

Mason City Iowa, USA 25 F3

Masqaṭ *see* Muscat

Massachusetts *state* USA
23 G3

Massawa *see* Mits'iwa

Massif Central *upland* France
73 C5

Massoukou Gabon 59 B6

Masterton New Zealand
133 D5

Matadi Dem. Rep. Congo 59 B7

Matagalpa Nicaragua 34 D3

Matamoros Mexico 33 E2

Matanzas Cuba 36 B2

Matara Sri Lanka 115 E4

Mataram Indonesia 120 D5

Mataró Spain 75 G2

Mato Grosso *upland* Brazil
43 E3

Matosinhos Portugal 74 C2

Matsue Japan 113 B5

Matsuyama Japan 113 B5

Matterhorn *peak* Italy/
Switzerland 77 B7

Maturín Venezuela 41 E1

Maun Botswana 60 D3

Mauritania *country* W Africa 56

Mauritius *country* Indian
Ocean 61 H4 123 B5

Mawlamyine Myanmar *prev.*
Moulmein 118 B4

Mayaguana *island*
The Bahamas 36 D2

Mayfield New Zealand 133 C6

Mayotte *overseas department*
France, Indian Ocean 61 G2

Mayyit, Al Baḥr al *see* Dead
Sea

Mazār-e Sharīf Afghanistan
104 D3

Mazatlán Mexico 32 C3

Mažeikiai Lithuania 88 B3

Mazury *region* Poland 80 D3

Mazyr Belarus *Rus.* Mozyr'
89 D7

Mbabane *administrative
capital of* Swaziland 61 E4

Mbaké Senegal 56 B3

Mbala Zambia 61 E1

Mbale Uganda 55 C6

Mbandaka Dem. Rep. Congo
59 C5

Mbeya Tanzania 55 B8

Mbuji-Mayi Dem. Rep. Congo
59 D7

McKinley, Mount *peak* Alaska,
USA *var.* Denali 18 C3

Mead, Lake *lake* SW USA
28 A1

Mecca *see* Makkah

Mechelen Belgium 69 C5

Mecklenburger Bucht *bay*
Germany 76 C2

Medan Indonesia 120 B3

Medellín Colombia 40 B2

Médenine Tunisia 53 F2

Medford Oregon, USA 26 A4

Medina *see* Al Madīnah

Mediterranean Sea Atlantic
Ocean 84-85

Meekatharra Australia
129 B5

Meerut India 116 D3

Megísti *island* Greece 98 B4

Mek'elē Ethiopia 54 C4

Mekong *river* SE Asia 106 D3

Mekong, Mouths of the
wetlands Vietnam 119 D3

Melanesia *region* Pacific Ocean
126 C3

Mirim, Lake see Mirim Lagoon
Mirim Lagoon *lagoon* Brazil/ Uruguay *var.* Mirim, Lake 44 C5
Mirtóo Pelagos *sea feature* Mediterranean Sea 87 C6
Miskitos Cayos *islands* Nicaragua 35 E2
Miskolc Hungary 81 D6
Miṣrātah Libya 53 F2
Mississippi *state* USA 30 C2
Mississippi *river* USA 16 C5
Mississippi Delta *wetlands* USA 30 C4
Missoula Montana, USA 24 B2
Missouri *state* USA 25 G4
Missouri *river* USA 17 C5
Mistassini, Lake *lake* Canada 20 D3
Mitau see Jelgava
Mitchell S Dakota, USA 25 E3
Mitchell River *river* Australia 130 C3
Mitilíni Greece 86 D4
Mito Japan 112 D4
Mitrovica see Mitrovicë/ Mitrovica
Mitrovicë/Mitrovica Kosovo *Serb.* Mitrovica, *prev.* Kosovska Mitrovica 83 D5
Mits'iwa Eritrea *var.* Massawa 54 C4
Mitumba, Monts *Mountain range* Dem. Rep. Congo 59 E7
Miyazaki Japan 113 B6
Mjøsa *lake* Norway 67 B5
Mljet *island* Croatia 83 C5
Mmabatho South Africa 60 D4
Mo Norway 66 C3
Mobile Alabama, USA 30 C3
Moçambique Mozambique 61 F2
Mocímboa da Praia Mozambique 61 F2
Mocoa Colombia 40 B4
Mocuba Mozambique 61 E3
Modena Italy 78 B3
Modesto California, USA 27 B6
Modohn see Madona

Modriča Bosnia & Herzegovina 82 C3
Mogadiscio see Mogadishu
Mogadishu *capital of* Somalia *Som.* Muqdisho, *It.* Mogadiscio 55 D6
Mogilëv see Mahilyow/Mogilëv
Mo i Rana Norway 66 C3
Mojave California, USA 27 C7
Mojave Desert *desert* W USA 27 C7
Moldavia see Moldova
Molde Norway 67 A5
Moldova *country* E Europe *var.* Moldavia 90
Molodechno see Maladzyechna
Molodeczno see Maladzyechna
Molotov see Perm'
Moluccas see Maluku
Molucca Sea see Maluku, Laut
Mombasa Kenya 55 C7
Monaco *country* W Europe 73 E6
Monclova Mexico 33 E2
Moncton Canada 21 F4
Mongo Chad 58 C3
Mongolia *country* NE Asia 108-109
Monroe Louisiana, USA 30 B2
Monrovia *capital of* Liberia 56 C5
Mons Belgium 69 B6
Montague Seamount *undersea feature* Atlantic Ocean 45 H1
Montana *state* USA 24 C2
Montauban France 73 C6
Mont Blanc *peak* France/Italy 62 D4
Mont-de-Marsan France 72 B6
Monte Cristi Dominican Republic 37 E3
Montego Bay Jamaica 36 C3
Montenegro *Country* SE Europe 83 D5
Monterey California, USA 27 B6
Montería Colombia 40 B2
Montero Bolivia 42 D4
Monterrey Mexico 33 E2
Montes Claros Brazil 43 G4

Montevideo *capital of* Uruguay 44 C5
Montgomery Alabama, USA 30 D2
Monthey Switzerland 77 A7
Montpelier Vermont, USA 23 G2
Montpellier France 73 C6
Montréal Canada 21 E4
Montserrat *overseas territory* UK, West Indies 37
Monywa Myanmar 118 A3
Monza Italy 78 B2
Moora Australia 129 B6
Moore, Lake *lake* Australia 129 B6
Moorhead Minnesota, USA 25 E2
Moosonee Canada 20 C3
Mopti Mali 57 E3
Morava *river* C Europe 82 E4
Moravská Ostrava see Ostrava
Moray Firth *inlet* Scotland, UK 70 C3
Moree Australia 131 D5
Morelia Mexico 33 E4
Morena, Sierra *mountain range* Spain 74 D4
Murghāb, Daryā-ye *river* Afghanistan/Turkmenistan 104 D4
Morioka Japan 112 D3
Mornington Abyssal Plain *undersea feature* Pacific Ocean 135 G5
Morocco *country* N Africa 52
Morogoro Tanzania 55 C7
Mörön Mongolia 108 D2
Morondava Madagascar 61 F3
Moroni *capital of* Comoros 61 F2
Morotai, Pulau *island* Indonesia 121 F3
Morova *river* Poland 80 C6
Morris Jesup, Kap *headland* Greenland 65 E1
Moscow *capital of* Russia *Rus.* Moskva 92 B4 96 B2
Mosel *river* W Europe *Fr.* Moselle 77 A5
Moselle *river* W Europe *Ger.* Mosel 72 E4

Mosgiel New Zealand 133 B7
Moshi Tanzania 55 C7
Moskva see Moscow
Mosquito Coast *coastal region* Nicaragua 35 E3
Moss Norway 67 B6
Mossendjo Congo 59 B6
Mossoró Brazil 43 H2
Most Czech Republic (Czechia) *Ger.* Brüx 80 A4
Mostaganem Algeria 52 D1
Mostar Bosnia & Herz. 82 C4
Mosul see Al Mawşil
Motril Spain 75 E5
Mottama, Gulf of *sea feature* Myanmar 133 C5
Motueka New Zealand 133 C5
Moulins France 72 C4
Moulmein see Mawlamyine
Moundou Chad 58 C4
Mount Gambier Australia 131 B7
Mount Isa Australia 130 B4
Mount Magnet Australia 129 B5
Mount Vernon Illinois, USA 22 B5
Mouscron Belgium 69 A6
Moyobamba Peru 42 B3
Moyu China 108 B2
Mozambique *country* SE Africa 61
Mozambique Channel *sea feature* Indian Ocean 61 F3
Mozyr' see Mazyr
Mpika Zambia 61 E2
Mtwara Tanzania 55 C8
Muang Không Laos 119 D5
Muang Xaignabouri see Xaignabouri
Mudanjiang China 110 E3
Mufulira Zambia 60 D2
Muğla Turkey 98 A4
Mulhouse France 72 E4
Mull *island* Scotland, UK 70 B3
Muller, Pegunungan *mountains* Indonesia 120 C3
Multan Pakistan 116 C2
Mumbai India *var.* Bombay 117 C5

München Germany *Eng.* Munich 77 C6
Muncie Indiana, USA 22 C4
Munich see München
Münster Germany 76 B4
Muqdisho see Mogadishu
Mur *river* C Europe 77 E7
Murchison River *river* Australia 129 B5
Murcia Spain 75 F4
Mures *river* Hungary/Romania 81 D7
Murfreesboro Tennessee, USA 30 D1
Murgab Tajikistan 105 F3
Murgap *river* Turkmenistan *var.* Murghab 104 C3
Murghab see Murgap
Müritz *lake* Germany 76 D3
Murmansk Russia 92 C2 96 C1
Murray *river* Australia 131 B6
Murray Fracture Zone *tectonic feature* Pacific Ocean 135 E2
Murray Ridge *Undersea feature* Arabian Sea 122 B3
Murwillumbah Australia 131 E5
Murzuq Libya 53 F3
Muş Turkey 99 F3
Muscat *capital of* Oman *Ar.* Masqaţ 103 E5
Musgrave Ranges *mountain range* Australia 129 D5
Musters, Lago *lake* Argentina 46 C6
Mu Us Shadi *Desert* China 109 E3
Mvonioälv *river* Finland/ Sweden 66 D3
Mwali *island* Comoros 61 F2
Mwanza Tanzania 55 B6
Mwene-Ditu Dem. Rep. Congo 59 D7
Mweru, Lake *lake* Dem. Rep. Congo/Zambia 59 D7
Myanmar *country* SE Asia *var.* Burma 118-119
Myeik Myanmar *prev.* Mergui 119 B5
Mykolayiv Ukraine *Rus.* Nikolayev 91 E4
Mykonos *island* Greece 87 D5
Mysore see Mysūru

Mysūru India *prev.* Mysore 114 D2
Mzuzu Malawi 61 E2

N

Naberezhnyye Chelny Russia *prev.* Brezhnev 93 C5
Nablus West Bank *var.* Nābulus, *Heb.* Shekhem 101 D6
Nābulus see Nablus
Nacala Mozambique 61 F2
Naga Philippines 120 E2
Nagano Japan 112 C4
Nagasaki Japan 113 A6
Nägercoil India 114 D3
Nagornyy Karabakh *region* Azerbaijan 99 G2
Nagoya Japan 113 C5
Nägpur India 116 D4
Naqqu China 108 C5
Nagykanizsa Hungary *Ger.* Grosskanizsa 81 C7
Nagyszombat see Trnava
Naha Japan 113 A8
Nain Canada 21 F2
Nairobi *capital of* Kenya 55 C6
Najaf see An Najaf
Najrān Saudi Arabia 103 B6
Nakamura Japan 113 B6
Nakhichevan' see Naxçıvan
Nakhon Ratchasima Thailand 119 C5
Nakhon Sawan Thailand 119 C5
Nakhon Si Thammarat Thailand 119 C6
Nakuru Kenya 55 C6
Nal'chik Russia 96 A4
Namangan Uzbekistan 105 E2
Nam Co *lake* China 108 C4
Nam Dinh Vietnam 118 D3
Namib Desert *desert* Namibia 60 B3
Namibe Angola 60 B2
Namibia *country* southern Africa 60
Nampa Idaho, USA 26 C3
Namp'o North Korea 110 E4
Nampula Mozambique 61 F2
Namur Belgium 69 C6

Nanchang China 111 C5
Nancy France 72 D3
Nänded India 116 D5 114 D1
Nanjing China 111 D5
Nanning China 111 B6
Nanortalik Greenland 64 C5
Nansen Basin *undersea feature* Arctic Ocean 137 G4
Nantes France 72 B4
Napier New Zealand 132 E4
Naples *see* Napoli
Napo *river* Ecuador/Peru 42 B2
Napoli Italy *Eng.* Naples 79 D5
Narbonne France 73 C6
Nares Strait *sea feature* Canada/Greenland 64 C1
Narew *river* Poland 80 E3
Narmada *river* India 116 D4
Narva Estonia 88 E2
Narva *river* Estonia/Russia 88 E2
Narva Bay *sea feature* Gulf of Finland *Est.* Narva Laht, *Rus.* Narvskiy Zaliv 88 E2
Narva Laht *see* Narva Bay
Narvik Norway 66 C3
Narvskiy Zaliv *see* Narva Bay
Naryn Kyrgyzstan 105 G2
Näshik India 116 C5
Nashville Tennessee, USA 30 D1
Nâsir, Buḥeiret *see* Nasser, Lake
Nassau *capital of* The Bahamas 36 C1
Nasser, Lake *reservoir* Egypt *var.* Nâsir, Buḥeiret 54 B2
Natal Brazil 43 H3
Natal Basin *Undersea feature* Indian Ocean 123 A5
Natitingou Benin 57 E4
Naturaliste Plateau *undersea feature* Indian Ocean 123 E6
Natzrat Israel *Eng.* Nazareth 101 A5
Nauru *country* Pacific Ocean 126 D3
Navapolatsk/Novopolotsk Belarus *Rus.* Novopolotsk 89 D5
Navassa Island *unincorporated territory* USA, West Indies 36 D3

Navoiy Uzbekistan *Uzb.* Nawoly 104 D2
Nawabshah Pakistan 116 B3
Nawoly *see* Navoiy
Naxçivan Azerbaijan *Rus.* Nakhichevan' 99 G3
Náxos *island* Greece 87 D6
Nay Pyi Taw *capital of* Myanmar 118 B3
Nazareth *see* Natzrat
Nazca Peru 42 B4
Nazrēt Ethiopia 55 C5
Nazwá Oman 103 E5
N'Dalatando Angola 60 B2
Ndélé Central African Republic 58 C4
N'Djaména *capital of* Chad 58 B3
Ndola Zambia 60 D2
Nebitdag *see* Balkanabat
Nebraska *state* USA 24-25 E3
Neches *river* S USA 29 H3
Neckar *river* Germany 77 B5
Necochea Argentina 47 D5
Neftezavodsk *see* Seýdi
Negēlē Ethiopia 55 C5
Negev *see* HaNegev
Negro, Rio *river* Argentina 47 C5
Negro, Rio *river* Brazil/Uruguay 44 C4
Negro, Rio *river* N South America 40 C1
Neiva Colombia 40 B3
Nellore India 115 E2
Neman *river* NE Europe *Bel.* Nyoman, *Lith.* Nemunas, *Ger.* Memel, *Pol.* Niemen 88 B4
Nemunas *see* Neman
Nemuro Japan 112 E2
Nepal *country* S Asia 117
Neris *river* Belarus/Lithuania *Bel.* Viliya, *Pol.* Wilja 88 C4
Ness, Loch *lake* Scotland, UK 70 C3
Netherlands *country* W Europe *var.* Holland 68-69
Netze *see* Noteć
Neubrandenburg Germany 76 D3

Neuchâtel, Lac de *lake* Switzerland 77 A7
Neumünster Germany 76 C2
Neuquén Argentina 47 C5
Neusiedler See *lake* Austria/ Hungary 77 E6
Neusohl *see* Banská Bystrica
Neutra *see* Nitra
Nevada *state* USA 26-27
Nevers France 72 C4
Nevşehir Turkey 98 C3
New Amsterdam Guyana 41 G2
Newark New Jersey, USA 23 F3
New Britain *island* Papua New Guinea 126 B3
New Brunswick *province* Canada 21 F4
New Caledonia *self-governing territory of special status* France, Pacific Ocean 126 C5
New Caledonia *island* Pacific Ocean 124 D3
New Caledonia Basin *undersea feature* Pacific Ocean 124 D4
Newcastle Australia 131 D6
Newcastle upon Tyne England, UK 70 D4
New Delhi *capital of* India 116 D3
Newfoundland & Labrador *province* Canada 21 F2
Newfoundland *island* Canada 21 G3
Newfoundland Basin *undersea feature* Atlantic Ocean 48 B3
New Georgia Islands *island group* Solomon Is 126 C3
New Guinea *island* Pacific Ocean 126 B3
New Hampshire *state* USA 23 G2
New Haven Connecticut, USA 23 G3
New Ireland *island* Papua New Guinea 126 C3
New Jersey *state* USA 23 F4
Newman Australia 128 B4

North Sea Atlantic Ocean 70 E2
North Siberian Lowland *lowlands* Russia 94-95
North Taranaki Bight *gulf* New Zealand 132 D3
North Uist *island* Scotland, UK 70 B3
Northwest Territories *territory* Canada 19 E3
Norway *country* N Europe 66-67
Norwegian Sea Arctic Ocean 137 G5
Norwich England, UK 71 E6
Noteć *river* Poland *Ger.* Netze 80 C3
Nottingham England, UK 71 D6
Nottingham Island *island* Hudson Strait 20 D1
Nouâdhibou Mauritania 56 B2
Nouakchott *capital of* Mauritania 56 B2
Nouméa *capital of* New Caledonia 126 D5
Nova Gradiška Croatia 82 C3
Nova Iguaçu Brazil 43 F5 45 F2
Novara Italy 78 B2
Nova Scotia *province* Canada 21 F4
Novaya Zemlya *islands* Russia 137 H4
Novaya Zemlya Trench *see* East Novaya Zemlya Trench
Novi Sad Serbia 82 D3
Novokuznetsk Russia *prev.* Stalinsk 96 D4
Novopolotsk *see* Navapolatsk/ Novopolotsk
Novosibirsk Russia 96 D4
Novosibirskiye Ostrova *islands* Russia *Eng.* New Siberian Islands 95 F1
Novo Urgench *see* Urgench
Novyy Margilan *see* Farg'ona
Nsanje Malawi 61 E3
Nsawam Ghana 57 E5
Nubian Desert *desert* Sudan 54 B3
Nu'eima West Bank 101 D7
Nuevo Laredo Mexico 33 E2
Nuku'alofa *capital of* Tonga 127 F5
Nukus Uzbekistan 104 C2

Nullarbor Plain *region* Australia 129 D6
Nunap Isua Island *coastal region* Greenland *Dan.* Uummannaruaq *Dan.* Kap Farvel 64 C5
Nunavut *Territory* Canada 19 F3
Nunivak Island *island* Alaska, USA 18 B2
Nuoro Italy 79 A5
Nuremberg *see* Nürnberg
Nürnberg Germany *Eng.* Nuremberg 77 C5
Nusa Tenggara *islands* East Timor / Indonesia 120 E5
Nuuk Greenland *var.* Godthåb 64 C4
Nyainqêntanglha Shan *mountain range* China 108 D5
Nyala Sudan 54 A4
Nyasa, Lake *lake* E Africa 51 D5
Nyeri Kenya 55 C6
Nyima China 108 C4
Nyíregyháza Hungary 81 E6
Nyitra *see* Nitra
Nykøbing Denmark 67 B8
Nyköping Sweden 67 C6
Nyngan Australia 131 D6
Nyoman *see* Neman

O

Oakland California, USA 27 B6
Oakley Kansas, USA 25 E4
Oamaru New Zealand 133 B7
Oaxaca Mexico 33 F5
Ob' *river* Russia 96 D4
Oban Scotland, UK 70 C4
Obihiro Japan 112 D2
Obo Central African Republic 58 D4
Oceania 124-125
Ocean Island *see* Banaba
Oceanside California, USA 27 C8
Ochamchira *see* Och'amch'ire
Ochamchire Georgia *prev.* Och'amch'ire, *Rus.* Ochamchira 99 E1
Och'amch'ire *see* Ochamchire

Ödenburg *see* Sopron
Odense Denmark 67 B7
Oder *river* C Europe 80 C4
Odesa Ukraine *Rus.* Odessa 91 E4
Odessa *see* Odesa
Odessa Texas, USA 29 E3
Odienné Côte d'Ivoire 56 D4
Odisha *region* India *prev.* Orissa 116 C5
Oesel *see* Saaremaa
Ofanto *river* Italy 79 D5
Offenbach Germany 77 B5
Ogaden *plateau* Ethiopia 55 D5
Ogallala Nebraska, USA 24 D4
Ogbomosho Nigeria 57 F4
Ogden Utah, USA 24 B3
Ogdensburg New York, USA 23 F2
Oger *see* Ogre
Ogre Latvia *Ger.* Oger 88 C3
Ogulin Croatia 82 B3
Ohio *state* USA 22 D4
Ohio *river* N USA 22 B5
Ohrid Macedonia 83 D6
Ohrid, Lake *lake* Albania/ Macedonia 83 D6
Ohře *river* Czech Republic (Czechia)/ Germany *Ger.* Eger 81 A5
Ōita Japan 113 B6
Okara Pakistan 116 C2
Okavango *river var.* Cubango southern Africa 60 C3
Okavango Delta *wetland* Botswana 60 C3
Okayama Japan 113 B5
Okazaki Japan 113 C5
Okeechobee, Lake *lake* Florida, USA 31 F4
Okhotsk Russia 97 G3
Okhotsk, Sea of Pacific Ocean 134 C1
Okinawa *island* Japan 113 A8
Oki-shotō *island group* Japan 113 B5
Oklahoma *state* USA 29 F1
Oklahoma City Oklahoma, USA 29 F2
Okushiri-tō *island* Japan 112 C2

Öland *island* Sweden 67 C7
Olavarría Argentina 46 D4
Olbia Italy 79 B5
Oldenburg Germany 76 B3
Oleksandriya Ukraine *Rus.*
Aleksandriya 91 E3
Oleněk Russia 97 E3
Ölgiy Mongolia 108 C2
Olhão Portugal 74 C4
Olita *see* Alytus
Olmaliq *see* Almalyk
Olmütz *see* Olomouc
Olomouc Czech Republic
(Czechia) *Ger.* Olmütz 81 C5
Olsztyn Poland *Ger.* Allenstein
80 D2
Olt *river* Romania 90 B5
Olympia Washington, USA
26 B2
Omaha Nebraska, USA 25 F4
Oman *country* SW Asia 103 D6
Oman, Gulf of *sea feature*
Indian Ocean 103 E5, 122 B3
Omdurman Sudan 54 B4
Omsk Russia 96 C4
Onega *river* Russia 92 C4
Onega, Lake *see* Onezhskoye
Ozero
Onezhskoye Ozero *lake* Russia
Eng. Lake Onega 92 B3
Ongole India 115 E2
Onitsha Nigeria 57 F5
Onslow Australia 128 A4
Ontario *province* Canada
18 B3
Ontario, Lake *lake* Canada/USA
17 D5
Oostende Belgium *Eng.* Ostend
69 A5
Opole Poland *Ger.* Oppeln 80 C4
Oporto *see* Porto
Oppeln *see* Opole
Oradea Romania 90 B3
Oran Algeria 52 D1
Orange River *river* southern
Africa 60 C4
Oranjestad Aruba 37 E5
Orantes *River* Asia 100 B3
Ordu Turkey 98 D2
Ordzhonikidze *see* Vladikavkaz
Örebro Sweden 67 C6

Oregon *state* USA 26
Orël Russia 83 A5
Orem Utah, USA 24 B4
Orenburg Russia 93 C6 96 B4
Orense *see* Ourense
Orestiáda Greece 86 D3
Orinoco *river* Colombia/
Venezuela 41 E3
Oristano Italy 79 A5
Orkney *islands* Scotland, UK
70 C2
Orlando Florida, USA 31 E4
Orléans France 72 C4
Örnsköldsvik Sweden 67 C5
Orantes *river* SW Asia 100 B3
Orissa *see* Odisha
Orosirá Rodópis *see* Rhodope
Mountains
Orsha Belarus 89 E5
Orsk Russia 93 D6 96 B4
Oruro Bolivia 42 C4
Ösaka Japan 113 C5
Osborn Plateau *undersea
feature* Indian Ocean 123 C5
Ösel *see* Saaremaa
Osh Kyrgyzstan 105 F2
Oshawa Canada 20 D5
Oshkosh Wisconsin, USA 22 B2
Osijek Croatia 82 C3
Oslo *capital* of Norway 67 B6
Osmaniye Turkey 98 D4
Osnabrück Germany 76 B3
Osorno Chile 47 B5
Oss Netherlands 68 D4
Ossora Russia 97 H2
Ostend *see* Oostende
Östersund Sweden 67 C5
Ostrava Czech Republic
(Czechia) *Ger.* Mährisch-
Ostrau, *prev.* Moravská
Ostrava 81 C5
Ostrołęka Poland 80 D3
Ostrowiec Świętokrzyski
Poland 80 D4
Ösumi-shotō *island group*
Japan 113 A7
Otago Peninsula *peninsula*
New Zealand 133 B7
Otaru Japan 112 D2
Oti *river* Africa 57 E4

Otranto, Strait of *sea feature*
Albania/Italy 79 E5
Ottawa *capital* of Canada
20 D4
Ottawa *river* Canada 20 D4
Ou *river* Laos 118 C3
Ouachita *river* SE USA 30 B2
Ouagadougou *capital* of
Burkina Faso 57 E3
Ouârâne *desert* Mauritania
56 D2
Ouargla Algeria 53 E2
Ouessant, Île d' *island* France
72 A3
Ouésso Congo 59 C5
Oujda Morocco 52 D2
Oulu Finland 66 D4
Oulu *river* Finland 66 D4
Oulujärvi *lake* Finland 66 E4
Ounasjoki *river* Finland
66 D3
Our *river* W Europe 69 E7
Ourense Spain *var.* Orense
74 C2
Ourinhos Brazil 44 D2
Ourthe *river* Belgium 69 D6
Outer Hebrides *island group*
UK *var.* Western Isles 70 B3
Outer Islands *island group*
Seychelles 61 H2
Ouyen Australia 131 C6
Oviedo Spain 74 D1
Owando Congo 59 C6
Owen Fracture Zone *tectonic
feature* Arabian Sea 122 B3
Owensboro Kentucky, USA
22 B5
Oxford England, UK 71 D6
Oxnard California, USA
29 C7
Oyem Gabon 59 B5
Oyo Nigeria 57 F4
Ozark Plateau *plain* Arkansas/
Missouri, USA 25 G5
Ózd Hungary 81 D6

P

Paamiut Greenland 64 B4
Pachuca Mexico 33 E4

Plata, Rio de la *river* Argentina/ Uruguay *var.* River Plate 44 B5 46 D4

Plate, River *see* Plata, Rio de la

Platte *river* C USA 25 E4

Plattensee *see* Balaton

Plenty, Bay of *bay* New Zealand 132 E3

Pleven Bulgaria 86 C1

Płock Poland 80 D3

Ploieşti Romania 90 C4

Plovdiv Bulgaria *Gk.* Philippopolis 86 C2

Plungė Lithuania 88 B4

Plymouth *capital of* Montserrat (currently abandoned) *see* Brades

Plymouth England, UK 71 C7

Plzeň Czech Republic (Czechia) *Ger.* Pilsen 81 A5

Po *river* Italy 78 B2

Pocatello Idaho, USA 26 E4

Po Delta *wetland* Italy 78 C3

Podgorica *capital of* Montenegro 83 C5

Pohnpei Island *island* Micronesia 126 C2

Pointe-Noire Congo 59 B6

Poitiers France 72 B4

Poland *country* E Europe 80-81

Polatsk *see* Polatsk/Polotsk

Polatsk/Polotsk Belarus *Bel.* Polatsk, *Rus.* Polotsk 89 D5

Pol-e Khomrī *see* Pul-e Khumrī

Polotsk *see* Polatsk/Polotsk

Poltava Ukraine 91 F2

Poltoratsk *see* Aşgabat

Polynesia *region* Pacific Ocean 127

Pomeranian Bay *bay* Germany/ Poland 80 B2

Pompano Beach Florida, USA 31 F5

Ponca City Oklahoma, USA 29 G1

Pondicherry *see* Puducherry

Ponta Grossa Brazil 44 D2

Pontevedra Spain 74 C1

Pontianak Indonesia 120 C4

Poona *see* Pune

Poopó, Lake *lake* Bolivia 42 C5

Popayán Colombia 40 B3

Poprad Slovakia *Ger.* Deutschendorf 81 D5

Porbandar India 116 B4

Pori Finland 67 D5

Porsgrunn Norway 67 B6

Portalegre Portugal 74 C3

Port Angeles Washington, USA 26 A1

Port Arthur Texas, USA 29 H4

Port Augusta Australia 131 B6

Port-au-Prince *capital of* Haiti 36 D3

Port Blair India 115 G2

Port Douglas Australia 130 D3

Port Elizabeth South Africa 60 D5

Port-Gentil Gabon 59 A6

Port Harcourt Nigeria 57 F5

Port Hardy Canada 18 D5

Port Harrison *see* Inukjuak

Port Hedland Australia 128 B4

Portland Australia 131 B7

Portland Maine, USA 23 G2

Portland Oregon, USA 26 B2

Port Lincoln Australia 131 A6

Port Louis *capital of* Mauritius 61 H4

Port Macquarie Australia 131 E6

Port Moresby *capital of* Papua New Guinea 126 B3

Porto Portugal *Eng.* Oporto 74 C2

Porto Alegre Sao Tome and Principe 44 D4

Port of Spain *capital of* Trinidad & Tobago 37 G5

Porto-Novo *official capital of* Benin 57 F5

Porto Velho Brazil 42 C3

Portoviejo Ecuador 40 A4

Port Said *see* Bür Sa'īd

Portsmouth England, UK 71 D7

Port Sudan Sudan 54 C3

Portugal *country* SW Europe 74

Port-Vila *capital of* Vanuatu 126 D5

Porvenir Chile 47 B7

Posadas Argentina 46 E3

Posen *see* Poznań

Poste-de-la-Baleine *see* Kuujjuarapik

Pöstyén *see* Piešťany

Potenza S Italy 79 D5

Poti Georgia 99 E2

Potosí Bolivia 42 C5

Potsdam Germany 76 D4

Póvoa de Varzim Portugal 74 C2

Powder *river* N USA 24 C2

Powell, Lake *lake* SW USA 24 B5

Poza Rica Mexico 33 F4

Poznań Poland *Ger.* Posen 80 C3

Pozo Colorado Paraguay 44 B2

Pozsony *see* Bratislava

Prag *see* Prague

Prague *capital of* Czech Republic (Czechia) *Cz.* Praha, *Ger.* Prag 81 B5

Praha *see* Prague

Praia *capital of* Cape Verde 56 A3

Prato Italy 78 B3

Pratt Kansas, USA 25 E5

Preăh Seihânŭ *see* Sihanoukville

Preschau *see* Prešov

Prescott Arizona, USA 28 B2

Presidente Prudente Brazil 44 D2

Prešov Slovakia *Ger.* Eperies, *var.* Preschau, *Hung.* Eperjes 81 D5

Prespa, Lake *lake* SE Europe 83 D6 86 A3

Presque Isle Maine, USA 23 G1

Pressburg *see* Bratislava

Preston England, UK 71 D5

Pretoria *judicial capital of* South Africa 60 D4

Préveza Greece 86 A4

Prijedor Bosnia & Herzegovina 82 B3

Prilep Macedonia 83 E5

Prince Albert Canada 19 F5

Prince Edward Island *province* Canada 21 F4

Prince Edward Islands *island group* South Africa 123 A7
Prince George Canada 19 E5
Prince of Wales Island *island* Canada 19 F2
Prince Rupert Canada 18 D4
Princess Charlotte Bay *bay* Australia 130 C2
Princess Elizabeth Land *region* Antarctica 136 D3
Príncipe *island* Sao Tome & Principe 59 A5
Pripet *river* Belarus/Ukraine 90 C1
Pripet Marshes *wetlands* Belarus/Ukraine 90 C1
Prishtinë *capital of* Kosovo *Serb.* Priština 83 D5
Priština *see* Prishtinë
Prizren Kosovo 83 D5
Prome *see* Pyay
Prossnitz *see* Prostějov
Prostějov Czech Republic (Czechia) *Ger.* Prossnitz 81 C5
Provence *region* France 73 D6
Providence Rhode Island, USA 23 G3
Providencia, Isla de *island* Colombia 35 E3
Provo Utah, USA 24 B4
Prudhoe Bay Alaska, USA 18 D2
Przheval'sk *see* Karakol
Pskov Russia 92 A4
Pskov, Lake *lake* Estonia/Russia *Est.* Pihkva Järv, *Rus.* Pskovskoye Ozero 88 D3
Pskovskoye Ozero *see* Pskov, Lake
Ptich' *see* Ptsich
Ptsich *river* Belarus *Rus.* Ptich' 89 D6
Pucallpa Peru 42 B3
Puducherry India *prev.* Pondicherry 115 E2
Puebla Mexico 33 F4
Pueblo Colorado, USA 22 D4
Puerto Aisén Chile 47 B6
Puerto Barrios Guatemala 34 C2
Puerto Carreño Colombia 40 D2

Puerto Cortés Honduras 34 C2
Puerto Deseado Argentina 47 C6
Puerto Maldonado Peru 42 C4
Puerto Montt Chile 47 B5
Puerto Natales Chile 47 B7
Puerto Plata Dominican Republic 37 E3
Puerto Princesa Philippines 120 E2
Puerto Rico *commonwealth territory* USA, West Indies 37 F3
Puerto San Julián Argentina 47 C7
Puerto Suárez Bolivia 42 D4
Puerto Vallarta Mexico 32 D4
Pula Croatia 82 A3
Pul-e Khumrī Afghanistan *prev.* Pol-e Khomrī 105 E4
Pune India *prev.* Poona 114 C1
Puno Peru 42 C4
Punta Arenas Chile *prev.* Magallanes 47 B7
Puntarenas Costa Rica 34 D4
Purmerend Netherlands 68 C3
Purus *river* Brazil/Peru 42 C3
Pusan *see* Busan
Putrajaya *administrative capital* of Malaysia 120 B3
Putumayo *river* NW South America 38 B3
Pyapon Myanmar 118 B4
Pyarnu *see* Pärnu
Pyay Myanmar *prev.* Prome 118 A4
Pyongyang *capital of* North Korea 110 E4
Pyramid Lake *lake* Nevada, USA 27 C5
Pyrenees *mountain range* SW Europe 62 C4

Q

Qaanaaq Greenland *var.* Thule 64 D1
Qābatiya West Bank 101 D7

Qaidam Pendi *basin* China 108 D4
Qalāt Afghanistan *prev.* Kalāt104 D5
Qalqīlya West Bank 101 D7
Qamdo China 108 D5
Qandahār *see* Kandahār
Qaqortoq Greenland 64 C4
Qara Qum *see* Karakumy
Qarshi *see* Karshi
Qasigiannguit Greenland 64 C3
Qatar *country* SW Asia 103 D5
Qattara Depression *see* Qaṭṭārah, Munkhafaḍ al
Qaṭṭārah, Munkhafaḍ al *desert basin* Egypt *Eng.* Qattara Depression 54 A1
Qausuittuq *see* Resolute
Qeqertarsuaq Greenland 64 B3
Qeqertarsuaq *island* Greenland 64 B3
Qian *see* Guizhou
Qilian Shan *mountain range* China 108 A4
Qimusseriarsuaq *bay* Greenland 64 C1
Qinā Egypt 54 B2
Qingdao China 110 D4
Qinghai *province* China *var.* Chinghai, Koko Nor, Qing, Tsinghai 108 D4
Qinghai Hu *lake* China *var.* Koko Nor 108 D4
Qingzang Gaoyuan *plateau* China *Eng.* Plateau of Tibet 110 A4
Qiong *see* Hainan
Qiqihar China 110 D3
Qira China 108 B4
Qitai China 108 C3
Qom Iran *var.* Kum 102 C3
Qondūz *river* Afghanistan 105 E4
Qondūz *see* Kunduz
Qo'qon Uzbekistan *prev.* Kokand, *var.* Khokand, 105 E2
Quba Azerbaijan *Rus.* Kuba 99 H2
Québec Canada 21 E4
Québec *province* Canada 20 D3

Queen Charlotte Islands *islands* Canada 18 D4

Queen Charlotte Sound *sea feature* Canada 18 D5

Queen Elizabeth Islands *islands* Canada 19 F1

Queensland *state* Australia 130 C4

Queenstown New Zealand 133 B6

Quelimane Mozambique 61 E3

Querétaro Mexico 33 E4

Quetta Pakistan 116 B2

Quezaltenango Guatemala 34 B2

Quibdó Colombia 40 B2

Quimper France 72 A3

Quy Nhon Vietnam 119 E5

Qing *see* Qinghai

Quito *capital of* Ecuador 40 A4

Qŭrghonteppa Tajikistan *Rus.* Kurgan–Tynbe 105 E3

Qyteti Stalin *see* Kuçovë

R

Raab *see* Győr

Raab *see* Rába

Rába *river* Austria/Hungary *Ger.* Raab 81 C7

Rabat *capital of* Morocco 52 C2

Race, Cape *coastal feature* Canada 21 H4

Rach Gia Vietnam 119 D6

Radom Poland 80 D4

Radviliškis Lithuania 88 C4

Ragusa Italy 79 D7

Rahimyar Khan Pakistan 116 C3

Raipur India 117 E5

Rājahmundry India 115 E1

Rājasthān *state* India 116 C3

Rājkot India 116 C4

Rājshāhi Bangladesh 117 G4

Rakaia *river* New Zealand 133 C5

Rakvere Estonia *Ger.* Wesenberg 88 D2

Raleigh North Carolina, USA 31 F1

Ralik Chain *islands* Marshall Islands 126 D1

Râmnicu Vâlcea Romania *prev.* Rîmnicu Vîlcea 90 B4

Ramallah West Bank 101 D7

Ramree Island *island* Myanmar 118 A3

Rancagua Chile 46 B4

Rānchi India 117 F4

Randers Denmark 67 A7

Rangiora New Zealand 133 C6

Rangitikei *river* New Zealand 132 D4

Rangoon *see* Yangon

Rankin Inlet Canada 19 G3

Rapid City South Dakota, USA 24 D3

Rarotonga *island* Cook Islands 127 G5

Rasht Iran 102 C3

Ratak Chain *islands* Marshall Islands 126 D1

Ratchaburi Thailand 119 C5

Rat Islands *island group* Alaska, USA 18 A2

Raukumara Range *mountain range* New Zealand 132 E3

Rauma Finland 67 D5

Ravenna Italy 78 C3

Rawalpindi Pakistan 116 C1

Rawson Argentina 47 C6

Razgrad Bulgaria 86 D1

Reading England, UK 71 D6

Rebecca, Lake *lake* Australia 129 C6

Rebun-tō *island* Japan 112 D1

Rechytsa Belarus 89 D7

Recife Brazil 43 H3

Recklinghausen Germany 76 G4

Red Deer Canada 19 E5

Redding California, USA 27 B5

Red River *river* S USA 30 B3

Red River *river* China/ Vietnam 118

Red Sea Indian Ocean 122 A3

Reefton New Zealand 133 C5

Regensburg Germany 77 C5

Reggane Algeria 52 D3

Reggio di Calabria Italy 79 D6

Reggio nell' Emilia Italy 78 B3

Regina Canada 19 F5

Rehoboth Namibia 60 C4

Reichenberg *see* Liberec

Reid Australia 129 D6

Reims France *Eng.* Rheims 72 D3

Reindeer Lake *lake* Canada 17 C4

Reni Ukraine 90 D4

Rennes France 72 B3

Reno Nevada, USA 27 B5

Resistencia Argentina 46 D3

Reşiţa Romania 90 B4

Resolute Canada *Var.* Qausuittuq 19 F2

Réunion *overseas department* France, Indian Ocean 123 B5

Reus Spain 75 G2

Reutlingen Germany 77 B6

Reval *see* Tallinn

Revel *see* Tallinn

Revillagigedo, Islas *island* Mexico 32 B4

Rey, Isla del *island* Panama 35 F5

Reykjavík *capital of* Iceland 65 E5

Reynosa Mexico 33 E2

Rēzekne Latvia *Ger.* Rositten, *Rus.* Rezhitsa 88 D4

Rezhitsa *see* Rēzekne

Rheims *see* Reims

Rhine *river* W Europe 62 D3

Rhode Island *state* USA 23 G3

Rhodes *see* Ródos

Rhodope Mountains *mountain range* Bulgaria/Greece *Gk.* Orosirá Rodópis, *Bul.* Despoto Planina 86 C3

Rhône *river* France/Switzerland 62 C4

Ribeirão Preto Brazil 45 E1

Riberalta Bolivia 42 C3

Rîbniţa Moldova 90 D3

Richfield Utah, USA 24 B4

Richland Washington, USA 24 C2

Richmond Kentucky, USA
22 C5

Richmond New Zealand
133 C5

Richmond Virginia, USA 23 E5

Richmond Range *mountain range* New Zealand 133 C5

Ricobayo, Embalse de *reservoir* Spain 74 D2

Riga *capital of* Latvia *Latv.* Rīga
88 C3

Riga, Gulf of *sea feature* Baltic Sea 88 C3

Riihimäki Finland 67 D5

Rijeka Croatia *It.* Fiume 82 A3

Rimah, Wādī ar *dry watercourse* Saudi Arabia
103 B5

Rimini Italy 78 C3

Rîmnicu Vîlcea *see* Râmnicu Vâlcea

Riobamba Ecuador 40 A4

Rio Branco Brazil 42 C3

Rio Cuarto Argentina 46 C4

Rio de Janeiro Brazil 45 F2

Río Gallegos Argentina 47 C7

Rio Grande Brazil 44 D4

Rio Grande *river* N America
16 B6

Rio Grande Rise *undersea feature* Atlantic Ocean 49 C6

Río Verde Mexico 33 E3

Rishiri-tō *island* Japan 112 D1

Rivas Nicaragua 34 D3

Rivera Uruguay 44 C4

Riverside California, USA
27 C8

Riverton New Zealand 133 A7

Rivne Ukraine *Rus.* Rovno 90 C2

Riyadh *capital of* Saudi Arabia *Ar.* Ar Riyāḍ 103 C5

Rize Turkey 99 E2

Rkîz Mauritania 56 C3

Road Town *capital of* British Virgin Islands 37 F3

Roanne France 73 D5

Roanoke Virginia, USA 23 E5

Roanoke *river* SE USA 31 G1

Robinson Range *mountain range* Australia 129 B5

Rochester Minnesota, USA
25 F3

Rochester New York, USA
23 E3

Rockford Illinois, USA 22 B3

Rockhampton Australia 130 D4

Rock Island Illinois, USA 22 B3

Rock Springs Wyoming, USA
24 C3

Rockstone Guyana 41 G2

Rocky Mountains *mountain range* Canada/USA 18-19 D4

Rodez France 73 C6

Ródhos *see* Ródos

Ródos *island* Greece *var.* Ródhos, *Eng.* Rhodes 87 E6

Ródos Greece *Eng.* Rhodes
87 E6

Rodosto *see* Tekirdağ

Roeselare Belgium 69 A5

Roma Australia 131 D5

Roma *see* Rome

Romania *country* SE Europe 90

Rome *capital of* Italy *It.* Roma
78 C4

Rome Georgia, USA 30 D2

Rønne Denmark 67 B8

Ronne Ice Shelf *ice feature* Antarctica 136 B3

Roosendaal Netherlands
68 C4

Rosario Argentina 46 D4

Roseau *capital of* Dominica
37 G4

Rosenau *see* Rožňava

Rositten *see* Rēzekne

Ross Ice Shelf *ice feature* Antarctica 136 B4

Ross Sea Antarctica 136 B4

Rostak *see* Ar Rustāq

Rostock Germany 76 C2

Rostov-na-Donu Russia 96 A3

Roswell New Mexico, USA
28 D2

Rotorua New Zealand
132 D3

Rotorua, Lake *lake* New Zealand 132 D3

Rotterdam Netherlands
68 C4

Rouen France 72 C3

Rovaniemi Finland 66 D3

Rovno *see* Rivne

Rovuma *river* Mozambique/
Tanzania 61 F2

Roxas City Philippines
121 E2

Rožňava Slovakia *Ger.* Rosenau, *Hung.* Rozsnyó
81 D6

Rozsnyó *see* Rožňava

Ruatoria New Zealand
132 E3

Ruawai New Zealand
132 D2

Rudnyy Kazakhstan 96 C4

Rudolf, Lake *see* Lake Turkana

Rügen *headland* Germany
76 D2

Rukwa, Lake *lake* Tanzania
55 B7

Rumbek South Sudan 55 B5

Rundu Namibia 60 C3

Ruoqiang China 108 C3

Ruse Bulgaria 86 D1

Russia *country* Europe/Asia *off.* Russian Federation
92-93 96-97

Russian Federation *see* Russia

Rustavi Georgia 99 F2

Rutland Vermont, USA 23 F2

Rutog China 108 B4

Rwanda *country* C Africa 55

Ryazan' Russia 93 B5

Rybinskoye Vodokhranilishche *Reservoir* Russia *Eng.* Rybinsk Reservoir 92 B4

Rybnik Poland 81 C5

Ryūkyū-rettō *island group* Japan 113 A8

Ryukyu Trench *Undersea feature* East China Sea
134 B2

Rzeszów Poland 81 E5 **Saale** *river* Germany 76 C4

S

Saarbrücken Germany 77 A5

Saare *see* Saaremaa

Saaremaa *island* Estonia *var.* Saare, Sarema, *Ger.* Ösel, *var.* Oesel 88 C2

Šabac Serbia 82 C3

Sasebo Japan 113 A6
Saskatchewan *province* Canada 19 F5
Saskatchewan *river* Canada 19 F5
Saskatoon Canada 19 F5
Sassandra *River* Côte d'Ivoire 56 D5
Sassari Italy 79 A5
Satu Mare Romania 90 B3
Saudi Arabia *country* SW Asia 102-103
Sault Sainte Marie Canada 20 C4
Sault Sainte Marie Michigan, USA 22 C1
Saurimo Angola 60 C2
Sava *river* SE Europe 82 C3
Savannah Georgia, USA 31 F3
Savannah *river* SE USA 31 E2
Savissivik Greenland 64 C2
Savona Italy 78 A3
Savu Sea *sea* Indonesia 120 E5
Sawhāj Egypt *var.* Sohâg 54 B2
Sawqirah Oman 103 D6
Saýat Turkmenistan 104 D3
Sayhūt Yemen 103 D7
Saynshand Mongolia 109 E2
Say 'ūn Yemen 103 C6
Scandinavia *geophysical region* Europe 48 D2
Schaffhausen Switzerland 77 B6
Schaulen *see* Šiauliai
Schefferville Canada 21 E2
Scheldt *river* W Europe 69 B5
Schiermonnikoog *island* Netherlands 68 D1
Schneidemühl *see* Piła
Schwäbische Alb *mountains* Germany 77 B6
Schwarzwald *Forested mountain region* Germany *Eng.* Black Forest 77 B6
Schwerin Germany 76 C3
Scilly, Isles of *islands* UK 71 B7
Scotia Sea *sea* Atlantic Ocean 136 A1
Scotland *national region* UK 70
Scottsbluff Nebraska, USA 24 D3

Scottsdale Arizona, USA 28 B2
Scranton Pennsylvania, USA 23 F3
Scutari, Lake *lake* Albania/ Montenegro 83 C5
Seddon New Zealand 133 C5
Seattle Washington, USA 26 B2
Ségou Mali 56 D3
Segovia Spain 75 E2
Segura *river* Spain 75 E4
Seikan Tunnel *tunnel* Japan 112 D3
Seinäjoki Finland 67 D5
Seine *river* France 72 C3
Sejong City *administrative capital* of South Korea 110 E4
Selfoss Iceland 65 E5
Semara *see* Smara
Semarang Indonesia 120 D4
Semey Kazakhstan *prev.* Semipalatinsk 96 D4
Semipalatinsk *see* Semey
Sendai Japan 112 D4
Senegal *country* W Africa 56
Senegal *river* Africa 56 C3
Sên, Stœng *river* Cambodia 119 D5
Seoul *capital* of South Korea *Kor.* Sŏul 110 E4
Sept-Iles Canada 21 F3
Seraing Belgium 69 D6
Seram, Pulau *island* Indonesia 121 F4
Serbia *country* SE Europe 82 B3
Serdar Turkmenistan *prev.* Gyzylarbat, prev. Kizyl-Arvat 104 B2
Serhetabat Turkmenistan *prev.* Gushgy, Kushka 104 C4
Serov Russia 96 C3
Serpent's Mouth, The *sea feature* Trinidad & Tobago/ Venezuela *Sp.* Boca de la Serpiente 41 F1
Serra do Mar *mountains* Brazil 44 D3
Sérres Greece 86 C3
Setesdal *valley* Norway 67 A6
Sétif Algeria 53 E1

Setúbal Portugal 74 C4
Seul, Lake *lake* Canada 20 A3
Sevana Lich *lake* Armenia 99 G2
Sevastopol' Ukraine 91 F5
Severn *river* Canada 20 B3
Severn *river* England/Wales, UK 71 D6
Severnaya Dvina *river* Russia *Eng.* Northern Dvina 92 C3
Severnaya Zemlya *island group* Russia 137 H3
Sevilla Spain *Eng.* Seville 74 D4
Seville *see* Sevilla
Seychelles *country* Indian Ocean 61 122 B4
Seyðisfjörður Iceland 65 E4
Seýdi Turkmenistan *prev.* Neftezavodsk 104 D2
Seyhan *see* Adana
Sfax Tunisia 53 F2
's-Gravenhage *capital* of Netherlands *Eng.* The Hague 68 B3
Shaan *see* Shaanxi
Shaanxi *province* China *var.* Shaan, Shan-hsi, Shaanxi, Shenshi, Shensi 111 C5
Shaanxi Sheng *see* Shaanxi
Shache China 108 A3
Shackleton Ice Shelf *ice feature* Antarctica 136 D3
Shandong *province* China *var.* Lu, Shantung 110 D4
Shanghai China 111 D5
Shangrao China 111 D6
Shan-hsi *see* Shaanxi
Shannon *river* Ireland 71 B5
Shan Plateau *upland* Myanmar 118 B3
Shantou China 111 D6
Shantung *see* Shandong
Sharjah *see* Ash Shāriqah
Shawnee Oklahoma, USA 29 G2
Shdanov *see* Mariupol'
Shebeli *river* Ethiopia/Somalia 55 D5
Sheberghān *see* Shibirghān

Smyrna *see* İzmir

Snake *river* NW USA 26 D4

Snowdonia *mountains* Wales, UK 71 C5

Sobradinho, Represa de *Reservoir* Brazil 43 G3

Sochi Russia 93 A7 96 A3

Société, Îles de la *islands* French Polynesia *Eng.* Society Islands 127 H4

Society Islands *see* Société, Îles de la

Socotra *see* Suquṭrá

Sodankylä Finland 66 D3

Sofia *capital* of Bulgaria *var.* Sofija, *Bul.* Sofiya 86 C2

Sofija *see* Sofia

Sofiya *see* Sofia

Sognefjorden *inlet* Norway 67 A5

Sohâg *see* Sawhāj

Sokhumi Georgia *Rus.* Sukhumi 99 E1

Sokodé Togo 57 E4

Sokoto Nigeria 57 F3

Sokoto *river* Nigeria 57 F3

Solāpur India 116 D5 114 D1

Sol, Costa del *coastal region* Spain 75 E5

Soligorsk *see* Salihorsk

Solomon Islands *country* Pacific Ocean 126

Solomon Islands *island group* PNG/Solomon Islands 124 C3

Solomon Sea Pacific Ocean 126 B3

Somalia *country* E Africa 54-55

Somali Basin *undersea feature* Indian Ocean 122 A4

Somaliland *Disputed territory* E Africa 55 D5

Sombor Serbia 82 C3

Somerset Island *island* Canada 19 F2

Somme *river* France 72 C3

Somoto Nicaragua 34 D3

Songea Tanzania 55 C8

Songkhla Thailand 119 C7

Sonoran Desert *see* Altar, Desierto de

Sopron Hungary *Ger.* Ödenburg 81 B6

Soria Spain 75 E2

Sorocaba Brazil 43 F5 45 E2

Sorong Indonesia 124 G4

Sotavento, Ilhas de *island group* Cape Verde *var.* Leeward Islands 56 A3

Soûr Lebanon *anc.* Tyre 100 A4

Sousse Tunisia 53 F1

South Africa *country* southern Africa 60-61

South America 38-39

Southampton England, UK 71 D7

Southampton Island *island* Canada 17 G3

South Andaman *island* India 115 G2

South Australia *state* Australia 131 A5

South Australian Basin *undersea feature* Southern Ocean 124 B5

South Bend Indiana, USA 22 C3

South Carolina *state* USA 31 F2

South Carpathians *see* Carpaţii Meridionali

South China Sea Pacific Ocean 119 E7

South Dakota *state* USA 24-25 E3

South East Point *coastal feature* Australia 131 C7

Southeast Indian Ridge *undersea feature* Indian Ocean 123 E6

Southeast Pacific Basin *undersea feature* Pacific Ocean 135 E5

Southend-on-Sea England, UK 71 E6

Southern Alps *mountain range* New Zealand 133 B6

Southern Cook Islands *islands* Cook Islands 127 G5

Southern Cross Australia 129 B6

Southern Ocean *ocean* 123 D7

Southern Upland *mountain range* Scotland, UK 70 C4

South Fiji Basin *undersea feature* Pacific Ocean 124 D4

South Geomagnetic Pole *pole* Antarctica 136 C3

South Georgia *overseas territory* UK, Atlantic Ocean 136 A1

South Indian Basin *undersea feature* Indian Ocean 123 E7

South Island *island* New Zealand 133 D5

South Korea *country* E Asia 110-111

South Orkney Islands *islands* Antarctica 136 A2

South Pole *ice feature* Antarctica 136 B3

South Sandwich Islands *overseas territory* UK, Atlantic Ocean 136 A1

South Shetland Islands *islands* Antarctica 136 A2

South Sudan *country* NE Africa 55 B5

South Taranaki Bight *bight* New Zealand 132 C4

South Uist *island* UK 70 B3

South West Cape *headland* New Zealand 133 A8

Southwest Indian Ridge *undersea feature* Indian Ocean 123 B6

Southwest Pacific Basin *undersea feature* Pacific Ocean 125 F4

Soweto South Africa 60 D4

Spain *country* SW Europe 74-75

Sparks Nevada, USA 27 C5

Sparta *see* Spárti

Spartanburg South Carolina, USA 31 E2

Spárti Greece *Eng.* Sparta 87 B6

Spencer Gulf *gulf* Australia 131 B6

Spitsbergen *island* Svalbard 65 F2

Split Croatia 82 B4

Spokane Washington, USA 26 C2

Spratly Islands *islands* South China Sea 120 D2

Spree *river* Germany 76 D3

Springfield Illinois, USA 22 B4

Springfield Massachusetts, USA 23 G3

Springfield Missouri, USA 23 F5

Springfield Oregon, USA 26 A3

Srebrenica Bosnia & Herzegovina 82 C4

Srednesibirskoye Ploskogor'ye *var.* Central Siberian Uplands, *Eng.* Central Siberian Plateau. *mountain range* Russia 97 E3

Sri Jayewardenapura Kotte *legislative capital of* Sri Lanka 115 E4

Sri Lanka *country* S Asia *prev.* Ceylon 115

Srinagarind Reservoir *Reservoir* Thailand 119 C5

Srpska, Republika *republic* Bosnia and Herzegovina 82 C3

Ssu-ch'uan *see* Sichuan

Stalinabad *see* Dushanbe

Stalingrad *see* Volgograd

Stalin Peak *see* Communism Peak

Stalinsk *see* Novokuznetsk

Stambul *see* İstanbul

Stanley *capital of* Falkland Islands 47 D7

Stanleyville *see* Kisangani

Stara Planina *see* Balkan Mountains

Stara Zagora Bulgaria 86 D2

Starbuck Island *island* Kiribati 125 F2

Stavanger Norway 67 A6

Stavropol' Russia 93 A7 96 A3

Steinamanger *see* Szombathely

Steinkjer Norway 66 B4

Stepanakert *see* Xankändi

Stettin *see* Szczecin

Stewart Island *island* New Zealand 133 A8

Štip Macedonia 83 E5

Stirling Scotland, UK 70 C4

Stockholm *capital of* Sweden 67 C6

Stockton California, USA 27 B6

Stœng Trêng *see* Stung Treng

Stoke-on-Trent England, UK 71 D6

Stolp *see* Słupsk

Storfjorden *fjord* Norway 65 F2

Stornoway Scotland, UK 70 B2

Stralsund Germany 76 D2

Stranraer Scotland, UK 70 C4

Strasbourg France *Ger.* Strassburg 72 E4

Stratford New Zealand 132 D4

Stratford-upon-Avon England, UK 71 D6

Stratonice Czech Republic (Czechia) 81 A5

Stromboli *island* Italy 79 D6

Struma *see* Strymonas

Strumica Macedonia 83 E5

Strymonas *river* Bulgaria/ Greece *var.* Struma 86 C3

Studholme New Zealand 133 B6

Stuhlweissenburg *see* Székesfehérvár

Stung Treng Cambodia *var.* Stœng Trêng 119 D5

Stuttgart Germany 77 B6

Subotica Serbia 82 D2

Suceava Romania 90 C3

Sucre *legal capital of* Bolivia 42 C5

Sudan *country* NE Africa 54 B3

Sudbury Canada 20 C4

Sudd *region* South Sudan 55 B5

Sudeten *mountains* Central Europe *var.* Sudetes, Sudetic Mountains, *Cz./Pol.* Sudety 81 B5

Sudetes *see* Sudeten

Sudetic Mountains *see* Sudeten

Sudety *see* Sudeten

Suez *see* As Suways

Suez, Gulf of *sea feature* Red Sea 101 A8

Suez Canal *canal* Egypt *Ar.* Qanāt as Suways 54 B1

Şuḩār Oman 103 D5

Sühbaatar Mongolia 109 E1

Suhl Germany 76 C5

Sukabumi Indonesia 120 C5

Sukhumi *see* Sokhumi

Sukkur Pakistan 116 B3

Sula, Kepulauan *island group* Indonesia 121 F4

Sulawesi *island* Indonesia *Eng.* Celebes 121 E4

Sulu Archipelago *island group* Philippines 121 E3

Sülüktü *see* Sulyukta

Sulu Sea Pacific Ocean 121 E2

Sulyukta Kyrgyzstan *Kir.* Sülüktü 105 E2

Sumatra *island* Indonesia 120 B4

Sumba, Selat *island* Indonesia 121 E5

Sumbawanga Tanzania 55 B7

Sumbe Angola 60 B2

Sumgait *see* Sumqayıt

Sumqayıt Azerbaijan *Rus.* Sumgait 99 H2

Sumy Ukraine 91 F1

Sunda, Selat *strait* Indonesia 120 D5

Sunderland England, UK 70 D4

Sundsvall Sweden 67 C5

Suntar Russia 97 F3

Sunyani Ghana 57 E4

Superior Wisconsin, USA 22 A1

Superior, Lake *lake* Canada/ USA 16 C3

Suquţrá *island* Yemen *var.* Socotra 103 D7 122 B3

Şūr Oman 103 E5

Surabaya Indonesia 120 D5

Surakarta Indonesia 120 D5

Sūrat India 116 C5

Surat Thani Thailand 119 C6

Sûre *river* W Europe 69 D7

Surfers Paradise Australia 131 E5

Surinam *see* Suriname

Suriname *country* NE South America *var.* Surinam 41

Surkhob *river* Tajikistan 105 E3

Surt Libya *var.* Sidra 53 G2

Surt, Khalīj *sea feature* Mediterranean Sea *Eng.* Gulf of Sirte, Gulf of Sidra 85 E4

Surtsey *island* S Iceland 65 E5

Susanville California, USA 27 B5

Suways, Qanāt as *see* Suez Canal

T

Suva *capital of* Fiji 127 E4
Svalbard *external territory*
Norway, Arctic Ocean 65 G2
Svay Riĕng *see* Svay Rieng
Svay Rieng Cambodia *var.* Svay
Riĕng 119 D6
Sverdlovsk *see* Yekaterinburg
Svetlogorsk *see* Svietlahorsk/
Svetlogorsk
Svietlahorsk/Svetlogorsk
Belarus *Rus.* Svetlogorsk
89 D6
Svyataya Anna Trough
undersea feature Kara Sea
137 H4
Swakopmund Namibia 60 B3
Swansea Wales, UK 71 C6
Swaziland *country* southern
Africa 61
Sweden *country* N Europe
66–67
Sweetwater Texas, USA 29 F3
Swindon England, UK 71 D6
Switzerland *country*
C Europe 77
Sydney Australia 131 D6
Sydney Canada 21 G4
Syeverodonets'k Ukraine 91 G1
Syktyvkar Russia 92 D4 96 C3
Sylhet Bangladesh 117 G4
Syracuse *see* Siracusa
Syracuse New York, USA
23 E3
Syr Darya *river* C Asia 104 D1
Syria *country* SW Asia 100–101
Syrian Desert *desert* SW Asia
Ar. Bādiyat ash Shām 101 C5
Szczecin Poland *Ger.* Stettin
80 B3
Szczeciński, Zalew *bay*
Germany/Poland 80 A2
Szechwan *see* Sichuan
Szeged Hungary *Ger.* Szegedin
81 D7
Szegedin *see* Szeged
Székesfehérvár Hungary *Ger.*
Stuhlweissenburg 81 C6
Szekszárd Hungary 81 C7
Szolnok Hungary 81 D6
Szombathely Hungary *Ger.*
Steinamanger 81 B6

Tabariya, Bahrat *see*
Tiberius, Lake
Tábor Czech Republic (Czechia)
81 B5
Tabora Tanzania 55 B7
Tabrīz Iran 102 C2
Tabuaeran *island* Kiribati
var. Fanning Island 127 G2
Tabūk Saudi Arabia 102 A4
Tacloban Philippines 120 F2
Tacna Peru 42 C4
Tacoma Washington, USA 26 B2
Tacuarembó Uruguay 44 C4
Tadmur Syria *Eng.* Palmyra
100 C3
Taegu *see* Daegu
Taejŏn *see* Daejeon
Tafassâsset, Ténéré du *desert*
Niger 57 G2
Taguatinga Brazil 43 F3
Tagus *river* Portugal/Spain *Port.*
Tejo, *Sp.* Tajo 74 C3
Tahiti *island* French Polynesia
127 H5
Tahoe, Lake *lake* W USA 27 B5
Tahoua Niger 57 F3
Taibei *see* Taipei
Taichung Taiwan *var.* Taizhong
111 D6
Taieri *129* New Zealand 133 B7
Taihape New Zealand 132 D4
T'ainan *see* Tainan
Tainan Taiwan *prev.*
T'ainan111 D6
Taipei *capital of* Taiwan *var.*
Taibei 111 D6
Taiping Malaysia 120 B3
Taiwan *country* E Asia *prev.*
Formosa 111
Taiwan Strait *sea feature* East
China Sea/South China Sea
var. Formosa Strait 111 D7
Taiyuan China 110 C4
Taizhong *see* Taichung
Ta'izz Yemen 103 B7
Tajikistan *country* C Asia 105
Tajo *see* Tagus
Takapuna New Zealand 132 D2

Takla Makan *see* Taklimakan
Shamo
Taklimakan Shamo *desert*
region China *var.* Takla
Makan 108 B3
Talamanca, Cordillera de
mountains Costa Rica 35 E4
Talas Kyrgyzstan 105 F2
Talaud, Kepulauan *island*
group Indonesia 121 F3
Talca Chile 46 B4
Talcahuano Chile 46 B4
Taldykorgan Kazakhstan 96 C5
Tallahassee Florida, USA
30 D3
Tallinn *capital of* Estonia *prev.*
Revel, *Ger.* Reval, *Rus.* Tallin
88 D2
Talsen *see* Talsi
Talsi Latvia *Ger.* Talsen 88 B3
Tamale Ghana 57 E4
Tamanrasset Algeria 53 E4
Tambo Australia 130 C4
Tambov Russia 93 B5
Tamil Nādu *state* India 114 D2
Tampa Florida, USA 31 E4
Tampere Finland 67 D5
Tampico Mexico 33 F3
Tamworth Australia
131 D6
Tanami Desert *desert* Australia
128 E3
Tananarive *see* Antananarivo
Tanega-shima *island* Japan
113 B7
Tanga Tanzania 55 C7
Tanganyika, Lake *lake* E Africa
51 D5
Tanger Morocco *var.* Tangiers
52 C1
Tanggula Shan *mountain*
range China 108 C4
Tangiers *see* Tanger
Tangra Yumco *lake* China
108 B5
Tangshan China 110 D4
Tanimbar Islands *see* Tanimbar,
Kepulauan
Tanimbar, Kepulauan *island*
group Indonesia *Eng.*
Tanimbar Islands 121 F5

U

Vienna *capital of* Austria *Ger.* Wien 77 E6

Vientiane *capital of* Laos *var.* Viangchan 118 C4

Vietnam *country* SE Asia 118-119

Vigo Spain 74 C2

Vijayawāda India 115 E1

Vila Nova de Gaia Portugal 74 C2

Vila Real Portugal 74 C2

Viliya *see* Neris

Viljandi Estonia *Ger.* Fellin 88 D2

Villach Austria 77 D7

Villahermosa Mexico 33 G4

Villa Mercedes Argentina 46 C4

Villarrica *peak* Chile 39 B6

Villavicencio Colombia 40 C3

Villeurbanne France 73 D5

Vilna *see* Vilnius

Vilnius *capital of* Lithuania *Pol.* Wilno, *Ger.* Wilna, *Rus.* Vilna 89 C5

Viña del Mar Chile 46 B4

Vinh Vietnam 118 D4

Vinnitsa *see* Vinnytsya

Vinnytsya Ukraine *Rus.* Vinnitsa 90 D2

Virgin Islands *unincorporated territory* USA, West Indies 37 F3

Virginia Minnesota, USA 25 F2

Virginia *state* USA 22-23

Virovitica Croatia 82 C3

Virtsu Estonia *Ger.* Werder 88 C2

Visākhapatnam India 117 E5

Visalia California, USA 27 C7

Visby Sweden 67 C7

Viscount Melville Sound *sea feature* Arctic Ocean 19 F2

Viseu Portugal 74 C3

Vistula *see* Wisła

Vitebsk *see* Vitsyebsk/Vitebsk

Viterbo Italy 78 C4

Viti Levu *island* Fiji 127 E4

Vitim *river* Russia 95 E3

Vitória Brazil 43 G5 45 G1

Vitória da Conquista Brazil 43 G4

Vitoria-Gasteiz Spain 75 E1

Vitsyebsk/Vitebsk Belarus *Rus.* Vitebsk 88 E5

Vjosës, Lumi i *river* Albania 83 D6

Vladikavkaz Russia *prev.* Ordzhonikidze, Dzaudzhikau 93 B7

Vladimir Russia 93 B5

Vladimirovka *see* Yuzhno-Sakhalinsk

Vladivostok Russia 97 G5

Vlieland *island* Netherlands 68 C1

Vlissingen Netherlands *Eng.* Flushing 69 B5

Vlorë Albania 83 D6

Vojvodina *region* Serbia 82 D3

Volga *river* Russia 96 A3

Volgograd Russia *prev.* Stalingrad 93 B6, 96 A3

Volkovysk *see* Vawkavysk

Vologda Russia 96 B2

Vólos Greece 86 B4

Volta *river* Ghana 57 E4

Volta, Lake *lake* Ghana 57 E4

Volta Redonda Brazil 45 E2

Vóreies Sporádes *island group* Greece *Eng.* Northern Sporades 86 C4

Vorkuta Russia 92 E3

Vormsi *island* Estonia *Ger.* Worms, *Swed.* Ormsö 88 C2

Voronezh Russia 93 B5

Võru Estonia *Ger.* Werro 88 D3

Vosges *mountain range* France 72 E4

Vostochno-Sibirskoye More Arctic Ocean *Eng.* East Siberian Sea 137 G2

Vostok Island *island* Kiribati 127 H4

Vrangel'ya, Ostrov *island* Russia *Eng.* Wrangel Island 97 G1

Vratsa Bulgaria 86 C2

Vršac Serbia 82 D3

Vukovar Croatia 82 C3

Vulcano, Isola *island* Italy 79 D6

Vyatka *river* Russia 93 C5

W

Wa Ghana 57 E4

Waag *see* Váh

Waal *river* Netherlands 68 D4

Wabash *river* C USA 22 B4

Waco Texas, USA 29 G3

Waddeneilanden *island group* Netherlands *Eng.* West Frisian Islands 68 C1

Waddenzee *sea feature* Netherlands 68 D1

Wadi Halfa Sudan 54 B3

Wādī Mūsá Jordan *var.* Petra 101 B7

Wad Medani Sudan 54 B4

Wagga Wagga Australia 131 C6

Wagin Australia 129 B6

Wahai Indonesia 121 F4

Wahībah, Ramlat Āl *Desert* Oman 103 E5

Waiau *river* New Zealand 133 A7

Waipawa New Zealand 132 E4

Wairau *river* New Zealand 133 C5

Wairoa New Zealand 132 E3

Waitaki *river* New Zealand 133 B6

Waiuku New Zealand 132 D3

Wakatipu, Lake *lake* New Zealand 133 D7

Wakayama Japan 113 C5

Wake Island *atoll* Pacific Ocean 124 D1

Wake Island *US unincorporated territory* Pacific Ocean 134 C2

Wakkanai Japan 112 D1

Wałbrzych Poland *Ger.* Waldenburg 80 B4

Waldenburg *see* Wałbrzych

Wales *national region* UK *Wel.* Cymru 71

Wilno *see* Vilnius

Windau *see* Ventspils

Windhoek *capital of* Namibia 60 C3

Windorah Australia 130 C4

Windsor Canada 20 C5

Windward Islands *see* Barlavento, Ilhas de

Winisk *river* Canada 20 B3

Winnemucca Nevada, USA 27 C5

Winnipeg Canada 19 G5

Winnipeg, Lake *lake* Canada 19 G5

Winston-Salem North Carolina, USA 31 F1

Winton Australia 130 C4

Wisconsin *state* USA 22 B2

Wismar Germany 76 C3

Wisła *river* Poland *Ger.* Weichsel, *Eng.* Vistula 63 E3 80 D4

W.J. van Blommesteinmeer *Reservoir* Suriname 41 H3

Włocławek Poland 80 C3

Wodzisław Śląski Poland *Ger.* Loslau 81 C5

Wolfsburg Germany 76 C3

Wollongong Australia 131 D6

Wolmar *see* Valmiera

Woods, Lake of the *lake* Canada/USA 20 A3

Woodville New Zealand 132 D4

Worcester England, UK 71 D6

Worcester Massachusetts, USA 23 G3

Worms *see* Vormsi

Wołkowysk *see* Vawkavysk

Wrangel Island *see* Vrangel'ya, Ostrov

Wrocław Poland *Ger.* Breslau 80 C4

Wuday 'ah Saudi Arabia 103 C6

Wuhai China *var.* Haibowan 109 E3

Wuhan China 111 C5

Wuliang Shan *mountain range* China 111 A6

Wuppertal Germany 76 A4

Würzburg Germany 77 C5

Wuxi China 111 D5

Wyndham Australia 128 D3

Wyoming *state* USA 24 C3

X

Xaignabouli Laos *prev.* Muang Xainabouri 118 C3

Xalapa Mexico *var.* Jalapa 118 C3

Xai-Xai Mozambique 61 E4

Xalapa Mexico 33 F4

Xam Nua Laos 118 D3

Xankändi Azerbaijan *Rus.* Khankendy, *prev.* Stepanakert 99 G2

Xánthi Greece 86 C3

Xiamen China 111 D6

Xi'an China 111 B5

Xiang *see* Hunan

Xiao Hinggan Ling *mountain range* China 110 D2

Xilinhot China 109 F2

Xingu *river* Brazil 43 E3

Xingxingxia China 108 D3

Xining China 109 E4

Xinjiang Uygur Zizhiqu *autonomous region* China *var.* Sinkiang 108 B3

Xinxiang China 110 C4

Xixón *see* Gijón/Xixón

Xizang Zizhiqu *see* Tibet

Xuzhou China 111 D5

Y

Yafran Libya 53 F2

Yakima Washington, USA 26 B2

Yaku-shima *island* Japan 113 B7

Yakutsk Russia 97 F3

Yala Thailand 119 C7

Yalong Jiang *river* China 111 A5

Yalta Ukraine 91 F5

Yamaguchi Japan 113 B5

Yambio South Sudan 55 B5

Yambol Bulgaria 86 D2

Yamdena, Pulau *island* Indonesia 121 G5

Yamoussoukro *capital of* Côte d'Ivoire 56 D5

Yamuna *river* India 117 E3

Yana *river* Russia 95 F2

Yangon Myanmar *Eng.* Rangoon 118 B4

Yangtze *see* Chang Jiang

Yaoundé *capital of* Cameroon 59 B5

Yap *island* Micronesia 126 A1

Yap Trench *undersea feature* Philippine Sea 124 B2

Yaqui *river* Mexico 32 B2

Yaren *de facto capital* Nauru 126 D2

Yarmouth Canada 21 F4

Yaroslavl' Russia 96 B2

Yazd Iran 102 D4

Yazoo *river* SE USA 30 C2

Yecheng China 108 A3

Yekaterinburg Russia *prev.* Sverdlovsk 96 C3

Yelisavetpol *see* Gäncä

Yellowknife Canada 19 E4

Yellow River *see* Huang He

Yellow Sea Pacific Ocean 110-111

Yellowstone *river* NW USA 24 C2

Yemen *country* SW Asia 1 03 C7

Yenakiyeve Ukraine 91 G3

Yengisar China 108 A3

Yenisey *river* Russia 96 D3

Yerevan *capital of* Armenia *var.* Erevan, Jerevan, *Eng.* Erivan 99 F2

Yevpatoriya Ukraine 91 F4

Yinchuan China 110 B4

Yining China 108 B2

Yogyakarta Indonesia 120 D5

Yokohama Japan 113 D5

Yopal Colombia 40 C2

York England, UK 71 D5

York, Cape *headland* Australia 130 C1

Yorkton Canada 19 F5

Youngstown Ohio, USA 22 D3

Ypres *see* Ieper

Yu *see* Henan

Yuba City California, USA 27 B5

Yucatan Channel *channel* Caribbean Sea 36 A2